COBBETT'S

PAPER AGAINST GOLD:

Containing the History and Mystery of the Bank of England, the Funds, the Debt, the Sinking Fund, the Bank Stoppage, the lowering and the raising of the value of Paper-Money; and shewing, that Taxation, Pauperism, Poverty, Misery and Crimes have all increased, and ever must increase, with a Funding System.

No. 1.]—COBBETT'S PAPER AGAINST GOLD.—[*Price Two-Pence.*

INTRODUCTION.

Botley, 8th February, 1817.

The time is now come, when every man in this kingdom ought to make himself, if possible, well acquainted with all matters belonging to the *Paper-Money System.* It is that System, which has mainly contributed towards our present miseries; and, indeed, without that System those miseries never could have existed in any thing approaching towards their present degree. In all countries, where a *Paper-Money,* that is to say, a paper which could not, at any moment, be converted into Gold and Silver, has ever existed; in all countries, where this has been the case, the consequence, first or last, has always been great and general misery, and, in most such cases, such misery has been productive of that confusion and bloodshed, which I most anxiously hope will be prevented, in this instance, by timely measures of a just and conciliatory character and by the good sense, patience and fortitude of the people.

To be able clearly to trace our miseries to this grand cause, *the Bank and the Paper-Money,* it is necessary, that we inquire into the origin of money, how it acts upon the affairs of men, how prices depend upon its quantity, and how money itself is changed in its quantity and value. Next it is necessary, that we come at a clear idea of the origin of Paper-Money and of its introduction into this country. Next, we ought to see the origin of the Bank and its Paper; to see how Loans have been made and how and by what means a Debt has been created. This compels us to go back and trace minutely the Bank and the Debt from their fatal birth to the present time; to show how they arose both together, and how they have gone swelling mountains high, side by side while taxes, pauperism, misery and, crimes have all gone on increasing in the same degree. We ought next to inquire, whether it be possible to lessen the Debt by that scheme, which has been called the Sinking Fund. Then we ought to enter into all the facts of that curious event, called the *Bank-Restriction,* which was a *Stoppage of Cash-Payments* at the Bank, in violation of the Bank Charter and of the laws of debtor and creditor. This transaction ought now to be clearly understood by every man in England.

All the *actors* in the transaction ought to be put forth in their true character; for it is to this transaction, that we may trace more immediately all those sudden changes in the currency, which have ruined the farmers, the tradesmen, the land-owners, and which have reduced the journeymen and labourers to such intolerable misery as that which they now endure, and which never was endured in England at any former period.

To enable every man, and especially the *youth,* of this country, to come at a competent knowledge on all these topics, was the original object of this work, and is now the object of its re-publication. It consists of a series of Letters, addressed to the *People of Salisbury,* in the year 1810 and 1811; because, at that time, those people were suffering severely from the failure of Country Banks. At the same time, there was a proposition before Parliament for making the Bank pay in Gold and Silver at the end of *two years.* This was proposed by the *Opposition;* but the *Ministers* said, that, though the Bank was able to pay, it would not be wise to make it pay, *till peace came.* I contended, that, for the Bank to pay in gold and silver was *impossible,* without *wiping away a part of the Debt;* or, without *plunging the country into ruin and misery.* The Bank does *not* pay; and, by only making *one step* towards it, the whole nation, all but fund-holders and tax-eaters, *have already been ruined.*

In the writing of this work the greatest pains were taken to make my statements and my arguments, not only as clear and as strong, but also, as familiar as possible, and, by these means, to render a subject, which has always been considered as intricate and abstruse, so simple as to be understood by every reader of common capacity; and, in this object, I hope I have succeeded, because I have had the satisfaction to witness numerous instances, where persons, who would generally be denominated illiterate, have, by the reading of this work, become completely masters of the whole subject.

The truth is, however, that the pride of those, who call themselves *learned men,* lead them to misjudge greatly as to the capacity of those, whom they call the illiterate, or *unlearned.* To arrange words into sentences in a grammatical manner, to arrive at correct results by the operations of figures, require a knowledge of *rules,* which knowledge must be acquired by art; but the capacity of receiving plain *facts* and of *reasoning* upon those facts has its natural place in every sound mind; and, perhaps, the mind the most likely speedily to receive and deeply to imbibe a fair impression is precisely that mind which has never been pre-occupied by the impressions of art or of school-education. And, if there be men to hold the doctrine, that the people in general *ought not* to understand any thing of these matters, such men can proceed upon no principle other than this, that popular ignorance is the best security for public plunderers and oppressors.

It will be seen, that the Letters, composing the greater part of this work, were written in, and dated from the "*State Prison, Newgate.*" For six years *before* the date of these Letters, I had been endeavouring to rouse my country to a sense of its danger from the Debt and Paper-Money, and had often foretold, that national ruin and misery would be the result. But, it was while I was shut up in Newgate, that I made my greatest effort. The *cause* of my imprisonment, and of the other heavy punishments inflicted on me, is pretty well known; but, as this work is chiefly intended for the use of *schools* and of *young persons* in general, and, as I hope it may be read many years after its author will have closed his eyes for ever, it is no more than justice to myself and to a family of children, to whom their father's character will always be as dear as their own lives, for me to make here, and to send forth, inseparable from this work, the following concise and undeniable record of facts, which record was published immediately after the expiration of my imprisonment, in the month of July, 1812.

ENGLISH LIBERTY OF THE PRESS,

As illustrated in the Prosecution and Punishment of WILLIAM COBBETT.

In order that my countrymen and that the world may not be deceived, duped, and cheated upon this subject, I, WILLIAM COBBETT, of Botley, in Hampshire, put upon record the following facts; to wit: That, on the 24th of June, 1809, the following article was published in a London news-paper, called the COURIER:— "The Mutiny amongst the LOCAL "MILITIA, which broke out at "Ely, was *fortunately* suppressed on "Wednesday, by the arrival of four "squadrons of the GERMAN LEGION CAVALRY from Bury, "under the command of General "Auckland. Five of the ringleaders "were tried by a Court-Martial, and "*sentenced to receive* 500 *lashes each*, "part of which punishment they re"ceived on Wednesday, and a part "was remitted. *A stoppage for their* "*knapsacks* was the ground of the "complaint that excited this mutinous "spirit, which occasioned the men to "surround their officers, and demand "what they deemed their arrears. "The first division of the German "Legion halted yesterday at New"market on their return to Bury." ——That, on the 1st July, 1809, I published, in the Political Register, an article censuring, in the strongest terms, these proceedings; that, for so doing, the Attorney General prosecuted, as seditious libellers, and by Ex-Officio Information, me, and also my printer, my publisher, and one of the principal retailers of the Political Register; that I was brought to trial on the 15th June, 1810, and was, by a Special Jury, that is to say, by 12 men out of 48 appointed by the Master of the Crown Office, found guilty; that, on the 20th of the same month, I was compelled to give bail for my appearance to receive judgment; and that, as I came up from Botley (to which place I had returned to my family and my farm on the evening of the 15th), a Tipstaff went down from London in order to seize me, personally; that, on the 9th of July, 1810, I, together with my printer, publisher, and the newsman, were brought into the Court of King's Bench to receive judgment; that the three former were sentenced to be imprisoned for some months in the King's Bench prison; that I was sentenced to be imprisoned for two years in Newgate, the great receptacle for malefactors, and the front of which is the scene of numerous hangings in the course of every year; that the part of the prison in which I was sentenced to be confined is sometimes inhabited by felons, that felons were actually in it at the time I entered it; that one man was taken out of it to be transported in about 48 hours after I was put into the same yard with him; and that it is the place of confinement for men guilty of unnatural crimes, of whom there are four in it at this time; that, besides this imprisonment, I was sentenced to pay a thousand pounds TO THE KING, and to give security for my good behaviour for seven years, myself in the sum of 3,000 pounds, and two sureties in the sum of 1,000 pounds each; that the whole of this sentence has been executed upon me, that I have been imprisoned the two years, have paid the thousand pounds TO THE KING, and have given the bail, Timothy Brown and Peter Walker, Esqrs. being my sureties; that the Attorney General was Sir Vicary Gibbs, the Judge who sat at the trial, Lord Ellenborough, the four Judges who sat at passing sentence, Ellenborough, Grose, Le Blanc, and Bailey; and that the jurors were, Thomas Rhodes of Hampstead Road, John Davis of Southampton-place, James Ellis of Tottenham Court Road, John Richards of Bayswater, Thomas Marsham of Baker Street, Robert Heathcote, of High Street, Marylebone, John Maud, of York Place, Marylebone; George Baxter, of Church Terrace, Pancras; Thomas Taylor, of Red Lion Square; David Deane of St. John Street; William Palmer, of Upper Street, Islington; Henry Favre, of Pall-Mall; and that the Prime Ministers during the time were Spencer Perceval, until he was shot by John Bellingham, and after that Robert B. Jenkinson, Earl of Liverpool; that the prosecution and sentence took place in the reign of King George the Third, and that, he having become insane during my imprisonment, the 1,000 pounds was paid to his son, the Prince Regent, in his behalf; that, during my imprisonment, I wrote and published 364 Essays and Letters upon political subjects; that, during the same time, I was visited by persons from 197 cities and towns, many of them as a sort of deputies from Societies or Clubs; that, at the expiration of my imprisonment, on the 9th of July, 1812, a great dinner was given in London for the purpose of receiving me, at which dinner upwards of 600 persons were present, and at which Sir Francis Burdett presided; that dinners and other parties were held on the same occasion in many other places in England; that, on my way home, I was received at Alton, the first town in Hampshire, with the ringing of the Church bells; that a respectable company met me and gave me a dinner at Winchester; that I was drawn from more than the distance of a mile into Botley by the people; that, upon my arrival in the village, I found all the people assembled to receive me; that I concluded the day by explaining to them the cause of my imprisonment, and by giving them clear notions respecting the flogging of the Local Militia-men at Ely, and respecting the employment of German Troops; and, finally, which is more than a compensation for my losses and all my sufferings, I am in perfect health and strength, and, though I must, for the sake of six children, feel the diminution that has been made in my property (thinking it right in me to decline the offer of a subscription), I have the consolation to see growing up three sons, upon whose hearts, I trust, all these facts will be engraven.

WM. COBBETT.

Botley, July 23, 1812.

PAPER AGAINST GOLD.

LETTER I.

Appointment of the Bullion Committee—Main points of the Report—Proposition for the Bank to pay in two Years—To merit the appellation of a Thinking People, we must shew that our Thinking produces Knowledge—Go back into the History of Paper Money—Definition of Money—Increase of Paper—What is the cause of this Increase?—Origin of the Bank of England—How it came to pass that so much Paper Money got afloat—Increase of Bank Notes wanted to pay the increase of the interest on the National Debt—Progress in issuing Bank Notes from 20 to 1 Pounds—Suspicion awakened in 1797 which produced the Stoppage of Gold and Silver Payments at the Bank of England.

GENTLEMEN,

DURING the last session of parliament, a Committee, that is to say, ten or twelve members, of the House of Commons, were appointed to inquire into the cause of the high price of Gold *Bullion*, that is, Gold *not coined;* and to take into consideration the state of the circulating medium, or money, of this country. This Committee have made a *Report*, as they call it; but, it is a great book, that they have written, and have had printed; a book much larger than the whole of the New Testament. Of this Report I intend to enter into an Examination; and, as you have recently felt, and are still feeling, some of the effects of Paper-Money, I think it may not be amiss, if, upon this occasion, I address myself to you. I have introduced myself to you without any ceremony; but, before we part, we shall become well acquainted; and, I make no doubt, that you will understand the distinction between Paper-Money and Gold-Money much too well for it to be in the power of any one ever again to deceive you; which understanding, will, in the times now fast approaching, be of great utility to all those amongst you, who may have the means of laying up money, however small the quantity may be.

The Committee above-mentioned, which, for brevity's sake, I call the Bullion Committee, sent for several persons, whom they examined as *witnesses*, touching the matter in question. There was SIR FRANCIS BARING, for instance, the great loan-maker, and GOLDSMIDT, the rich Jew, whose name you so often see in the news-papers, where he is stated to give grand dinners to princes and great men. The *Evidence* of these, and other money-dealers and merchants, the Bullion Committee have had printed; and, upon this evidence, as well as upon the Report itself, we shall have to make some remarks.

The result of the Committee's inquiries is, in substance, this; *that the high price of gold is occasioned by the low value of the paper-money; that the low value of the paper-money has been occasioned* (as, you know, the low value of apples is) *by the great abundance of it; that the only way to lower the price of the gold is to raise the value of the paper-money, and that the only way to raise the value of the paper-money is to make the quantity of it less than it now is.* Thus far, as you will clearly see, there was no conjuration required. The fact is, that, not only do these propositions contain well-known, and almost self-evident truths; but, these truths have, during the last two or three years, and especially during the last year, been so frequently stated in print, that it was next to impossible that any person in England, able to read, should have been unacquainted with them. But, having arrived at the conclusion, that, in order to raise the value of the paper-money, *its quantity must be lessened;* having come to this point, the rest of the way was more difficult; for, the next object was, to point out *the means of lessening the quantity of the paper-money,* and this is an object, which, in my opinion will never be effected, unless those means include the destruction of the whole mass.

Not so, however, think the Gentlemen of the Bullion Committee. They think, or, at least, they evidently wish to make others think, that it is possible to lessen the quantity of the paper-money, and to cause guineas to come back again and to pass from hand to hand as in former times; they would fain have us believe, that this can be done without the total destruction of the paper-money; and, indeed, they have actually recommended to the House of Commons to pass a Law to cause the Bank in Threadneedle Street, London, commonly called the Bank of England, *to pay its notes in real money,* at the END OF TWO YEARS from this time. Two years is a pretty good lease for people to have of this sort. This Bank *promises to pay* on *demand.* It does this upon the face of every one of its notes; and, therefore, as a *remedy* for the evil of want of gold, to propose, that this Bank should *begin* to pay in two years' time, is something, which I think, would not have been offered to the public in any age but this, and, even in this age, to any public except the public in this country. The notes of the Bank of England bear, upon the face of them, a promise that the Bankers, or Bank Company, who issue the notes, will *pay* the notes upon *demand.* Now, what do we mean by *paying* a note? Certainly we do not mean, the giving of *one note for another note.* Yet, this is the sort of payment, that people get at the Bank of England; and this sort of payment the Bullion Committee does not propose even to begin to put an end to in less than *two years* from this time.

Gentlemen; we, the people of this country, have been persuaded to believe many things. We have been persuaded to believe ourselves to be "the *most thinking* people in Europe;" but to what purpose do men think, unless they arrive at useful knowledge by thinking? To what purpose do men think, if they are, after all their thinking, to be persuaded, that a Bank, which has not paid its promissory notes in gold for *thirteen years and a half,* will be able to pay them in gold at the end of *fifteen years and a half,* the quantity of the notes having gone on regularly *increasing?* If men are to be persuaded to believe this, to what purpose do they think? But, before I proceed any further in my remarks upon the Report of the Bullion Committee; before I proceed to lay before you the *exposures* now made by the labours of this Committee; the facts now become *evident* through this channel; the *confessions* now made by these members of the House of Commons: before I proceed to lay these before you, and to remark upon the remedies, proposed by the Committee, it will be necessary for me to go back into the *history of the paper-money;* because, without doing this, I shall be talking to you of things, of which you will have no clear notion, and the reasonings, relating to which, you will, of course, not at all understand. It is a great misfortune, that any portion of your time, should be spent in reading or thinking about matters of this kind; but, such is our present situation in this country, that every man, who has a family to preserve from want, ought to endeavour to make himself acquainted with the nature, and with the probable consequences, of the paper-money now afloat.

Money, is the *representative,* or the *token* of property, or *things of value.* The money, while used as money, is of no other use; and, therefore, a bit of lead or of wood or of leather, would be as good as gold or silver, to be used as money. But, if these materials, which are every where found *in such abundance,* were to be used as money, then would be so much money made that there would be no end to it; and, besides, the money made in one country would, however there enforced by law, have no value in any other country. For these reasons *Gold* and *Silver*, which are amongst the most *scarce* of things, have been, by all the nations that we know any thing of, used as money.

While the money of any country consists of nothing but these scarce metals; while it consists of nothing but gold and silver, there is no fear of its becoming *too abundant*; but if the money of a country be made of lead, tin, wood, leather, or paper; and if any one can make it, who may choose to make it, there needs no extraordinary wisdom to foresee, that there will be a great abundance of this sort of money, and that the gold and silver money, being, in fact, no longer of any use in such a state of things, will go, either into the hoards of the prudent, or into the bags of those, who have the means of sending or carrying them to those foreign countries where they are wanted, and where they will bring their value.

That a state of things like that here spoken of, does now exist in this country, is notorious to all the world. But while we are all acquainted with the fact, and while many of us are most sensibly feeling the *effects*, scarcely a man amongst us takes the trouble to inquire into the *cause*: yet, unless the cause be ascertained, how are we to apply, or to judge of a *remedy?* We see the country abounding with paper-money; we see every man's hand full of it; we frequently talk of it as a strange thing, and a great evil; but never do we inquire into the cause of it.

There are few of you who cannot remember the time, when there was scarcely ever seen a bank note among Tradesmen and Farmers. I can remember, when this was the case; and, when the farmers in my country hardly ever saw a bank note, except when they sold their hops at Weyhill fair. People, in those days, used to carry little bags to put their money in, instead of the paste-board or leather cases that they now carry. If you look back, and take a little time to think, you will trace the gradual increase of paper-money, and the like decrease of gold and silver money. At first there were no bank notes under 20 pounds; next they came to 15 pounds; next to 10 pounds: at the beginning of the last war, they came to 5 pounds; and, before the end of it, they came down to 2 and to 1 pounds. How long it will be before they come down to parts of a pound, it would, perhaps, be difficult to say; but in Kent, at least, there are country notes in circulation to an amount so low as that of seven shillings. It is the *cause* of this that is interesting to us; the cause of this change in our money, and, in the *prices* of goods of all sorts and of labour. All of you who are forty years of age can remember, when the price of the gallon loaf used to be about ten pence or a shilling, instead of two shillings and sixpence or two shillings and ten pence, as it now is. These effects strike you. You talk of them every day; but the *cause* of them you seldom, if ever, either talk or think of: and it is to this cause that I am now endeavouring to draw your attention.

You have, during the last seventeen years, seen the quantity of paper money rapidly increase; or in other words, you have, day after day, seen less and less of gold and silver appear in payments, and, of course more and more of paper-money. But, it was not till the year 1797, that the paper-money began to increase so very fast. It was then that the *two* and *one* pound notes were first made by the Bank of England. It was then, in short, that paper-money became completely predominant. But, you will naturally ask me, "what was the cause of *that?*" The cause was tha the Bank of England *stopped paying its notes in gold and silver.* What! stop paying its notes? Refuse to pay its *promissory notes?* The Bank of England, when its notes were presented, *refuse to pay them?* Yes: and, what is more, an Act of parliament brought in by Pitt, was passed, to protect the Bank of England against the legal consequences of such refusal. So that, the people, who held promissory notes of the Bank, and who had, perhaps, given gold or silver for them, when they went to the Bank for payment, were told, that they could have no gold or silver, but that they might have other notes, *more paper*, if they pleased, in exchange for the paper they held in their hands and tendered for payment. From that time to this, the Act of parliament, authorising the Bank of England to refuse to pay its notes in gold and silver, has been in force. At first it was passed for *three months;* next till the parliament should meet again; then it was to last to the end of the *war*; then, when *peace* came, it was continued just for a year, till things should be settled; then, as things were not quite settled, it was continued till parliament should meet again; and, as this present war had begun by that time, the act was made to continue till *six months after the next peace.*

The *reasons* given upon the different occasions, it will be very material to notice; for, it is this stoppage in the payment of gold and silver at the Bank of England upon which the whole question turns. Every thing hangs upon this; and, when we come to examine that part of the Report which treats of the Bank's reviving its payments in gold and silver, we shall find it of great use to us to recur to the *reasons*, the divers, the manifold reasons that were given, at different times, for suspending those payments. Since that suspension took place, you have seen the gold and silver disappear; you have seen, the paper has supplied the place of gold; paper-money makers have set up all over the kingdom; and might not this well happen, when, to pay paper-money nothing more than paper-money was required? But, the *reasons* given for this measure of suspension; the reasons given for the passing of an Act of Parliament to protect the Bank of England against the demands of its creditors are seldom recurred to, though, as you will presently see, without recurring to those reasons, and without ascertaining the *true* cause of the passing of that Act of Parliament, we cannot form so good a judgment relative to the *remedy* now proposed; namely, that of the Bank of England's reviving its payments in gold and silver. This is the remedy, which the Bullion Committee propose; and, you will say, a very good remedy it is; a very good remedy indeed; for people who have, for so long a time, not paid their notes in gold and silver, to begin to pay their notes in gold and silver, is a very good remedy; but, the thing to ascertain, is, *can the remedy be applied?* This is the question for us to discuss. It required nobody to tell us, that *paying in gold and silver* would be an effectual remedy for the evils arising from *not paying in gold and silver;* but, it required much more than I have yet heard to convince me, that to pay again in gold and silver *was possible.*

The chief object of our enquiries being this; *Whether it be possible, without a total destruction of all the paper money, to restore gold and silver to circulation amongst us;* this being the chief object of our enquiries, we should first ascertain *how the gold and silver was driven out of circulation,* and had its place supplied by a paper-money; for, unless we get at a clear view of this, it will be next to impossible for us to reason satisfactorily upon the means of bringing gold and silver back again into circulation.

Some people suppose, that paper *always* made a part of the currency, or common money, of England. They seem to regard the Bank of England as being as old as the Church of England, at least, and some of them appear to have full as much veneration for it. The truth is, however, that the Bank of England is a mere human institution, arising out of causes having nothing miraculous, or supernatural, about them; and that both the institution and the agents who carry it on, are as mortal as any other thing and any other men, in this or in any other country. THE BANK, as it is called, had its origin in the year 1694, that is, a hundred and sixteen years ago; and it arose thus: the then King, WILLIAM III, who had come from Holland, had begun *a war* against France, and, wanting money to carry it on, an act was passed (which act was the 20th of the 5th year of his reign) to invite people to make voluntary advances to the government of the sum of 1,500,000 pounds, and for securing the payment of the interest, and also for securing the re-payment of the principal, *taxes* were laid upon beer, ale, and other liquors. Upon condition of 1,200,000*l.* of this money being advanced, within a certain time, the subscribers to the loan were to be incorporated; and, as the money was advanced in due time, the incorporation took place, and the lenders of the money were formed into a trading Company, called "THE GOVERNOR "AND COMPANY OF THE BANK "OF ENGLAND." Out of this, and other sums borrowed by the government in the way of mortgage upon the taxes, there grew up a thing called the *Stocks*, or the *Funds* (of which we will speak hereafter); but the Bank Company remained under its primitive name, and as the *debt* of the nation increased, this Company increased in *riches* and in consequence.

Thus, you see, and it is well worthy of your attention, the Bank had its rise *in war* and *taxation*. But, we must reserve reflections of this sort for other occasions, and go on with our inquiries how *gold and silver have been driven out of circulation* in this country, or, in other words, how it came to pass that so much paper-money got afloat.

The Act of Parliament, which I have just referred to, points out the manner in which the Bank Company shall carry on their trade, and the articles in which they shall trade, allowing them, amongst other things, to trade in gold, silver, bills of exchange, and other things, under certain restrictions; but, as to what are called *bank notes*, the Company was not empowered to issue any such, in any other way, or upon any other footing, than merely as *promissory* notes, for the amount of which, in the coin of the country, they were liable to be sued and arrested. Having, however, a greater credit than any other individuals, or company of individuals, the Bank Company issued notes to a greater amount; and, which was something new in England, they were made payable, not to any *particular person*, or his *order*, and not at any *particular time;* but to the *bearer*, and on *demand*. These characteristics, which distinguished the promissory notes of the Bank of England from all other promissory notes gave the people greater confidence in them; and as the Bank Company were always ready to pay the notes in Gold and Silver, when presented for payment, the notes became, in time, to be looked upon as being as good as gold and silver. Hence came our country sayings:—"*As good as the Bank;*" "*As solid* "*as the Bank;*" and the like. Yet, the Bank was, as we have seen, merely a company of mortal men, formed into an association of traders; and their notes nothing more than written promises to pay the bearer so much money in gold or silver.

We used to have other sayings about the Bank, such as, "*As rich as* "*the Bank;*" "*All the gold in the* "*Bank;*" and such like, always conveying a notion, that the Bank was a *place*, and a place, too, where there were great heaps of money. As long as the Company were ready and willing to pay, and did actually pay, their notes in gold and silver, to all those persons who wished to have gold and silver, it is clear that these opinions of the people, relative to the Bank, were not altogether unfounded;

for, though no bit of paper, or of any thing which has no value in itself, can be, in fact, so good as a bit of gold; still, if it will, at any moment, whenever the holder pleases, bring him gold or silver to the amount written upon it, it is very nearly as good as gold and silver; and, at the time of which we are speaking, this was the case with the promissory notes of the Bank Company. But, it must be evident, that though the Company were ready, at the time now referred to, to pay their notes in gold and silver, they had never in their money-chests a sufficiency of gold and silver to pay off *all* their notes, if they had been presented all at once. This must be evident to every man; because, if the Bank Company kept locked up as much gold and silver as their notes amounted to, they could get nothing by issuing their notes, and might full as well have sent out their gold and silver. A farmer, for instance, who is generally using a hundred pounds of money to pay his workmen, might lend the hundred pounds and get interest for it, if he could persuade his workmen to take promissory notes of his own drawing, instead of money, and, if he were sure, that these promissory notes would not be brought in for payment; but, if this was not the case, he would be compelled to keep the hundred pounds in his drawer ready to give to those who did not like to keep his promissory notes; and, in such case, it is clear, that the money would be of no use to him, and that he might full as well have none of his notes out.

Just so with the Bank Company, who, at no time, could have in hand gold and silver enough to pay off *all* their notes at once; nor was this necessary as long as the people regarded those notes as being equally good with gold and silver. But, it is clear, that this *opinion of the goodness* of the Company's notes, or rather, the *feeling of confidence*, or, still more properly perhaps, the *absence of all suspicion*, with respect to them, must, in a great degree, depend upon the *quantity* of notes seen in circulation, compared with the quantity of gold and silver seen in circulation. At first, the quantity of notes was very small indeed; the increase of this quantity was, for the first twenty years, very slow; and, though it became more rapid in the next twenty years, the quantity does not appear to have been large till the war which took place in 1755, before which time the Bank Company put out no notes under 20 pounds in amount. Then it was that they began to put out 15 pound notes, and afterwards, but during the same war, 10 pound notes. During all this time, loans, in every war, had been made by the government. That is to say, the government had borrowed money of individuals, in the same way as above-mentioned, in the year 1694. The money thus borrowed was never payed off, but was suffered to remain at interest, and was, as it is now, called the NATIONAL DEBT, the interest upon which is annually paid out of the taxes raised upon the people. As this debt went on increasing, the bank-notes went on increasing, as, indeed, it is evident they must, seeing that the interest of the Debt was, as it still is and must be, *paid in bank-notes*.

It is not simply the quantity of bank-notes that are put into circulation, which will excite alarm as to their solidity; but, it is that quantity, if it be great, *compared with the quantity of gold and silver*, seen in circulation. If, as the bank-notes increased, the circulating gold and silver had increased in the same proportion; then, indeed, bank-notes would still have retained their usual credit; people would still have had the same confidence in them. But, this could not be. From the nature of things it could not be. The cause of the increase of the bank-notes, was, the increase of the interest upon the National Debt; and, as it grew out of an operation occasioned by poverty, it would have been strange indeed had it been accompanied with a circumstance, which would have been an infallible indication of riches.

Without, however, stopping here to inquire into the cause of the coin's not increasing with the increase of paper, suffice it to say, that such was the fact. Year after year we saw more of bank-notes and less of gold and silver; till, in time, such was the quantity of bank-notes required to meet the purposes of gold and silver in the payment of the interest of the still increasing Debt, and in the payment of the taxes, many other banks were opened, and they also issued their promissory notes. The Bank Company's notes, which had never before been made for less sums than 10 pounds, were, soon after the beginning of PITT's war, in 1793, issued for *five pounds*, after which it was not to be supposed, that people could have the same opinion of bank-notes that they formerly had. Every part of the people, except the very poorest of them, now, occasionally, at least, possessed bank-notes. Rents, salaries, yearly wages, all sums above five pounds, were now paid in bank-notes; and, the government itself was now paid its *taxes* in this same sort of currency.

In such a state of things it was quite impossible that people should not begin to perceive, that gold and silver was better than bank-notes; and that they should not be more desirous of possessing the former than the latter; and, the moment this is the case, the banking system must begin to tremble; for, as the notes are payable to the *bearer*, and payable on *demand*, it is very certain, that no man, with such a preference in his mind, will keep in his possession a bank-note, unless we can suppose a man so absurd as to keep a thing, of the goodness of which he has a suspicion, while, for merely opening his mouth or stretching forth his hand, he can exchange it for a thing of the same nominal value, and of the goodness of which it is impossible for him or any one else to entertain any suspicion. "Public Credit," as it has been called, but, as it may more properly be called, "*The credit of bank-notes*," has been emphatically denominated, "SUSPICION ASLEEP." In the midst of events like those of 1793 and the years immediately succeeding; in the midst of circumstances like those above-mentioned, relating to the bank-notes, it was impossible that SUSPICION should sleep any longer. The putting forth of the 5 pound bank-notes appears to have rouzed it, and, in the month of February, 1797, it became broad awake. The stoppage of payment on the part of the Bank Company was the immediate consequence; but, a particular account of that important event, which totally changed the nature of all our money transactions, and which will, in the end, produce, in all human probability, effects of the most serious nature, must be the subject of a future Letter. In the mean while I am,

Your Friend,

WM. COBBETT.

State Prison, Newgate, Thursday, 30th August, 1810.

LETTER II.

What are the Funds and Stocks and National Debt?—Necessity of clearly understanding what these words mean—Meaning of them—Inquiry into the Origin of the Funds and Debt—The English Revolution—Act of Parliament, 4th William III. Cap. 3, begins the Funding and Debt System—First Loan to Government—Nature of Funds and Stocks and National Debt—Explanation of how "Money is put in the Funds"—Illustration in the case of Messrs. Muckworm and Company, and that of Farmer Greenhorn—The Funds shown to be NO PLACE, nor any thing of a mystical nature.

GENTLEMEN,

HAVING in the foregoing letter, taken a sketch of the History of the Bank of England, and of its Notes, from their origin down to the time *when that Bank stopped paying its notes in gold and silver*, the next thing to do, in our regular course of proceeding, will be to inquire into, and clearly ascertain, the *cause* of that stoppage; for it is very evident, that without ascertaining this cause, we shall not be able to come to any thing like a decided opinion with regard to our main question, namely, WHETHER THERE BE ANY PROBABILITY THAT THIS BANK WILL BE ABLE TO RETURN TO THEIR PAYMENTS IN GOLD AND SILVER, in which question every man of us, from the highest to the lowest, is so deeply interested.

But, it is necessary for us to stop a little where we are, and not go on any further with our inquiries into the cause of the stoppage at the Bank of England, until we have taken time to look a little at the FUNDS and the NATIONAL DEBT. These are words which are frequently made use of; but, like many other words, they stand for things which are little understood, and the less, perhaps, because the words are so very commonly used. As in the instance of *Shrove Tuesday* or *Shrovetide*, words which we all, from the oldest to the youngest, make use of; but as to their *meaning*, we content ourselves with supposing (or appearing to suppose), that they contain a commandment for us to eat Fritters and Pancakes, and to murder poor unoffending cocks; whereas they mean, the Tuesday, or the time *for going to confess our sins to*, and to *get absolution from the Priests; to shrieve*, being a word equal in meaning *to confess*, and *shrove* to *confessed*; and the use of them in the case here mentioned having been handed down to us from the days of our forefathers, when the Catholic worship was the worship of the country.

Monstrous, however, as is the perversion of the meaning of words, in this instance, it is scarcely more so than in the case of the *Funds* and the *National Debt*; but, there is this very important difference in the two cases; that, while, in the former, the perversion is attended with no mischief to either individuals, or to the nation, in the latter, it is attended with great mischief to both; with the ruin and misery of many a thousand of widows and orphans, and with woes unnumbered to the nation at large. But, if a right understanding of the meaning of these words be, in all cases where words are used, of some consequence, it is of peculiar consequence here, where, as may have been gathered from the preceding letter, we shall find the *Funds*, the *Stocks*, and the *National Debt*, to be so closely interwoven with the *Bank Notes*, as to be quite inseparable therefrom in every possible state or stage of their existence.

The word FUND means, a *quantity of money put or collected together*. The word STOCK, as applied to such matters, has the same meaning. Both words may admit of meanings somewhat different from this; but, this is the meaning which plain men commonly give to these words; and it is, too, the fair and sensible meaning of them. Now, we shall presently see, in what degree this meaning belongs to what are commonly called the *Funds*, or the *Stocks*, into the origin and progress of which, we are now going to inquire; and, an inquiry it is, worthy of the undivided attention of every true Englishman; every man who wishes to see the country of his forefathers preserved from ruin and subjugation.

Soon after the ENGLISH REVOLUTION; that is to say, soon after our ancestors, who had too much spirit to be *dragooned* out of their liberty and their property, had driven away king James the Second, and had brought over the Prince of Orange and made him king in his stead, and had, at the same time, taken measures for stripping the family of Stuart of the crown for ever, and putting it upon the heads of his present Majesty's family; soon after this Revolution, the existence of Funds, Stocks, and a National Debt began, under the auspices of that same Prince of Orange, who was then become our King William III. and who appears to have lost but very little time in discovering the effectual way of obtaining money from the English, without resorting, as the Stuarts had, to those means, the use of which had, ever and anon, excited commotions against them; which had brought one of them to the scaffold; and which, at last, after driving another from the land, had for ever stripped them of their crown. The real motives for creating a National Debt we shall, by-and-by, perhaps, have occasion to notice; but, at present, our business is to get at a clear notion of *the way in which it was created.*

William the Third was hardly seated upon the throne before a war was begun against France, and, in the 4th year of his reign, being the year 1692, an act of parliament was passed imposing "Certain Rates and Duties "upon Beer, Ale and others Liquors, for *securing certain Recompences and Advantages* in the said "Act mentioned, to such Persons as "shall voluntarily advance the sum "of *Ten Hundred Thousand Pounds* "towards carrying on the *War against* "*France.*" This is the Title of the Act, being Chapter 3rd of the 4th year of William and Mary. These are the very words; and fatal words they were to England.

In the body of this Act, it is enacted, that the persons, who shall advance the million of pounds, shall, out of the rates and duties imposed by the act, receive a certain *interest,* or annual payment, for the use of the money so advanced. They were to have, and they had, their money secured to them by the way of *annuity for life or lives;* and, they were to have certain advantages in cases of survivorship; and the annuities were to be redeemed upon certain conditions and at certain times. But, it will be quite useless for us to load our subject with a multitude of words, and to ring the changes upon all the quaint terms, which, as appertaining to these matters, have, one would think, been made use of for no other purpose than that of confusing the understandings of plain men. The light wherein to view the transaction is this: The Government was (no matter how, or from what cause) got into a war with France; and, for the alledged purpose of pushing on this war with "*vigour*" (it is odd enough that the very word was made use of, just as it is now) they borrowed a million of pounds of individuals, and, at the same time, imposed taxes upon the whole nation for the purpose of paying the interest of the money so borrowed; or, in other words, the nation's taxes were *mortgaged* to the lenders of this million of pounds.

The lenders of the money, who, in time, became to be called *fund-holders,* or *stock-holders,* did, as the work of lending and fund-making advanced, make their loans in various ways, and the bargains between them and the government were of great variety in their terms, and in the denominations made use of; but, it was always the same thing in *effect:* the government borrowed the money of individuals: it mortgaged taxes for the payment of the interest; and those individuals received for their money, promises, or engagements, no matter in what shape, which enabled them to demand annually, half-yearly, or quarterly, the share of interest due to each of them; and any single parcel of interest, so received, is what is, in the queer language of the funding trade, called a "*dividend.*" No matter, therefore, what the thing is called; no matter how many nick-names they choose to give to the several branches of the Debt. We daily see, in the newspapers, what is called the "PRICE OF STOCKS," as in the following statement, which is in all the newspapers of this day:

Bank Stock 257 5$\frac{1}{2}$
3 per Cent. Red. 68$\frac{1}{4}$ $\frac{5}{8}$ $\frac{3}{8}$ $\frac{1}{2}$
3 per Cent. Con. 67$\frac{7}{8}$ 8 7$\frac{7}{8}$
4 per Cent. 85 4$\frac{7}{8}$ 5$\frac{1}{8}$ 4$\frac{7}{8}$
5 per Cent. Navy 99$\frac{3}{8}$ $\frac{1}{2}$ $\frac{1}{4}$ $\frac{3}{8}$
Long Annuities 18$\frac{1}{2}$
Omnium 2$\frac{5}{8}$ $\frac{7}{8}$ dis.
Excheq. Bills 1 dis. 5 prem.
Bank Stock for open. 257$\frac{1}{2}$
Consols for——68$\frac{1}{2}$ $\frac{1}{4}$ $\frac{3}{8}$

These are names, which the dealers, or jobbers, in Stocks give to the several classes of them. But, as I said before, let us avoid confusing our heads with this worse than Babylonish collection of names, or sounds, and keep fully and clearly and constantly in our sight, these plain facts: FIRST, that *the Funds, the Stocks,* and *the National Debt,* all mean one and the same thing; SECONDLY, that this Debt is made up of the *Principal* money lent to the Government at different times since the beginning of the thing in 1692; THIRDLY, that the *Interest* upon this principal money is paid out of the taxes; and, FOURTHLY, that those persons who are entitled to receive this interest, are what we call *fund-holders,* or *stock-holders,* or, according to the more common notion and saying, have "*money in the funds.*"

Being here in the elementary, the mere horn-book, part of our subject, we cannot make the matter too clear to our comprehension; and, we ought, by no means, to go a step further, till we have inquired into the sense of this saying about people's "*having money in the Funds;*" from which any one, who did not understand the thing, would naturally conclude, that the person who made use of the saying, looked upon *the Funds,* as a *place,* where a great quantity of gold and silver was kept locked up in safety. Nor, would such conclusion be very erroneous; for, generally speaking, the notion of the people of this country is, that the *Funds* or the *Stocks* (they are made use of indiscriminately,) is a PLACE, where money is kept. A place, indeed, of a sort of mysterious existence; a sort of financial Ark; a place not, perhaps, to be touched, or even seen; but, still the notion is, that of a place, and a place, too, of more than mortal security.

Alas! *the Funds* are no place at all! and, indeed, how should they, seeing that they are in fact, one and the same thing with the *National Debt?* But, to remove, from the mind of every creature, all doubt upon this point; to dissipate the mists, in which we have so long been wandering about, to the infinite amusement of those who invented these terms, let us take a plain common-sense view of one of these *loaning* transactions. Let us suppose, then, that the Government wants a *loan,* that is, wants to *borrow money,* to the amount of a million of pounds. It gives out its wishes to this effect, and, after the usual ceremony upon such occasions, the loan is made, that is, the money is lent, by Messrs. Muckworm and Company. We shall see, by-and-by, when we come to talk more fully upon the subject of loans, what sort of a way it is, in which Muckworm pays in the money so lent, and in what sort of money it is that he pays. But, for the sake of simplicity in our illustration, we will suppose him to pay in real good money, and to pay the whole million himself at once. Well: what does Muckworm get in return? Why, *his name is written in a book; against his name is written that he is entitled to receive interest for a million of money;* which book is kept at the Bank Company's house, or shop, in Threadneedle Street, London. And, thus it is that Muckworm "*puts a million of money into* "*the Funds.*" "Well," you will say, "but *what becomes of the money?*" Why, the Government *expends it,* to be sure: what should become of it? Very few people borrow money for the purpose of locking it up in their drawers or chests. "What? then, "the money all *vanishes;* and *nothing* "*remains in lieu of it but the lender's* "*name written in a book?*" Even so: and this, my good neighbours, is the way, that "*money is put into the* "*Funds.*"

But, the most interesting part of the transaction remains to be described. Muckworm, who is as wise as he is rich, takes special care not to be a fund-holder himself; and, as is always the case, he loses no time in *selling* his *stock,* that is to say, his *right to receive the interest of the million of pounds.* These funds, or stock, as we have seen, have no bodily existence, either in the shape of money or of bonds or of certificates or of any thing else that can be seen or touched. They have a being merely in *name.* They mean, in fact, *a right to receive interest;* and, a man, who is said *to possess, or to have, a thousand pounds' worth of stock,* possesses, in reality, nothing but *the right of receiving the interest of a thousand pounds.* When therefore, Muckworm *sells* his million's worth of stock, he sells the right of receiving the interest upon the million of pounds which he lent to the government. But, the way in which sales of this sort are effected is by parcelling the stock out to little purchasers, every one of whom buys as much as he likes; he *has his name written in the book* for so much, instead of the name of Muckworm and Company; and, when Muckworm has sold the whole, his name is crossed out, and the names of the persons, to whom he has sold, remain in the book.

And, here it is that the thing comes home to our very bosoms; for, our neighbour, farmer Greenhorn, who has all his life long been working like a horse, in order to secure his children from the perils of poverty, having first bequeathed his farm to his son, sells the rest of his property (amounting to a couple of thousands of pounds), and, with the real good money, the fruit of his incessant toil and care, purchases two thousand pounds worth of Muckworm's Funds, or Stocks, and leaves the said purchase to his daughter. And, why does he do say? The reason is, that, as he believes, his daughter will always receive the interest of the two thousand pounds, without any of the risk, or trouble, belonging to the rents of house or land. Thus neighbour Greenhorn is said to have "put two thousand "pounds in the funds;" and thus his daughter (poor girl!) is said to "*have* "*her money in the funds;*" when the plain fact is, that Muckworm's money *has been spent by the government,* that *Muckworm has now the two thousand* pounds of poor Grizzle Greenhorn, and that she, in return for it, has *her name written in a Book,* at the Bank Company's house in Threadneedle street, London, in consequence of which she is entitled to receive the interest of the two thousand pounds; which brings us back to the point whence we started, and explains the whole art and mystery of making loans and funds and stocks and national debts.

It will be very useful to show the *effect* of this "putting money in the "funds," with respect to the party, who is said to put it in. I do not know of any duty more pressing upon me, than that of showing, in this plain and practical way, what have been, what are, and what must be, the consequences to those, who thus dispose of their property; especially if they have no property of any other sort. But, this will be found to belong to another part of our subject; and, as we have now seen what the Funds and the Stocks *really are;* as we have blown away the mist in which we had so long been wandering; as the financial Ark is now no more in our sight than any veritable box made of deal boards and nails; as we are now satisfied, that there is nothing mystical in the words Funds and Stocks, and that, so far from meaning *a place where a great quantity of money is kept,* they are not the name of any place at all, nor of any thing which has a corporeal existence, and are the mere denominations, or names, of the several classes, or parcels, of Debt, which the government owes to individuals: in short, as we have now, let us hope, arrived at a complete knowledge of the *nature* and *origin* of the Funds and the Stocks and the National Debt, which, as was before said, are, in fact, all one and the same thing, it is time that we proceed to enquire into their *progress,* and to see how that progress is connected with the increase of the Bank Notes and with the stoppage of the payment of those notes in gold and silver. To do justice, however, to this copious and interesting theme, especially when coupled with what it will be necessary to say as to the schemes for *arresting* the progress of the Debt, will demand a separate Letter.

In the mean while,
I am with perfect sincerity,
Your Friend,
Wm. COBBETT.

State Prison, Newgate, Thursday, 6th Sep. 1810.

LETTER III.

Danger of exciting Popular Discontents against Country Paper-Money Makers—Description of the National Debt—Progress of the Debt—The different Denominations of it of no Consequence—Cost of the Anti-jacobin War—Progress of the National Expences—Progress of the Revenue or Taxes—The Effect of Taxation—Taxes cause Poverty and Misery in a Country—Not like Rents—Increase of Revenue no Proof of National Prosperity—What are the Signs of National Prosperity—Increase of the Poor Rates in England—Cost of the Tax-Gatherers sufficient to support 92,500 Families.

GENTLEMEN,

A LONDON print, which is what is called a ministerial newspaper, and which I, in the discharge of my duty as a public writer, am compelled to read, but which, for the sake of your morals, I hope none of you ever see, has most harshly spoken of that part of our paper money, which is issued by the Bankers, whose shops are in the country. The writer of this print has described that paper, namely, the country bank notes, as "*destructive* "*assignats;*" and, in another of his publications, he calls them "*vile* "*rags;*" and then again "*dirty rags.*" These hard words, besides that they are unbecoming in sober discussion, can do no good, and may do a great deal of harm, if they have any effect at all upon the minds of the people; and, therefore we will make a remark or two upon their tendency, before we proceed with the topic mentioned at the close of the last letter.

Assignats was the name given to the French revolutionary paper-money, the distresses occasioned by which are fresh in the recollection of most people; and, to give the same name to our country bank-notes was, therefore, to proclaim, as far as this writer was able to proclaim, that these notes *being more than one half of all our circulating medium*, were as bad, if not worse, than the paper money of France, which produced so much individual misery to so many millions of people. Not that this was betraying any *secret* to the world; for, it is beyond all comprehension foolish to suppose, that all the world, particularly our sharp-sighted enemy, are not fully acquainted with our situation in this respect, more especially now that the Bullion Report is abroad; but, what I find fault of, is, that this description of country-bank-notes, as contradistinguished from the London bank-notes, has a tendency to excite popular hatred, and, in cases that may happen, popular violence, against that part of our paper-money makers, called country bankers; than which nothing can be much more unjust in itself, or be more likely to lead to universal confusion, the experience of the world having proved that commotion, when once on foot, is seldom limited to the accomplishment of its original object; and, we may venture to affirm, that nothing was ever better calculated to render popular commotion violent, and to push it beyond its natural bounds, than the hatred and revenge, which it would seem to be the object of the print above mentioned to excite in the minds of the people.

The country paper-money makers

are not, as we shall soon see, any more to blame than are the paper-money makers in town. Paper-money making is a trade, or calling, perfectly innocent in itself, and the tradesmen may be very moral and even very liberal men. Amongst them, as amongst men of other trades, there are, doubtless, sharpers and even rogues, and, the trade itself may be one that exposes men to the temptation of becoming roguish; but it does not follow, that *all* the paper-money makers, or, that the paper-money makers *in general,* are men of dishonest views. It is therefore, not only illiberal, but unjust in the extreme, to condemn the whole of the trade in a lump, to call their wares "*destructive assignats, vile rags, dirty rags,*" and the like, whence it is, of course, intended that it should be understood, that all the issuers of them ought to be regarded as pests of society and treated accordingly; when the truth is, as we shall presently see, the fault is not in individuals, but in the system.

Having thus endeavoured to put you upon your guard against the tendency of this very unjust representation of our country bankers, and their money, an endeavour, which, it appeared to me, ought not to be delayed, we will now proceed with our subject, and, as was proposed, at the close of the last Letter, inquire into the *progress* of the Funds and Stocks; or, in more proper terms, into the INCREASE OF THE NATIONAL DEBT.

We have before seen what is the *nature* of this debt: we have also seen *how it began:* we shall, by-and-by have to show the *effects* of it: but what we have to do, at present, is to inquire into, and ascertain, how it has gone on increasing, and what is now its amount. We shall next inquire into the schemes for *lessening* the Debt; and then we shall distinguish what is called Redeemed from Unredeemed debt; but, first of all, let us leave all other views of it aside, and confine our attention merely to the sums borrowed. We have before seen, that the money has been borrowed in various ways, or under various denominations. In some cases the money borrowed was to yield the lender 3 per centum, that is to say 3 pounds interest, yearly, for every hundred pounds of principal. In some cases the lendor was to receive 4 per centum; in some cases 5 per centum; and in some cases more. Hence come the denomination of 3 *per cents* and 4 *per cents,* and so forth. But, to the people, who have to pay the interest, these distinctions are of no consequence at all, any more than it would be to either of us, whether our bakers' bills were made out upon brown paper or upon white. We shall see afterwards what we have to pay yearly in the shape of *interest,* which is the thing that touches us home; but, let us first see what the principal is, and *how it has gone on increasing;* bearing in mind, that, as was shown in the foregoing Letter, page 17, the borrowing, and, of course, the Debt, began in the year 1692, in the reign of William the Third, and that the loan made in that year amounted to one millions of pounds.

When QUEEN ANNE, who succeeded William, came to the throne, which was in the year 1701, the Debt was . . .	£16,394,702
When GEORGE I. came to the throne in 1714, it was	54,145,363
When GEORGE II. came to the throne, in 1727, it was	52,092,235
When GEORGE III. came to the throne, in 1760, it was . .	146,682,844
After the AMERICAN WAR, in 1784, it was	257,213,043

W. MOLINEUX, Printer, Bream's Buildings, Chancery Lane.

B

At the latter END OF THE LAST WAR; that is to say, the first war against the French Revolutionists, and which, for the sake of having a distinctive appellation, we will call the ANTI-JACOBIN WAR: at the end of that war, in 1801, the Debt was 579,931,447

At the PRESENT TIME; or rather, in January last: 811,898,082

That is to say, *eight hundred and eleven millions, eight hundred and ninety eight thousand, and eighty two;* and these in *pounds*, in English pounds, too! There are, in the accounts, laid before the parliament (from which the last mentioned sum is taken) some *shillings* and *pence* and even FARTHINGS, in addition; but though these accountants have been so nice, we will not mind a few farthings. Part of this Debt is what is called *funded* and a part *unfunded;* part is called Irish Debt, part Emperor of Germany's Debt, and another part the Prince Regent of Portugal's. But *interest upon the whole of it is payable in England;* and that is all that we have to look after; it being of no consequence to us what the thing is called, *so that we have to pay for it.* So that we are taxed to pay the interest of it, what matters it to us what names the several parts of it may go by? I hope, that there is not, at this day, a man amongst you, who is to be amused with empty sounds: I hope that your minds are not now-a-days, after all that you have seen, to be led away from the object before them by any repetition of mere names. *So long as we are taxed to pay the interest upon the Debt,* that man must be exceedingly weak, who is to be made to believe, that it is of any consequence to any of us by what name that debt is called.*

Such, then, has been the *progress* of the National Debt; and, it is well worthy of our attention, that it has increased in *an increasing proportion.* It is now nearly *six times* as great as it was when the present king came to the throne; and, which ought to be well attended to, *more than two thirds of the whole of the debt* has been contracted in carrying on, against the French, that war, which, at its commencement, was to succeed by means of *ruining the finances of France.* When the ANTIJACOBIN WAR began, in 1793, the Debt was, at the utmost 257,213,043*l.* It is now 811,898,082*l.* Such has, thus far, been the financial effect; such has been the effect as to money-matters, of the wars against the Jacobins. How many times were we told, that it required but *one* more campaign; *one* more; only *one* more *vigorous* campaign, to put an end to the war; to destroy, to annihilate, for ever, the *resources* of France. Alas! those resources have not been destroyed. They have increased in a fearful degree; while we have accumulated hundreds of millions of Debt in the attempt. How many writers have flattered us, from time to time, with the hope, nay, the certainty, (if we would but persevere) of triumphing over the French by the means of our *riches!* To how many of these deceivers have we been so foolish as to listen! It is this credulity, which has led to the present state of things; and, unless we shake it off at once, and resolve to look our dangers in the face, we shall, I greatly fear, experience that fate which our deceivers told us would be experienced by our enemy. PITT, it is well known, grew into favour with the nation in consequence of his promises and his plans to pay off the National Debt; and, this same PITT, who found that Debt 257 millions, left it upwards of 600 millions, after having, for twenty years, had the full power of managing all the resources of the nation; after having, for nearly the whole of that time, had the support of three fourths,

* There is, besides the above, the INDIA DEBT; but of that we will speak another time.

if not more, of the Members of the House of Commons; after having, of course, adopted whatever measures he thought proper, during the whole of that time. He found the Debt *two hundred* and fifty odd millions, and he left it *six hundred* and fifty odd. This was what was done for England by that PITT whose own *private debts* the *people* had to pay, besides the expence of a *monument* to his memory! This is what every man in England should bear constantly in mind.

Having now seen *how the National Debt has increased*, let us next see how the EXPENCES, of the Nation have increased; and, then take a look at the increase of the TAXES; for in order to be able to form a correct opinion upon the main points, touched upon by the Bullion Committee, we must have a full view, not only of the *Debt* but of the *Expences* and the *Taxes* of the nation.

When QUEEN ANNE came to the throne, in 1701, the whole Expences of the year, *including the interest on the National Debt* amounted to .	£5,610,987	Peace
When GEORGE I. came to the throne, in 1714, and just after Queen Anne had been *at war eleven years* .	6,633,581	Peace
When GEORGE II. came to the throne, in 1727, . .	5,441,248	Peace
When GEORGE III. came to the throne in 1760 . .	24,456,940	War
After the END OF THE AMERICAN WAR and at the beginning of PITT's Administration, in 1784 . . .	21,657,609	Peace
At the latter End of the last, or ANTI-JACOBIN WAR, in 1801, . . .	61,278,018	War
For the last year, that is the year 1809,	£82,027,288, 5*s*. 1¾*d*	War.

Now, without any thing more than this, let me ask any of you, to whom I address this Letter, whether you think it possible for the thing *to go on in this way for any great length of time*? If the subject did not present so many considerations to make us serious, it would be quite impossible to refrain from laughing at the scrupulousness that could put *five shillings and a penny three farthings* at the end of a sum of millions that it almost makes one's head swim but to think of. Laughable, however, as we may think it, those who have such accounts made out, think it no laughing matter. It is, on the contrary, looked upon by them, perhaps, as no very unimportant part of the system.

Upon looking at the above progress of the Expenditure, it is impossible to avoid being struck with the increase, *during the present reign*. The year 1760 was a time of war as well as the present; but, as we see, a year of war then, cost only 24 millions; whereas a year of war now costs 82 millions. We see, too, that a year of war now costs 20 millions more than a year of war cost only ten years ago. What, then, will be the cost if this war should continue many years longer, and if, as appearances threaten, the enemy should take such measures, and adopt such a change in his mode of hostility, as to add greatly to the expensiveness of our defence? This is a very material consideration; and, though it will hereafter be taken up, still I could not refrain from just touching upon it in this place. Am I told, that *our money is depreciated* or *fallen off in value*; and that the increase in our Expences is more *nominal* than real; that the increase is in name; merely in the figures, and not in the thing; for that a pound is not worth any thing like what a pound was worth when the king came to the throne? Am I told this? If I am

I say, that we are not yet come to the proper place for discussing matters of this sort; that we shall come to it all in good time; but, that, in the meanwhile, I may hope to hear no more abuse of our doctrines, from those, at least, who, in this way, would reconcile our minds to the enormous increase in the Nation's yearly Expences.

Having now taken a view of the increase of the *Debt*, and also of the yearly *Expences* of the nation, let us now see how the *Revenue*, or *Income*, or, more properly speaking, the TAXES; that is to say, the money received from the people, in the course of the year, by the several sorts of Tax-gatherers; let us now see how the amount of these has gone on increasing.

When QUEEN ANNE came to the throne, in 1701, the yearly amount of the taxes was	£4,212,358
When GEORGE I. came to the throne in 1714, it was - - - - -	6,762,643
When GEORGE II. came to the throne in 1727, it was - - -	6,522,540
When GEORGE III. came to the throne in 1760, it was - - -	8,744,682
After the AMERICAN war, in 1784, it was	13,300,921
At the close of the Anti-Jacobin war, in 1801, it was - - - - -	36,728,971
For the last year, that is 1809, it was - - -	70,240,226

It is quite useless to offer any comments upon this. The figures speak too plainly for themselves to receive any assistance from words. As to the *correctness* of these statements, there may, perhaps, be found some little inaccuracies in the copying of the figures, and in adding some of the sums together; but, these must be very immaterial; and, indeed, none of the questions, which we have to discuss, can possibly be affected by any little error of this sort. I say this in order to bar any cavil that may, possibly, be attempted to be raised out of circumstances, such as I have here mentioned.

Thus, then, we have pretty fairly before us, a view of the increase of the *Debts*, the *Expences*, and the *Taxes*, of the nation; and a view it is quite sufficient to impress with serious thoughts every man, whose regard for his country is not confined to mere professions. There are persons, I know, who laugh at this. *They* may have reason to laugh; but *we* have not. The pretence is, that taxes *return again* to those who pay them. Return again! In what manner do they return? Can any of you perceive the taxes that you pay coming back again to you? All the interested persons who have written upon taxation, have endeavoured to persuade the people, that, to load them with taxes does them no harm at all, though this is in direct opposition to the language of every Speech that the King makes to the Parliament during every war; for, in every such Speech, he expresses his deep *sorrow*, that he is compelled to lay new burdens upon his people.

The writers here alluded to, the greater part of whom live, or have a design to live, upon the taxes, always appear to consider the nation as being *rich* and *prosperous* in a direct proportion to the *quantity of taxes*, that is raised upon it; never seeming to take into their views of riches and prosperity the *ease* and *comfort* of the people who pay those taxes. The notion of these persons seems to be, that, as there always will be more food raised and more goods made in the country than is sufficient for those, who own, and who till the soil, and who labour in other ways, that the surplus, or super-abundance, ought to fall to *their* share; or, at least, that it ought to be *taken away in taxes*, which produce a luxurious way of living, and luxury gives *employment* to the people; that is to say, that it sets them to work *to earn their own money back again*. This is a mighty favour to be sure.

The tendency of taxation is, to create a class of persons who do not labour; to take from those who do labour the produce of that labour, and to give it to those who do not labour. The produce taken away is, in this case, totally *destroyed*; but, if it were expended, or consumed, amongst those who labour, it would produce something in its stead. There would be more, or better cloth; more or better houses; and these would be more generally distributed; while the growth of vice, which idleness always engenders and fosters, would be prevented.

If, by the gripe of taxation, every grain of the surplus produce of a country be taken from the lowest class of those who labour; they will have the means of *bare existence* left. Of course, their clothing and their dwellings will become miserable, their food bad, or in stinted quantity; that surplus produce which should go to the making of an addition to their meal, and to the creating of things for their use, will be *annihilated* by those who do nothing but eat. Suppose, for instance, a community to consist of a farmer, four cottagers, a taylor, a shoemaker, a smith, a carpenter, and a mason, and that the land produces enough for them all and no more. Suppose this little community to be seized with a desire to imitate their betters, and to keep a sinecure placeman, giving him a tenth of their produce which they formerly gave to their shoemaker. The consequence would be, that poor CRISPIN would die, and they would go barefooted, with the consolation of reflecting that they had brought themselves into this state from the silly vanity of keeping an idle man. But, suppose the land to yield enough food for all ten of them, and enough for two more besides. They have this, then, besides what is absolutely necessary to supply their wants. They can spare one of their men from the field, and have besides, food enough to keep him in some other situation. Now, which is best, to make him a second carpenter, who, in return for his food, would give them additional and permanent convenience and comfort in their dwellings; or, to make him a sinecure placeman or a singer, in either of which places he would be an annihilator of corn, at the same time, that in case of emergency, he would not be half so able to defend the community. Suppose *two* of the cultivators became sinecure placemen, then you kill the carpenter or some one else, or what is more likely, all the labouring part of the community, that is to say, all but the sinecure placemen, live more miserably, in dress, in dwellings, and in food. This reasoning applied to *tens*, applies equally well to *millions*, the causes and effects being, in the latter case, only a little more difficult to trace.

Such is the way in which *taxes* operate; the distinction between which operation and the operation of *rents* being this, that in the latter case, you *receive* something of which you have the particular enjoyment, for what y give; and, in the former case you receive nothing. It is by no means to be understood, that there should be no persons to live without what is generally called labour. Physicians, Parsons, Lawyers, and others of the higher callings in life, do, in fact, labour; and it is right that there should be persons of great estate, and without any profession at all; but then, you will find, that these persons *do not live upon the earnings of others*: they all of them give something in return for what they receive. Those of the learned profession give the *use of their talents and skill*; and the landlord gives *the use of his land or his houses*.

Nor ought we to look upon all Taxes as so much of the fruit of our labour lost, or taken away without cause. Taxes are necessary in every community; and the man, whether he be statesman, soldier, or sailor, who is in the service of the community, gives his services in return for that portion of the taxes which he receives.

We are not talking against *taxes in general;* nor, indeed, will we stop here to inquire, whether *our taxes*, at their present amount, be necessary; or, *whether, by other counsels, they might, in great part, at least, have been avoided.* These are questions, which, for the present, we will wholly pass over, our object being to come at a correct opinion with regard to the *effect* of heavy taxation upon the people who have to support it, reserving for another opportunity our remarks and opinions as to the *necessity* of such taxation in our particular case.

By national *prosperity* the writers above alluded to mean something very different indeed from that which you and I, who have no desire to live upon the taxes, should call national prosperity. They look upon it, or, at least, they would have us look upon it as being demonstrated in the increase of the number of chariots and of fine-dressed people in and about the purlieus of the court; whereas, reflection will not fail to teach us, that this is a demonstration of the increase of the taxes, and nothing more. National prosperity shews itself in very different ways: in the plentiful meal, the comfortable dwelling, the decent furniture and dress, the healthy and happy countenances, and the good morals of *the labouring classes of the people.* These are the ways in which national prosperity shows itself; and, whatever is not attended with these signs, is not national prosperity. Need I ask *you*, then, if heavy taxation be calculated to produce these effects? Have our labourers a plentiful meal of food fit for man? Do they taste meat once in *a day?* Are they decently clothed? Have they the means of obtaining firing? Are they and their children healthy and happy? I put these questions to you, Gentlemen, who have the means of knowing the facts, and who must, I am afraid, answer them all in the negative.

But, why need we here leave any thing to conjecture, when we have the undeniable proof before us, in the accounts, laid before Parliament, of the amount of the *Poor-Rates*, at two different periods, and, of course, at two different stages in our taxation; namely, in the year 1784, and in the year 1803? At the former period, the taxes of the year, as we have seen above, amounted to £.13,300,921; and then the Poor Rates amounted to £.2,105,623. At the latter period, the taxes of the year (as will be seen from the Official Statement in Register, Vol. IV. page 1471) amounted to £41,931,747; and the Poor Rates had then risen to £5,246,506. What must they, then, amount to at this day, when the year's taxes amount to upwards of 70 millions of pounds?

Here, then, we have a pretty good proof, that *taxation* and *pauperism* go hand in hand. We have seen what was produced by the ANTIJACOBIN WAR. The taxes continued nearly the same from 1784 to 1793, the year in which PITT began that war; so that, by the ANTIJACOBIN WAR alone the poor rates were augmented, in nominal amount, from £.2,105,623 to £.5,246,506; at which we shall not be surprized, if we apply to this case the principle above illustrated in the supposed community of ten men, where it is shown, that, by taking the produce of labour from the proprietors of it, and giving it to those, who do not labour and who do not give the proprietors of such produce any thing in return, *poverty*, or, at least, a *less degree* of *ease* and *enjoyment*, must be the consequence.

The poor-rates alone are now equal in amount to *the whole of the national expenditure*, including the interest of the Debt, when the late king came to the throne; and, the charges of *managing* the taxes; that is to say, the wages, salaries, or allowances, to the *Tax-Gatherers* of various descriptions; the bare charge which we pay on this account amounts to very little short of as much as the whole of the taxes amounted to when King William was crowned.

This charge; that is to say, *what we pay to the Tax-gatherers*, in one shape or another, is stated in the account laid before Parliament for the last year, at £.2,886,201, a sum equal to a year's wages of 92,500 labourers at *twelve shillings a week,* which may, I suppose, be looked upon as the average wages of labourers, take all the kingdom through. Is this *no evil?* Are we to be persuaded, that, to take the means of supporting 92,500 families, consisting, upon the usual computation (5 to a family), of 461,000 souls; that to take away the means of supporting all these, and giving those means to support others, whose business it is to *tax* the rest, instead of adding to the stock of the community by their labour; are we to be persuaded that this is *no evil;* and that, too, though we see the poor rates grown from 2 millions to 5 millions in the space of 10 years? Are we to be persuaded to believe this? Verily, if we are, it is a great shame for us to pretend to laugh at the Mahomedans.

Having now taken a view of the *progress* of the National *Debt* together with that of the National *Expences* and *Taxes;* and having (by stepping a little aside for a moment) seen something of their effect upon National *prosperity,* we will, in the next Letter, agreeably to the intention before expressed, inquire into the schemes for *arresting* this fearful progress; or, as they are generally denominated, plans for *paying off,* or *reducing,* the National Debt; a subject of very great importance, because, as we must now be satisfied, the *bank notes have increased with the Debt,* and, of course, the reducing of the Debt would, if it were accomplished, tend to the reduction of the quantity of bank-notes, by the excess of which it is, as the Bullion Committee have declared, that the gold coin has been driven from circulation.

I am, Gentlemen,
Your faithful Friend,
WM. COBBETT.

State Prison, Newgate, Tuesday, 11th Sept. 1810.

LETTER IV.

Schemes for paying off the National Debt—Former Sinking Funds—Origin of Pitt's Grand Sinking Fund—Changes made by Pitt's sway in the state of this Country—Grand Sinking Fund Act—Purposes of it—The Commissioners and their manner of proceeding—How they would buy up Grizzle Greenhorn's share of the Debt—What Redemption means—Commissioners step into Grizzle's shoes—We still are taxed for the Interest—Evils of the Grand Sinking Fund—What would be really redeeming—American mode of Redeeming—Statement of the Increase of the Interest on the Debt—Clause in Pitt's Grand Sinking Fund Act for ceasing to pay Interest, in 1808, upon Stock bought up.

GENTLEMEN,

OUR next business is to inform ourselves correctly with respect to the Schemes, which, at different times, have been on foot for PAYING OFF THE NATIONAL DEBT, and about which *paying off* we have, all our lives long, heard so much.

We have seen how the Debt has gone on increasing from its first existence to the present day; we have seen how the Expences of the nation and the Taxes of the nation have gone on increasing with the debt; we have also seen that the increase of the Bank-Notes has kept pace with the rest, till those notes have, at last, *driven the gold coin out of circulation.* This last, is the evil, for which the Bullion Committee have endeavoured to find out a remedy, and such a remedy they appear to think that they have found, in an Act of Parliament, which they propose to be passed for causing the Bank Company to pay their promissory notes in gold and silver in two years' time. One of our principal objects, in this discussion, is, to enable ourselves to form a correct opinion as to the *practicability of this remedy*, even at the end of two years; and, as we have, from what has already been shown, good reason to believe, that the quantity of bank notes, the excess of which has driven the gold out of circulation, cannot be lessened unless the Debt be also diminished, it is necessary for us to ascertain what has been done or attempted, and what is likely to be done, in the way of causing such diminution.

From very early stages of the Debt; indeed, almost from the very beginning of it, there were measures proposed for *paying it off*, the idea of an everlasting Debt, and an everlasting mortgage upon the nation's means, being at first, something too frightful for our upright and sensible ancestors to bear. Propositions, and even provisions, were at different times accordingly made for paying off parts of the Debt, and some comparatively small sums were, in the early stages of the progress, actually paid off; the Debt became less, and less interest was, of course, paid upon it. Still, however, as *new wars* came on, new sums were borrowed; and, as lending money to the government was found to be a profitable trade; as so many persons of influence found their advantage in the loaning transactions, the money was always easily enough raised. But, yet there continued to be a talk of *paying off* the Debt; and, in time, a part of the yearly taxes were set aside for that purpose, which part of the taxes so set aside was called a SINKING FUND.

These being words, which, as belonging to our present subject, are of vast importance, it is necessary for us to have a clear notion of their meaning. The word *fund*, as was before observed in Letter II. page 20, means *a quantity of money put together for any purpose*; and, in the instance before us, the word *Sinking* appears to have been prefixed to the word Fund in order to characterize, or describe, the particular purpose, or use, of the taxes so set apart; namely, the purpose of *sinking*, or *reducing*, or *diminishing*, or *lessening*, the Debt. So that the *Sinking Fund*, of which we have all heard so much, and of which most of us have known so little, means, in other words, in words better to be understood, a *Lessening Fund*; and whether the thing has, in its operation, hitherto, answered to its name, we shall by-and-by see, if, indeed, we have not seen enough to satisfy us upon this point in the increasing of the Debt, as exhibited in the foregoing Letter.

The amount of taxes thus set apart, or, to use the words with which we must now grow familiar, the Sinking Funds, which were, time after time, established, were in many cases, applied to other purposes than that for which they were destined, or intended. Indeed, they seem, for many years, to have been very little better than purses made up at one time and spent again at another, without answering any rational purpose at all; and, accordingly, the nation does not appear to have paid any great attention to them, or to have considered them as of any consequence, until the year 1786, when the present GRAND SINKING FUND was established by Pitt, who, but a little while before, had been made Prime Minister, and whose system has continued to this day.

Gentlemen, we are now entering upon a part of our subject, which not only demands an uncommon portion of your attention, but, into the discussion of which you will, I hope, carry such a spirit of impartiality as shall subdue all the prejudices of party and dissipate all the mists of ignorance which have therefrom arisen. It is, even yet, impossible to mention the name of Pitt, without exciting feelings that struggle hard against reason, and that, in some minds, overcome it. During his administration, the nation was divided into two parties, so hostile to each other, that both were easily made subservient to his views; and, it is, with every man who really loves his country, matter of deep regret, that the same, or nearly the same, divisions continue to the present day.

It is not for me, who, at one time, really looked upon PITT as the greatest minister that England ever saw, to reproach others, *who may still be as ignorant of the truth, as I was then,* for their attachment to his memory, for their high opinion of the schemes of his inventing, and for their blind adoration of those schemes; but when they have, as I have, taken a fair and full view of all his measures; when they have compared his deeds with his professions, his performances with his promises; when they have seen, that he added threefold to our Taxes and our Expenditure, and that, notwithstanding this, the power and the territory of France were extended in proportion to the sacrifices he called upon us to make for what he called resisting her; when they see, that the standard of national misery, the poor-rates, rose, during his sway, in almost a triple degree; when they see, that the war at the outset of which he relied, in no small degree, for success upon the *destruction of French assignats,* did, at the end of four years, cause the stoppage of gold and silver payments at the Bank of England, and that its prolongation has led to a state of things, in which a public print devoted to the government, has described the largest class of *English* bank-notes as "*destructive assignats;*" when they see this, and when they see, that, the National Debt, which he himself called "*the best ally of France;*" when they see, that that Debt, which he found at 200 millions and odd, he left at 600 millions and odd, while France, during his wars against her, had exchanged her assignats for gold, and had extended her territory and her sway to a degree which made that nation, whose power our forefathers despised, an object of continual dread to England; when the former partizans of PITT see this, as they must, aye, and *feel* it too, will they still persist in asserting the wisdom of his plans; and, above all, will they, when they see the Debt tripling in amount under his hands, still persist in asserting the *efficacy* of his *Sinking Fund,* and, upon that bare assertion, reject all inquiry into either the nature or the effect of that celebrated scheme?

Let us hope, that, in a country boasting of the thoughtfulness of its people, there can be but very few persons so besotted as this; and, indeed, it is due to the country to say, that there do not appear to be any such left, excepting amongst those who live upon the taxes, and whose perverseness arises not from their want of information. But, be this as it may, I am satisfied that you, my Friends and Neighbours, who, like me, have no interests separate from those of our country, will not, whatever may have been your prejudices heretofore, wilfully shut your eyes against the truth; and that you will accompany me in this inquiry with that great attention, which, as I before observed, the subject demands.

Pitt's *Sinking Fund* was begun in the year 1786, by an Act of Parliament (being Chapter XXXI of the 26th year of the reign of George III.) entitled—"*An Act for vesting "certain sums in Commissioners, at "the end of every Quarter of a Year, "to be by them applied to the Reduc- "tion of the National Debt.*" In virtue of this Act a certain part of the taxes was, in each year, to be paid to certain persons named in the Act, as Commissioners for managing the concern; and, these taxes, together with the accumulations upon them, have been, as formerly, called a *Sinking Fund.*

It is no matter what was th *amount* of the sum, or sums, of money, thus to be set apart out of the taxes, and to introduce particulars of that sort would only embarrass our view. Suffice it to know, that certain sums of money, being a part of the taxes, were set apart, and, that, with this money, together with its growing interest, the Commissioners, appointed by the Sinking Fund Act, were, at stated periods, and with certain limitations in their powers, to *redeem* the Debt as fast as they could, the word *redeem* having now come into fashion instead of the word *pay off*. It is of no consequence what were the periods, what were the days of the week or the times of the moon, when this work of redemption was to be performed. The *effect* is what we have to look after; but, in order to have a clear view of even that, we must see the *manner* of doing the thing, the manner of redeeming or paying off the Debt; for, without that, we shall be continually exposed to be bewildered and deceived; and, indeed, we shall be quite unable to form any thing like a clear notion of what the Sinking Fund really is.

The Commissioners, with the money thus put under their care and management, were to *purchase up stock* from individuals, which stock would then become *the property of the nation*. But, stay. We must go gently on here, or we lose ourselves in a moment. We must, indeed, not proceed a step further, till we have gone back to Letter II, at pages 18, 19, and have taken another look, and refreshened our memories as to what STOCK means. Having done so, and read on to the end of the first paragraph in page 19, we may proceed by repeating, that the Commissioners were to go to work with the money lodged in their hands, out of the taxes, and *purchase up Stock*. We have seen, in the pages just referred to, *how Stock is made;* we have seen how MUCKWORM lent his money to the government; we have seen how he got *his name written in a book* in return for his money; we have seen that Stock is nothing that can be seen, heard, smelled, or touched; we have seen that it signifies the *right of receiving interest* upon money lent to the government, which money has been long ago expended; we have seen the operation by which Muckworm became possessed of stock: and, lastly, we have seen our neighbour, FARMER GREENHORN, purchase two thousand pounds worth of MUCKWORM's stock, which the former bequeathed to his poor daughter GRIZZLE.

Now, then, observe, the whole of the Stock, of which the National Debt is made up, is exactly the same sort of thing as this two thousand pounds worth of Stock, belonging to Grizzle Greenhorn. There is a book, in which a list of the names of all those persons is written, who have, like Grizzle, a right to draw interest from the government out of the taxes; against each name in this list is placed the amount of the sum for which the person has a right to draw interest. Some have a right to draw interest for more and some for less. And these sums make up what is called the National Debt. Of course, the Sinking Fund Commissioners, in order to pay off the National Debt, or any part of it, must *purchase up Stock from individuals;* or, in other words, *pay them off their share of the Debt*. If, for instance, Grizzle Greenhorn has a mind to have her two thousand pounds to lay out upon land, or do any thing else with, she sells her stock, and, if it so happen, she may sell it to the Commissioners; and thus, as they pay her for it with the nation's money, it is said, that, by this transaction, they have *redeemed* (by which I should mean *paid off*) two thousand pounds of the National Debt. Grizzle, who was the creditor, has got her money again; she has no longer any right to draw interest for it; and of course, you would think, that these two thousand pounds worth of debt were paid off, and that the nation, that we the people, had no longer any interest to pay upon it; you would naturally think, that we were *no longer taxed to pay the interest upon this part of the Debt.*

Greatly, however, would you be deceived; cruelly deceived, if you did think so; for, notwithstanding the Commissioners have *redeemed* these two thousand pounds, we have still to pay the interest of them every year; *we are still taxed for the money wherewith to pay this interest, just in the same way as if the two thousand pounds worth of Debt had not been redeemed at all, but still belonged to Grizzle Greenhorn!* This is an odd way of *redeeming;* an odd way of *paying off;* do you not think it is, Neighbours? We have before seen, that the National Debt is a mortgage upon the taxes. It is constantly called so in conversation, and in writings upon the subject. But, should not either of you, who happened to have a mortgage upon your land or house, think it strange if, after you had *redeemed* a part of the mortgage, you had still to pay interest upon the part redeemed as well as upon the part unredeemed? TO REDEEM, as applied to money engagements, means to *discharge,* to *set free* by payment. This is the meaning of the word redeem, as applied to such matters. It sometimes means to *rescue* or to *ransom,* from captivity, from forfeiture, or from peril of any sort, by paying a price. But, in every sense, in which this word is used, it always implies the *setting free* of the object on which it operates; and, when applied to a mortgage, a bond, a note of hand, or a Debt of any sort, it implies the *paying of it off.* How, then, can the two thousand pounds worth of Debt, purchased from Grizzle Greenhorn, by our Sinking Fund Commissioners, be said to be *redeemed* by us, if we are still *taxed to pay the interest upon it,* and, of course, if it be not discharged, and not set free?

Nothing, at first sight appears more plausible, nothing more reasonable, nothing more clear, than the mode above described, of redeeming the Debt by purchasing from the several individuals, who, like Grizzle Greenhorn, own the Stock or the Debt, their respective shares thereof. And, the operation is as simple as any thing can be. For, the Sinking Fund Commissioners, having, for instance, received two thousand pounds from the Tax-gatherers, in virtue of the Sinking Fund Act, go and purchase Grizzle's stock; they give her the two thousand pounds; her right to draw interest from us ceases; her share of the Stock or Debt is redeemed or paid off; *and her name is crossed out of the Book.* Ah; but, alas! *the names of our Sinking Fund Commissioners are written in the Book instead of hers!* Aye; we have to pay the interest of the two thousand pounds *to them* instead of to her; and our taxes on account of this which is called the *redeemed* part of the Debt, are just as great as they were before this curious work of redemption began.

"Well then," you will say, "what "does this thing mean; and what "can it have been intended for?" Why, to speak candidly of the matter, though the thing was an invention of PITT, under whose sway so much mischief came upon this nation, I believe, that the thing was well meant. I believe that it was intended to free the nation from its Debt. But, I am satisfied, that it has been productive of no small part of the evils, which England and which Europe have experienced since its invention; for, by giving people renewed confidence in the solidity of the Funds or Stocks, it rendered government borrowing more easy; and, of course, it took from the Minister that check to the making of wars and the paying of foreign armies, for the want of which check the Expences and Taxes and Debt of the country have been so fearfully augmented, to say nothing, at present, about the dreadful changes which those wars have made in our affairs both at home and abroad.

To produce such effects was, however, certainly not the *intention* of the scheme. The intention was, that the Sinking Fund Commissioners should, with the money put into their hands out of the taxes, purchase up Stock, or parts of the Debt, belonging to individuals; that the parts, so purchased up, *should not cease to exist;* that they should be written in the Great Book under the name of the Commissioners; that the Commissioners should receive the interest upon them, instead of its being received by individuals as before; that this interest, as fast as it came into the hands of the Commissioners, should, like the money paid to them annually out of the taxes, be laid out in purchasing up more Stock from individuals; and that the thing should go on thus, till the last of the Stock, or Debt, got into the hands of Commissioners; when, of course, the government might burn the Great Book, and the National Debt would be paid off.

This scheme was very pretty upon paper; it made a fine figure in the newspapers and pamphlets of the day; and looked quite solemn when embodied into an Act of Parliament. There was, to be sure, when people looked into the matter more closely, something rather whimsical in the idea of a nation's *paying interest to itself:* something very whimsical in a nation's GETTING MONEY by *paying itself interest upon its own Stock.* Many persons thought so, at the time, and some said so; but the formidable tables of figures made out by court calculators, and the flowery and bold speeches of PITT, soon put all such persons out of countenance, and reduced them to silence; or exposed them to the charge of faction and disaffection and disloyalty. The country, infatuated with its "Heaven-born Minister," became deaf to the dictates of common sense; and, with as much fondness as the mother hangs over her smiling babe, it cherished and fostered the fatal delusion.

As the execution of the Sinking-Fund Act proceeded, more and more of the Stock, or parts of the Debt, became of course entered in the Great Book in the names of the Commissioners. Hence arose a new denomination in our national money accounts; namely, the *redeemed* debt; that is, the parts of the debt, as aforesaid purchased up by the Commissioners, was now called the "*redeemed* debt;" a phrase which contains a contradiction in itself. But, still it was unavoidable; for, it was not *paid off;* it was *bought up*, but we had still, and *have* still, to *pay interest upon it;* and, therefore, it could not be said to be paid off; for, it would be folly too gross to pretend that we had paid off a debt or a mortgage, for which we were still paying interest. If, indeed, the parts of the debt, which were purchased up by the Commissioners, had been, at once, done away, and we had ceased to pay interest upon them, then those parts would have been *really redeemed.* If, for instance, Grizzle Greenhorn's two thousand pounds worth of Stock had been crossed out of the Great Book, and had not been inserted in it again under any other name, that two thousand pounds worth of the debt would have been redeemed in reality. This is the way in which the Sinking Fund of the American States operates. They raise yearly a certain sum in taxes; with that sum they purchase up part of their debt; and then that part of the debt *ceases to exist* in any shape whatever. The next year they raise a like sum in taxes, and again purchase up parcels of the debt. And, thus they proceed, having every succeeding year, *less and less interest to pay upon their debt.* This is *real* redemption: this is real paying off. But, the way in which we proceed bears no resemblance to it; nor has any thing in common with it, except it be the *name.*

Let us, before we proceed any further, take a view of the *increase of the interest that we have to pay upon the debt.* We have seen in Letter III. page 25, how the debt itself has gone on increasing. But, we have not yet taken a look at the increase of the INTEREST; though this is very material, and, indeed, it is the only thing, belonging to the debt, worthy of our attention. The statement of the amount of the debt itself is of no practical use, except as it serves to illustrate, to render more clear, the part of the subject upon which we now are. For as we have seen, the Debt is nothing more than a right possessed by certain persons, called Stock-Holders, to draw interest from the nation; or, in other words, to take annually, or quarterly, part of the taxes raised upon the people at large. Let us, therefore, take a look at the progress of this interest.

When QUEEN ANNE came to the throne, in 1701, the annual interest on the National Debt was	£1,310,942
When GEORGE I. came to the throne, in 1714	3,351,358
When GEORGE II. came to the throne, in 1727	2,217,551
When GEORGE III. came to the throne, in 1760	4,840,821
After the AMERICAN WAR, in 1784, and just before the making of Pitt's Sinking Fund	9,669,435
At the latter end of the ANTI-JACOBIN WAR, in 1801	21,778,018
For the LAST YEAR, that is 1809	32,870,608

There are included in this sum "*charges for management;*" and, as we have before seen, there is some of the Debt (small portions) called the loans, or debts, of the *Emperor of Germany*, and of the *Prince Regent of Portugal*, which, it is *possible*, they may repay us; but, this is, as it is called in the account laid before Parliament, during the last session, the "Total charge *on account of Debt,* "payable in Great Britain." And, let me ask any sensible man, what consequence it can be to us, what the Debt is called; what consequence by what name the different sorts of it may go, so that the interest upon it still goes on increasing, and so that we have to pay the whole of that interest out of the taxes?

When PITT's Sinking Fund was established, there was a time fixed, when the interest should *begin to be diminished.* I mean, a time was fixed, when the people should no longer pay taxes to defray the interest upon the Stock, or parts of the Debt, which should *after that time be purchased up by the Commissioners.* The time so fixed was 1808, *two years ago.* The *year* was not *named* in the Act; but, it was known to a certainty; because this ceasing to pay interest was to begin, when the interest upon the Stock, or parts of the Debt, bought up, together with the sums paid to the Commissioners out of the taxes, should amount to a certain sum (four millions annually); and, as the sums to be paid to them were fixed, it was a mere question of arithmetic when the paying of interest would cease, agreeably to the terms of the Act; as expressed in the XXth clause, as follows: "And be it further enacted by "the authority aforesaid, that whenever the whole sum annually receivable by the said Commissioners, including as well the quarterly sum "of two hundred and fifty thousand "pounds herein before directed to be "issued from the exchequer, as the "several Annuities and Dividends of "Stock to be placed to the Account "of the said Commissioners in the "Books of the Governor and Company of the Bank of *England*, by "virtue of this Act, shall amount in "the whole to FOUR MILLIONS ANNUALLY, the Dividends due on such "Part of the Principal or Capital "Stock as shall *thence-forth* be paid "off by the said Commissioners, and "the Monies payable on such Annuities for Lives or Years as may "*afterwards* cease and determine, "SHALL NO LONGER BE "ISSUED AT THE RECEIPT "OF HIS MAJESTY'S EXCHEQUER, but shall be CONSIDERED AS REDEEMED by Parliament, and shall remain to be disposed of as Parliament shall direct." In *what way* it might have been supposed, that Parliament, in its wisdom, would *dispose* of these parcels of *redeemed debt*, I shall not, for my part presume to hazard a conjecture; but, as was before observed, it was easy, (the *sums being given*) to ascertain the time, when the provision in this clause would begin to operate; and, that time was, *the year* 1808.

There was another Act, passed seven years later, (1792), allotting more of the taxes to the same purpose (Chapter 52 of the 32nd year of this king's reign); and still the same provision was made; namely, that, when the produce of the Sinking Fund should amount to 4 millions annually, *all the Stock, or parts of the Debt, that should be purchased up by the Commissioners after that time*, SHOULD NO LONGER HAVE INTEREST PAID UPON IT OUT OF THE TAXES; but that *these parts* of the Debt should (mark the words) "be *considered* AS RE-"DEEMED." And so they would. They really, in *that case* would have been *redeemed*; but the word *redeemed* is now applied, even in the Accounts laid before Parliament, to those parts of the Debt, bought up by the Commissioners, the dividend, or interest, on which parts, IS STILL ISSUED AT THE EXCHEQUER; that is to say, *is still paid out of the taxes!* And all this goes on amongst "the *thinking*" people of England!

But, what was done, in the long expected year 1808? What was done, when *the year of promise* came? This is the most interesting part of this most curious history; but, as to bring to a close the whole of the discussion, relating to the Sinking Fund, would extend this letter to double its present length, I think it better to make the remaining part of it the subject of another Letter, beseeching you, in the meanwhile, to make up, by your patience in the perusal, for whatever want of clearness may be discovered in the writer.

I remain, Gentlemen,
Your faithful friend,
Wm. COBBETT.

State Prison, Newgate, Thursday, September 14, 1810.

LETTER V.

"I would inculcate one truth with peculiar earnestness; namely, that a *Revolution* is *not* the ne-"cessary consequence of a *National Bankruptcy*.—*Pursuits of Literature*.

Digression respecting the use of Bank-Notes as a Political Support to the Government—Mr. Addington's Notion of convincing Buonaparté by the means of a Tax—Answer of the Moniteur—Advice given to Mr. Addington in the Register in 1803—Passage quoted from a Government News-paper describing Bank-Notes as necessary to the Existence of the Government—Same Doctrine promulgated by Mr. Paine in his Rights of Man—How different is this from what the World has been told—Effect of it to encourage the Enemy—Resume the subject of the Sinking Fund—No Interest taken off in 1808—Addington's Act of 1802—George Rose quoted to prove that it was clearly held forth to the Nation that Taxes would be repealed in consequence of the Sinking Fund—P.S. Sir John Sinclair's Pamphlet.

GENTLEMEN,

BEFORE we resume the discussion, relating to *Pitt's Grand Sinking Fund*, which want of room obliged us to break off, at the close of the last letter, I think it may be useful to submit to you here an observation or two, calculated to obviate any unfounded apprehensions that might otherwise be excited by the apparently inevitable fate of the paper-money; and this I deem the more necessary, as publications are daily appearing, from the pens of ignorant or interested persons, the evident tendency, and, indeed, object, of which is, to persuade the public, that the existence of the government; that the existence of law and order; that the safety to persons and property; nay, that the continuance of the very breath in our nostrils, depend upon the credit of the Bank Notes.

The author, from whose writings I have taken my motto to this present Number of my work, was, you see, of a very different opinion; and, I have quoted his sentiment upon the subject, because his work is well known to be of what is called the ANTI-JACOBIN kind, that is to say, a work the tendency of which is to prevent men like you from having any thing to say or to do, any more than your horses, in the affairs of government. This writer, who, however, might mean well, and who is certainly a very clever man, so far from supposing that the existence of the government depended upon the credit of bank-notes, is, you see, fixed in his opinion, and an opinion that he wishes "to inculcate with peculiar earnestness," that a REVOLUTION, thereby meaning a change in the form of government, is *not* the necessary consequence, even of a *National Bankruptcy;* that is to say, not only a total discredit of all the paper-money and especially the Bank of England Notes, but also an utter inability to pay, in any way whatever, the interest upon the National Debt, or any part of it.

This is my opinion also, as it always has been since I turned my attention to the subject. At the beginning of the present war, MR. ADDINGTON, who was then the Prime Minister, told the House of Commons, that one of his principal objects in laying on the Property Tax and other war taxes, was, "to convince "Buonaparté, that it was *hopeless* for "him to contend with our *finances.*" To which the MONITEUR, or French government-newspaper, replied: "*Pay "your bank notes in gold and silver,* "and then we will believe you, without your going to war."*

Whether the Minister made good his promise; whether he has convinced Buonaparté, that, it was "*hopeless* for him to contend with our "*finances,*" *you,* Gentlemen, are as likely to be able to judge as any body that I know. I, for my part, blamed the Minister for holding out such a *motive* for his taxing measures. I said to him: The true way of convincing your enemy, that this war upon your finances will be useless, is to state explicitly to the world, that you are not at all afraid of the consequences of what is called a national bankruptcy; for, while you endeavour to make people believe, that such an event *cannot possibly happen,* they will certainly think that you regard it, if it should happen, as *irretrievable ruin and destruction;* and, therefore, as you never can quite overcome their apprehensions, the best way is to be silent upon the subject, or, *to set the terrific bug-bear at defiance.* To Buonaparté's exultation at our approaching bankruptcy the answer is always ready: France has been a bankrupt; France has not paid her paper-money in specie; yet France is not the weaker for that; France is, in spite of her ruined finances, in spite of the long pamphlets of Sir Francis D'Ivernois and Mr. Rose, in spite of the longer speeches of Lord Mornington, Lord Auckland and Mr. Pitt, in spite of the innumerable columns of figures which these noblemen and gentlemen have drawn up in battle array against her; in spite of all this, France is yet powerful, yea, much more powerful than she was before she experienced what is called a national bankruptcy. What ground, therefore, have the French to rejoice at our finances being about to undergo a similar operation?

Such were *my* sentiments and my reasoning upon this subject, seven

---

* Register, Vol. III. page 948. June, 1803

years ago; a time, when to pronounce the word *depreciation*, as applied to bank-notes, was sure to expose a man to charges very little short of *treason*, which charges were made by those very persons, who have now declared the greater half of our bank-notes to be "*destructive assignats*," and who have called them "*vile* and *dirty rags*." My opinion was, and it still is, that the total destruction of the paper-money would not cause any change injurious to this kingdom; and, indeed, I should have a most hearty contempt for the constitution and for the whole form and composition of our government, if I thought that their existence depended upon the credit of bank-notes. There are however, those who think just the reverse; and these are, too, writers, who appear to be entirely devoted to the government: one of whom goes so far as to say, that the government has *no other trust-worthy support* than that which it derives from the bank-notes. "The "human mind," says he, "is sen-"sible only of the present good, or "evil, and has too little thought to "anticipate consequences, and *if it* "*was not for the immediate personal* "*interest of a very large and informed* "*part of the community in the Nation-*"*al Debt, Patronage and Paper Cur-*"*rency*, GOVERNMENT COULD "HAVE NO EXISTENCE, stand-"ing insulated on the pure basis of "duty, and remote national and res-"pective good. The conduct of Swe-"den, America, Ireland, and the "Jacobins of England, in their par-"tiality for France, exemplify a want "of sense to execute the maxims of "EPICURUS: The paper currency "of Bank Notes (there should be no "Country Bank) offers to Govern-"ment a *most indestructible support*, "because IT MAKES THE DAI-"LY BREAD OF EVERY IN-"DIVIDUAL DEPEND SUB-"STANTIALLY ON THE "SAFETY OF GOVERN-"MENT, whereas money, which "may be *hoarded*, separates the in-"dividual from the public safety. In "the present revolutionary state of "the world, I think our paper cur-"rency a most *miraculous mean of* "*salvation*, and the man who would "*propose the payment of Bank Notes* "*in specie at any period*, to separate "individual property from public "safety, might as well propose *the* "*burning of the Navy to protect the* "*commerce of the world*."*

Gentlemen, do you remember the writings of PAINE? Do you remember the *Rights of Man* for the writing of which the author was *prosecuted* by the then Attorney General who is now the Lord Chancellor? Do you remember the *Rights of Man*, the author of which was prosecuted, and, being absent, was *outlawed*; the publishers of which were prosecuted all over the kingdom; the circulating of which was forbidden by Proclamation; and, to counteract the principles of which ASSOCIATIONS were formed of the rich and the powerful? Well, it was in this very work, that the doctrine here laid down by this government writer, was first started. PAINE said, that *the existence of the government depended upon the existence of the bank-notes*; and that, the question was not, *how long the British government would stand*; but, *how long the Funding System would last*. PAINE'S mode of reasoning was, if I am correct in my recollection, as nearly as possible, like that of this government writer. He laid it down as an admitted fact, that the people (owing to causes that he stated) must be *wholly indifferent about the fate of the government*; but, that, as so many of them were, either by holding *Stocks* or *Bank-notes*, interested in the fate of the government, they would, *while the Stocks and Bank-notes lasted*, continue to support the government, whatever might be their *feelings* towards it. But, that, when, from whatever cause, the Funding System should fail, not a soul would be found to lift a finger, or, even to

* MORNING POST news-paper: 14th Sept. 1810.

express a wish in favour of the existence of the government.

Just the same, or rather more, is now said by this government writer; a writer, one half of whose pages are filled with invectives against those whom he calls the friends of the Emperor of France. But, how is it possible for any thing to be written more agreeable to the Emperor Napoleon than what this writer has put forth? Until now the world has been told that we entertained a real *love for our government*; that we were attached to our constitution because it afforded such fine *protection* to our *persons* and our *property*; that we loved the constitution, because it insured to us the enjoyment of *liberty*, and defended us against every species of *oppression*; that we had made numerous sacrifices, and that we were ready to make as many more, nay, even "to spend our *last shilling* and shed the *last drop of our blood*," for the sake of these *liberties* and in defence of *a king*, whom we so *dearly loved*, and in gratitude for the blessings enjoyed during whose reign, we held a Jubilee. Until NOW, this is what the world has been told. But NOW it is told, by this loyalty-professing writer, that the only motive whence we support the government at all, is, to preserve the value of the Bank-notes that we hold; that, if it was not for the immediate personal interest of so many people in *the National Debt*, and for *patronage* and *paper currency*, the Government could have *no existence;* that we support the government because without its existence, the bank-notes would fall, and because, by the number of bank-notes, we are thus made to depend upon the safety of Government *for our daily bread;* and that, therefore, the man who would propose the payment of bank-notes in gold and silver *at any period*, might as well propose *the burning of the Navy*, or, in other words, the giving up of the country to France.

What, Gentlemen! are we never, then, to see gold and silver again? Every Minister; every Member of Parliament; every one of those, who endeavoured to palliate the measure of protecting the Bank Company from paying their notes in Gold and Silver; every one of them "*lamented* the *necessity*," as they called it, of the measure. But, NOW, behold, we are told that it was a *good thing;* and not only a good thing, but that *the government could not exist without it!* Gentlemen, we call ourselves a "*thinking* people;" but, believe me, that this is what would not have been said to any other civilized people upon earth.

We might here easily show how encouraging a prospect doctrines of this sort hold out to our enemy, and how strong an inducement to use all those means, whether in the way of attack or of menace, which are likely to destroy the credit of the paper-money, that being, if these doctrines be sound, the sure and certain way of destroying our government. But, another opportunity will offer for observations upon these matters; and, it is now time that we return to our inquiry into the SINKING FUND.

In the last Letter, page 50, having stated the provisions, made in the Acts of 1786 and 1792, for the nation's *ceasing to pay interest* upon the Stock that should be redeemed, or bought up by the Commissioners, after the year 1808; or, in other words, the nation's ceasing to *pay taxes* on account of the Stock, or part of the Debt, which should be bought up after that time: having stated these provisions, we were proceeding to inquire—*What was done in the long-expected year*, 1808? What was done *when the year of promise came?*

Why, my Neighbours, *nothing at all was done:* just nothing at all in the way provided for. The nation ceased to pay no *dividends of interest;* and, of course, this work of redemption caused *none of its taxes to be taken off.* "Well," say you, "but is "it possible, that, after such a solemn "proceeding; after the *express* and "*positive* declaration in two Acts of

"Parliament, that the dividends of "interest *should* cease to be paid in "1808; is it possible that, after "that, all the dividends did continue "to be paid, *just the same as if those* "*Acts had never been passed?*" O, yes! It is not only *possible* to be so, but it *is* so. All the dividends have continued to be paid; and *are paid to this day.* The above-mentioned provisions, in the Acts of 1786, and 1792 were *repealed.* The Parliament undid what it had before done. It did away the provisions, which it had made in 1786 and 1792. It passed another Act, which said that those provisions should not be carried into effect; or, in other words, that which was *law* before was no *longer law.*

This new Act was passed in the month of June, 1802, ADDINGTON, the successor and the friend of PITT, being then Minister. This Act (which is Chapter 71 of the 42d year of the reign of George III.) is entitled—"An Act to amend and "RENDER MORE EFFECTUAL two Acts passed in the "twenty-sixth and thirty-second "years of the reign of his present "Majesty, for the reduction of the "National Debt." This Act, which was to render those two Acts *more effectual*, sets out by stating, that the said two Acts had been by experience found "to be attended with *most be-*"*neficial consequences* to the *public* "*credit* of the country;" and having made that declaration, it sets to work, and repeals the two provisions abovementioned; and, of course, when the year 1808 came, when the year of expectation arrived, *no dividends* ceased to be paid, and *interest* upon the whole of the Debt was still paid, and is still paid to this day.

Gentlemen, it is hardly to be believed, that any men, who, like PITT and his associates and supporters, had invented and caused to be passed, the two first mentioned Acts, could propose the last mentioned Act, that is to say, the Act of 1802. Not only, however, did they propose it, but the ANTI-JACOBIN writers laughed in our faces and called us fools, if not levellers and jacobins, if we ventured to express any doubt at all of the wisdom and justice of any of these successive measures; and, these writers stoutly denied, *that it ever was intended to take off any of the taxes in 1808*; and, of course, they maintained, that we, who felt disappointment, in this respect, were fools for our pains, and, indeed, they expressed themselves thus, that we "were "*nature's fools*," and not the fools of the Minister.

Never, surely, were any portion of mankind treated with such barefaced contempt as the people of England were, at the time referred to, by the venal writers of newspapers, pamphlets, magazines, and reviews, who, seeing the people terrified out of their senses, by alternate alarms within and without, seemed to think that he was the best man, who could show the greatest degree of scorn for their understanding and character. Had not this been their persuasion, would they have dared to tell us, that *none but fools ever expected the Sinking Fund to produce a repeal of Taxes*, when it must still remain in the memory of every man, who was then at all conversant in political matters, that the *repeal of taxes*; the *lessening of the taxes*; the making of their *burthens less*, was the promise held forth to the people by the supporters of PITT; nay, when it is notorious, that PITT owed the establishment of his tremendous power to the opinion which the people entertained, that he had discovered, and would put in practice, the means of *reducing the load of their Taxes?* This, as the great end of his schemes, was so much talked of; it is so well known, that this was so distinctly stated in the speeches in parliament, and so many times repeated, that I am almost ashamed to trouble you with any proof of the fact; yet, considering that the point is of great importance, I will put the matter beyond all dispute by a reference to a work on the increase of the *Resources* of the kingdom, published in 1799, under the name of GEORGE ROSE, who was then a Secretary of the Treasury, and who is now Treasurer of the Navy and a Privy Counsellor, and who, in the execution of the work about to be cited, was, doubtless, assisted by PITT himself. Indeed, this must have been the case; or, at least, it must be believed, that nothing, upon such a subject, and under the name of his official Secretary, would be published without PITT's previous approbation. In this work, which is entitled, "A "Brief Examination into the In-"crease of the Revenue Commerce, "and Manufactures of Great Britain, "from 1792 to 1799;" in this work the hopeful effects of the Sinking Funds of 1786 and 1792 are pointed out, and the writer says:—"By the "operation of these sinking funds, "without any further intervention of "Parliament, the one existing before "the war, will attain its *maximum* "(4,000,000*l.* a year) most pro-"bably, in 1808, in no case later "than February 1811. As the *di-"vidends* due on such parts of the "old debt as shall be paid off after "the sinking fund shall have attained "its *maximum*, and the annuities "which shall afterwards fall in, will "be at the disposal of Parliament, "*the period of REPEALING "TAXES annually, to an amount "equal thereto, cannot be delayed "more than nine, ten, or eleven years.*"

Need I ask you, Gentlemen, whether you have heard of any *repealing of taxes?* Whether you have *felt* your *load of taxation lightened?* Whether you pay *less* taxes, than you paid when this placeman wrote his book in 1799? No: These questions I need not put to you; nor need I ask you what are your feelings towards those, who fed you with hopes of a diminution of your burdens; nor need I, perhaps, say one more word upon the subject of the *Sinking Fund,* not to have seen through which by this time would argue a much greater want of discernment than I am disposed to attribute to any part of my countrymen, and especially to you, whose discerning faculties have, as to matters of this sort, been, of late, pretty well sharpened by experience. Nevertheless, with the hope of leaving no possibility of bewildering any body in future, with regard to the nature or effect of the *Sinking Fund,* I shall add some additional remarks; but, as these remarks will open to us quite new views of the matter, and will extend to some length, I shall postpone them to my next; and I remain, in the mean while,

Your faithful Friend,

WM. COBBETT.

State Prison, Newgate, Monday, September 17, 1810.

P. S. A pamphlet, entitled, "OBSERVATIONS ON THE REPORT OF "THE BULLION COMMITTEE," has just been published by Sir JOHN SINCLAIR, who is, it seems, a member of Parliament, and who is said to have been recently made a Privy Counsellor. So much of such gross ignorance, in so short a compass, I do not recollect to have met with in the course of my reading, except, perhaps, in the Morning Post newspaper, or in the British Critic Review. Such a publication would be wholly unworthy of serious notice, were it not pretty evidently the vehicle of the sentiments and views of others. For this reason, some of its prominent absurdities will be noticed, when I come to that part of my subject, to which they more particularly belong. In the mean time, in order to furnish the means of judging of this writer's depth of understanding, take the following specimen from a former work of his, and compare his theory with the practice now before our eyes. "The "PUBLIC DEBTS of a nation, not "only *attract riches from abroad,* "with a species of magnetic in-"fluence, but they also *retain money "at home,* which *otherwise would be "exported,* and which, if sent to "other countries, might possibly be "attended with pernicious consequences to the State, whose wealth "was carried out of it. If France, "for example, maintained its wars "*by borrowing money*, and England "*raised all its within the year*, "the necessary consequence would "be that all the loose and unemployed money of England, would "*naturally be transmitted to France*, "where it would be placed out to advantage." This is quite sufficient. The next time that Sir JOHN thinks of writing upon matters of this sort, he will do well to go, previously, and take a lesson of Mrs. DE YONGE. She will be able to tell him for a certainty, whether National Debts have a tendency to *keep money at home*, to *prevent it from being exported*, and to *bring money from abroad*. She will also be able to give him a lesson upon *depreciation*, in a way, which, perhaps, will make the thing comprehensible even to him.

LETTER VI.

"It is not altogether improbable, that, when the nation becomes heartily sick of its Debts, and is cruelly oppressed by them, some daring projector may arise with *visionary schemes for their discharge*; and, as "public credit will begin, by that time, to be a little frail, the least touch will destroy it, and in this manner "it will *die of the Doctor*. But, it is more probable, that the breach of national faith will be the necessary "effect of wars, defeats, misfortunes, and public calamities, or even, perhaps, of victories and conquests."—HUME on Public Credit.

Saying that a Man writes from a Prison is not a satisfactory Refutation of his Arguments—Proceed with the subject of the Sinking Fund—Alledged grounds of Addington's Act in 1802—The Time when it was to begin to yield us Relief, to wit 45 Years—Mr. Brand's Answer to an Argument of mine—He denies that Interest is paid upon the Redeemed Stock—Acts of Parliament and Public Accounts say the contrary—Examination of the Example stated by Mr. Brand—Great Error in regarding things as alike which are essentially dissimilar in their Properties—Consequence of this Error shown in the supposed case of Thrifty—Grand Fallacy in supposing that what we pay to support the Sinking Fund, would otherwise be of no use to us—Conclusion of the subject of the Sinking Fund—*P. S.* Mr. Randall Jackson's Speech at the Bank Company's House, in Threadneedle Street.

GENTLEMEN,

IT was naturally to be expected, that those venal men, who for want of industry to "labour with their "hands the thing that is good," and from a desire to live upon the labour of others, have chosen the occupation of writing, instead of obeying the voice of nature, which bade use the brush and not the pen, to blacken shoes and not paper; it was naturally to be expected that those venal men, who gain their livelihood by serving the corrupt and by deceiving the weak, and the number of whom, in this Town, is unfortunately, but too great; it was naturally to be expected that this description of men would feel alarmed at the progress of these Letters, which, by making honest and useful truths so familiar to the minds of the people, threatened literary venality with destruction. Accordingly these instruments of Corruption have shewn their anger and resentment against me; but, the only *answer* they have offered to me is this: "that I "discharge my gun from a *stone-bat*"*tery*;" meaning that I write from a *prison*; therein giving the public a specimen of their *wit* as well as of their *manliness*. This is always the way; it is the constant practice of those, who, while they are, from whatever motive, impelled *to oppose* a writer, want either the *materials* or the *ability* to shew that he is wrong; and, Gentlemen, you may lay it down as a maxim, that when any publication is answered by abuse, and especially personal abuse, the author of such publication *is right*, or, at least, that his abusers *want the ability to shew that he is wrong*. Facts and reasoning, if erroneous, always admit of refutation: but, if correct, no one can refute them; and, if erroneous, to refute may still require some ability; whereas, *to abuse* the person from whom they have proceeded, is within the power of every one, a gift not denied to any creature capable of uttering articulate sounds or of making marks upon paper. The great cause, however, of abuse in such cases, is the *weight of the truths*, against which such abuse is opposed: for it is here as in common verbal disputes, he who has the truth clearly on his side, is always seen to be in good temper, while his opponent scarcely ever fails to discover impatience and anger, and, in but too many cases, to give way to personal invective and false accusation; and, be you well assured, Gentlemen, that even the venal men, above-described, *answer* me by saying *that I write from a prison*, only because they have *no other answer to give*.

Leaving them in the full possession and unenvied enjoyment of all the advantage and of all the honour which such a mode of answering can give, let us proceed with our inquiry into the effects of the SINKING FUND, just casting our eye back first, and refreshing our memory as to the foregone facts; namely, that the Sinking-Fund Acts of PITT, which provided for the cutting off some part of the interest upon the Debt in 1808; that those provisions, which led the poor nation to hope for a taking off of part of its taxes in 1808; that these provisions, which, as we have seen, were held forth to the *believing* people of England, in the pamphlet of GEORGE ROSE, as the sure and undoubted pledge for the taking off of taxes in 1808, or thereabouts; that these provisions, in order to *begin* to taste the benefit of which, the people were to pay *a million a year of additional taxes* for *twenty-two years;* that these provisions; yes, we must bear in mind, that these provisions, after the people had gone on *hoping* for *sixteen years* out of the twenty two: that these provisions, were, by ADDINGTON'S Act of 1802, *repealed, done away*, made of *no more effect than if they never had been enacted by the Parliament*.

"Well," you will say, "but upon "what *ground* was this measure "adopted? What end was it pro-"posed to answer?" Oh! why it was to pay off the Debt, *new* as well as *old;* for, by this time, the Debt contracted since the existence of the Sinking Fund, was become greater than the one contracted before. It was to pay off the Debt, new as well as old, *sooner* than they would have been paid off, if this new Act had not been passed. And it was said, in support of the measure, that it would be *better for us* (good God, what a "*thinking*" people we are!) not to have any of our taxes taken off in 1808; but to go on paying interest upon the whole of the Debt, as before, till our Sinking-Fund Commissioners had bought up *the whole* of the Stock, and that, *then* (Oh, then!) *then*, my boys, huzza! for, *then* we should be completely *out of Debt*.

"*Thinking* people" of England, *when* do you *think* that that *then* was to arrive? *When* do you think that it was supposed that our Commissioners would have bought up the whole of the Stock existing when the new Act was passed? *When* do you think that the day, the happy day, the new day of promise was to come? *When* do you think we were, according to this Act for rendering the Sinking Fund "MORE EFFECTUAL;" when, aye *when* do you think, that we were, according to this *improved* plan, to *begin* to feel the effects of it, in the lessening of our taxes? How many years do you think we were to wait; how many years to keep paying additional taxes for the purpose of paying off the Debt, before we began to taste of *any redemption of Taxes* in consequence of it? Only FORTY FIVE! Forty Five years only had we to wait; and *now* we have only THIRTY NINE to wait, and to pay taxes all the time, *over and above the interest upon the Debt;* only *thirty nine* years before we shall cease to pay interest upon the whole of the Debt existing in 1802; about *five eighths* of the Debt, *now* existing. We have been waiting ever since the year 1786; we have been waiting for *twenty four years;* we have been paying taxes all that time, *over and above the interest of the Debt;* we have, for twenty four years, been paying taxes for the purpose of paying off the Debt; and, now, at the end of these twenty four years, those of us who are alive have the consolation to reflect, that we have only *thirty nine* years more *to wait and to pay these Sinking Fund taxes,* before we shall begin to taste the fruit of all this patience and all these sacrifices, and that, at the blessed time here mentioned, *some* of our taxes will be taken off, ... unless another Act should be passed, between this time and that, for rendering the last made Act "MORE EFFECTUAL."

Gentlemen, need I say more? Certainly it is not *necessary;* but, there are still some views to take of this matter, which having taken, we may defy all the world to puzzle us upon this subject again.

We have seen, that we *still pay interest upon the whole of the Debt;* we have seen, in Letter IV. p. 69, that, *since the Sinking Fund was established,* the interest we pay has increased from *nine* millions and upwards to *thirty-two* millions and upwards; and, we humbly think, at least I do, that so long as I am compelled *to pay interest* for a Debt, it is no matter *to whom,* or under *what name,* I pay it. This is an obvious truth. There is something so consummately ridiculous in the idea of a nation's *getting money* by paying interest *to itself* upon its *own stock,* that the mind of every rational man naturally rejects it. It is, really something little short of madness to suppose, that a nation can *increase its wealth;* increase *its means of paying others;* that it can do this by *paying interest to itself.* When time is taken to reflect, no rational man will attempt to maintain a proposition so shockingly absurd. I put the thing in this way in an Article, published by me in 1804,* and I requested the late REV. JOHN BRAND, who had written a great deal upon the subject, to look at the Article, and to tell me what sort of answer he could find to this part of it. He did so, and the following was his answer:

"I have looked at your observations on the Sinking Fund; and the following is my answer to your great argument; namely, "that the "Debt said to be redeemed is an "imaginary discharge, *because* IN-"TEREST *thereon continues to be* "*paid.*"——If the interest *does continue* to be paid, the *conclusion is just;* and this is the fundamental principle of much of what you have said.——It is, reduced, therefore, to a question of fact, and I should say *the interest does not continue to be paid.* The same *tax continues to be levied,* it is paid also *away,* but it is paid for another purpose; it is yearly applied to the paying off more principal; *no part of it is applied to the payment of interest.* ——Take an example in a private concern, A has on his estate a mortgage of £.70,000 at 3 per cent. which he has the liberty to pay off as he pleases. He *determines* to *diminish his expenditure* by £.1,000 a year, at the end of the year he pays the interest £.2,100, and part of the principal £.1,000, his payment that year is £.3,100, and this sum he continues to pay annually till the debt is annihilated; it is now reduced to £.69,000; at the end of the second year there will be due for interest £.2,070, being

* REGISTER, Vol. V. page 591.

"30 less than the year before; when, "therefore, the second payment of "£.3,100 is made, it will consist of "two parts, £.1,030 for principal, "and £.2,070 for interest.——The "interest of the 1,000 paid off the "first year does not continue to be "paid in the second, and the £.30 "interest of the part of the capital "*redeemed* or *paid off* is now applied "to *the payment of more capital.*—— "Such mortgager at the end of the "year has actually paid off £.1,000, "of year two £.2,030, and of year "three £.3,060 18s. And that he "continues to pay annually the same "sum on account of debt, that is, on "account of principal and interest "jointly, does not in the least affect "this conclusion.

Now, in the first place, you see, MR. BRAND takes up "a *new position*," as most combatants do, when they are afraid to meet their antagonist. He is obliged to say, that we DO NOT *continue to pay interest* upon the part of the Debt, which is bought up, or, as it is called, *redeemed*. Aye! but, what say the *Acts of Parliament?* They say, that interest is continued to be paid thereon: they say, that, when any Stock, or parts of the Debt, are bought up, or redeemed, by the Commissioners, "the *dividends thereon* shall be *received by the said Commissioners*," or by the Bank on their account. And, what is the language of the Accounts, laid before Parliament? Why, in the account of the nation's *Expenditure* of last year, there is the following item: "INTEREST on Debt of Great Britain REDEEMED, £.4,443,519." So that, either the Acts of Parliament and the Public Accounts make use of misnomers, or, I was right in calling it *interest*. Besides, how completely does this denial of MR. BRAND dissipate all our fine dreams about the *gains* of the Sinking Fund? Is it not the commonly received notion, that we *gain money* by this fund? Are we not continually told, by the venal writers of the day, about what the Fund *yields?* Were we not told by them, less than six weeks ago, that this Fund had *produced* such and such sums? And, what is meant by a Fund's *yielding* and *producing*, if you cast the notion of *interest* aside? In what other way is it to *yield?* In what other way can it *produce an addition to its amount?* Yet, on the other hand, it is impossible to adhere to this notion of *interest*, without falling into the gross absurdity, before mentioned, of supposing that the nation can *get money;* that it can *increase its means of paying others*, by paying interest *to itself*, by becoming the *lender of money to itself*, by becoming *its own creditor;* an absurdity, which, as we have seen, MR. BRAND dared not risk his reputation in attempting to support.

We now come to MR. BRAND'S "*example* in a *private* concern." And here, Gentlemen, suffer me once more, and in a more pressing manner than before, to solicit your attention; because we have now before us the ground work of all the sad delusion, which has so long existed and which does still exist, upon this subject.

It is a natural propensity of the mind of man to assimilate things, which he wishes to understand, with things which he does understand. Hence the application of the terms *mortgage*, *redemption*, and others, to the Debt of the Nation. But, in this work of assimilation, *or bringing things to a resemblance for the purposes of illustration*, we ought to take the greatest care, not to make use of violence, not to regard as *alike*, things which are *essentially different in their properties;* for, if we do this, error must be the result, and I think, you will find, that this has been done by all those, who have reasoned like MR. BRAND; that is to say, *the whole* of those writers and speakers, who have held forth the Sinking Fund as likely to produce relief to the country.

We know, we daily see, that *private persons* pay off *encumbrances upon their estates;* and, we know very well and very familiarly, how fast the money of private persons increases *by being permitted to lie at compound interest*. This very common portion of knowledge appears to have been quite enough for our Financiers, who had, therefore, nothing to do but to look into *interest tables*, where they would not fail to find, that a million a year set apart, in 1786, would, at compound interest, pay off the then existing Debt, in the space of *sixty-years* from that time. They ask no more. This quite satisfies them. They have no doubts upon the subject; and, accordingly, they set apart the million a year; that is to say, they make a law for applying, as we have seen, a million a year of taxes, raised upon the nation, to the paying of the nation's Debts. But, where is the real *similarity* between this proceeding and the proceeding of the *individual* as supposed by Mr. Brand, Mr. M'Arthur, Mr. Pitt and others; for they have all made use of the same sort of illustration? Where is the *similarity* in the cases?

MR. BRAND'S individual, to whom, for the sake of clearness, we will give the name of THRIFTY, *diminishes his expenditure* by a thousand a year; that is, he, instead of spending it upon beer, wine, bread, beef, and servants, pays it annually to GOLDHAIR, who has the mortgage upon his estate. Now, this you will clearly see, is to be a thousand a year SAVED by THRIFTY; and, besides this, he resolves to pay to GOLDHAIR (who has the mortgage on the estate, mind) as much more every year as will make each payment equal to what he formerly paid on account of the interest of the whole debt. This is an odd sort of way to do the thing, but it is THRIFTY'S humour, and there can be no doubt, that, in time, he will, thus, pay off his mortgage. But again, I ask, what *similarity* there is in the case of THRIFTY and the case of A NATION?

THRIFTY, we are told, "*determines to diminish his expenditure.*" Can a NATION do this? THRIFTY knows to a *certainty* what his income and what his expenditure will be; the former is *fixed*, and over the latter he has *complete controul*. Is this the case with a NATION? Prudent THRIFTY does not, and indeed, *the supposition will not let him* contract a debt with SILVERLOCKS, while he is clearing off with GOLDHAIR. Is this the case with A NATION? But suppose, for argument's sake, that, as to all these, there is a perfect similarity; still is there a point of dissimilarity, which nothing can remove. THRIFTY, we are told, SAVES a thousand pounds a year. *How* does the saving arise? Why, he has less beer, wine, bread, beef, and servants than he had before. His saving, then, is made from the brewer, the wine-merchant, the baker, the butcher, and the footmen; or, rather, it is made from the public; it is made from *the nation*; it is made from *a third party*. But where is the NATION to find *a third party* from whom to make *its* saving?

But, what we are now going to view is the GRAND FALLACY. In this case of THRIFTY it is supposed, that he makes retrenchments from *useless* expences; that "he *determines* to *diminish his expences* by a thousand a year," and that, what he WASTED before, what HE GOT NOTHING BY THE USE OF BEFORE, he now applies to the paying off of his mortgage. This is very rational, and very efficient it would be; but, is this the case with A NATION? Would the money, which is collected from the people *in taxes*, for the purpose of supporting the Sinking Fund, be *wasted*, if not collected from them? Would it be *squandered away* by the several individuals who pay it, in the same manner that THRIFTY'S thousand a year is supposed to have been wasted, before he began the work of redemption? Would it, in short, be of *no advantage* to them, if it were not taken away to be given to the Sinking Fund? Oh, yes! And it would produce a compound interest, too, in the hands of individuals, as well as in the hands of the Sinking Fund Commissioners. What has the nation *gained*, then, by paying millions to Commissioners, instead of keeping those millions in their own hands? **SINCE THE YEAR 1786, THE NATION HAS PAID UPWARDS OF 160 MILLIONS INTO THE HANDS OF THE SINKING-FUND COMMISSIONERS**; that is to say, so much money has been *collected from the people in taxes* for the purpose of redeeming Debt; and, if this sum had been left in the people's hands, would it have been of *no use to them?* Would it not, at any rate, have *helped* to prevent the Debt; *since that time*, from being **AUGMENTED IN THE SUM OF 600 MILLIONS.**

Let us give the thing one more turn, and then, it is, I think hard, if we may not safely quit it for ever.

THRIFTY is supposed to take his thousand a year out of what he before *wasted*; out of his *superfluities*. But, does our Sinking Fund money; do the taxes that we pay towards the Sinking Fund, come out of our *superfluities?* And, why suppose that THRIFTY *wasted* any money before? Why suppose that *he had any money to waste?* Is THRIFTY's being *in debt*, and having his *estate encumbered*; are these reasons sufficient for concluding, that he had it in his power to "*determine* to *diminish* his "expences?" Are they not rather reasons sufficient for concluding, that he was in circumstances of distress? Yes; and if, when we have come to that rational conclusion, we suppose him persuaded to believe, that he will get out of debt by *borrowing from* SILVERLOCKS *all the money that he pays off with* GOLDHAIR, and loading his estate with a new mortgage, *with the addition of the cost of bonds and fees*, then we shall have before our eyes "an *example* in a private "concern," pretty well calculated to illustrate the celebrated scheme, which we have now been discussing, and of which I now flatter myself that a single word more need never be uttered to any man of only common sense.

I am, Gentlemen,

Your faithful Friend,

WM. COBBETT.

State Prison, Newgate, Thursday, 20th Sept. 1810.

P. S.—FRIDAY, 21st SEPT.—I have just seen, in the Public Prints, a report of a Speech, said to have been delivered yesterday at the Bank Company's House, in Threadneedle-street, by Mr. RANDALL JACKSON. I shall not, as I said before, suffer any publications of the day to interrupt the course of my discussion. In my next LETTER, which will open the way to that memorable transaction, *the Stoppage of Gold and Silver payments at the Bank of England*, I shall, in all likelihood, have occasion to notice Mr. Jackson's Speech, not so much on its own account, as because it appears to have been highly applauded by the people at the head of the Bank Company, for whom, perhaps, Mr. JACKSON, who, it seems is a *lawyer*, made it in the way of his profession. One word, however, I must beg leave to add upon the part of this Gentleman's speech, in which, as the reporter says, he alluded *to me*, as one who had exulted at the appearance of the Bullion Report, because that Report, coming from such *high authority*, had put the *stamp of correctness on my opinions*. Never did *I say* this; never did I *think* this. Never did I look upon the Bullion Committee as a *high authority*; and, meanly indeed should I think of myself, if I thought any thing, that they could say or do, capable of adding the smallest weight to my opinions. No: what I exulted at was, that my principles and doctrines, as to paper-money, had, at last, produced *practical effect*, a proof of which was contained in the Bullion Report; and that, it was now more likely than before, that such measures would, in time be adopted, as would be likely to secure the country from the natural consequences of that overwhelming CORRUPTION, and that want of love for the real Constitution, which I regarded as the fruit of the Paper-money System, and which, years ago, I *proved*, as I think, to have proceeded, in great part, from that poisonous and all-degrading root. This was the cause of my exultation. I looked upon the Bullion Report as tending to this great object; and, as I prefer the accomplishment of this object, as I look upon the happiness and honour of my country as of far greater value to me than any other worldly possession, I said, and I still say, that the Bullion Report has given me more pleasure than I should derive from being made the owner of the whole of Hampshire. As for any idea of a *party* nature, I shall, I am sure, be believed when I say, that I did not care one straw to what party the Committee belonged. If I had a wish as to party it certainly would be, that *no change of ministry* should take place; for, (without prejudice to the OUTS, who, I think, would do the thing full as well with a little more time) I am quite satisfied that the present men will do it as neatly and as quickly as any reasonable man can expect.

LETTER VII.

"REAL MONEY can hardly ever multiply too much in any country: because it will always, as IT increases, be the *certain sign of the increase of* TRADE, of which it is the measure, and consequently of the soundness and vigour of the whole body. But this PAPER MONEY may, and does increase, without any increase of Trade; nay often when Trade greatly declines. FOR IT IS NOT THE MEASURE OF THE TRADE OF ITS NATION, BUT OF THE NECESSITY OF ITS GOVERNMENT; and it is absurd, *and must be ruinous*, that the same cause which naturally exhausts the *wealth* of a Nation should likewise be the only *productive cause of money*."—BURKE.

Review of the Ground over which we have passed in the foregoing Letters—Opening the Way into the History of the Bank's Stoppage in 1797—Vague Notion about the Increase of Bank-Notes being a Sign of an Increase of Trade and Wealth and Prosperity—This Notion examined—Mr. Randle Jackson's Speech inveighing against those who have recommended that he and his Partners shall be compelled to Pay their Promissory Notes in two Years—His Notion that an Increase of Bank Notes naturally arises from an Increase of Trade—Abuse heaped upon those who wish the Bank to pay its Notes—Such Persons called Riflers and accused of wishing to destroy the Credit of Old England—An Increase of Promissory Notes is a Proof of an Increase of Debt—Five Ways in which Bank-Notes get out into circulation—Absurdity of supposing that an Increase of Promises-to-pay are a Sign of an Increase of the Means of Paying—N.B. An Account of the Distresses arising from the Failure of the Banks at Salisbury and Shaftsbury.

GENTLEMEN,

IN the foregoing Letter, we closed the discussion relative to the *Sinking Fund*; and that brought us to a point, to a sort of stage, or resting place, on our way, from which point it will be advantageous for us to take a brief review of the ground over which we have passed; for, when the design of the writer is to serve the cause of *truth*, and especially when the truths he wishes to make apparent, have been industriously enveloped in darkness; in such a case, every other quality in writing ought to yield to that of *clearness*.

It was stated, at the out-set of our inquiries, that the *Chief Object* of them was, to ascertain, or, at least, to enable ourselves to form a decided opinion, "*Whether it be possible, "without a total destruction of all* "*the paper-money, to restore Gold* "*and Silver to circulation amongst* "*us.*" In pursuit of this object, it became necessary for us to make some preliminary inquiries as to *the cause of the Gold and Silver having gone out of circulation.*

The cause, the *immediate* cause, that is to say the cause which came close before the effect, was the *increase of the paper-money.* This cause was evident to every one; but, then, it became us to inquire what had been *the cause of that increase;* otherwise our inquiries would have been as useless as would be those of a farmer, who, upon finding a score of his sheep dead, should content himself with ascertaining that they had been killed with a knife, without making any inquiry as to the person by whom the destructive instrument had been used. Common sense, therefore, dictated to us to inquire into the cause, or causes, of the increase of the paper-money; and, in order to come at a clear understanding with respect to these causes, we were obliged to go back to the inauspicious origin of the paper-money system, that fatal system, whence arose the National Debt, that Debt which even PITT himself, the great abettor of the system, called "*the* "*best ally of France.*"

During this retrospect, we have seen, that the Bank of England is merely a Company of traders, whose charter arose out of a loan which they made to the Government, and that, at its institution, it never entered into the mind of man, that these traders were ever to be protected by law from paying, in the king's coin, their *promissory notes,* as they have been from February 1797 to the present day. We have seen, in proceeding to inquire into the cause of this *non-payment* or *stoppage,* on the part of the Bank, in 1797, that the Bank-notes have *gone on increasing in quantity,* and that these notes, of which, for more than half a century, there were none under 20 pounds, appeared, in the war of 1755, in the shape of 15 pounds and 10 pounds; and, during PITT's war against the French revolution, which war he carried on, in part at least, for the avowed purpose of *destroying the finances of France,* we have seen that they appeared in the shape, first, of 5 pounds, and, at last, in the shape of 2 pounds and 1 pound. We have, in order the better to understand the history of the Bank Stoppage in 1797, and the better to estimate its consequences, taken a view of the *Funds* and *Stocks* and *National Debt;* we have seen how they arose; we have described their nature; we have traced them in their dreadful progress; we have seen how the National Debt has gone on increasing, from the reign of William the Third to the present day; we have seen how exactly the increase of the National *Expenditure* and the *Taxes* and the *Poor Rates* have kept pace with the increase of the Debt; and, in the three last Letters, we have seen an ample developement, a clear exposure, of the schemes for "*redeeming,*" or "*pay-* "*ing off,*" that Debt, and we have seen, that during the operation of those schemes of redemption, the Debt has gone on increasing, and, that the *interest* we pay upon the Debt, has, since the Grand Scheme of PITT has been in force, been augmented from 9 millions a year to 32 millions a year.

This is what we have seen and what we have done. And having now, to use the sportsman's language, made good our ground, we may begin to move forwards towards the interesting history, of the stoppage of gold and silver payments at the Bank of England, in 1797.

Our first step, in opening the way into this history, must be to obtain a clear notion with regard to the manner, in which bank notes are issued, or put out into circulation among the people; or, rather, with regard to the *immediate* causes of putting them out. For unless we have a clear understanding upon this point, we shall have but a confused idea of the *more distant* causes, of their increase.

There, is, apparently, a vague, or indistinct, notion, floating in the minds of some men, that the increase of the bank notes is an indication, or sign, of an increase of TRADE, of WEALTH, and of PROSPERITY, which, as you must have perceived, are, by such persons, always jumbled and confounded together, for want of proper attention to the facts and principles, which we have stated and laid down in Letter III, from page 23 to page 37. But, we must not suffer ourselves to fall into this confusion; and, indeed, does not common sense reject the notion, that an increase of *promissory notes*, which necessarily argues the want of the means of the person, issuing them, to pay in specie; does not common sense, does not the plain understanding of every plain man, reject, with scorn, the notion, that such an increase is a sign of increasing *wealth* and *prosperity* in the person, or body, or community, by whom the issue is made? Why does our neighbour NEEDY give a note of hand in payment of his rent or of his taylor's bill? Why, because he has not the money in his pocket or his drawer. And, are we to be made to believe, that the circumstance of his not having money to pay what he owes is a proof of his *wealth* and *prosperity?* We have been persuaded to believe many things; but, I think, that, at this day, we shall not be persuaded to believe this. At the time of the *numerous bankruptcies*, in 1793, just after PITT's war broke out, PITT asserted, that they were a sign of *national prosperity*, and was almost *huzzaed* for the assertion; but, we have had time now to experience, time to *feel*, the worth of PITT's assertions, predictions, plans, and measures; and, with the benefit of this lesson, we shall not, now, be so easily persuaded, that *bankruptcy* is a sign of prosperity; though, it must, I think, be allowed, that it is full as true a sign of prosperity as that which has now been discovered in the *increase of promissory notes*, which increase is, and must be, always an infallible sign of a want, in a greater or a less degree, of the means to make payment *in money*.

As to the *increase of Trade*, that, indeed, will demand, as we shall hereafter more fully see, a certain increase of circulating medium, or money, as must be evident to every man, who reflects, but for one moment, upon the subject; because, where there are ten purchases of a pound each to be made (supposing them to be made in the same space of time) twice as much money will be wanted as where there are only five purchases of a pound each to be made. But, the increase of *trade*, that is to say, the increase of purchases and sales, or, in other words, *the increase of* MONEY'S WORTH *things*, though it is a very solid reason for the increase of *money*, is no reason at all for the increase of *promissory notes*, and especially of promissory notes which will *not bring money in exchange for them.* The man, who is in a great way of trade, gives more promissory notes than a man in a small way; but, he has proportionate means, and, at any rate, does not give notes without possessing the value of them in goods, or property of some kind, in *money's-worth* things; and of course his notes are *convertible into money*; but, is this the case with the notes of the Bank? Is this the case with the notes of *any* of our Banks? Such a man stands in need of no law to protect him against the demands of the holder of his notes; but there is a law to protect the Bank of England against the demand of any holder of its notes, who may wish to have guineas in exchange for those notes. And, can the increase of such notes be regarded as a sign of the increase of trade?

Yet this is a favourite fallacy with those, who either do not understand the matter, or who, while they do understand it, wish to deceive the world, and the people of this country in particular. This same fallacy was put forth with great assurance, at the House of the Bank in Threadneedle-Street, London, no longer ago than last Friday, by the Gentlemen, a Mr. RANDALL JACKSON, mentioned in the Postscript to the last Letter, page 73, in a speech, the whole of which (together with the speeches of the GOVERNOR OF THE BANK and of a Mr. PAYN, a Country Banker), as reported in the Morning Chronicle, of Saturday last, will be found in the APPENDIX, A, and which I beg leave to recommend to your attentive perusal.

MR. JACKSON, who is, it would seem, a proprietor of Bank Stock; that is to say, one of the Bank Company; that is to say, one of the persons in whose name the Bank-notes are issued; that is to say, one of the persons, who put forth the promissory notes of the Bank; that is to say, one of the persons who derive a profit, who get rich, from the putting out of those notes; MR. JACKSON most loudly inveighs against the Bullion Committee, and, indeed, pretty roundly abuses them; pretty roundly abuses a Committee of the House of Commons, for having recommended to the House to pass a law *to oblige him and his partners to pay their notes agreeably to promise*; and, this he does, you will observe, at the very time that he is railing against the revolutionists of France, for their *levelling principles*, and insinuating, that there are such levellers now at work in England; all which may be very natural in MR. JACKSON; for, who that is protected by law from the payment of his promissory notes, would wish that law to be repealed, and its place supplied by a law to compel him to pay? It may be very natural for a gentlemen, so situated, to abuse the Committee; but, it would be very foolish in the people; very foolish in the holders of his notes; very foolish in *his creditors*, to join in such abuse. Upon this part of his speech, however, we shall find a more suitable place for extending our remarks, and also for noticing what he said about the vast increase of Country Banks, without seeming to perceive, that that increase has been owing solely to the law which protected, and still protects, the Bank of England against the Gold and Silver demands of its creditors. Upon these parts of his speech, and upon his assertions respecting a debt said to be due to the Bank *from the public*; upon his statement of the causes of the Bank stoppage; upon the *wonderful unanimity* of all the speakers at this Meeting of the partners of the Bank Company, in declaring, that there would be NO GOOD *in their paying of their promissory notes in Gold and Silver*; upon all these topics, and upon some others, brought forward at the Bank Company's Meeting, we shall find, hereafter, a more suitable opportunity for making and applying our remarks, which, indeed, belong to other parts of our subject, and, therefore, we will, at present, confine ourselves to the only topic, introduced into these speeches, which belong to the part of our subject now immediately before us; namely, the notion, that *the increase of bank-notes naturally arises from an increase of trade.*

Since, however, I have digressed so far, I take the liberty to continue on a little further for the purpose of noticing a paragraph, in a newspaper of this very morning (Monday, 24th Sept.), which imitates MR. JACKSON in abusing those, who are desirous of seeing the Bank Company once more pay their promissory notes in Gold and Silver. "We are happy," says this writer, "to find, that the opinion "we have more than once expressed "upon this subject is sanctioned by "the first authorities in the Country, "and that the mischievous idea of "*throwing open the Bank immediately to be rifled by the engrossers and exporters of guineas*, is *universally reprobated.* Sir John Sinclair has "taken up the pen upon the subject, "and most ably does he treat it. "Neither the authority of the Committee, nor the clamours of those "*who wish to destroy the public credit* "*of Old England* have been sufficient to intimidate that *highly* informed and *much respected* Gentlemen from coming forward to vindicate *truth* and dispel a *most mischievous delusion*." What Gentlemen! is a recommendation to pass a law to oblige the Bank Company to *begin to pay its promissory notes in gold and silver, at the end of two years*; is this to be called "*throwing open*" the Bank to be "*rifled?*" Are you and all of us, who hold bank notes, to be denominated "*riflers*," or *robbers*, because we may wish to be paid the amount of those notes in gold and silver? Is a desire to see the Bank pay its promissory notes upon demand, agreeably to the words written in them, and to see the king's coin once more come back into circulation amongst us; is this desire to be attributed to a "*wish to destroy the* "*public credit of old England?*" Gentlemen, this language shows two things: first, that those who use it entertain a most hearty contempt for the people of England; and, second, that their cause is so very bad, that they dare not even attempt to offer in support of it any thing bearing the shape of an argument.

Leaving the Bank Company to the support of these railers, let us now, with the calmness and candour which belong to the cause of truth, return to our inquiry, *whether the increase of the bank notes has arisen from an increase of trade*, and, if not, *what has been the real cause, or causes, of that increase of bank notes which has driven the gold and silver out of circulation.*

We have seen, that a *real* increase of *trade* means, an increase in *purchases* and *sales*, or, in other words, an increase in commodities, or things, which are really *worth money*. Consequently an increase of trade will naturally demand an increase of money; but, what it demands is an increase of *real* money, seeing that the increase of the trade itself is no other than an increase of *money's worth* things; and, that the increase of its demand will not be for paper, or for notes not convertible into money. Precisely the contrary; and, in private concerns, we every day see, that it is the *falling off* of a man's real trade, it is the *lessening* of his quantity of money's worth things, that induces him to have recourse to the issue of paper, paper which he cannot turn into money. In a word, it is DEBT that makes a man give promissory notes. An increase of trade always implying an increase of money's worth things, *brings, of itself, an increase of real money*, unless that money be by some unnatural cause withheld from circulation. It is just the same with a nation, whose increase of money's worth things will *bring to it* an exactly proportionate increase of real money, if that money be not kept back, or driven out again, by some unnatural cause; but, DEBT, and the attendants upon debt, lead to the issuing of bank notes, or, to paper of some sort or other, or, to a something, no matter what it be, which has not a real value in itself. Real money is the *representative of MONEY'S WORTH THINGS*: promissory notes are the *representatives of DEBT*; and, this we shall clearly see, as we proceed in examining into the way, or rather, the divers ways, in which bank notes *get out into circulation amongst the people.*

The bank notes have in them nothing of a mystical nature. They are the joint work of paper-maker, an engraver, a printer, and the person who puts his name, in writing, at the bottom of them. Being thus brought to perfection, they are delivered at the Bank Company's House, or Shop, FIRST, to any persons, to whom the Company may owe money, for *work done* to their buildings, or to others for keeping their books, or for paper, or for printing, or, in short, for any services performed for them. A SECOND way, in which the notes get out, is through what is called *discounting*; that is to say, loans of bank notes made to private persons, for which the borrower leaves in possession of the Company a note of hand or bill of exchange, that is to say, an engagement to pay back again as much as he receives together with interest for the time, or, rather, the interest is deducted when the loan is made. A THIRD way, in which the notes get out, is through the advances, or loans, which the Bank makes to the Government, by way of anticipation upon the taxes, before they come in. A FOURTH way is through the payment of the interest of Exchequer Bills, or Navy Bills, which are a sort of promissory notes, given by the government, and upon which the Bank sometimes pays the interest, and, at other times, discounts them, or purchases them of the holders at the current price; but, in every case, a fresh parcel of bank notes, get, through the means of these bills, into circulation. A FIFTH way, in which the notes get out, is through the payment of the *dividends or the interest, of the Stock*, or *National Debt*, which dividends are paid quarterly; and, as we have before seen, the amount is *three times as great* as it was at the beginning of PITT'S war against the Jacobins of France, which we have called the ANTI-JACOBIN WAR.

Now, without enumerating any more of the ways, in which bank-notes get into circulation, is it not as clear as the Sun at noon-day, that they are always the *representatives of* DEBT? Is it not a fact that no one can deny, that the increase of them proceeds from the *increase of Debt*, and not from the *increase of trade?* Away, then, with the nonsense of those dreamers, who would persuade us that an issue of *promissory notes* proceeds from an increase of *money's worth* things! Away, with the idle talk about an increase of things of real value calling for an increase of *paper promises!* Away, away, with the confused, the childish notion, that *an increase of the means of paying* produces an increase of *promises to pay!* As well might any one tell you, that the increase of the paper of the Salisbury* and Shaftesbury banks arose from the *increase of the means of*

---

* The scenes at SALISBURY, on account of the failure of the Banks at that city and at Shaftesbury, have been truly distressing. At Salisbury in particular, where the greatest part of the sufferers live, the poor people were, in many cases, without victuals or drink for some time, and many persons, in a respectable way of life, were for many days together, obliged to sit down to dine upon little more than bread, no meat being to be purchased with the only sort of money (if a debased paper ought, for a moment, to go by that name) which was, generally speaking, in possession of the people. Many persons, in the lower ranks of life, who had gathered together a few pounds, the fruit of long labour and anxious care, of frugality, and of forbearance from enjoyment; the fruit, in short, of an exercise of all the domestic virtues, and destined to be the provision, as the saying is, "against a rainy day," that is, to be the source of comfort in sickness or in old age; many persons of this description, the heart ache of one of whom ought to give us more pain than to see fifty thousand Public Robbers swinging from so many gibbets; many persons of this description; many of these very best of the people, saw their little all vanish in a moment, and themselves reduced to the same state with the improvident, the careless, the lazy, the spendthrift, the drunkard, and the glutton, looking back upon a life of labour and of care, and looking forward to the misery and disgrace of a workhouse! To describe the scene, when the Meetings of Creditors took place, at Salisbury, would be impossible. The Council Chamber of the city (for no other place, except the Cathedral, would have contained a twentieth part of them), was surrounded with such multitudes, and so eager were they, in pressing forward, that some were in danger of their lives; and the constables, from necessity, perhaps, laid their staves about the heads of many of those who came to demand their due, particularly, as I am informed, on the 7th of this month. What a scene was this! Here, PITT, if he had still been alive, might have seen a specimen of the fruits of his system! The holders of the notes, were, I understand, each of them compelled to be at the expence of an *affidavit*, and obliged also, to attend in person, or *by an attorney*, at the Meeting of Creditors, and also for the receipt of the dividends whenever any shall take place. It is easy, therefore, to conceive *what portion of payment* will ever fall to the lot of hundreds of poor men and women, living at a distance from Salisbury, and scattered about in country places, where a news-paper is hardly ever seen. One of the banks was called the *Salisbury and Shaftesbury bank*, and part of the notes are *dated* at

paying their debts, an assertion, which, with the present scenes before your eyes, might be a little more impudent, but not a whit more contrary to truth than the assertion above noticed, and, I trust, completely refuted.

I am, Gentlemen,

Your faithful friend,

WM. COBBETT.

State Prison, Newgate, Monday, 24th September, 1810.

---

one place, and part at the other. Those notes, which were *dated* at the latter place, were to be proved at meetings to be held there; so that, many of the poor fellows, who had brought their notes to Salisbury, were told, that *they must carry them to Shaftesbury*, a place at *twenty miles distance!* The holder of each note, was, I understand, compelled, in order to have a claim to any dividend, to *swear* that *he* had *given the full value of the note*; so that, *one man could not demand payment of the note of any other man*; and, people could *not sell the notes for any thing below their nominal value.* It is evident, that, under circumstances like these, a great portion of the *poor* people who hold any of these notes, will lose the whole amount of them. I have two men, for instance, who had the misfortune to be of this number, James Gullingham and William Hurckett, the former of whom had a *five pound* note, and the latter a *one pound* note, both issued under the name of Bowles, Ogden, and Wyndham, and both which notes I have now lying upon the table before me. These men are at twenty-eight miles distance from Salisbury; to present the notes at the Meeting would have required three days absence from home in the midst of harvest, besides their expences at Salisbury and upon the road, which, without the expence of the affidavit, would have amounted to more than the one pound note of Hurckett, to say nothing about the expences attending the receipt of the dividends. Indeed, upon the circumstances being related to me, I was quite satisfied that any attempt of poor Gullingham to recover his debt from Messrs. Bowles, Ogden, and Wyndham, even supposing them to pay 20 shillings in the pound, would be a losing concern, and that the best way was for me to take the debt off their hands. I intend to send the pretty little bits of paper down to them, with a request, that they will paste them upon two little boards, and hang them up in their cottages, not only by way of ornament, but as a lesson to their neighbours and their children. I dare say, that there are many considerate masters who will act in like manner; but, it must be manifest to every one, that hundreds of poor families will suffer, and very severely suffer, from this one failure. What, then, must be the consequence, *if these failures should become general*; and, does it not become every one, who wishes to see the peace and independence of the country preserved, to use his utmost endeavours to convince the public of the necessity of measures to restore to circulation the gold and silver coin, and thereby to prevent, if possible, those dreadful convulsions, in which the issue of a paper currency, not convertible into specie, have but too frequently, not to say, invariably, ended?

Entered at Stationers' Hall.

Printed by W. MOLINEUX, 5, Bream's Buildings, Chancery Lane; Published by WM. COBBETT, Jun. No. 8, Catherine Street, Strand: and Retailed at No. 192, Strand.

LETTER VIII.

"That provisions and labour should become dear by the increase of *trade and money*, is in many respects "an inconvenience; but an inconvenience that is unavoidable, and the effect of that *public wealth* and "*prosperity* which are the end of all our wishes. It is compensated by the advantages which we reap from "the possession of those PRECIOUS METALS, and the weight *which they give the nation in all foreign* "*wars and negociations*; but there appears no reason for increasing that inconvenience by *a counterfeit* "*money*, which *foreigners will not accept of* in any payment, and which any great disorder in the state "*will reduce to nothing*."——*Hume.*

Further Observations respecting the fallacious Notion that Paper Money is the Consequence of an Increase of Trade and of National Prosperity—Sir John Sinclair's Idea about Roads and Canals—Exemplification in the Instances of France and the American States—Destruction of the Paper Money in both those Countries, the dawn of National Prosperity—Our own history shows the Influence of a National Debt in producing Bank Notes—Our Bank was the Offspring of the Debt—The Bank was necessary in order to pay the Interest of the Debt—Boldness of Mr. Jackson and Sir John Sinclair in asserting that Paper Money is necessary to Trade, and is a Mine of National Prosperity—What would Hume have said if he had been told that Scotland would produce a Man to assert what Sir John Sinclair has asserted?—The "LO HERE!" and the "LO THERE!"—The real cause of the increase of the Bank Notes—That Increase shown to have kept pace with the Increase of the Debt—Conclusion of this part of our subject.

GENTLEMEN,

IN the foregoing Letter we opened the way towards the history of the Stoppage of Gold and Silver, or, *Real-money payments*, at the Bank of England, in the year 1797, by showing the divers ways, in which bank-notes get out into circulation, or, in other words, the divers motives for making those notes; and by clearly showing also, in reasoning upon general principles, that it is *Debt* and not *Wealth*, that generates promissory notes, of whatever sort they may be, or by whomsoever issued. So fond, however, have we been upon this subject, and such great pains, for so long a time, have been taken to make us believe, that the increase of the paper-currency proceeds from an increase of *Trade*, or of something *favourable* to us, that I should not be perfectly satisfied with myself, were I to hasten forward, without first submitting to you all the observations that have occurred to me upon this part of our subject.

When those, who, from whatever motive, have written in favour of the Paper System, have had to account for the vast increase in the quantity of the bank-notes, they have always had recourse to our "*increasing* "*trade*" and "*wealth*" and "*pros-* "*perity*" and "*improvement*;" and they have, like SIR JOHN SINCLAIR, bid us look at the increase of *turnpike roads* and *canals* and *harbours* and new *inclosures*. Now, this reference to roads, canals, harbours, and enclosures is singularly unhappy; for, the Emperor Napoleon, in his annual speeches, to his Corps Legislatif, or Parliament, tells them of new roads

W. MOLINEUX, Printer, Bream's Buildings Chancery Lane.

and canals, compared to which ours are not worth naming, while we know pretty well that he has, during this war even, made a harbour and an arsenal and *a fleet too*, where there was before no semblance of maritime means, to get at which fleet, or, rather, to *attempt* to get at it, has cost us all the lives and all the millions of taxes expended in the Walcheren Expedition; and, while we *see*, that, as to *agricultural improvements*, France is able *to let us have bread*. Therefore, as this is the case in France, and as these same writers assure us, that the people of France are in a state of *extreme misery*, methinks that new canals and roads and harbours and agricultural improvements should not, by these writers, at any rate be cited as proofs of National prosperity.

But, what have these exertions of genius and industry; these efforts of the bodily or mental faculties of a people; what have these to do with *paper-money?* There is no *paper-money in France*. Yet the French make roads and canals and harbours and agricultural improvements. There is no *paper-money*, by which we always mean, paper *not convertible into gold or silver at the will of the holder;* there is no paper of this kind in the AMERICAN STATES; yet, it is pretty notorious, that there are improvements going on in those States, some of which are truly astonishing, and one instance in particular, I cannot help giving you, just as I found it published in the London news-papers of the 11th of last month* Having seen and admired this wonderful, and, perhaps, unparalleled, instance of prosperity and happiness proceeding from the united exertions of genius and industry; and, being at the same time, aware, that something approaching towards it must necessarily be going on in other parts of the country, you have only to know, that there is no such thing as a *paper-money* in any part of that country; for, then your conclusion must be, that a paper-money is not necessary to create, or to aid the operations of, genius and industry; and, history, at once to inform and console you, affords you these further facts, that both in France and America, there *has been* a paper-money; that, in both countries, that money has met with its *total destruction;* and that, since such destruction, both countries have flourished much more than they did while that money was in existence.

What have the partizans of the Paper System to offer in answer to this? Will any one of them venture to look these facts in the face? I do not believe they will. They will, I should suppose, rather choose to confine themselves to a dull re-assertion of their former assertions, interspersed, may be, with a seasoning of abuse upon those, by whom their ignorance, or insincerity, is detected and exposed. But, without resorting to the instances furnished in foreign countries, have we not, in the history of our own finances, quite a sufficient proof, that paper-money, or, indeed, *bank-notes of any sort*, are not the re-

* It is now a little more than five years, since a number of German families, styling themselves "THE HARMONY SOCIETY;" went to the United States, with the view of forming a distinct settlement. They soon planted themselves in the wilderness of BUTLER COUNTY, in the north-western corner of PENSYLVANIA. The following account of the origin and progress of their settlement is copied from the Mirror, a paper published in the neighbourghood of this frugal, industrious and thriving people.—The Association of Harmony had its origin in Germany upwards of 20 years ago; and feeling themselves much oppressed on account of their religion, they concluded to seek a country where they could exercise their religion without hindrance or oppression.—They chose the United States of America. In the year 1804, in December, about 20 families arrived in Zelinople, in the neighbourhood of which, Mr. George Rapp, with some others, bought about 4,700 acres of land, and during that fall built nine log-

presentatives of any thing but *Debt?* In every country, of which we have any knowledge, a *Government-Debt* has been accompanied with *bank-notes*, or *payments in paper*, of some sort or other, no matter under what name. The *Debt*, in England, did, as we have seen (Letter II, p. 17), begin in the year 1692; and there appeared, at first, no intention to pay either the interest or the principal in any thing but the usual gold and silver-coin of the country. People lent their guineas and crown pieces, and there was not the smallest notion of their being repaid in any thing but guineas and crown pieces. But, it was soon found, that to pay the interest of its *Debt*, the government needed something other than gold and silver; which, indeed, any one might have foreseen, because the *Debt* itself necessarily arose from the *want of gold and silver* within the reach of the government. It was, therefore, supreme folly to suppose, that the government, who had borrowed people's guineas from want, would long have guineas enough to carry on wars and to pay those people too. Accordingly, in only *two years* after the *Debt* began, the *Bank was established;* the Bank made notes; these notes, as far as they went, supplied the place of real money; and, very soon, by giving all possible countenance and support to

houses.—In the year 1805, in the spring, the Society consisted of about 50 families: they laid out the town of Harmony on their own land, and in that spring built twelve log-houses 94 feet by 18, built a large barn, cleared 25 acres round the town, and 151 acres for corn, and 50 acres for potatoes; a grist-mill was built this year, the race 3-8ths of a mile long, and 15 acres cleared for meadow, the other ground sowed with wheat and rye; in the fall and winter, 30 houses more were built.—In the year 1806 an inn was built two stories high, 42 by 32 feet, and some other houses; 300 acres cleared for corn, 58 acres for meadow; an oil-mill was built, and a tannery, a blue dyer's shop, and a frame barn 100 feet long. In the year 1807, 300 acres were cleared for grain and a meadow, a brick store-house built, a saw-mill and beer-brewery erected, and four acres of vines planted: in this year the Society sold 500 bushels of grain, and 3,000 gallons of whiskey manufactured by themselves of their own produce.—In the year 1808, a considerable quantity of ground cleared, a meeting-house built of brick, 70 feet long and 55 feet wide, another brick-house built, some other buildings and stables for cattle, pot-ash, soap-boiler and candle-drawer shops erected, a frame barn of 80 feet long built. Of the produce of this year was sold 2,000 bushels of grain; and 1,400 bushels were distilled.—In the year 1809, a fulling-mill was built, which does a great deal of business for the country, also a hemp-mill, an oil-mill, a grist-mill, a brick-warehouse 46 feet by 36, and another brick-building of the same dimensions, one of which has a cellar completely arched under the whole, for the purpose of a wine-cellar. A considerable quantity of land cleared this year. The produce of this year was 6,000 bushels of Indian corn, 4,500 bushels of wheat, 5,000 bushels of oats, 10,000 bushels of potatoes, 4,000lbs. of hemp and flax, 100 bushels of barley brewed into beer, and 50 gallons of sweet oil, made from the white poppy. Of the produce of this year will be sold, 3,000 bushels of corn, 1,000 bushels of potatoes, 1,000 bushels of wheat; 1,200 bushels of rye will be distilled.—In the year 1810 will be erected a barn 90 feet long, a school-house 50 feet by 44 wide, a grist-mill with three pair of stones, one of which will be burrs, and some small brick-houses for families.—The society now consists of 780 persons, comprising 140 families, they have now 1,600 acres of land cleared, 203 acres whereof are in meadow, and possess at present 6,000 acres of land.—There are different tradesmen members of of this society, who work for the country as well as the society, to wit: Twelve shoemakers, six taylors, twelve weavers, three wheel-wrights, five coopers, six blacksmiths, two nail-smiths, three rope-makers, three blue dyers, ten carpenters, four cabinet-makers, two sadlers, two waggon-makers, twelve masons, two potters, one soap-boiler, a doctor and apothecary, but neither *parson* nor *lawyer*, and in a short time a hatter and a tin-plate worker are expected.—During the last year the shoemakers alone worked for the country to the amount of 112 dollars and 8 cents, the coopers to the amount of 207 dollars, the sadlers to the amount of 739 dollars 54 cents, the tannery 675 dollars, the blacksmiths 100 dollars.

the Bank, the government got great part of the interest of its *Debt* paid in bank notes. Thus were the bank-notes, from the very outset, as, indeed, *all promissory notes* must be, the *representatives of Debt*, and not of *wealth*, of *prosperity*, or of *trade*; and, if this was the case, at a time when these notes were *convertible into gold and silver*, shall we *now* look upon them in a better light?

In spite, however, of the voice of history and of reason, and even in spite of common sense, there are (as in the instances of MR. RANDALL JACKSON and SIR JOHN SINCLAIR) men to be found, so ignorant or so hardy as to hold up bank-notes, promissory notes, and promissory notes, too, *not convertible into real money*: there are men to be found to hold up this *paper-money*, which, as we have clearly shewn, is always issued in consequence *of Debt*, in consequence of *a want of real money*, and which paper-money is, as BURKE (See the Motto to Letter VII, page 76) well describes it, "not the *measure of the* " *trade* of its nation, but of the *neces-* " *sities of its government*:" there are men to be found, who, like MR. JACKSON, insist that an increase of paper-money is called for by an increase of *trade*; and, who, like the bolder BARONET, scruple not to assert, that " the *abundance of circulation*" (speaking of bank-notes not convertible into gold and silver) " *is the great source* " *of our opulence and strength, and a* " MINE *of national prosperity*;" yea, who have the boldness to call promissory notes, which are issued only because the issuers are not able to pay in money, a *mine* of national prosperity; and, who are hardy enough to make this assertion at the very moment when they themselves are declaring, that it would *be ruinous* to attempt to force the issuers of such notes to pay them in money when presented.

HUME, as will be seen from that passage of his Essay on Money, from which I have taken my motto, observes, that there is an *inconvenience* in the increase of *real* money, which, as was shown in the last Letter, is naturally produced by an increase of trade; and he calls bank-notes (though, observe, convertible into gold and silver, as they were in his time), *counterfeit* money. What, then, would he have said of our present bank-notes; what would he have said of bank-notes not convertible into gold and silver; and what would he have said, if he had been told, that Scotland would produce a man, who would tell the people of Great Britain, and in print too, that *such* bank-notes are a mine of *National Prosperity?*

We have now, I think, said quite enough to convince any man, whose faculties enable him to distinguish falsehood from truth, that the notion of an increase of trade demanding an increase of paper-money is one of the most gross delusions, that either ignorance or an intention to deceive ever attempted to practise upon mankind. We have, in short, clearly shown, that the increase of bank-notes, and of promissory notes of every description, are produced by *Debt*, are the offspring and *representatives of Debt*, and that *real* money, and real money only, is the representative of *property*, or *wealth*, or things of *real value*, and, of course, that an increase of *trade*, which is only another term for an increase of *money's-worth things*, demands, and if there be no unnatural cause to prevent it, will, of itself, *bring into circulation* an increase of *real money*.

To acknowledge this truth would, however, have been so manifestly injurious to the Paper Money System, that it is not surprizing that the partizans of that system (which is but another name for those who have profited, and do still profit, from it) should have taken uncommon pains to avoid the acknowledgment, and even to maintain, with their utmost ability, any opinion of a contrary tendency. Hence all the absurdities, that we find in the various speeches and pamphlets, uttered and written upon the subject, and in which the increase of the bank-notes, and now of the paper-money, have been, at different times, attributed to almost every cause but the real one. At one time it was the enterprize in commerce; at another, the enterprize in roads and canals; at another, the "*pressure* of the war," which was, as a distant cause, true; at another, it was a "temporary alarm;" at another, it was *speculations abroad;* at another it was the "*influx* of "wealth;" at another, it was *Jacobinism;* and *now*, there are three causes, an *increase of trade*, the *embarrassment to trade* occasioned by Napoleon's commercial warfare against us, and *the exportation of gold!* These last-mentioned causes, which any one may hear from, perhaps, the three first persons whom he meets in Threadneedle Street, do, to be sure, most admirably *accord* with each other! But, it is the lot of falsehood to contradict itself.

In the meanwhile, however, very great is the mischief which arises from this misguiding of the public mind. The people, while amused with this "*Lo here!* and *Lo there!*" see not that which they ought to see; they see not the *real* cause of the increase of the paper-money, the *real cause of the gold and silver having gone out of circulation;* and, of course, they use no endeavours, they express no wish to see adopted any measures, calculated to remove that cause, and to relieve their country from this, the most formidable of all the dangers with which it is threatened.

That this *real* cause is no other, than *the increase of the Debt contracted by the government,* cannot, I think, be doubted by any one, who has gone patiently through the foregoing Letters, and who must have seen, that, *as the Debt increased, the bank-notes became of greater amount in the whole,* and of sums smaller and smaller, till, at last, they came down to *a single pound.* At first, and for half a century, there were no bank-notes for a sum less than *twenty pounds.* When the Debt got to about 70 millions, there were *fifteen pound-notes* made; before it reached 150 millions, there were *ten pound-notes* made; before it reached 300 millions, there were *five pound-notes* made; and before it had reached 500 millions, there were *two pound-notes* and *one pound-notes* made. Since it reached 500 millions, there have been, in some parts of the country, notes made to represent silver-coins, and the Silver Tokens, issued from the Bank of England, the *intrinsic* value of which is *less* than the *nominal*, have been circulated over the country, while the gold-coin, of every value, has almost wholly disappeared, is notoriously exported, and while English guineas, not one of which is seen by hardly any man in England, in the course of a month, make part of *the common current coin* on the continent of Europe, in the *American States*, and more especially *in France;* aye, in that very country, which Pitt and his associates told us, over and over again, was in "*the very gulph of* "*bankruptcy;*" and which we were, year after year, induced to believe would be totally ruined by the fall of that paper-money, the place of which has been, in a great part, supplied by our guineas!

Thus, then, we have seen, both from reason and experience, that it is *Debt* which produces bank-notes, and paper-promises of every sort; and, having seen the manner in which these paper-promises get out amongst us, and how their increase has kept pace with the increase of our *Debt*, we shall, in the next Letter, proceed to trace this increase to that grand and memorable effect, the Stoppage of Gold and Silver-payments at the Bank of England, in 1797.

I am, Gentlemen,
Your sincere Friend,
Wm. Cobbett.

State Prison, Newgate, Thursday, 27th Sept. 1810.

LETTER IX.

"The consternation was general through the whole kingdom. Thousands of families were utterly ruined, and "reduced from opulence to beggary. Despair seemed to have seized upon the country, in which so many "*suicides* were never before heard of."—HISTORY OF THE SOUTH SEA BUBBLE.

This Letter a Digression from the regular Line of the Discussion—Death of Abraham Goldsmidt the great Jew Money-Dealer—Effect of it described, as to the Funds—He and Sir Francis Baring called the Pillars of the City—The Corporation of London thought nothing of—Perilous State of the Country, if such be the Pillars of its Credit—Goldsmidt's Character—His Charities—His princely Entertainments—His Transactions with Sir John Peter at the Exchequer Bill Office—The Motive for the Act of Self-Murder—A Hint at the Reasons why this Jew has been so praised; and why benevolent Jew Characters have been introduced into some of our modern Stage Plays—The Cause of Goldsmidt's committing the Act—History of the Loan-Transaction—What Omnium and Discount is—Progress of the Fall of the Price of Stocks—News-paper Puffs to keep them up—What must be the State of the Country if such trifling Causes produce Discredit—"Capital, Credit, and Confidence"—What Security have we that Things will not become worse?—The Effect upon the Minds of our Enemies—Can it be supposed that People will purchase Stock, or hold Stock if the Fabric be so frail?—May not Napoleon cause a Combination against the Funds?—Of the Remedy or Expedient talked of—The Loan-Makers have no Claim to Compensation for any Loss they may sustain—The famous and immortal Loyalty Loan in the Days of Pitt—This Case different from that of the present Loan-Makers—Conclusion of the Digression.

GENTLEMEN,

THE death of ABRAHAM GOLDSMIDT, the *rich Jew*, mentioned in Letter I, page 2, and who is said to have shot himself on Friday last, the 28th of September; this death is, in the history and progress of the Paper-Money System, an *incident* of some importance, and at this time, worthy of our particular attention; because the circumstances connected with it afford, perhaps, a more striking and satisfactory illustration, than any other that can be imagined, of the *loan-making transactions*. In inquiries, which are of an intricate nature, it is always advantageous to be able to combine *practice* with principle; and, we shall, I think, find in the circumstances just alluded to, such a developement, such a practical exemplification, of some of the principles which we have laid down, as could scarcely have been derived from any other source. The present Letter will, indeed, turn us a little aside from the direct line of our pursuit, and may be considered as a *Digression;* but, it will not tend to *confuse* us, and the matter of it will be found of great use to us during the rest of our inquiry.

The news-papers, and particularly those which praise the government unceasingly, have stated, that, when the intelligence of this man's death reached the city of London (he having shot himself at his house, or rather palace at the village of MORDEN in Surrey) all was confusion and consternation. They tell us, that "The Stock Exchange, Capel-court, "and even the Royal Exchange, were "crowded, all persons eagerly making "inquiries about this event, and *for-"getting almost every thing* else.—"Little or no business was done. We "question whether *peace* or *war* sud-"denly made *ever created such a "bustle.**" We are told, that "*Words* "would be inadequate to express the "surprize, the *alarm* and the *dismay* "that were visible.†" We are further told, that the moment the intelligence reached the City of London, "the "FUNDS felt the effect, and three

* COURIER Newspaper, 28th Sept. † Ibid.

"per cent. Stock fell from 66½ to "63¾;*" that is to say, hundreds of millions of this sort of property instantly lost in value about 3 pounds in every hundred. We are told, in another place, that "the Ministers sent "off a Messenger, with the melan"lancholy tidings, to *the King* and "to the *Prince of Wales*.†"

And all this for the death of a Jew merchant? The *king* and the *heir apparent* to be informed of it by a royal Messenger! And, is it really true, that this man's having shot himself made the citizens of London forget almost every thing else? Is it really true, that such an event put business nearly at a stand? Is it really true, that it produced an effect equal to *peace* or *war* suddenly made? And is it true; is there truth in the shameful fact, that a Jew Merchant's shooting himself produced *alarm* and *dismay* in the capital of England, which is also called, and not very improperly, perhaps, the emporium of the world?

If all this be true, it is high time that we become acquainted with the reasons why such a person was thought of so much consequence; and that we consider well the tendency of a system, that could make his life, or his death, an object of national importance. One of the public prints presents us with the following disconsolate reflection: "The *mutability of* "*human affairs* has been strongly "evinced during the last few weeks.— "SIR FRANCIS BARING and MR. A. "GOLDSMIDT, who were considered "as the PILLARS OF THE CITY, "are both dead within that time. "The effects their deaths have had "*on the funds of the country* will "best bespeak *the support they gave* "*them* while they lived.‡" What! The *Pillars of the City of London!* The Corporation of that famous City, the Mayor, Aldermen, Sheriffs, Common Counsellors, and the Liverymen; all these; the whole of this admirably constituted body, to which, upon so many occasions, the people of the kingdom have been indebted for the preservation of their liberties; the whole of this body sinks out of sight, and all the Companies of industrious and ingenious Tradesmen along with it; they all become nothing, at the mention of the names of a couple of dealers in funds and paper-money! With eyes very different indeed do I view the parties; and, though I desire not the death of either, and am as sorry as you, my neighbours, to hear of the untimely death of any man, I have not the smallest hesitation in saying, that I look upon the life of SIR FRANCIS BARING, or that of GOLDSMIDT, as being of no more, if so much, value to England, as that of any one of your apprentices, or plough-boys; and, I have no doubt, that, before we arrive at the close of this Series of Letters, you will see good reason for believing, that my opinion is founded in a just estimate of the nature and tendency of the professions of these several parties.

But, are these writers aware of the import of their words, when they tell us, that the two persons above-mentioned were the PILLARS *of the City*; that they *gave support to the funds of the country*; and that their deaths have *occasioned these Funds to fall?* Are these writers aware of the tendency of such declarations? Do they consider what it is that they are saying; what it is they are proclaiming to the people and to the world? If they do, and if they expect to be believed, their intention *must be* to destroy all confidence in the Funds and Stocks: for what man in his senses can possibly confide in that which leans for support upon the life of individuals, and of individuals, too, who,

* TIMES Newspaper, 29th Sept.
† COURIER Newspaper, 28th Sept.
‡ TIMES Newspaper, 29th Sept.

from the perils of their very calling, are liable to be driven to commit acts of suicide? In some cases, we are *compelled* to leave our property dependent upon the lives of individuals; but, no man with his intellects perfect ever does this from *choice*; and, if these writers should make the public in general believe, or, if the public from any other cause should believe, that the Funds stand in need of the support of individuals, it is a pretty clear case, that the price of them must fall very low, before many people will be inclined to dispose of their solid property in order to purchase Stock. They must come down to almost nothing, and the purchase must be a sort of gambling; for no man will lay out his money in Stock, as men hitherto have done, if it should become matter of general belief, that the Funds are in any degree dependent upon the lives, and, of course, upon the *will* of individuals.

We will now see (for it is very curious) what has been said as to the *cause* of GOLDSMIDT'S putting an end to his life; and, that will let us into matter essentially belonging to our subject. But, before we proceed any further, I think myself called upon to make a few remarks upon what has, in some of our newspapers, been said about the *character* of this man; for, though I have no desire to say any harm of him, or to cause people to believe harm of him, I think it wrong; I think it very unjust towards my readers; I think it an act of treason to the morals of my country, to stand by, with pen in hand, and to see spread abroad amongst the people such *unqualified praises* of a man, who has terminated his existence by *suicide*, and especially when I do not believe those praises to be *founded in truth*.

We are told of his *acts of charity*; his *subscriptions to charitable undertakings*; his *name*, we are told, was always seen foremost upon such occasions. But, why tell us of this again, if every individual act has been carefully *printed* and *published* before. There are cases, in which a man's acts of charity may get out to the world in spite of him; but, he is very unlucky when his name is *printed* upon every trifling occasion, which has been the case with this man's charities. Besides, what has he given, put it all together? Not, perhaps, the odd shillings and pence upon the the enormous sums that he has gained by his dealings with the government; and, is any man so blind as not to perceive, that motives very different indeed from those of charity might dictate his gifts? A man, acquiring such immense wealth, must see, that something was necessary to keep the public from *grudging*; and, though I do not take upon me to say, that GOLDSMIDT'S donations proceeded from this motive, I cannot help thinking that they frequently did, when I recollect how many paragraphs, stating the nature and amount of his charities, I have, at different times, read in the newspapers.

> "Who builds a Church to God, and not to fame,
> "Will ne'er inscribe the marble with his name."

One of his eulogists says: "he had "done so many kind and generous "actions—his benevolence was so "*enlarged*—his public and private "character was so *princely*, embrac-"ing *men of all persuasions*—he was "so *unostentatious* in his habits, and "so mild and cheerful in his man-"ners;—in short, a man more truly "amiable in all the relations of life "*never existed*. He was *incessantly* "employed in acts of *friendship*; and "though like every man of extensive "dealings, he had to encounter the "bitterness of opposition and envy, "we never heard even from his most "active rivals, any other than the "most favourable testimony to his "virtues. He died in the 53rd year "of his age.—We understand that

"that which preyed most acutely on "his feeling, and wrung from him "many an agonizing exclamation, "was the manner in which he had "been treated *by some persons who* "*had been under the greatest obliga-* "*tions to him.* He had, for years, "been a man the most looked up to "in the monied market—his com- "mand of money had been immense "—his credit unbounded. This was a "proud situation; but elevated as he "was, it inspired him with *nothing* "*like hauteur or insolence*—he was still "the same affable man, increasing in "kindness, if possible, with his in- "creasing wealth*." The much greater part of this has not, I am satisfied, a particle of truth in it. Never was any thing more *ostentatious* than the acts of *benevolence*, as they are called, of this man, who, as I observed years ago, merely tossed back to the miserable part of us, in the shape of alms, the fractions of the pence, upon the immense sums of money that he got by his traffic in loans and bills and funds. The public, if it has any memory all, must remember the accounts that were given of his *entertainments*, at which even princes were present; and at which, probably, as much was consumed in an evening as would have maintained the whole village of Morden for a year. Of these entertainments the most pompous accounts were published in all the newspapers of the day; and, from the manner of the publication, there can be but little doubt of its having been *paid for.* As to his having shewn his hospitality to men of *all persuasions*, that is precisely what a man does, who is more intent upon *securing the favour of men in power*, than upon cultivating real friendship; and, indeed, I have, for my part, very little doubt, that the cost of the entertainments of GOLDSMIDT was always put down amongst the necessary out-goings of his trade.

* MORNING POST Newspaper, Oct. 1.

Thus far, however, what I have stated may be called matter of *opinion*. What I am now going to state is matter of fact, and of fact, too, that the people of England should have been made fully acquainted with long ago. I allude to this man's transaction with SIR JOHN PETER in the funding of Exchequer Bills, and which transaction is related in a Report made by a COMMITTEE of the House of Commons, which was ordered to be printed on the 14th of May last, and which will be found at page 193 of the Appendix to Vol. XVII of the Parliamentary Debates. And here, Gentlemen, we shall have a view of something of no small interest to us as belonging to the Inquiries, in which we are engaged.

In Letter VII, at page 85, mention was made of *Exchequer Bills*; and they were described as one sort of the promissory notes, issued by the government in payment of persons, to whom they owe money. They are like other promissory notes, with this difference, that they bear *an interest* of so much upon each hundred pounds every day, the rate of which interest varies according to circumstances. In short, an EXCHEQUER BILL, which derives its name from the place whence it issues, is like a bank-note, not convertible into money at the will of the holder, except that the bank-note does not bear interest, and the Exchequer Bill does. You will easily perceive, that these Exchequer Bills, while out, form a part of the National Debt. They belong to what is called *Unfunded Debt*; and, they are sometimes paid off and taken up, as a private person pays off and takes up his notes of hand. But, sometimes, the government, like the private person, finds it inconvenient to pay off these bills; and, in such cases, it *funds* them; that is to say, it makes an advantageous offer to the holders of them to *exchange them for Stock*; and when this is done, the amount of such Exchequer Bills is, of course, *added to the great mass of the permanent National*

Debt; which, as you will perceive, is a way of *borrowing money* that occasions much less *talk* and *noise* than would be occasioned by a new loan. The *loan*, this year was for 14 millions; but, then, there were Exchequer Bills funded to the amount of eight millions, so that the addition to the permanent or funded Debt, has, in fact, in this one year, been 22 millions.

I have just said, that when the government finds it inconvenient to pay off and take up Exchequer Bills, it makes an advantageous offer to the holders of them, by which these holders are induced to give them up, and to take Funds or Stock, in lieu of them. The Bills are brought by the holders to a certain place, called the Exchequer Bill Office, where they are received, and where the voucher is given which procure the holder stock in exchange for them. Upon these occasions, there is generally a great struggle of the Bill-holders *to get first into the office*; because when the quantity of Bills to be funded have been presented and received, all the rest must, for the present, at any rate, still remain with the holders; and, as there is *an advantage* in getting them funded, it is evident enough, that there must always be an anxious rivalship in pursuit of that object.

Upon an occasion of this sort, in the month of March last, ABRAHAM GOLDSMIDT attended, amongst others, with a view of getting into the Exchequer Bill office; and, being unable to get in at *the common door*, so early as some others, he went to a passage leading to another part of the office, where he met SIR JOHN PETER, one of the Paymasters, or persons who conduct the business of the office. "*To this person, he delivered his* "*pocket-book, containing Exchequer* "*Bills to the amount of* 350,000 "*pounds, and then went away.* SIR "JOHN PETER carried in the book "and the bills; and, in consequence "of this, GOLDSMIDT's bills were "funded; while the bills of other "persons, who had attended from "the earliest hour, and had got in "amongst the very first, and whose "bills were actually *received*, had "their bills *returned* without being "funded." It appears also, from the Report, that, upon a previous day, this GOLDSMIDT, with a few others, had found out and used the means of getting into the Office *before the door was opened* to the public. The Committee state, that the same Paymaster, "SIR JOHN PETER, according to an "*arrangement previously made*, did, "on the first day of funding, before "the doors were open to the public, "take into the office with him, Mr. "GOLDSMIDT, Mr. SUTTON, and "Mr. GILLMAN, as appears from "the evidence of Mr. Gillman and "Mr. Sutton. The other Paymaster "in attendance, MR. PLANTA, says "that he found those *gentlemen* in "the Board Room upon his arrival "at the office; that he knew it to be "a *great impropriety;* that he ex-"pressed *indignation at the proceed-*"*ing*, and ordered the doors to be "immediately thrown open to the "public. The names, however, of "the gentlemen so introduced *stand* "*amongst the very first on the books* "*of that day.*" The Committee reprobate these proceedings, as partial, unjust, and foul; and recommend means for preventing the like in future.

Now, Gentlemen, this is quite enough to enable you to judge of the real character of GOLDSMIDT, who is so extolled by our courtly news-writers, who have, doubtless, their reasons for what they do; you will, from these facts alone, facts which cannot be denied, be able to judge, whether this man is deserving of the character, which, with so much industry, is given him; whether he was that kind, benevolent, disinterested, generous, and noble-minded man, which he has been represented to be;

or, whether with all his outward show of liberality and generosity, he was, as to his essential practices, still a money-loving, a money-amassing Jew, and nothing more; and if any additional proof of this were wanting, what need we but the simple fact of his having killed himself, *because he was losing a part of his immense wealth*; a truly Jew-like motive for the commission of an act—at which human nature shudders? Gentlemen, how much more to be respected and to be pitied are hundreds and thousands of your industrious and honest neighbours, who had their *all* snatched from them in a moment, and who, after a life of labour and of abstinence, saw themselves deprived of the means of buying a dinner; and that, too, observe, without any fault of theirs, without any greedy speculation, any desire on their part to gain by over-reaching their neighbours, or to possess any thing which was not the fair fruit of their labour? What value are we to set upon the *princely feasts* of a man, who could creep in at a back door to get the preference in funding Exchequer Bills? What value are we to set upon *friendship*, such as he would, doubtless, entertain for such men as SIR JOHN PETER? And, as to his *charities*; as to what he used to give to the miserable part of our countrymen, under the name of charities, it is very probable, that the whole of what he bestowed in this way in the course of his life, did not amount to half so much as the sum that he gained in consequence of his proceeding above-noticed with SIR JOHN PETER.

Gentlemen, the *reasons* why he has been so much praised by many of our news-writers would amuse you; and it would also entertain you to learn the real cause of the fine benevolent *Jewish characters*, which are to be found in some of our *modern plays*. if indeed, a feeling of shame for your country did not overpower your propensity to laugh at at these offerings of literary venality at the shrine of Mammon. But, having now bestowed quite as much time as it merited in remarks upon the *character* of the departed Jew, but which remarks were demanded by truth, we will now proceed to those matters, connected with his death, which are of much greater consequence to us, and a clear understanding of which will be found to be greatly useful in the course of the remainder of our Inquiries. Indeed, these matters not only relate to our subject, but they are strongly illustrative of some of the most important parts of it.

The cause of GOLDSMIDT'S committing the act of self-murder is stated as follows: "The cause of this rash "act it is not difficult to assign:—"Mr. Goldsmidt was a joint con-"tractor for the late loan of 14 mil-"lions with the house of Sir Francis "Baring, and taking the largest pro-"bable range that he had dealt "amongst his friends one half of the "sum allotted to him, the loss sus-"tained by the remainder, at the rate "of 65*l.* per thousand, which was "the price of Thursday, was more "than any individual fortune could "be expected to sustain. Ever since "the decline of *Omnium* from par, "Mr. Goldsmidt's spirits were pro-"gressively drooping; but when it "reached 5 and 6 per cent. discount. "without the probability of recover-"ing, the unfortunate gentleman ap-"peared evidently restless in his dis-"position, and disordered in his "mind; and, as we have reason to "believe, not finding that cheerful "assistance amongst his monied "friends which he had experienced "in happier times, he was unable to "bear up against the pressure of his "misfortunes; and hence was driven "to terminate a life which till then "had never been chequered by mis-"fortune. The moment intelligence "of the distressing event reached the

"the city, which was about the period "of the opening of the Stock Exchange, the Funds suddenly felt "the effects, and the Three per Cent. "Stock fell in a few minutes from "66½ to 63¾: *Omnium* declined "from about 6½ to 10¼ *discount*, and "then remained steady at that price "for some time."* What to do with all these cant words one hardly knows; but, taking along with us what we have before seen, we shall be able, with a little explanation, to understand them.

In Letter II, page 18, and onwards, we saw something of the manner, in which *Loans* are made to the government; but, we must here speak of the transaction a little more in particulars. The Loan-Maker bargains with the Minister to lend so many millions of money, upon condition of receiving so much Stock means, and we have seen what Stock remains. But, this Stock (as will be seen in Letter II, page 18,) is of several sorts: 4 *per cents.*, 3 *per cents.*, and so on. And the Loan-Maker generally agrees to take some of each sort. As soon as the Loan is made, he begins to sell his Stock, as we have seen, in page 20, to such people as our good neighbour, FARMER GREENHORN; but, when he sells it, *all the sorts of it are put together*, and hence it is called OMNIUM, that being a Latin word, meaning THE WHOLE TOGETHER, or ALL TOGETHER. When the Omnium will sell for more than has been given for it, it is said to be at a *premium;* and when it will not sell for so much as has been given for it it is said to be at a *discount*, that word meaning, to *count back*, or to *refund;* so that, in these transactions, to sell at a *premium* means to *gain* by the sale, and to sell at a *discount* means to *lose* by the sale; *premium* means *gain*, and *discount* means *loss*.

Applying this to what we have before seen, respecting the cause of the death of GOLDSMIDT, it will be perceived, that he was losing 6 per cent, or 6 pounds in the hundred, upon his part of so immense a transaction as that of a Loan of 14 millions. It is said, you will observe, that he and the BARINGS took the Loan between them; and it is supposed, that a great part of his share remained unsold, at the time when the fall in the price took place. His loss, if the price did not mend, would, of course, be immense; and, it appears, that the thought of such a loss was more than his mind could bear; which latter is by no means wonderful, seeing that his soul was set upon gain; that all his views and notions of happiness centered in wealth. The lover, whose passion is too strong for his reason, destroys himself, because the object of that passion is dearer to him than life. GOLDSMIDT destroys himself, because wealth is dearer to him than life. And yet, we are to be told, of the *princely munificence* of this man! Never was there a nation so much insulted as this!

In most cases there is a considerable *gain* made by LOAN-MAKERS, who have, indeed, in many cases, become so rich by these transactions as to be enabled to surpass in expences the gentry and the nobility of the kingdom, which, as we shall by-and-by see, is one of the great evils of the National Debt. How it has happened, that so great a loss has hitherto been experienced upon the *present* Loan, it would be very difficult, perhaps, for any one to tell. It has been asserted, in the public prints, that there was a *combination* against the Loan-Makers; but, this is perfect nonsense; for, *all Stocks* fell at the same time; and, what a fine state must that thing, called PUBLIC CREDIT, be in, if *any combination* of individuals can injure it?

The progress of the fall in the price of Stocks, and particularly of

* TIMES Newspaper, Sept. 29

the Omnium, upon this occasion is very curious; and, it will be of great use to us to take a look back into the public prints, and see the attempts there made to keep up the prices; attempts which come very fairly under the denomination of *puffing*. These attempts are worthy of the greatest attention; for, trifling and even stupid as they appear, and as they are *in themselves*, they will, if I mistake not, be hereafter referred to as being amongst the most *significant* signs of the times.

These attempts began with a paragraph, inserted in *all* the daily newspapers, stating the *amount of the fortune* of Sir FRANCIS BARING'S family, who, it will be recollected, were now become the part owners of the OMNIUM along with GOLDSMIDT. The paragraph, of the 11th of September, was as follows: "Yesterday "morning, at one o'clock, died at his "house at Leigh, Sir Francis Baring, "bart. in his 74th year. He was "physically exhausted, but *his mind* "*remained unsubdued* by age or in-"firmity to the last breath. His bed "was surrounded by nine out of ten, "the number of his sons and daugh-"ters, all of whom he has lived to see "established in *splendid independ-"ence*. Three of his sons carry on "the *great commercial house*, and "which, by his *superior talents and* "*integrity*, he carried to so great a "height of respect—and the other "two sons are *returned from India* "*with fortunes*. His five daughters "are all most happily married, and "in addition to all this, it is supposed "he has left *freehold estates to the* "*amount of half a million*. Such has "been the result of the honourable "life of this English Merchant."

On the 17th of September, the following was published: "Stocks "experienced this morning *a con-"siderable depression*: Omnium was "at $5\frac{1}{2}$ discount. The *death of Sir* "*Francis Baring is said to have been* "*the chief cause of it.*"

On the 19th: "The sudden and "rapid decline of the Stocks merits, "it may be supposed, some notice. "Consols, which begun yesterday at "$66\frac{3}{8}$, closed at $65\frac{1}{4}$; and Omnium "left off at $6\frac{1}{2}$ discount. *Various* "*causes were assigned* for this effect "(a descent upon Heligoland, a sub-"sidy to Russia,) all equally impro-"bable. We can *do no more at pre-"sent* than state the fact, though *we* "*strongly suspect that we know the* "*cause*."

On the 20th: "Stocks were better "this morning; and *the attempts to* "*continue the depression of the Funds* "are likely to be defeated, as they "*ought to be*."

On the 22nd: "Yesterday being "a holiday, no business was pub-"licly transacted in the Funds, but "several private bargains were made "at an advanced price. Consols "were done at $66\frac{1}{2}$ which is a material "rise. There is reason to hope that "a few days will *dispel the alarm* "which was raised and propagated "beyond what any *just cause* could "warrant, by *persons desirous of fish-"ing in troubled waters*; by certain "*writers, eager to convert public con-"fusion to the promotion of their poli-"tical views*, and by certain *jobbers*, "*anxious to make it subservient to* "*their pecuniary interests*. The *er-"roneous* idea so industriously cir-"culated by certain individuals that "there is a *depreciation of the Bank-"currency*, has undoubtedly con-"tributed, in some degree with other "circumstances of pressure, to pro-"duce the late depression in the "funds."

Now, it must be observed, that these paragraphs were *circular*; that is to say, they went through all the daily news-papers, or, at least, nearly all of them, and for aught I know, to the contrary, through the weekly news-papers too; so that, there is not the smallest doubt of the puffing having been carried on at the instigation of some interested party.

But, Gentlemen, what a state, I again ask, must that thing, called PUBLIC CREDIT, be in, if it can be affected in this way? First SIR FRANCIS BARING's death causes the Funds to fall, and the fall in the Funds causes the death of GOLDSMIDT, and then the death of GOLDSMIDT causes the Funds to fall lower still! What is all this talk about combinations; about attempts to continue the depression; about an alarm, beyond any just cause; about the Funds being depressed by persons desirous of fishing in troubled waters, by certain writers eager for public confusion; by certain jobbers anxious to promote their own interest; by certain individuals who have insidiously circulated erroneous ideas about the depreciation of Bank-notes? What is all this talk? What does all this mean? Is it come to this at last, that this PUBLIC CREDIT, which was to defend us against all the warlike operations of France; is it come to this, that this PUBLIC CREDIT, this defence of the country, is to be destroyed, or, at least, materially affected, by the tricks of money-Jobbers, the opinions (and the *erroneous* opinions too) of political writers, or by the death of a Jew? If this be the case, let those who have what they call *money in the Funds*, let the GRIZZLE GREENHORNS, look to themselves.

At the peace of Amiens, when we reminded PITT and his associates of the promise they had made us never to make peace without obtaining "*indemnity for the past and security* "*for the future*," and, when we proved to them, that, while they acknowledged that they had obtained no indemnity for the past, they had left us more insecure than ever for the future. When we pointed out to them, the consequences of their war, which had put into the hands of France so many countries, and so much of maritime means; and of their peace, which had left all these terrible means in her hands: when we pointed out this to them, what was their answer? Why this: that, though France had acquired a great extent of *territory*, her acquisitions in point of *strength* did not surpass ours, which consisted of an immense mass of CAPITAL, CREDIT, and CONFIDENCE; the changes upon which words were rung over and over again, till the speech became full as enlivening and instructive as a peal of the three bells of Botley Church. But, what becomes of these fine things, if the scribbling of a news-paper writer, or of a pamphleteer, or if the sudden death of a Jew, is capable of so materially affecting them? What, in that case, becomes of that Capital, Credit, and Confidence, which were to counterbalance all the acquisitions of France, and were to prove a never-failing defence to England? True said the adherents of PITT, who wished still to find something to say by way of apology for his ruinous measures; "true," said they, "France "has made conquests; she has gained "sea-ports; she has acquired and "now quietly possessess, the means "of rearing a navy; but, look at the "immense CAPITAL of England; "look at her CREDIT; look at the "CONFIDENCE which she possesses; "look at these pillars of national "strength." It was not easy to see, however long one looked, that these things were pillars of national strength; but, if they were; if they were the pillars, upon which this nation was to depend, what are we to think of our situation, when we are told, as we are in the above-cited publications, and, indeed, as we are told every day, that the Funds, which are said to be the barometer of national CREDIT, can be, nay *have been*, and still *are*, lowered in their value by such trifling things as the erroneous opinion of a writer on politics, or the death of a Merchant or a Jew? If what we have been told about the importance of CREDIT be true; if it be our defence against the enemy, what must our situation be, if what we are *now* told be true, namely, that this CREDIT has been shaken by such contemptible means? PITT and his associates told us, that CAPITAL, CREDIT, and CONFIDENCE, which is using three words instead of one, merely for the sake of the *sound;* they told us that these were the *pillars* of the nation; and, as we have seen above, our newspapers now tell us, that SIR FRANCIS BARING and GOLDSMIDT were the *pillars* of our CREDIT; so that, at last, we come to this comfortable conclusion—that the defence and preservation of the country depended upon SIR FRANCIS BARING and GOLDSMIDT, one of whom has *died* and the other *shot himself* within the last three weeks! And this is the effect, is it, of the PITT system of what is called Public Credit?

If what we are now told *be true,* what security have we, that things will *stop* where they are? What reason have we to conclude, or to suppose, that the same causes will not continue to operate, 'till the whole of the Funds are annihilated; that is to say, until nobody will give any thing at all for any sort of the Stock? We are told, that the fall, which has already taken, has, in part, been the consequence of *combinations of individuals,* which must mean, combinations *not to purchase;* and, who is to *put an end* to such combinations? Who is to prevent the force of them from *increasing*? Then, again, we are told, that the fall has partly been produced by *jobbers intent upon their own interests;* and, who, let me ask, is to alter the nature of these jobbers; who can say, or even guess, when these interested jobbers will be pleased to desist from their selfish and mischievous practices? If the causes of the fall be such as have been stated to the public in the above-cited and other publications, who will pretend to say when or where, the fall will stop? And, I should be very glad to hear any reason, why, if those alledged causes be founded in truth, the Funds should not continue to fall, till they are not worth owning; till it is not worth GRIZZLE GREENHORN'S while to have her name written in the Great Book.

We here see, that these boasted friends of their country; these men of such high-flying loyalty; these writers who accuse of *Jacobinism* all those who cannot believe, and who will not say, that the Paper-money is as good, if not better, than Gold and Silver; we here see, that these boasted friends of their country, who apparently, would eat Buonaparté raw, if they could get at him; we here see these outrageously-loyal writers proclaiming to that same Buonaparté what must delight him more than almost any thing that he could hear, namely, that such is the state of our public credit, such the state of our pecuniary resources, such the confidence in our funds, such the confidence in the security of our government-bonds, that this confidence is shaken by a combination of jobbers, or the death of a Jew. How much abuse has been, at various times, heaped upon those, who have expressed their doubts as to the durability of the Paper-money system! Nay, the Bullion Committee themselves have been very grossly abused for their Report upon the subject; by which Report, their opponents say, they have *injured the credit* of the country. They are charged with having *injured the credit of this country,* because they have recommended that the Bank of England should *pay its notes in Gold and Silver.* What, then, are those men doing, who now assert, that a *combination of individuals;* that the *tricks of interested jobbers;* that the *erroneous opinions of political writers:* what are the men doing, who assert, that these things are capable of causing the government securities to fall in value; and, who scruple not to tell us, that the men, who were the *pillars* of the Public Funds, *are dead?* What are these writers doing; and how will they now be able to hold up their heads and complain of the endeavours of others to destroy what they call public credit, which, if it admit of destruction by the means of the pen, must assuredly fall for ever under the pens of these writers?

If what these writers say be true; if the stocks are to be lowered in value by combinations of individuals, by the errors of writers, by the reports of committees, or by the death of a Jew; if this be true, can it be thought, that people will long be disposed to become proprietors of stock? Can it be thought, that they will, like our neighbour GREENHORN, put their money in the Funds? Can it be expected, that fathers and mothers will make provision for their children, or their grand-children, by purchasing stock, liable to be lowered in value by such causes? Nay, can it be expected, that any man in his senses, who is now the owner of stock, will not dispose of it as soon as possible, and at almost any rate? For, is it possible to regard as safe property; is it possible to regard as any property at all, a thing the value of which may be lowered ten per cent, in the space of ten days, and, of course, which may be lowered to almost nothing; is it possible to regard as any *property* at all, a thing the value of which may be thus reduced by the combinations of individuals, the trickery of jobbers, the errors of political writers, or the death of a Jew, or of any other individual or number of individuals? Is it possible to regard such a thing as property? Common sense says, no; and yet the statement of these causes, a statement, which, if it have any effect at all, must tend to the discredit, and, indeed, to the destruction, of the Funds; this statement comes from the pens of those, who cry out JACOBIN against every man, who ventures, in however modest a way, to express his doubts of the solidity of the Funding System.

These writers, in their eagerness to abuse those, to whom they impute the fall of the Funds, seem to have overlooked the conclusions that would naturally be drawn from their premises, else they would have perceived what a dangerous thing it was to declare to our powerful and sharp-sighted enemy that a combination of individuals was capable of shaking our Funds. That enemy is, by these same writers, represented as being all-powerful by his intrigues in other countries; and, is it too much to suppose, that it might be possible for him to find the means of forming combinations against the Funds in England? If combinations of individuals can pull down the value of our Government securities, is it to be believed, that our enemy will not be disposed, and that he will not endeavour, to form such combinations? And, if we are asked, where he will find individuals so base, have not these writers pointed them out to him; or, at least, have they not told him, in terms that admit not of misunderstanding, that there are such individuals in England, in London, and now actually at work; and that these individuals have caused the Funds to fall, have caused the Government securities to lose part of their value? Let these writers, therefore, confess that these statements of theirs have proceeded from error; or,

Entered at Stationers' Hall.
LONDON:—Printed by WM. MOLINEUX, Bream's Buildings, Chancery Lane.

at any rate, that they are *untrue;* or let them for ever hold their tongue as to complaints against those, who entertain doubts of the solidity of the paper-money system.

Here, Gentlemen, I should have concluded this already-too-long Letter; but, an article, which I find in the public prints of this morning (Tuesday, 2nd October) induces me to add some observations upon the subject of the *remedy* or *expedient,* which has been more than hinted at. The article alluded to, is as follows: "The state of the Funds was a little "improved yesterday; and as no "bad consequences beyond those of "the first *shock* had arisen from Mr. "Goldsmidt's death, *it is hoped that* "*things will soon be restored to their* "*former level.* The result of the "conferences of the leading Loan-"holders, with *the Chancellor of the* "*Exchequer and the Lords of the Trea-*"*sury,* on Saturday, has not yet been "made known. Mr. Goldsmidt's "house continues to discharge, with-"out reserve or hesitation, all the de-"mands made on it. The account "at the Stock Exchange was not set-"tled nor declared yesterday, in con-"sequence of the attendance of Mr. "Nathan Solomons, Mr. Goldsmidt's "broker, at the funeral, which took "place, according to the Jewish rites, "about noon yesterday. His body "was placed by the side of that of "his brother Benjamin. Yesterday "morning early *Mr. Perceval came* "*to town from his house at Ealing,* "and soon after sent off letters to the "Governor and Deputy-Governor of "the Bank, Mr. Wish, the *Chairman* "*of the Commissioners of Excise,* the "*Treasurer of the Ordnance,* and a "number of other *official Gentlemen;* "they all attended Mr. Perceval, and "he was with them during the whole "of the day."

These conferences will not, I trust, as some persons appear to suppose, lead to any application of the public money, that is to say, of the taxes, to the *assisting,* as it is called, of these Loan-holders. The Loan-holders, or Loan-makers, have never been known to *return to the people* any part of the immense *profits,* which they, from time to time, have made upon their loaning transactions. We see, from one of the above-quoted passages, that SIR FRANCIS BARING has gained enough to lay out *half a million of money in freehold estates.* Great part of this was, it is reasonable to suppose, gained by the many loans to Government, in which he has been at different times concerned. Well, then, if these profits, these immense *gains,* be considered as fairly belonging to him, or his heirs and successors; and, if we view the not less immense gains of GOLDSMIDT in the same light; if the *gains* be theirs, ought not the *loss* to be theirs also? Upon any other principle, what a sort of bargain would a government-loan be? A bargain where all the chance of gain would be on one side, and all the chance of loss on the other. If the loan-maker gained, well; but, if he lost, the people must make good his loss. Is this the way that dealings take place between man and man? Is there any one of you, Gentlemen, who would sell a load of wheat to a miller, leaving him the chance of gaining by it, and, if he happened to lose by it, would give him back again the amount of his loss? Oh, no! You would keep

E

W. Molineux, Printer, Bream's Buildings, Chancery Lane.

the whole of the price of your wheat, and leave the miller to console himself in counting his gains upon other occasions.

But, if contrary to my wish and expectation, "*relief*," as it is called, were to be given to those persons, in *what way* could it be done? The loan is made and ratified in virtue of an ACT OF PARLIAMENT. There can be no alteration made in the bargain; there can be no change in the terms of payment; there can be no abatement in the demands of the government, without another ACT OF PARLIAMENT, previously passed.—Those who made the loan must pay the 14 millions into the King's Exchequer, let what will be their loss upon the transaction, unless indeed, the whole of their property, *real* and *personal*, be insufficient for the purpose; and, in that case, the people have a right to expect, that the government will take care to hold back from the loan-makers, or to recover from them, so much of the new Stock as will not leave the loan-makers a farthing in the people's debt.

During PITT's Anti-jacobin War, which, as you will bear in mind, was to succeed by producing the destruction of the paper-money in France; during that war, which was to diminish the power of France, and to restore the Bourbons by the means of ruin to the French finances; during that famous war, which was to plunge, and which, as PITT told us, did plunge France ,"*into the very* "*gulph of Bankruptcy*;" during that renowned war, there was what was called a "LOYALTY LOAN." People were *invited* in the name of *loyalty*, to come forward and lend their money to the government, for the purpose of carrying on the Anti-jacobin war with vigour; and, at the same time, no very unintelligible hints were given, in some of the public prints, that those who had it in their power to lend, and did not lend, upon this occasion, were deficient in point of *loyalty*, an imputation not very pleasant at any time, and, at the time to which we are referring, *singularly inconvenient*. The LOYALTY LOAN was accomplished; but, owing to some cause or other, it did not prove to be a *profitable concern* for the lenders; and, as in the case of the present loan, as far as it has gone, the loan fell to a discount, and a *loss* was sustained upon it. Such loss, one might have expected, would have been not only contentedly, but gladly sustained, as a sacrifice upon the altar of loyalty; and this, it was said by PITT, would have been the case, but that he and his associates in the ministry, did not think it wise to suffer loyalty so *disinterested* to experience any *loss*. An act, therefore, was passed for making good to the lenders whatever they would otherwise have lost by their ardent affection for their king and country, and loyalty was thus prevented from costing them any thing.

The case, however, of these loyal and devoted persons was somewhat different from that of the makers of the present loan. The Loyalty Loan men had never *gained* any thing by loan-making. They had not got their half million's worths of freeholds and their palace-like mansions. They had made *a bargain*, and they ought, in my opinion, to have been held to that bargain; because, if there had been a *gain* instead of a loss, they would have put that gain in their pocket, and would, doubtless, have looked upon it as doubly blessed, being the profits of trade and of loyalty too; and further, because, they had put their names down upon a list, which was to hold them forth to the world as men ready to make *sacrifices* for their king and country, in contradistinction to those, whose names were not put upon the list. But, still, though nothing, in my opinion, can ever fully reconcile to principles of justice, the compensating of these people for their losses by that loan, there is great difference between th-?

case and the case of the present loan-makers or holders, who have no claim whatever to any compensation at all, or to any relief, or to the adoption of any measure, that shall cost the people one single shilling. If they lose by this loan, they have gained by other loans. If they cannot pay without the sale of their goods and chattles, why should not their goods and chattles be sold, as well as the goods and chattles of those, who out of pure loyalty, have set up papers for the purpose of writing me down, and whose names I have never once mentioned, on whose papers I have never set my eyes, and who have killed themselves in their foolish attempts to wound me? Why should not the loan-makers, if they cannot make good their bargain, have their goods and chattles, sold as well as these loyalty writers? I am, however, reasoning here, against an unfounded surmise; for, it appears from the above quoted publications, that the family of BARING is very rich and in perfect credit, and that the concerns of GOLDSMIDT are in a flourishing way, seeing that his house is able to meet all the demands upon it, of every sort, without the least delay or hesitation. This being the case, there can be *no need of any interference on the part of the government*, who will doubtless see, that the bargain is fulfilled agreeably to the terms.

I have now done with this accidental occurrence, the notice of which, so much at length, forms a Digression from the regular line of our progress, by which, as we shall see by-and-by, will have afforded us practical knowledge, of great use in our future inquiries.

I am, Gentlemen,
Your faithful friend,
WM. COBBETT.

State Prison, Newgate, Tuesday, 2nd October, 1810.

LETTER X.

"They" (the French Revolutionists) "forget that, *in England*, not one shilling of Paper Money of any "description is received but of *choice*; that the whole has had its origin *in cash*, actually deposited; and "that it is convertible, at pleasure, *in an instant*, and without the smallest loss, into cash again. *Our* "*Paper is of value in commerce, because in law it is of none.* It is powerful on Change, because in Westminster hall it is impotent. In payment of a debt of twenty shillings, *a creditor may refuse all the paper* "*of the Bank of England*. Nor is there among us a single public security, of any quality or nature whatsoever, that is *enforced by authority*. In fact it might be easily shewn, that our paper wealth, *instead of* "*lessening the real coin, has a tendency to increase it*; instead of being a *substitute* for money, it only "*facilitates its entry*, its *exit*, and its *circulation*; that it is the symbol of prosperity, and not the badge "of distress. *Never was a scarcity of cash, and an exuberance of paper, a subject of complaint in this* "*nation.*"—*Burke*. Reflections on the French Revolution. Written and published in 1790.

"But, whatever momentary relief, or aid, the Minister and the Bank might expect from this low contrivance of "*Five Pound Notes*, it will *increase the inability of the Bank to pay the Higher Notes*, and hasten "the destruction of all; for, even the small taxes that used to be paid in money, will now be paid in those "notes, and the Bank will *soon* find itself with scarcely any other money than what the hair powder-"guinea tax brings in.—"—*Paine's* Decline and Fall of the English System of Finance. Written and published in March, 1796.

"When the situation of the Bank of England was under the consideration of the two Houses of Parliament, "in the year 1797, it was *my* opinion, and that of many others, that *the extent, to which the Paper-Cur*"*rency had been carried*, was the *first* and *principal*, though not the sole cause, of the many difficulties "to which that Corporate Body was then, and had, of late years, from time to time, been exposed, in "supplying the cash, necessary for the commerce of the kingdom."—*Charles Jenkinson, Earl of Liverpool*, Letter to the King, published in 1805.

Horrid Passage from the Morning Post News-Paper—Such are the Writers by whom the Paper-Money System and its Patrons are supported—Such are the Answers that are given to these Letters—Bank Paper asserted to be the only Sort of Currency calculated to exert the Energies of an Island—Proceed in tracing the Increase of Debt and Notes to that grand Effect, the Bank Stoppage—Table shewing the annual Increase of the Debt and Interest from 1793 to 1797—Increase in the Number and Amount of Payments at the Bank demanded small Notes—Hence came the Five Pound Notes—Burke's Picture of the English Bank Paper—Paine's Prediction—Lord Liverpool the Historian of Paine's Prophecy.

GENTLEMEN,

In returning to our subject, we must bear in mind, that, in Letter VIII, and in the foregoing Letter, we saw clearly, that bank-notes, as well as all other promissory notes, ought to be considered as *representatives of debt*, while *real money* ought to be considered as the representative of *property*, or things of *real value*. At the close of Letter VIII, we saw how the increase in the quantity of bank-notes had *kept pace with the increase of the National Debt;* and we proposed, when we should resume the subject, to trace this joint increase to that grand and memorable effect, THE STOPPAGE OF GOLD AND SILVER PAYMENTS AT THE BANK OF ENGLAND in 1797.

But, before we enter upon this interesting matter, will you give me leave again to give you a specimen of the way, in which my Letters are *answered* by the venal writers in London? To do this will not be without its utility, both now and hereafter. It will be useful to shew you what sort of writers those are, who are opposed to me; and, though it may not be so useful to posterity, it will, nevertheless, be of some use, and will be very curious, for our children to see what manner of men those were, who wrote in favour of the Paper-money System. The passage I am about to lay before you was published in a news-paper, printed for the use of "The *Fashionable World,*" under the date of the 6th of this month, and its words are these. "To the People of the United "Kingdom.—The detestable characters *exposed lately in the pillory,* "may be considered the *real representatives* of the *Corsican Tyrant* "and his Ministers, *who boast* of the "*monstrous vice* which excites such "horrors in every British bosom, and "who, fearful of your valour, are "exerting every artifice to subvert "your empire, *betray your virtue,* and "extirpate your people. COBBETT, "the oracle of the Jacobins, *abuses* "*the British Papers for speaking ill* "*of such infamous monsters,* whose "detestable practices must annihilate "every virtuous principle from the "human breast; and he tells the "British People, in effect, that *if* "*they are to be robbed by taxes and* "*oppressed by power,* it is of no consequence *whether they are conquered* "*by a French Vere-street gang,* or "governed by a *virtuous British Sovereign and his respectable Ministers.* "Such is the profound reasoning of "an *apostate low-minded* scribe, who "is impelled by a *savage passion* "revenge for Ministerial deserved "*contempt,* and by *foolish* and *base* "hopes of conciliation with the *Corsican Monster,* who often rewards, "but never has been known to forgive. "He publishes weekly an *infernal* "Register, to excite *mutiny in the* "*army and the fleet,* to seduce the "*loyalty of British subjects,* to con-"*found the good sense of the yeomanry* "by low *cunning* and *artful sophistry,* and above all, *to destroy Public* "*credit and Bank Paper, as the best* "*bond of individual and public security, and the only medium of currency to suit and exert the energies* "*of an insular and commercial people.* "Such a man, whom *reading and* "*writing made a corporal,* but whom "sense and reason will never make a "politician or an honest patriot, may "be the *proper oracle of a Vere-street* "*gang of regal French ruffians,* but "his councils of liberty, economy, "and reform, must be regarded as the "treacherous delusions of *a French* "*spy,* when offered to a free, virtuous "and happy nation."*

Such, Gentlemen, is the language of my opposers. *Such* is the sort of men who dislike me. *Such* are the *answers* that are given to my statements and my reasoning upon a sober and most important subject of political economy. The abuse here heaped

* Morning Post, Saturday, Oct. 6, 1810.

upon a person, whom our Commander in Portugal, in his public dispatches, recognizes as *an* "*Emperor*," and who, in our courts of justice, has been recognized as a "*Sovereign* of "France," to say nothing of our negociations and treaties with him; the abuse here heaped upon Napoleon, who is not only called a *monster*, but is distinctly charged with "*boasting* "*of the monstrous vice*," for being guilty of which several infamous wretches have lately stood in the pillory in London, can, surely, not meet with the approbation of any man upon earth; for, one would fain hope, that there is not another man like this writer. Yet is it a serious consideration for the country, that such an accusation should be thus boldly put forth in our public news-papers, and in a news-paper, too, which, from its uniform praises of the men at present in power, is called a *ministerial* newspaper, and is, in general, looked upon as a sort of *half official* print. As far as concerns this particular article, every man in England will be ready to acquit the ministers; and, indeed, every one will readily believe that it must meet with their sincere reprobation. But, this may not be the opinion *abroad*; and, I leave you to guess what an impression such a publication is calculated to give the world of *our national character*.

There is one declaration here, about the paper-money, that I wish you to bear in mind; namely that "bank-"paper is the *best bond* of individual "and public security, and *the only* "*medium of currency to suit and* "*exert the energies of an insular and* "*commercial people*." So that, according to this writer, the return of gold and silver would be no good at all, and we ought, indeed, to desire to get rid of it, if we had any; though, upon the trial of De Yonge (of which we shall see more by-and-by), both the Attorney General and the Judge so decidedly declared *the exportation of the coin* to be a most *mischievous* practice; and though this writer himself, little more than two months ago, *congratulated* his readers upon the prospect of seeing bank-paper destroyed, which paper he called, in his print of the 19th of July, "*destruc-*"*tive assignats*," and afterwards, "*vile* "*dirty rags*;" aye, that very paper, which he now asserts to be "the *best* "*bond* of individual and public secu-"rity, and the *only medium* of cur-"rency to suit and exert the *energies* "of an insular and commercial "people."

Let us now leave our opponents; let us leave the paper-money system and its patrons to receive all the *support* that writings like the above can give, while we proceed in tracing the increase of the National Debt and that of the bank-notes to that grand and memorable effect, *the stoppage of gold and silver-payments at the Bank of England* in **1797**, from which time our *paper-money* began, because it was then that the bank-notes ceased to be convertible into coin, and have remained in that state to this day.

We have already seen, that, at the beginning of Pitt's war with the Republicans of France in **1793**, our National Debt amounted to about **250** millions, because it did not increase during the peace preceding that war. Its amount, at the close of the American war, was **257** millions (See Letter III. page 26), and the annual interest paid upon it was **9** millions and about a half. The debt, and, of course, the interest along with it, decreased a little before the beginning of Pitt's war against the Jacobins of France; so that, when that war was begun, both Debt and Interest were somewhat less than at the conclusion of the American war. We will, however, take them at what they were at the last-mentioned period; and, in order the more clearly to shew the progress of the cause of the great increase of bank-notes, and finally, of the Stoppage of Gold and Silver-payments at the Bank, we will state the annual increase of the Debt and Interest, from the beginning of the war to the year 1797, when the Stoppage took place, which statement is not only very curious, but is of singularly great importance.

	DEBT. £.	INTEREST. £.
Before the Anti-Jacobin war began (in 1793), the amount was	257,213,043	9,669,435
In that same year was added	6,250,000	252,812
Amount at the end of 1793	263,463,043	9,922,247
In the year 1794 was added	15,676,525	773,324
Amount at the end of 1794	279,139,567	10,695,571
In the year 1795 was added	25,609,897	1,227,415
Amount at the end of 1795	304,749,464	11,922,986
In the year 1796 was added	41,303,699	1,850,373
Amount at the end of 1796	346,053,163	13,773,359
In the year 1797 was added	67,087,668	3,241,790
Amount at the end of 1797	413,140,831	17,015,149

Thus, then, we see, that the first four years and a half of PITT's war with the Jacobins, or Republicans of France, nearly doubled the Debt and the Interest, or (which is the same thing to the people), the *annual charge on account of Debt,* which, together with interest, includes management and Sinking fund-allowance. Four years and a half of the Anti-jacobin war nearly doubled these; and, according to the principles we have before laid down, in Letters VII and VIII, the bank-notes would necessarily increase in the same proportion as the Debt and Interest increased; because, every quarter of a year, the *dividends* to be paid at the Bank, became greater and greater.

Before the Anti-Jacobin war began, the *dividends of a year,* amounted, as we see above, to 9,669,435*l.* To obviate all pettifogging cavil here, let me state, that this sum was not *wholly* dividends, or interest; but consisted, partly, of "*charges for management,*" paid to the Bank of England; and also of charges on "*account of the* "*Sinking Fund.*" But, as was observed before, this is of no consequence to the people, who pay the taxes, out of which *the whole* sum comes; and, I only make the distinction to avoid a cavilling charge of misrepresentation, or error. When, therefore, we speak of the amount of the *Interest* of the National Debt, let it be understood, that we include these charges; and that, by the word *Interest* is meant the *annual charge on account of the Debt.*

To resume, then; before the Anti-Jacobin war began, the dividends, or interest, of one year amounted, as we have seen, to 9,669,435 pounds; and before the nation got to the end of the fifth year of that war, a year's dividends, or interest, amounted to 17,015,149 pounds; not much short of double. The Bank, therefore, having nearly twice as much to pay yearly in interest of the Debt; having, to speak in round numbers, 17 millions to pay under this head, where it had but 9 millions to pay before the beginning of PITT's Anti-Jacobin war; having twice as much to issue on this great score as it had previous to the war, was, of course, compelled to increase the quantity of its *paper-promises,* or the quantity of its *Gold and Silver-coin*; because, as we have before seen (Letter VII. page 77), an increase in the number and amount of payments must necessarily demand an increase of the money, or medium, in which those payments are made; and, why this increase, at the Bank of England, would take place in *paper-promises*, and not in Gold and Silver-coin, we have seen in Letters VII and VIII, where it was shewn that an increase of Debt must produce an increase of paper-promises, or notes, when once a paper-system has begun.

That the experience of the times, of which we are now speaking, perfectly corresponded with the principles here stated, we shall now see by adverting a little to the manner, in which the payments of interest at the Bank were formerly made.

It has before been observed, that, when the National Debt first began, the whole of the Interest was paid in Gold and Silver, there being then no such thing as bank-notes, and *no such thing as a Bank*, in this country. It has also been observed, that, very shortly after the Debt came into existence, it produced its natural offspring, *a Bank*, which issued its *promissory notes*, and in which promissory notes the interest of the Debt was, in part, at least, paid. *At first*, it appears, that the Bank *paid an interest upon its notes, or bills*; but, this was soon left off; and, from that time, the bank-notes, or bills, became part of the circulating medium of the country.

When the Stock owners, or Public Creditors, as they are sometimes called, went to the Bank to receive their dividends, or interest, they might have either bank-notes, or Gold and Silver, according to their choice.—Some persons chose the coin, and some the paper. But, as the Debt increased, and, of course, the amount of the dividends, or interest, it was evident, from what has already been said, that the Bank would possess a less and less quantity of Gold and Silver in proportion to the quantity of its paper. And, further, the payments of interest having, as we have seen above, become nearly double in amount to what they were in 1793, previous to the Anti-Jacobin war, it is natural to suppose, that there would be double the number of Stock-holders, and, of course *double the number of payments to make*. Therefore, as, at every payment, the receiver had his choice of paper or Gold and Silver-coin, there were double the number of chances against the Bank; and, at any rate, as there were, as yet, no bank-notes of an amount less than TEN POUNDS, there must necessarily be, upon every payment an issue of Gold and Silver from the Bank, to the amount of every demand, or part of a demand, *falling short of ten pounds*.

This the Bank could bear before the Anti-Jacobin war; but, when that war had nearly doubled the Debt, the Interest, and the number of the payments, on account of Interest; when this increase had taken place, the Bank found it necessary, not only to augment the general quantity of its notes; it found it necessary not only to add to the total amount of its notes; that is to say, to put out a greater sum in notes, than it had out before the Anti-Jacobin war; but, it also found it necessary to put out some notes of a *lower amount* than it already had, in order to pay *the parts of ten pounds*, which we have just mentioned.

Hence came the FIVE POUND NOTES. And, you will perceive, Gentlemen, that causes precisely similar had formerly produced the FIFTEEN POUND NOTES and the TEN POUND NOTES; namely, an increase of the National Debt, and, of course, an increase of the dividends, or interest; these being always paid at the Bank, after the establishment of the Bank Company.

Here let us stop for a little and look back at the MOTTO, or, rather MOTTOS, to this Letter.

In the FIRST, the passage from BURKE, we have a picture of English Bank Paper previous to the war; aye, to that very war, which that very picture and others in the same publication greatly tended to produce, and were, without, I believe, any bad motive, *intended* to produce. Look well at that picture, Gentlemen. Look at he triumphant contrast there exhibited between the money of England and that of France, which latter country had then a paper-money. And, when you have viewed that picture in all its parts; when you have fully examined the contrast; then turn your eyes to what is now exhibited to the world: then see what English Bank Paper now is, and what in this regard is the state of France, where all the paper-money has, long ago, been destroyed, and where there is no currency but that of Gold and Silver-coin, part of which coin consists of English Guineas, those guineas the absence of which all men of sense and of public-spirit so sorely lament, and the practicability of causing the return of which is, as you will bear in mind, the chief object of our Inquiries.

In the SECOND motto, the passage from PAINE, (the mortal antagonist of Burke as to every thing else) we have an opinion as to the consequences of the Bank having made 5 pound-notes. We have a prediction as to the *inability* which it will produce in the Bank *to pay its higher notes*. This prediction was, it appears, written in March 1796, and it was published in England, in or about, the month of June of that year; which was, as we shall see by-and-by, only about *nine months* before the *stoppage of gold and silver-payments at the Bank* actually took place.

In the THIRD motto, the passage from the late LORD LIVERPOOL, we have the opinion, not only of the writer himself, who upon such a matter, is no very mean authority, but, as he asserts, of *many others* (doubtless, persons of distinction, as to rank, at least); we have an opinion, thus sanctioned, that the *increase of the paper-currency* was the *first* and *principal* cause of the Stoppage of Gold and Silver-payments at the Bank; and which opinion perfectly corresponds with that of PAINE, there being this distinction in the merits of the two writers, that Lord Liverpool only recorded what PAINE had foretold: the former was the historian, the latter the prophet; and, it is not a little curious, that Lord Liverpool, a clerk in whose office had written under a feigned name, a sham life of PAINE, should become the recorder of the truth of PAINE's predictions, and that too in "a *Letter to the King*," in whose name the very work containing the predictions had been prosecuted as A LIBEL.

Here are three writers, all of whom of great understanding and experience, and the two former of abilities scarcely ever surpassed in any age or country, all opposed to each other as to every other question; each one hating the other two, and each one hating the other one: yet all agreeing as harmoniously as their bones would now agree, if they happened to be tumbled together; all agreeing as to these principles respecting paper-money.

Having now traced the increase of the Debt down to the putting forth of the 5 pound bank-notes, we will rest here, and resume the subject in our next.

I am, Gentlemen,

Your faithful friend,

WM. COBBETT.

State Prison, Newgate, Monday 8th October, 1810.

LETTER XI.

"These *five pound-notes* will circulate chiefly among little shopkeepers, butchers, bakers, market people, "renters of small houses, lodgers, &c. All the high departments of commerce, and the affluent stations of "life were already overstocked, as Smith expresses it, with the bank-notes. No place remained open "wherein to crowd an additional quantity of bank-notes but among the class of people I have just men- "tioned, and, the means of doing this could be best effected by coining five pound-notes. But no new "supplies of money can, as was said before, now arrive at the Bank, as all the taxes will be paid in "paper. What, then, would be the consequence, were the Public Creditors to demand payment of their "Dividends in Cash, or demand Cash for the bank-notes in which the Dividends are paid; a circumstance "always liable to happen."—*Paine.* Decline and Fall of the English System of Finance. Published in "1796.

"I should stop here, but there is a subject of so great importance, and so nearly connected with the Coins "of your Majesty's realm, that I should not discharge my duty if I left it wholly unnoticed; I mean what "is now called *Paper currency*; which is carried to so great an extent, that it is become highly inconve- "nient to your Majesty's subjects, and may prove, in its consequences, if no remedy is applied, dangerous "to the credit of the kingdom. It is certain, that the smaller Notes of the Bank of England, and those "issued by country Bankers, have supplanted the Gold Coins, usurped their functions, and driven a great "part of them out of circulation: in some parts of Great Britain, and especially in the southern parts of Ireland, small Notes have been issued to supply the place of Silver Coins, of which here is certainly a "great deficiency."—*Charles Jenkinson, Earl of Liverpool,* Letter to the King. Published in 1805.

Progress from Five to One Pound Notes—Suspicion begun soon after the Five Pound Notes—Paine's Prediction as to People going to the Bank—Lord Liverpool's Opinion agreeing with that of Mr. Paine—History of the Bank Stoppage of Gold and Silver Payments—Enormous increase of the Debt in 1797—Other cause—Alarmists—Meeting of Parliament in Oct. 1796—Alarm of Invasion—Arming Acts—Mr Fox's Opinion of the Alarm—Exaggerated Representations of the Venal Prints—French Fleet appears off the Coast of Ireland—Effect of the Alarm begins to be felt at the Bank of England—Venal Prints change their Tone all of a sudden, and accuse the Jacobins of exciting Alarm—Run upon the Bank becomes serious—Increased by a Report of a French Fleet with Troops on board, being off Beachy Head—Followed immediately by the landing of Tate and his Raggamuffins in Wales—Bank receives its finishing blow—Vain attempts to check the Run upon the Bank—Order of Council issued—Disappointment of the Crowd at the Bank in Threadneedle Street.

Gentlemen,

IN the foregoing Letter, we traced the National Debt, and the Interest thereon, in their progressive increase from the year 1793 to 1797 inclusive, in which latter year we shall find that the Stoppage of Gold and Silver-payments, at the Bank of England, took place. We have seen, that, in the course of the aforementioned period, the amount of Debt and Interest was nearly doubled; we have seen that the Bank of England, had, of course, nearly double the sum to pay in Dividends, or Interest; we have seen how this increase of payments at the Bank of England produced a new family of notes, so low in amount as Five Pounds, there having been before the Anti-Jacobin War, no Bank Notes under Ten Pounds; we shall soon see how the same still growing and ever-prolific cause brought forth, at last, a still more numerous and more diminutive litter; and, when we have gone through the history of the Two and One Pound Notes, we shall want scarcely any thing further to convince us, that, in such a state of things, it was next to impossible for Gold and Silver to remain in circulation.

It was observed in Letter I, page 6, that when notes, so low in amount as Five Pounds came to be issued; when rents, salaries, yearly wages, and almost all the taxes came to be paid in paper; when this became the case, and when, of course, every part of the people, except the very poorest, possessed occasionally, bank-notes, it was impossible that men should not begin to think, that there was some difference between Gold and Silver and Bank-notes, and that they should not become more desirous to possess the former than the latter. In other words, it was impossible, that men should not begin to have some *suspicion* relative to the Bank-notes; and, it is very clear, that the moment such suspicion arises, there is an end to any paper-money, which is convertible into Gold and Silver at the will of the bearer, who will, of course, lose not an instant in turning that of which he has a *suspicion* (however slight) into that of which it is impossible for any one to have a suspicion.

Thus it happened in 1797, as PAINE, in his pamphlet, published only the year before, had foretold, in the words of the first of my mottos to this Letter. He there told his readers how the issuing of the Five Pound Notes would operate; he pointed out how this measure would keep real money from the Bank; and he asked what must be the consequence, if (as it *might any day happen*) the people should go to the Bank and *demand cash for the notes.* This did happen the very next year; and, as he foretold in another part of his pamphlet, those who went to present their notes *first* came *best off.* LORD LIVERPOOL, in the passage, which I have selected for my second motto to this Letter, had when he wrote, *seen the thing happen;* he had seen the fulfilment of what Mr. PAINE had foretold, and spoke, therefore, of the "*dangerous*" consequences of an excessive issue of paper, with the fact before his eyes. Experience, which, says the proverb, "makes fools wise" had taught his Lordship in 1805, what he might have learnt from Mr. PAINE in 1796. Nevertheless, the opinions of Lord Liverpool have some weight, and are worthy of attention with us in England; because, though his talents and mind were of a cast quite inferior to those of such men as HUME and PAINE and BURKE, and though there is nothing in what he has said, which I had not said, in the Register, years before, still as being a man of great experience in business, as having during this whole reign been a great favourite at court, and especially as having, upon this occasion, *addressed himself directly to the King,* his opinions, though of no consequence elsewhere, are worthy of some notice in this country, and may possibly, in some minds, tend to produce that conviction, which, in the same minds, a stupid and incorrigible prejudice would have prevented from being produced by all the powers of HUME or PAINE.

But, we must now return to the Bank, and see *how* it happened that the people went to demand money in payment of the notes in 1797. That it did happen we all know; but, there are not a few of the people forming the present population of the country, who have forgotten, or, who have never known, the true history of the *Stoppage of Gold and Silver-payments at the Bank of England;* yet, without a knowledge of this history, and a thorough knowledge of it too, we cannot possibly pursue our inquiries to a satisfactory result.

We have seen abundant arguments to prove, that paper-money, that promissory paper of every sort, is the offspring and representative of *Debt;* that a National or Public Debt never can fail to bring forth bank-notes, or paper-promises of some sort or other; that, of course, as the Debt increases and its Interest increases, there will be, and must be, an increase of the paper in which that interest is paid; and in the last Letter, p. 131, we saw, in the Table of Increase of the Debt and Interest from the beginning of the Anti-Jacobin War to the year 1797, we here saw, in practice, the cause of the making of the FIVE POUND bank-notes. But, as we have since seen, that measure was not sufficient. We saw, at p. 134, that it was o *avoid paying in Gold and Silver* the sums, or part of sums, from TEN to FIVE pounds, which must have induced the Bank to make and put out notes so low as FIVE POUNDS. If you look again at that Table, gentlemen, you will see how the increase went on; you will see, that it was *greater and greater every year.* In the year 1793, the addition of the annual Interest was (speaking in round numbers) only 250 *thousand pounds;* but, in the year 1797, the addition was, 3¼ *millions;* that is to say, a third part of as much as the whole amount of the Interest previous to the Anti-Jacobin war. Thus did this war of PITT against the Republicans of France cost, in only *one year,* nearly as much, in addition to Debt, as the cost of the whole of the American War, the extravagant expenditure of which had, till now, been proverbial.

There were, however, *other causes* at work, at the time of which we are now speaking; causes operating upon the paper system from without; causes which must be here fully stated; for, besides that a knowledge of them is essential to our inquiry, it is demanded by justice towards those who opposed the ruinous measure of PITT, and who foretold their consequences; and this demand is, in a peculiar manner, addressed to ME, who, from being so situated as to be unable to come at, or even suspect, the truth, while many circumstances conspired to make me take for truth that which was false, was not only one of the dupes of the system but who, unintentionally, contributed according to the degree of my talents, towards the extension of the circle of duplicity.

Credit is a thing wholly dependent upon *opinion.* The word itself, indeed, has the same meaning as the word *belief.* As long as men *believe* in the riches of any individual, or any company, so long he or they possess all the advantages of riches. But, when once *suspicion* is excited, no matter from what cause, the *credit* is shaken: and a very little matter oversets it. So long as the *belief is implicit,* the person, towards whom it exists, goes on, not only with all the appearances, but with all the advantages of wealth; though, at the same time, he be insolvent. But, if his wealth be not *solid;* if he have merely the *appearance* of wealth; if he be unable to pay so much as he owes, or in other words, if he be *insolvent,* which means neither more nor less than *unable to pay.* When an individual is in this situation, he is liable, at any moment, to have his insolvency exposed. Any accident, that excites alarm in the minds of his creditors, brings the whole upon him at once; and he who might otherwise have gone on for years, is stopped in an instant.

Thus it will happen to Companies of Traders as well as to individuals; and thus it did happen to the Bank Company, at the time we are speaking of, and at which time an *alarm of invasion* prevailed through the country.

From the very out-set of the war, the inventors and supporters of it had been, from time to time, propagating *alarms* of various sorts, by the means of which alarms, whether they themselves believed in them or not, they were enabled to do things, which never had before been either known or heard of or dreamt of in England. The mode of reasoning with the peo- was this: You see, that, in France, the revolution has deprived the people of both *property and life;* there are those who wish to cause a revolution in England: the measures taken, or proposed, are absolutely necessary to prevent the accomplishment of this wish: therefore, you have your choice, either to submit quietly to these measures, whatever *portion* of your *liberty* or *property* they may take away, or let in upon you a revolution which will take away *all your property* and your *lives* into the bargain. There was no room for hesitation; and thus were the people determined, and with this view of the matter did they proceed, until the time above referred to, the ministers being, probably, full as much alarmed as the people, and certainly not with *less cause.*

At times, however, especially after the war had continued for three or four years, the effect of alarm seemed to grow very faint. Danger has been so often talked of, that at last, it was grown familiar. In the year 1796, however, things began to wear a serious aspect. All the minister's predictions and promises had failed; his allies, to whom and for whose support so many millions had been paid by the people of this country, had all laid down their arms or had gone over to the side of France; the assignats in France had been annihilated without producing any of the fatal consequences which PITT had so confidently anticipated, and upon which, indeed, he had relied for success; and a negociation for peace, opened at the instance of England, had produced nothing but a convincing proof of high pretensions of the enemy, and of his confidence in his cause and resources.

When the parliament met, therefore, in October 1796, the ministers and their adherents seem to have been full of real apprehension. They failed not to renew the signal of *alarm*, in which, indeed, they were kept in countenance by the enemy, who had openly declared his attention of invading the country. The subject was mentioned in the King's speech, upon a part of which a motion was grounded on the 18th of October, for the bringing in of bills for the raising men with all possible speed, for the purpose of defending the country against invasion. In virtue of a resolution passed in consequence of this motion, three acts were passed with all possible rapidity, the first for providing an *augmentation for the militia* to be trained and exercised in a particular manner; the second for raising a certain number of men in the several counties of England and Scotland (there were two Acts), for the *service of the regular Army and the Navy*; and the third for raising a *provisional force of cavalry* to be embodied, in case of necessity, for the defence of these kingdoms;* which acts were finally passed on the 11th of November 1796. When this measure was under discussion, MR. FOX, Mr. SHERIDAN, and others opposed it upon the ground of its not being necessary, and MR. FOX, who called it a *requisition*, after the French manner, observed that, if it was necessary to our safety, it was the conduct of the ministers and of the last parliament who confided in them, which had brought us into that miserable situation, "a parliament," he said, "which "had done more to destroy every "thing that is dear to us, than in "better days would have entered into "the mind of any Englishman to "attempt, or to conceive; a parliament "by whom the people had been drained "so much, and from whom they had "had so little benefit; a parliament "that had diminished the dearest "rights of the people so shamelessly "and so wickedly; a parliament whose "conduct it was that had given rise "to this measure." MR. FOX added, that he did not believe that invasion would render any such measure necessary; that the real resources of the country consisted of the people's attachment to the constitution, and that, therefore, the proper measure to be adopted would be to allow them to possess the spirit of that constitution. The minister and his partizans contended, however, that there was real cause for alarm; and PITT said, that as to the constitution "it still pos- "sessed that esteem and admiration "of the people, which would induce "them to defend it against the designs "of *domestic foes*, and the attempts of "*their foreign allies*;" thus, according to his usual practice, proceeding upon the assumption, that there was a party in the country in *alliance*, as to wishes, at least, *with the enemy*.

While these measures were before parliament, the venal part of the press was by no means inactive. Representations the most exaggerated were made use of in speaking of the temper and designs of the enemy, always insinuating that the opponents of the Minister were ready to join the enemy

* 37 George III. Chapters 3, 4, 5, and 6.

or, at least, wished him success. The French were exhibited as being quite prepared; and a descent was held forth as something almost too horrible to be thought of. This was useful for the purpose of making the Arming Acts go down; but the alarmists did not seem to be aware of its cutting another way; and, least of all do they appear to have imagined, that it would set people to thinking of what effect *invasion* might produce upon *bank notes.*

In the mean while, the negociations for peace were broken off by the month of December, which gave rise to new *alarm.* This was soon followed by the appearance of a French naval force, with troops on board, off the coast of Ireland; and, though its return back to France, without attempting a descent, might, one would think, have tended to quiet people's fears, it was, on the contrary, made the ground-work of a still more general and more vociferous alarm. There were now no bounds to the exaggerations of the venal prints. From the first week in January, (1797) to the third week in February, the people were kept in a state of irritation hardly to be conceived. Addresses to them, in all shapes and sizes, were published, calling upon them to *arm* and *come forth* at once, not waiting for the slow process of the Militia and Cavalry Acts. "Already," were we told, "the opposite coast was crowded with "hostile arms; forests of bayonets "glistened in the sun; *despair* and "*horror* were coming in the rear." It was next to impossible that this should not make people think of what was to become of them; make them reflect a little as to what they were *to do* in case of invasion; and it required but very little reflection to convince them, that money, at all times useful, would, in such a case, be more useful than ever. Whence by a very natural and easy transition, they would be led to contemplate the *possibility* of real money being *rather* better than paper. That's enough! There needs no more! Away, in an instant, they go to the Bank, where the written promises tell them the bearer shall be paid *on demand.*

This effect of the alarm, an effect of which neither PITT nor any of his adherents seem ever to have had the smallest suspicion, and, indeed, when MR. FOX cautioned them against it, they effected to laugh at what he said; this effect of the alarm, raised and kept up by the minister and the great Loaners and men of that description; this effect of the alarm began, it appears, to be sensibly felt, at the Bank of England, immediately after the appearance of the French fleet off the coast of Ireland; and, as it afterwards appeared, from official documents, the drain had become so great by the end of the third week in February, that the Directors saw the impossibility of going on, unless something could be done to put a stop, or, at least, greatly to check, the run upon them for cash. The people were, in short, now doing precisely what PAINE, only about ten or eleven months before, had advised them to do, and the consequence was precisely what he had predicted.

It was now extremely curious to hear the language of the *venal news-papers,* who had, for months before, been endeavouring to excite *alarm,* and who abused MR. FOX and his party, called them Jacobins, and, sometimes, traitors, because they said that the alarm was *false,* and was invented for bad purposes. These very news-papers now took the other side. They not only themselves said, that the alarm was *groundless;* but they had the impudence, the unparalleled, the atrocious impudence, to *accuse the Jacobins,* as they called them, *of having excited the alarm,* for the purpose of injuring *public credit!*

This change of tone was begun on the 17th of February by those notoriously venal prints, those prints so far famed above all others in the annals of venality;—the "TRUE BRITON" and the "SUN." The thing was begun in "An Address to JOHN BULL," in which the "*most thinking* people," who were still all in frying confusion to get on with the levies of additional militia, and parish-men for the army and navy, and the provisional cavalry; the "*most thinking* people," while all hurry and bustle about this, were told by these shameless writers, who had almost called the people traitors for not making greater haste to arm; the people were, by these same writers, now told, that alarm might be *pushed too far;* that, if so pushed, it might do us *an injury equal to invasion;* that every one must see, that *the French wished to ruin our credit*; that, of course, to shew an *eagerness to sell out of the funds* was to *favour the designs of the enemy;* that it was, besides, the greatest nonsense in the world for people to suppose that their property was *not safe in the Bank of England;* that no apprehension need be felt, and that the people who had money in the funds, might safely rely upon the *wooden walls of Old England.* Though, observe, the whole country was actually in movement, down to the very beadles, in order to raise men for defence by *land.*

"The evidence of facts" was before the people's eyes. The alarm was not to be allayed by assertions like these. And, though the venal prints grew more and more positive in their assurances, that there was now no danger from invasion; though they (on the 21st of February) assured the people, that it was "an *error* to suppose that the enemy was at our "gates," and that "a *panic* might do "infinite mischief to public credit," people still kept carrying their notes softly to Threadneedle-street, they kept on selling out of the Stocks: and, a report, on the day last-mentioned, of the appearance of *a French fleet, with Troops on board,* off BEACHY HEAD*, immediately followed by the famous landing of TATE and his handful of raggamuffins in WALES,* appears to have given confidence in bank-paper the finishing blow.

All, as appears from the documents, and as we shall by-and-by see, was consternation in Threadneedle-street. The diminution of the gold became greater and greater every day. In vain did the venal prints cry out against alarm. They had cried "*wolf,*" till the people had believed them. They had called upon them to "stand "forward in *defence of the constitu-* "*tion,*" 'till they had convinced them it was time for every man to think a little about taking care of himself. In vain did these venal writers now call aloud against alarm; in vain did they say, (24th February) that the Beachy Head-report "arose from a "mistake in the signals; that the re- "sources of the country were *undi-* "*minished*; that it was *degrading* to "suppose that we had *not a sufficient* "*force to annihilate the enemy;* that "the *panic was shameful, unmanly,* "*mean*, and *dastardly;*" In vain did they assert (24th February), that "in- "vasion was more to be *desired* than "*dreaded;*" in vain did they exclaim: "Let us, for *God's* sake, not give "way to our fears *so as to injure* "*public credit.*" In vain did they (25th February) aver, "that the *alarm* "*was groundless;* that they were *sure* "no attack was *meditated;* and that "they were convinced it *never would* "*be.*" In vain did they again exclaim; "for *God's* sake let not the "gloomy despondency of a few men "in the city *give a fatal blow to pub-* "*lic credit.*"

In vain were all these efforts: SUSPICION, to use PAINE's emphatical expression, was no longer ASLEEP. It was broad awake, and to stay its operations was impossible. To excite fears in the breasts of the people was a task to which the venal prints had been adequate; but to remove

* "PORTSMOUTH, FEB. 20.—An account reached this place, this morning at half "past ten, A.M. of *several French transports,* "*convoyed by armed vessels, having been seen*

those fears, or to impede the progress of their effects upon the mind, was too much for any human power to accomplish. The run upon the Bank continued to increase, until the day last mentioned, Saturday, November the 25th of February 1797, a day which will long be remembered, and which will be amongst the most memorable in the annals of England, as being the *last* (hitherto at least) on which the Bank of England was compelled, at the will of the bearer, to pay its promissory notes in gold and silver, agreeably to the tenor of those notes; until the evening of that day the run continued, but, on the next, though it was *Sunday*, an Order was issued from the PRIVY COUNCIL requiring the Directors of the Bank *to forbear issuing any cash in payment*, until the sense of Parliament could be taken upon the subject, which memorable instrument was in the following words*, to which I must beg of you, Gentlemen, to pay particular attention.

We shall, by-and-by, see *whence* it was that "Mr. Chancellor of the "Exchequer" received his information, and *what sort of information* it was that he did receive; but, for the present, we will, in order to avoid making this Letter too long, content ourselves with seeing what the Bank Company did in consequence of this *Order not to pay their creditors;* this requisition *not to pay their promissory notes when presented;* this *Order to forbear issuing cash in payment*.

The run had been very great on the *Saturday*, and people would scarcely suspect, that the *Sunday*, especially by such a godly ministry as PITT'S was, would have been spent in labour of any sort. It would, however, naturally give people time to *think* a little; it would afford them leisure to reflect on the consequences of being without a farthing of cash in case of invasion. Accordingly, on the *Monday* morning, they appear to have been quite prepared for furnishing

"*off Beachy Head.* The intelligence came "by the signal posts, and Admiral Sir P. "Parker immediately on receiving it, ordered two ships of the line and five frigates to slip their cables and proceed to "sea. This squadron is now out of sight, "and all the other ships are getting in readiness.---The sensation that this made in "the City may be easily conceived. It "spread a *very general alarm;* but it was "soon contradicted. Letters, written as "the post was setting out, stated that the "alarm had been occasioned by a *mistaken* "*signal*, and that instead of a fleet of 300 "*French transports*, it was no more than a "signal that 3 *privateers* had been discovered off Beachy Head.---Such, however, "is the consequences of the state of alarm "*into which Government has thrown the country* "*by the cry of a threatened Invasion*."--- "MORNING CHRONICLE, 22 Feb. 1797.

* "On Saturday the *public mind received* "*the shock of a new alarm.* An express arrived from Lord Milford, informing the "King's Ministers that a body of French "troops, amounting to about 1200, had "been landed at Fiskard out of the ships "which we stated had approached the "coast of Pembroke. Ministers took the "earliest opportunity of announcing the "fact to the Lord Mayor."---MORNING "CHRONICLE, 26 February, 1797.

* *At the Council Chamber, Whitehall, Feb. 26, 1797.*

By the LORDS of his MAJESTY'S Most Honourable PRIVY COUNCIL.

Present,

The LORD CHANCELLOR (Rosslyn)
LORD PRESIDENT
DUKE of PORTLAND
MARQUIS CORNWALLIS
EARL SPENCER
EARL of LIVERPOOL (Charles Jenkinson)
LORD GRENVILLE
Mr. CHANCELLOR of the EXCHEQUER

Upon the *representation of the Chancellor of the Exchequer*, stating that from the result of the information which *he has received*, and of the enquiries which it has been his duty to make respecting the effect of the *unusual demand for specie*, that have been made upon the metropolis, in consequence of *ill-founded or exaggerated alarms* in different parts of the country, it appears that unless some measure is immediately taken, there may be reason to apprehend a *want of a sufficient supply of cash to answer the exigencies of the public service.* It is the unanimous opinion of the Board, that it is indispensibly necessary, *for the public service*, that the Directors of the Bank of England should *forbear issuing any cash in payment* until the sense of Parliament can be taken on that subject, and the proper measures adopted thereupon, themselves with real money, if it was to be had at the Bank. Let us, however, as to this fact, take the words of the venal writers themselves. "Yesterday-morning," says the TRUE BRITON of *Tuesday*, the 28th of February, "a *great run* seemed to have "been *meditated* upon the Bank, as "A CROWD OF PEOPLE ASSEMBLED THERE AS SOON "AS THE DOORS OPENED. "This design was HAPPILY *defeated* by a Resolution of the Privy "Council, transmitted to the Bank "Directors on Sunday, and, in consequence, *they had Hand-bills ready* "*for delivery*, a copy of which, with "the Order of the Privy Council annexed, our readers will find, as an "Advertisement in the front of our "Paper."*

Such, Gentlemen, was the manner in which the *Stoppage of Gold and Silver payments at the Bank of England* took place; such was the manner of that event, which produced the evils, for which the Bullion Committee have proposed *a remedy*. Upon the Order of Council there is much to observe, before we proceed further; but, having laid before you a plain narrative of the event, it will be best to reserve those observations, 'till my next, and, in the meanwhile,

I remain, Gentlemen,

Your sincere friend,

WM. COBBETT.

State Prison, Newgate, Monday,
15th October, 1810.

---

for maintaining the means of circulation, and *supporting the public and commercial credit* of the kingdom at this important conjuncture; and it is ordered, that a copy of this minute be transmitted to the Directors of the Bank of England, and they are *hereby required*, on the grounds of the exigency of the case, to conform thereto until the sense of Parliament can be taken as aforesaid.

W. FAWKENER.

* "*Bank of England, February* 27, 1797.

In consequence of an order of his Majesty's Privy Council notified to the Bank last night, a Copy of which is hereunto annexed.—The Governor, Deputy Governor, and Directors of the Bank of England think it their duty to inform the Proprietors of Bank Stock, as well as the Public at large, that *the general concerns of the Bank are in the most affluent and prosperous situation*, and such as to *preclude every doubt as to the security of its notes*.—The Directors mean to continue their usual discounts for the accommodation of the Commercial Interest, *paying the amount in Bank notes*, and the *Dividend Warrants* will be paid in the *same manner*.

FRANCIS MARTIN, *Secretary*.

Entered at Stationers' Hall.

LONDON: Printed by WM. MOLINEUX, Bream's Buildings, Chancery Lane.

LETTER XII.

"Every victim of injustice and cruelty" (speaking of the *French* government) "*bequeaths his revenge to his* "*connections, to his friends, and to his relations*; or (if all these should be involved in the same common "fate with himself) every such execution raises detestation and abhorrence, even in the breast of ordinary spectators, and *unites the public opinion against a Government*, which exists only by the daily practice of *robbery* and *murder*. From this disgusting scene, let us turn our eyes to *our own situation*. THERE "the contrast is striking in all its parts. HERE we see nothing of the character and genius of *arbitrary* "*finance*; none of the *bold frauds of bankrupt power*; none of the wild struggles and plunges of *des-* "*potism in distress*; no lopping off from the capital of debt; no *suspension of interest*; no robbery, under "the name of loan; no raising the value; no *debasing the substance of the coin*. HERE we behold "*public credit of every description rising* under all the disadvantages of a general war; an ample re- "venue, flowing freely and copiously from *the opulence of a contented people*."—*Lord Mornington* "(now *Marquis Wellesley*). Speech in the House of Commons, 21st January 1794.

The interest of the national funded debt is paid at the Bank in the same kind of paper in which the taxes are "collected. When people find, as they will find, a reservedness among each other in giving gold and silver "for bank-notes, or the least preference for the former over the latter, they will go for payment to the "Bank, where they have a right to go. They will do this as a measure of prudence, each one for himself, "and *the truth, or delusion of the funding system will be then proved*."—*Paine*. Decline and Fall of the English System of Finance. Published in 1796.

The great object, however, is to open the Bank of England, and to enable it to carry on its pecuniary "transactions to the extent which its resources will admit of, on the solid principle of giving either cash or "paper at the option of the applicant. *Until that is done, neither public or private credit, nor agricul-* "*ture, nor commerce, nor manufactories, nor the income of the nation, can go on prosperously*."—*Sir John Sinclair*. Letter, published in 1797.

---

he Impression made upon the Country by the Stoppage of Gold and Silver Payments at the Bank---Ridiculous Situation of the Ministers in complaining of False Alarms---Jacobins now accused of causing the Run upon the Bank---Foolishness of this Accusation---Mr. Wilberforce answered by Mr. Fox---Now was the Time for Mr. Pitt's Adherents to leave him---They had been warned by Mr. Fox and others---King's Speech and Language of the Minister at the Opening of the Session during which the Stoppage took place---If the Minister's Adherents had now quitted him it might have prevented the present Dangers---Mr. Pitt's Humiliation in the House of Commons---Questions put to him upon the subject of the Legal Tender, by Mr. Combe and Mr. Nicholls---His Inability to determine on what Measures he should propose.

GENTLEMEN,

HAVING, agreeably to the inten- m expressed, traced the increase of e Debt and of the Bank-Notes down that grand and memorable effect, e *stoppage of Gold and Silver-pay- ents at the Bank of England*, our xt object must naturally be to know hat *impression* that event produced on the nation, and what *measures* ere adopted in consequence of it; in her words, to continue the history of e *stoppage* down to the time, when e evil of paper-money produced the rming of the Bullion Committee.

The impression made upon the na- n in general was such as might have en expected, after all the *flattering accounts* which had been given of the national resources. The ORDER OF COUNCIL does, you will perceive, ascribe the event to "*ill-founded* and "*exaggerated alarms*, in different "parts of the country." But, supposing this to have been the chief, and only cause, with what face could the ministers complain of these alarms; seeing that they themselves had done their utmost to excite them? They had not only proposed and carried through the Arming Bills, but they had been writing to the magistrates, in every part of the kingdom, calling upon them for internal preparations "while" (Morning Chronicle, 22nd February 1797) "Contractors had

MOLINEUX, Printer, Bream's Buildings, Chancery Lane.

"put every town into commotion by "inquiries as to the number of *Ovens*, "the quantity of *grain*, and the *State* "*of the Provisions*." Nay, the preamble of the Arming Acts itself proclaimed, that the measures were become necessary, "in order to pre-"vent, or repel, any attempt, *which* "*the enemies of the country might* "*make to effect a descent upon the* "*kingdom*." After all this it was, that the Privy Council spoke, in a sort of complaining tone, of "*ill-*"*founded* and *exaggerated* alarms"!

When the matter came before Parliament, the Opposition did, certainly, not spare the Minister and his adherents, who had the confidence to hold the same tone as to the *alarm;* and whose opinion of the minds of the people was such, that they scrupled not to repeat the assertions of the venal prints, and to ascribe the *injury* (for they *then* acknowledged it to be an *injury*) which Public Credit had sustained to *unfounded* alarms, excited by the *internal enemies* of the country, which, in a contrary sense, some members were malicious enough to believe. GENERAL WALPOLE (in the Debate of the 1st of March) made an admirable exposure of them in this way, to which no answer was given, but that they were not *always* to feel alarm, because they had *once* felt it; though the fact was that they were proclaiming alarm, with all their might, 'till the Bank, as it afterwards appeared, *represented to them secretly, that the alarm, if continued, would take away all their cash.* MR. SHERIDAN, in adverting to the speech of GENERAL WALPOLE, who had remarked upon MR. WINDHAM'S not having *signed* the Order of Council, said, "that he believed it proceeded "from the *reflections* it contained "against the alarmists," and he added, that "even amidst the wreck "of public credit, it was impossible "not to laugh at the juggling tricks "and miserable shifts to which ministers had recourse."

The venal part of the press, now that it was impossible any longer to disguise the state of the credit of the Bank, began a regular new attack upon the *Jacobins*, whom it had before reviled for endeavouring *to check* the alarm, and whom it now accused of *causing* the alarm. The notoriously venal prints before-mentioned (TRUE BRITON and SUN), which had, to the last moment, abused the Jacobins for (as they said) propagating the *false* notion of the Bank not having gold to answer their notes. These prints, never equalled in venality, I believe, by any prints in the world, the MORNING POST only excepted, now abused those same unfortunate Jacobins for *not acknowledging the necessity* of the Order in Council. They (3rd March 1797) again accused the Jacobins of having caused "a *distrust* of the Bank," and of having formed a design to *ruin the credit of the country*, in which "they "had *so far* succeeded, at least, as to "*persuade* the people, in *some parts* "*of the country*, that gold was *pre-*"*ferable* to Bank notes."

Gentlemen, pause here for a moment, and contemplate the *foolishness* as well as the injustice of such observations as these. You will bear in mind, that the Jacobins, as they were called, were, by these same writers, constantly represented as men without learning, without sense, without property, and, of course, without influence. How, then, were they to have the power of producing such an effect upon the minds of the nation; and, upon the minds of those, too, who *held the bank-notes* and who *owned the Stock?* The Jacobins, as these venal prints had the impudence to call them, had not been able to persuade the people to check MR. PITT in his ruinous career of war and expenditure; they had not been able to prevent any one of the measures of that Minister; they had not been able to persuade the people to do any one thing that they wished them to do, and, at the very time we are speaking of, they were out-voted, in the parliament, *four to one*. Yet, to these same Jacobins was now ascribed that run upon the Bank, which produced the Order in Council; which produced an order, issued by the king's *Privy Council*, to encourage a Company of Merchants to refuse illegally, to pay their promissory notes, when duly presented. The Jacobins, as they were still called with a degree of impudence not to be adequately described; the Jacobins, who were represented as defeated and put down, and as being held in abhorrence by the people, were, nevertheless, at the same moment, represented as having such power over the mind of that same people, as to cause them to make a run upon the Bank, which was called "stabbing the country in its vitals." Mr. Fox, in answer to Mr. WILBERFORCE, who (March 1, 1797) attributed "much of "the *public calamity* to the *conduct* "*of the Opposition*, and to the conduct of those who had proceeded to "lengths which the Opposition would "not *avow*; in answer to this MR. FOX said: "this reminds me of a "scene in Ben Johnson, where it appears, that an Imposter had played "his tricks very successfully for a "long time upon his dupes, and, "when he was detected, the dupes "became very angry, not at the Impostor, but at those who had detected him."

Now was the time for those, who had been deluded into a support of Mr. PITT's measures, to make a frank and manly acknowledgement of their error, and to join Mr. Fox in demanding a change of system. They had, when war was first contemplated, received the most solemn assurances, that the *resources* for *vigorous preparation* (at first preparation only was talked of) were *ample*, even from the *excess* of the revenue;* they had been, when, after the war had begun and had brought, at once, very disastrous effects as to pecuniary matters, told that those effects were *completely removed*, and that the revenue was in a *favourable state*;† they had been told, that the war could not be of long duration; they had been told that the situation of France, in every respect, and especially in respect to her finances, was desperate beyond description; the French system had been repeatedly described to them as one that could not last above a few months, having in itself the seeds of inevitable destruction; they had been assured, that all the powers of Europe would join us against France; they had been told, that, if there were no other cause of ruin to our enemy, that enemy must be ruined by the loss of all his colonies (which we had taken), and by the annihilation of his naval force, which seemed to have been nearly completed by the fourth year of the war; they had had, year after year, exhibited to them such pictures of the finances of France compared with those of England, as to make them believe that France must speedily become *bankrupt*, while England was (and partly in consequence of the war) becoming, every day, more and more rich, that her commerce was daily increasing, and that her *credit*, which was always firmly established, was now *built upon a rock*; they had, even in the King's Speech, made at the beginning of the session of which

* "Gentlemen of the House of Commons. It is a great *consolation* to me to "reflect, that *you will find ample resources* "for effectually defraying the expence of "*vigorous preparations*, from the excess of "the *actual revenue beyond the ordinary expenditure*."——KING'S SPEECH, 13th Dec. 1792.

† "I feel too sensibly the repeated proofs "which I have received of the affection of "my subjects not to lament the necessity "of any additional burthens. It is, however, a *great consolation* to me, to observe "the favourable state of the Revenue, and "the *complete success of the measure which was* "*last year adopted for removing the embarrassments affecting commercial credit*."—— KING'S SPEECH, 10th January 1794.

we are now speaking, and during which the stoppage took place, at the beginning of that very session they had been told, in the King's Speech, of the SOLIDITY of the pecuniary resources of the country,* while the Minister and his adherents echoed back the assertion. Upon this last occasion, which, Gentlemen, is worthy of particular attention, the time being only *four months* before the Bank-stoppage actually took place; upon this occasion, SIR WILLIAM LOWTHER, who seconded the address, and who is now a Lord, I believe, said "if we regarded our *finances*, they were ABUNDANT "in the EXTREME, and such as "were adequate to any emergency "of the country." LORD MORPETH, son of the earl of Carlisle, who moved the address to the king in answer to his speech, said "As to "our *internal situation*, we have "witnessed it, for some time past, "with *joy* and *exultation*; and have "reason to congratulate his Majesty "and the people at large, upon our "*auspicious prospects* in that re-"spect." And Mr. PITT himself said, "As to our *resources*, they fur-"nish, indeed, in a moment like the "present, a subject of *peculiar con-"gratulation* and *well-grounded con-"fidence*. .... Our "resources remain as yet, *untouched*, "and we shall be able to bring them "into action with a degree of concert "and effect, worthy of the character "of the British nation, and of the "cause in which they will be em-"ployed. These resources have in "them, NOTHING HOLLOW "OR DELUSIVE. They are the "result of an accumulated capital, of "gradually increasing commerce, of "HIGH AND ESTABLISHED "CREDIT; and they have been "produced while we have been con-"tending against a country, which "exhibits, in every respect, *the re-"verse of this picture*."†

Such, Gentlemen, was the language of the Minister and his adherents at the beginning of that session, during which, took place the memorable event, recorded in the foregoing Letter; and before you proceed any further, I beg you to look well at it. I beseech you to consider it well. If you do so, you never will be deluded again by any high-sounding assertions, let them come from what quarter they will. These, which I have just quoted, are memorab'e words. They are precious matter for history. They go a great way in enabling any one to judge of the character of Mr. PITT, as a *statesman*, and especially as a *political economist*. Gentlemen, there is no such thing as answering me here. No one can contradict me. What I have laid before you is indubitably true; and, as such, I am sure, it will have weight upon your minds, whatever your prejudices heretofore may have been.

The adherents of Mr. PITT had been told all that we have now taken a hasty review of; and, though they ought never to have believed it, having constantly been warned against the delusion by Mr. FOX, Mr. SHERIDAN, Mr. NICHOLLS, Mr. HOBHOUSE, Mr. GREY, Mr. TIERNEY, and others, but especially by the three former; though they ought not to have believed, and would not, had it not been for the blinding influence of the fears excited in their minds, have believed in those delusive assertions and predictions; still, if they did believe in them, they were not (if they looked upon the principle of the war as being *just* and *wise*) to be

* "It is a *great satisfaction* to me to observe, that, notwithstanding the temporary embarrassments, which have been experienced, the state of the commerce, manufactures, and revenue of the country proves the real extent and SOLIDITY *of our resources*, and furnish you such means as must be equal to *any exertions* which the present crisis may require."—KING'S SPEECH, 6th October 1796.

† See Parliamentary Debates, 6th Oct 1796.

blamed for supporting the minister; but, when experience had undeceived them; when they saw the proof of their error; when clearly established facts told them that they were in the wrong course; when they had before their eyes, that which could not possibly leave a doubt in any man's mind, that the system which they had so long supported was ruinous to their country; when they saw the Bank of England stop payment of its notes, and take shelter under an Order of the Privy Council, immediately followed by an *Act of Indemnification*, that is to say, an act to shelter the parties concerned from the penalties of the law; when the adherents of Mr. PITT saw this; when they beheld these effects, this mighty ruin, which that adherence had brought upon their country; when they beheld this, they ought to have withdrawn their support; and, if they had done this, though I am very far from saying, that they could have restored Gold and Silver-payments at the Bank, and am still less inclined to say, that they would have put a stop to the workings of the French revolution, I am decidedly of opinion, that there was yet time to give such a turn to that revolution as to render it less violent in itself, less severe towards Europe in general, and infinitely less dangerous to this country; as we, in all likelihood, never should have seen an Emperor in France, and, of course, should not have had to dread, and to guard against, the effects of his ambition and his power. It must, I think, be now clear to all the world, that to Mr. PITT, supported by the great mercantile and monied bodies, BUONAPARTE owes his rise and his greatness; and, that, instead of being, as Mr. PITT once called him, "the *child* and *champion* of *Jacobinism*," he may be truly called the child of Mr. PITT and the *Paper-System*, that system, the effects of which we shall, every day, feel more and more; that system, of the evils of which almost every man seems now to be thoroughly convinced; that system, of which to prevent, or, at least, retard the still greater evils, the Bullion Committee have proposed that *remedy*, into which we shall, by-and-by, have to examine.

Mr. PITT, who was in the House of Commons, *boldness* personified; who never seemed to feel as men in general do upon being defeated in argument, or at being detected and exposed as to points of fact; who always appeared to increase in boldness in proportion as he was worsted in the contest, does, however, seem to have, for a while at least, felt himself humbled upon this occasion, and to have been as the vulgar saying is, completely *chop-fallen;* and, after what we have seen him (in the above-quoted passages) assert, only *four months* before, well might he feel humbled; well might he feel afraid to open his mouth in the presence of those, who had so often told him that such would be the result of his system, and whom he had, as often, reproached with the *want of love for their country;* and even at whose opinions not only himself but his underlings had been accustomed to laugh. To come to the House of Commons, that scene of his long-enjoyed triumph; to come to that bench, whence he had so long been in the habit of dictating to all around him, and of dealing out his sarcasms upon all who dared question his infallibility; to come to the same bench, and thence to deliver a Message from the King, (27th February 1797) *announcing the Stoppage of Gold and Silver-payments at the Bank of England*; to do this, and to look Mr. Fox in the face, seemed to be too much even for Mr. PITT; to come down to the House, and say, that *necessity* had compelled him to issue an Order of the King's Council to forbid, or to protect, the Bank of England *from paying the just demands of its creditors*, was more than he was able to do without faultering, and it is, perhaps, more than any other man upon earth, under similar circumstances, would have been able to do at all.

His confidence seems, for once, to have failed him; and, what is upon record as to the debate, clearly proves, that he did not know what to do; that he literally was *at his wit's end.* Having delivered the Message, and laid a copy of the Order of Council upon the table, he moved for the Message to be taken into consideration the next day; and, at the same time, gave notice of a motion for appointing a Committee to inquire into the concerns of the Bank, an inquiry, he said, which "would greatly tend "*to confirm the solidity* of the Bank "capital." He also said, that he meant to declare by law, that "notes "instead of cash would be *taken by* "*the public in payment of the sums* "*due to them by the Bank.*" Mr. Alderman Combe asked him, whether he meant "that bank-notes "were to be taken only by the *re*-"*ceivers of the revenue*, or, that they "were to become *a legal tender* in "*all* money-transactions." He answered, that, "in the first instance, "he meant only to propose, that *they* "*should be taken on the part of the* "*public,*" leaving future measures to be decided upon, after the Committee should have made their report. Mr. Combe asked him "whether it was "*his opinion*, that this measure would "be *resorted to in the end.*" He answered, that "he had *no opinion* "upon the subject." Mr. Fox asked him, "if he *disclaimed* the opinion." He replied, that "he said *nothing* "*about it at all.*"

Look at him, Gentlemen! See there the man, who had the management of the affairs of this country for twenty years, and during whose administration more persons were, I believe, promoted to the peerage, than during any century before. Look at him. See him, who, only *four months* before, had boasted that our "resources "were *untouched*," and that there was "nothing *hollow* or *delusive* in "our finances." Look at him now, not able to *say;* nay, not able to *give an opinion*, whether he shall propose Bank-notes to be made a *legal tender*, or not! Mr. Nicholls (of whose great understanding upon this subject we shall see many proofs by-and-by) "pressed him for an answer to the "question which had been put to him, "whether it was his intention that "the notes of the Bank of England "should be declared *a legal tender* "from the Bank *to the public credi-* "*tor?* If so, he was about *to pro-* "*claim an act of insolvency.* And, "considering it in this light, he re-"probated his silence, as an instance "of most atrocious arrogance. After "animadverting, in the severest terms, "on the confiding majorities in that "House, who supported the Minis-"ter in every measure, however wild, "and sanctioned every part of his "conduct, however insolent, he con-"cluded with repeating the question, "*whether or not bank-notes were to* "*be declared a legal tender to the* "*public creditor.*" After the treatment which this gentlemen had frequently received at the hands of Mr. Pitt and his adherents, it could surprize no body to see him give way, upon this occasion, to a degree of asperity, which, without taking these circumstances into view, might not have been fully justified by the conduct of Mr. Pitt upon this particular occasion, who, in answer to Mr. Nicholls, said, that he was "per-"plexed by the observations and "questions of the learned gentleman, "who to an *intricacy* which it was "impossible to unravel, added an "exertion of voice much beyond "what he was accustomed to, and an "asperity of language which even "exceeded that of the other honour-"able gentle-gentleman (Mr. Sheri-"dan). He hoped that he would "not persist in thinking it atrocious "arrogance in him, if he did not attempt to answer what he conceived it would be unpardonable arrogance in him *to attempt to understand*. When a man obtruded his opinion, with too much rashness or too much positiveness, then he might be accused of arrogance; but he did not perceive that the man who *altogether declined giving an opinion*, could incur the imputation. But the learned gentleman seemed to be as ignorant of the forms of the House as of the common mode of business. He might have known that though it would be sometimes convenient to ask and to communicate information by question and answer, that, no discussion can regularly take place, except *when a motion was before the House*."

This was a very poor evasion; but, in fact, he could give no answer to the question, unless he had been ready to make a full and fair acknowledgment of his *not knowing what to do*. Nothing could be plainer than the question; nothing more distinct; nothing more intelligible to any man, who understood the common meaning of the frightful words, LEGAL TENDER. But, how was an answer to be given? Even if the minister had made his mind up to go that length. Even if he had screwed his courage up to the contemplation of such a measure, how was he to find face to propose it *all at once?* To propose such a measure required time, even with such a man as MR. PITT. It, at any rate, required time for him to look round him in the House. It required time for him to discover how his adherents felt, and whether they were still to be depended upon. It also required time to break the matter to the public, and to afford an opportunity for the press, and for the minister's monied friends out of doors to exert their influence. It not only required time to see what *could* be done, but what *dared* to be attempted.

To obtain this time the scheme of a Committee of Inquiry was resorted to, the result of which inquiry and an account of the measures adopted, we shall see in the next Letter. In the meanwhile, I am,

Gentlemen,

Your faithful friend,

WM. COBBETT.

State Prison, Newgate, Thursday, October 18, 1810.

LETTER XIII.

"But it was urged that the Bank had temporary difficulties to encounter, and that it behoved them to adopt some mode of granting relief to that important public body. The House of Commons, however, knew nothing of this. No application was made to them by the Bank; nor did it appear even that application had been made for the Order in Council; on the contrary, it appeared that this facetious Council, instead of examining the Directors of the Bank, acted entirely upon the authority of the Chancellor of the Exchequer. Nay, what added to his surprize was, that *not one of the Bank Directors* who had seats in that House, had ever *come forward and expressed an opinion upon the subject*. Some information was certainly necessary before the House sanctioned so novel and dangerous a measure. They had heard of the Bank a short time ago lending two millions to Government, and they had also heard of the dividends on Bank Stock increasing Was it not material to be informed therefore how they had come to stop payment at a time when their affairs seemed to be going on so prosperously?"—MR. SHERIDAN. Speech 28th Feb. 1807.

Alledged Ability of the Bank—Proceedings out of Doors for what is called Support of Public Credit—Mansion House Meeting—Brook Watson—Quarter Sessions Resolutions—Privy Council Resolutions—Representations of the Venal Prints relative to these Resolutions—Real Origin of the Mansion House Meeting—Directors prevail upon Mr. Pitt to have a private Meeting of Bankers at his House—Plan of a public Meeting there laid—Peep behind the Curtain—Meeting of the Bank Proprietors—Declaration of the Governors, Mr. Bosanquet and Mr. Thornton—These Declarations compared with the private Minute of the Bank, expressing their Alarm for the Safety of the House, and for calling upon Mr. Pitt to know when he would interfere

GENTLEMEN,

WHEN we look at the boast, referred to in the words of my Motto, and consider how many boasts of the same sort the Minister had uttered, and which he had continued in the habit of uttering, down almost to the very hour of the Bank Stoppage, we cannot help wondering that he could no longer endure his existence. What, then, will be the astonishment of posterity, to hear him, in a few months after that event, speak of it and of the measures growing out of it, as the happy means of *safety to the country;* and what will be their shame to find, that he was still confided in and supported?

As we proceed with the history of the measures of *remedy* which were now adopted, we must not fail to pay particular attention to the *opinions* and *doctrines*, at this time expressed and laid down by the Minister and his adherents, especially by those of his adherents, who had a more immediate interest in the concerns of the Bank of England. We must take care to bear in mind what they *then* said as to the *origin* of the Order of Council for the Stoppage of Gold and Silver-payments at the Bank; what they said as to the *nature* and *necessity* of the measure; what they said as to the *ability* of the Bank to resume its payments; and what they said as to the *time* of such resumption. What they *then* said, as to all these points, we must take care to bear in mind; because, we shall have to compare it with what the same persons have said since, and have to shew how in this case, as well as in so many others, the nation has been led on, by degrees, to acquiesce in what, if proposed to it all at once, would have made it shrink with affright, or fired it with indignation.

Before the House of Commons met, the day after the Message and Order of Council had been laid before it, that is to say, on the 28th of February 1797, the Anti-Jacobin adherents of the Minister had been hard at work *out of doors.* A meeting had been called in the Mansion House of the City of London consisting of *Merchants, Bankers,* and others, the Chairman being the Lord Mayor, whose name was BROOK WATSON, who then or very soon afterwards filled the lucrative office of *Commissary General to the Army,* and who was, in a very few years after that, made a *Baronet.* The persons assembled upon this occasion proclaimed their resolution *not to refuse* bank-notes in payment of any sums due to them, and to use their utmost endeavours to make *all their payments* in the same manner; * which, as you will perceive, Gentlemen, was neither more nor less than resolving, that they would do their utmost to keep up their own credit and consequence, and, in fact, to preserve themselves from instant ruin.

Similar Resolutions were passed in the country, where the Quarter Sessions happening to be then taking place, the Resolutions were sent forth *from the Bench*, with, of course, something of a *magisterial* weight and

---

* MANSION-HOUSE, LONDON.—*February* 27, 1797.—At a meeting of Merchants, Bankers, &c. held here this day, to consider of the steps which it may be proper to take, to prevent Embarrassments to Public Credit, from the effects of any ill-founded or exaggerated Alarms, and to support it with the utmost exertions at the present important conjuncture—The LORD MAYOR in the Chair;—RESOLVED UNANIMOUSLY,—That we, the undersigned, being highly sensible how necessary the preservation of Public Credit is at this time, do most readily hereby declare, that we will not refuse to receive Bank Notes in payment of any sum of money to be paid to us; and we will use our utmost endeavours to make all our payments in the same manner. —BROOK WATSON.

The resolution lies for signing at the following places; London Tavern, Bishopsgate-Street; Crown and Anchor Tavern, Strand; St. Albans Tavern, St. Alban's Street; Three-Crown Coffee-House, in Three-Crown Court, Borough; and at Lloyd's Coffee-house.

authority, as will be seen in the instance of the magistrates of Surrey, who, with *Lords Grantley* and *Onslow* at their head, appear to have led the way.* The *Privy Council* (pray read their *names* all over) had also a meeting upon the subject, and it was quite curious to see the Judges and great pensioners, and even the *Ministers themselves*, not excepting the *Lord High Treasurer*, publishing their promises to receive and to pay bank-notes, and, as far as depended on them individually, to support the circulation of those notes.†

These Meetings and their Resolutions furnished the venal prints with the pretence for asserting, that the alarm was at an end; that the people had had time to reflect, and that reflection could not fail to convince them, that there was no room for suspecting the solidity of the Bank. The meetings and resolutions (to which latter, in London, there were soon obtained thousands of signatures) were represented as having been perfectly *voluntary;* that they were the spontaneous effects of *pure public-spirit*, working in the breasts of *loyal* and disinterested men, and, of course, that those who did not come forward to resolve, or to sign, were *disloyal* men.

Gentlemen, stop with me here for a minute. Some of *you* may have been induced, by these venal writers, to think ill of all those of your neighbours, who disapproved of MR. PITT and his deeds; some of *you* may have been thus led, by the representations of these writers, to hate your honest neighbours, to stigmatize them as Jacobins, and to suspect them, in fact, of treasonable designs; some of *you* may, from this corrupt and deadly

---

* SURREY.—At the General Quarter Session of the Peace of our Sovereign Lord the King, holden at Saint Mary, Newington, by adjournment, in and for the said County, on Thursday, the 2nd day of March 1797.——We, whose names are hereunto subscribed, being desirous to contribute, as far as we can, to the support of the public and commercial credit of the kingdom, at this important crisis, do hereby agree and bind ourselves to receive the Notes of the Bank of England in all payments as Money, and to support, as far as depends on us individually, their circulation for the public benefit.

Grantley,	Edward Layton,
Onslow and Cranley,	John Morgan,
John Frederick,	Peter Broadley,
Joseph Shaw,	M. Nolan,
Thomas Evance,	George Shepley,
Rd. Carpenter Smith,	Thomas Barrow,
George Griffin Stonestreet,	Francis Lawson,
	John Jos. Shermer,
James Bulcock,	Robert Forrest,
William Hill,	John Pardon,
Robert Burnett,	Edward Morris,
Gideon Fournier,	Vitruvius Lawes,
Benjamin Robertson,	Samuel Marryatt,
Jonathan Stonard,	W. D. Best,
James Fielding,	Arthur Onslow.

Ordered, That the Clerk of the Peace do cause the above to be forthwith advertised in the Morning Papers.—*By the Court*,

LAWSON.

† At the Council Chamber, Whitehall, the 28th of February 1797,—Present—The Lords of His Majesty's most Honourable Privy Council.—We, whose names are hereunto subscribed, being desirous to contribute, as far as we can, to the support of the public and commercial credit of this Kingdom, at this important crisis, do hereby agree and bind ourselves to receive the Notes of the Bank of England in all payments as Money, and to support, as far as depends on us individually, their circulation.

J. Cantuar',	Sydney,
Loughborough, C.	Grenville,
Chatham, P.	Onslow and Cranley,
Dorset,	Walsingham,
Leeds,	Kenyon,
Montrose,	Malmesbury,
Roxburgh,	Auckland,
Portland,	St. Helen's,
Townshend,	Henry Addington,
Cornwallis,	W. PITT,
Bute,	HENRY DUNDAS,
Pembroke,	Cha. Townshend,
Westmorland,	C. F. Greville, V. C.
Chesterfield,	J. C. VILLIERS,
Sandwich,	James Greville,
Drummond Hay Kinnoul,	R. P. Arden,
	Wm. Wynne,
Macclesfield,	THOMAS STEELE,
Spencer,	A. Macdonald,
Liverpool,	S. Douglas,
Mornington,	W. Windham.
Gower Sutherland,	

source, have had your minds so poisoned, and so perverted from their natural bias, as to have contributed towards those fatal divisions in the nation, the effect of which, it is to be feared, your children's children will rue. Of such of you, therefore, as answer to this description, let me beg the earnest attention, while I develope the true source of the above-mentioned meetings and resolves, which, as you have seen, were described, by the venal writers, as being *perfectly voluntary*, and flowing from *pure public-spirit*.

You will bear in mind, that the Order in Council was signed on Sunday, the 26th of February, and that it was laid before the House of Commons on Monday the 27th, on which last-mentioned day, the Mansion House Meeting, Mr. BROOK WATSON in the Chair, took place. The next, Tuesday the 28th, the Minister, in opening the way for his first motion about the law to sanction the Order in Council, said, *in allusion to this meeting:* "With respect to the "first step to be considered, the state "of the Bank, that already has, in a "great measure, been ascertained by "the *confidence of public opinion.* Of "this public opinion, the most *unequi-"vocal and satisfactory proofs have "been afforded, even within the short "space that has elapsed since the mi-"nute of* Council has been issued. It "has been *clearly evinced*, that there "is no doubt entertained with respect "to the solidity of the Bank to "answer all the demands of its "creditors." Thus he appeared to consider the resolution of the Meeting of the Bankers and Merchants as expressive of the opinions and feelings of the nation at large, and, of course, as being a voluntary act, an act of *their own*, an act not, by any means, dictated *by him*, or by *the Bank*, nor hatched or contrived by them. Thus the thing appeared to the world; thus it appeared to the "*most thinking* "people in all Europe;" this was its outside look; but, let us now take a peep behind the curtain.

For a while, no official documents were laid before Parliament, relating to the Stoppage. This was avoided by one means or other. But, it could not be for ever avoided; and, at last, some of the papers were laid before the House of Commons; but, by the time that these got printed, the public was lulled again, and the papers passed with little or no notice. Amongst these papers, was a minute of the BANK DIRECTORS, respecting an "Interview with the Chancellor of "the Exchequer (Mr. Pitt) on the "24th of February 1797;" which, you will observe, was on the *Friday before*, the Bank having issued Gold on Saturday for the last time. On the Thursday, the run upon the Bank had been very hard; and, the measure of Stoppage of cash-payments seems to have *then* been looked upon as settled. With this measure in their eye, the Bank Directors and Mr. Pitt did what we shall see recorded in the following minute of the Bank Directors' proceedings, under the date just mentioned, of the 24th of February 1797. "The Governor and "Deputy Governor this day waited "on Mr. Pitt, to mention to him, "that it would, in the present cir-"cumstances, be *highly* requisite, that "some *general meeting of the bankers "and chief merchants of London* "should be held, in order to bring "on *some resolution* for the support "of the public credit in this alarming "crisis; and they took the liberty *to "recommend* to Mr. Pitt, to have *a "private meeting* of some of the chief "bankers at *his house to morrow*, at "three o'clock, in which *the plan* for "a more *general meeting* on Tuesday "or Wednesday next might be laid; "in the *propriety of which Mr. Pitt "agreed*, and said he would *summon "a previous meeting for to-morrow "accordingly.* This was communi-"cated by the Governor to the "Committee."

Thus, Gentlemen, were "the *most* "*thinking* people in Europe" treated. Here you see the origin; here you see the real cause, of the public *spirited meeting* at the Mansion House; here you see how those pure and disinterested persons were put in motion. You have, heretofore, seen the *show*; but, you have now seen, as to this part of it, the funnels, pullies, pegs and wires; and the only misfortune is, that you see them a little too late; though, I trust that the exposition may yet do some good, and at any rate, it must, I should think, make you a little less credulous in future, a little less inclined to believe every word that comes forth under appearances like those above described.

While Meetings were going on in such a jovial way, in all other quarters, it would have been strange indeed if the Bank itself had not had its meeting. This took place on Thursday, 2nd of March. The Order of Council had been issued on the Sunday, 26th of February; it had been laid before the House of Commons on the 27th; on the same day the Meeting had taken place at the Mansion-House; on the 28th. (as we shall presently see) the conduct of the Bank began to be discussed in parliament, and it had been asserted there, that the Order of Council was the sole work of the *government*, and not of *the Bank*; the manifest intention of which was to cause it to be believed, that the government *forced* the Bank *not to pay its creditors* agreeably to its promissory notes; and, that the Bank neither *wanted* nor *wished* any such measure *on its own account*. Declarations to this amount had been made in parliament; but, it appears, that a repetition of them at a Bank Meeting was thought necessary; and accordingly a meeting took place; or, to use their own language, "A "COURT OF PROPRIETORS was "held" on the day just-mentioned, namely, the 2nd of March.

At this meeting at the Bank, where one might have expected to see the Directors and Proprietors clothed in sack-cloth and ashes, the first thing done was, the passing of a vote of THANKS to the Directors for having acted *agreeably to the Order of Council*, that is to say, for having availed themselves of this Order to refuse payment of their promissory notes, to refuse payment of their just debts legally demanded. They had been guilty of a violation of the law, and for that violation they were *thanked* by their constituents, the stock Proprietors, who in fact, were the *Debtors* of the holders of Bank-notes! Having, with an *unanimous* voice dispatched this part of the business of the day, the GOVERNOR of the Bank took, it appears from the report of the proceedings, the opportunity of publicly declaring (in a way that might get into print) that the Bank Directors had *made no application to the government* for an order for the stoppage of Cash-payments at the Bank. Mr. BOSANQUET, who it seems, was a Director, declared, that the measure "was *not adopted* "*at the instance of those concerned in* "*the direction of the Bank*;" and Mr. THORNTON, also a Director, said, "that he wished it to be understood "*explicitly*, that the Order in Coun- "cil *was not issued at the instance of* "*the Bank Directors*." Mr. BOSANQUET called the stoppage "a great "*state measure*;" a measure dictated by "*national* policy." He said it was "meant to operate only for a *short* "*time*;" and that "he *earnestly hoped*" (how different from the language of Mr. Randle Jackson and the present governor of the Bank); yes, he EARNESTLY HOPED, "that the "Bank, which was *quite able*, would "soon be PERMITTED to pay its "notes in cash, in the same manner "that it had formerly done."*

* The following is the Report, taken entire, from the Morning Chronicle of the 3d of March, 1797.

When, Gentlemen, you have read through the report of the Bank Proceedings of the day here referred too, and I beseech you *to read every word of it*, you will, doubtless, be astonished at the hardihood of men, who could, under such circumstances, hold such language. What! *thank* the Directors for not paying their promissory notes! *Thank* them for this! The Proprietors of Bank Stock, who were the persons composing the Meeting upon this occasion, were the persons who owed the amount of the Bank-notes; they were the debtors of the note-holders; the Directors were their agents. So that, here we see a parcel of people, who had issued great quantities of

---

"Yesterday a Court of Proprietors was held at the Bank,—The GOVERNOR of the Bank, after the Order in Council, of the the 26th of February, was read, stated, that the Court of Directors had thought it their duty to acquiesce in the Order, and hoped they had acted in conformity to the opinion and wishes of the Proprietors of Bank Stock.—MR. HARMAN moved, "that it is the opinion of this Court, that the *thanks* of the Proprietors of Bank Stock are due to the Court of Directors for *their acquiescence in the Order in Council*, and for their speedy communication thereof to this Court." The motion was put and carried unanimously.—MR. ALLERDYCE asked, *whether the application had been made from the Bank to Government, for the Order in Council*, to prohibit them from issuing specie?—The Governor of the Bank replied, that *no such application had been made by the Court of Directors*, but that the Bank having experienced an unexampled drain of specie for some time past, that Court had thought it their duty to acquaint the Minister of the Country with the circumstance, that he might take what measures he might deem necessary, and at the same time remove all responsibility, for such measures from the Direction. He added, that a Secret Committee of the House of Commons had been appointed to enquire into the state of the Bank accounts, and that the Court of Directors were *fully persuaded that the result of that enquiry would be a report of the perfect solidity of the Corporation.*—MR. SANSOM wished to be informed whether there was any precedent for the House of Commons appointing a Committee to enquire into the affairs of the Bank? In his opinion, if a Committee was to be appointed it ought to be a Committee chosen from the Proprietary; but after the assurance which they had from the Directors of the solidity of the Bank capital, he saw no necessity for any enquiry at all.—A Proprietor stated, that there was a precedent for the measure on the Journals of the House of Commons, in 1696.—MR. MANNING said, he had examined into the proceedings of the House of Commons, in 1696, and found that there was not the smallest resemblance between that and the present measure. At that time the Bank had been established for only two years, their Notes were at a discount all over the Kingdom, and the Silver-coinage was called in, circumstances which were totally different from the present.—MR. BOSANQUET begged leave to trouble the Court with a very few words. He said that the Order in Council was to be considered *entirely as a great state-measure*, which was *not adopted at the instance of those concerned in the direction of the Bank*. The Court of Directors, in the present state of public affairs, had considered it to be their duty to keep the Minister of the Country informed respecting the situation of the Bank. For some time past there had been an *an unexampled ruin* for specie upon the Bank, and this they *communicated to the Chancellor of the Exchequer, leaving him to adopt what measures he might think proper.* The consequence was the Order in Council, of the 26th of February, was issued. It would have been *absurd* in the Directors of the Bank to have resisted this Order, because the Minister must have been supposed to be in possession of a great deal of information *to which they had no access*, and to be in the knowledge of circumstances of which they were not aware; besides, that there was no knowing what might have been the consequences had the unusual drain for cash, which they had experienced, been continued for any length of time.—They *complied*, therefore, with the Order of his Majesty's Council, understanding it to have been *dictated by national policy*, and *meant to operate only for a short time*. He had no hesitation in saying that the affairs of the Bank were in a state of the *greatest affluence of prosperity*, that they had even a considerable *surplus*, and that he *earnestly hoped* they would SOON BE PERMITTED *to pay their Notes in cash* in the same manner as they had formerly done.—MR. THORNTON wished it to be understood explicitly, that the Order in Council was *not issued at the instance of the Bank Directors*; that their accounts were not tendered to the House of Commons for examination, and that they neither *asked nor wished for the partnership and guarantee of Government*.—There being no other business before the Court, they adjourned to yesterday fortnight, when the dividends become due.

promissory notes, assemble together, and *thank*, aye, and *publicly thank*, their agents for having refused, *illegally refused, payment of those notes!* Gentlemen, our venal prints may talk as they please; they may refer us to what instances they choose; but any thing equal to this, any such instance of cool assurance, I defy them to produce from the history of the world, or, even from the works of imagination.

But, as yet, we have not seen these proceedings in their true colours. We have seen them in colours pretty strong; but we have not seen them as they will appear when we have taken another look at the Bank-documents, which were afterwards laid before parliament, and which, as was before observed, never got out fairly to the knowledge of the people. We have seen these Bank Directors making public declarations, that *they* had no hand at all in the Stoppage; that they did not *apply* for the Order in Council; that it was a measure of *the government*; that it was a *state*-measure; and that they *earnestly hoped* soon to be PERMITTED to *resume their payments in cash.* This is what they told *the public* on the 2nd of of March. And, it was not only at the Bank-meeting that this declaration was made. It was repeatedly made in the House of Commons; but, we will, at present, confine ourselves to what was said by the Bank Directors themselves.

Such, then, were their declarations on the 2nd of March. Now, then, let us see what they had been at *in secret* with the Minister, during the *nine days before.* On the 21st of February, they, observing, with great uneasiness, the large and constant decrease in their cash, held a particular consultation on the subject, and perceiving that their cash was reduced to a certain sum, of which certain sum, be it observed, *they do not state the amount*, they came to a resolution to go to Mr. Pitt, and tell him "how "their cash was circumstanced," they did so, and Mr. Pitt observed to them (and you will laugh heartily at the observation) "that the alarm of "invasion was *now become much* "*more general than he could think* "*necessary*," they then pressed Mr. "Pitt to make some declaration in "parliament, upon this subject, "in "order to *ease the public mind*."— This is a pretty specimen enough of the intercourse that existed between these parties, and will serve to explain the reason for many of the speeches that we have at different times heard.* MR. PITT, however,

---

* *Resolution of the Court of Directors, and Deputation's Interview with the Chancellor of the Exchequer, 21st February 1797.*

The Committee observing with great uneasiness, the large and constant decrease in the cash, held a particular consultation on that subject this day; and on examination into the state of the cash *since the beginning of this year*, they found that in the course of the month of January there had been a decrease of l. and since the beginning of this month a farther loss of l. and that the cash was now reduced to between l. and about l. value, in bullion and foreign coin, about the value of l. in silver-bullion. Perceiving also, by the constant calls of the bankers from all parts of the town for cash, that there must be *some extraordinary reasons for this drain*, arising, probably, from the alarms of an expected invasion; the Committee, after maturely considering the matter, resolved to send a notice to the Chancellor of the Exchequer, of the situation of matters at the Bank; and to explain exactly to him *how the cash is circumstanced*, that he may, if possible and and proper, strike out some means of *alleviating the public alarms*, and stopping this apparent disposition in people's minds for having a large deposit of cash in their houses. The Governor, Deputy Governor, with Mr. Darell and Mr. Bosanquet, were deputed to wait upon Mr. Pitt; who went to him; and after describing to him the anxiety of mind which all the Directors were under on this subject, they explained to Mr. Pitt the exact particulars abovementioned. Mr. Pitt seemed aware that this unusual drain of cash from the Bank must arise from the alarm of an invasion, which he observed was *now become much more general than he could think necessary*. He said, that by all his informations he could

did, it seems press them, in his turn, "to endeavour to obtain *a supply of* "*gold from abroad,*" and the Governor told him they would do what they could in that way.

On the 22nd of February they had another interview with Mr. PITT, and they gave GOLDSMIDT and ELIASON orders for the *purchase of gold at Hamburgh.* But we no where find any account of the success of this order, which was, besides, rendered useless by the Order of Council, which rendered Gold *unnecessary.**

On the 24th of February they had another interview with Mr. PITT; and what they say as to this interview we must pay particular attention to. At a Committee consisting of the whole Court, it appeared that the cash was going away faster than ever "which gave *such an alarm for the SAFETY OF THE HOUSE*" (mark the words) that no time was lost in sending a deputation to Mr. PITT, to ask him how far they might venture to go on paying cash, and "when "HE would think it necessary to "INTERFERE." Mr. PITT told them, that this was an affair of such *importance*, that he must be prepared with some resolution to bring forward in the Council: †

not learn of any hostile preparations of consequence making in France to invade this country, except the fleet which was refitting at Brest, after being driven off from the coast of Ireland; but that he could not answer that no partial attack on this country would be made by such *a mad* and *desperate* enemy as we had to deal with. The deputation pressed on Mr. Pitt to declare something of this kind in Parliament, in order to *ease the publicmind.* Mr. Pitt also mentioned, that he hoped the Committee would, in the present situation of matters, think it necessary to *endeavour at obtaining a supply of gold from foreign countries*, which the Governor told him they were considering about, and should do *what they could* therein.

* *Interview with the Chancellor of the Exchequer, 22nd of February* 1797.—Messrs. Goldsmidt and Eliason attended the Committee this day, and were directed to give farther orders to Hamburgh *for the purchase of gold*; and were told that an application would immediately be made to the minister to order a frigate or armed sloop to go to Hamburgh to take in such gold as might be bought, and also to desire that the restriction on the captains of the packets, not to take any gold on board at Hamburgh for this country, might be taken off. The Governer and Deputy Governor waited on Mr. Pitt on this subject, who promised to apply to the Admiralty for directions about sending out a frigate or armed sloop; and that he would apply to the Postmaster General to give the orders to the captains of the packets.

† *Interview with the Chancellor of the Exchequer, 24th of February* 1797.—At a Committee of the whole Court held this day, it appeared that the loss of cash yesterday was above '.and that about .. were already drawn out this day, *which gave such an alarm for THE SAFETY OF THE HOUSE*, that the Deputy Governor and Mr. Bosanquet were desired to wait on Mr. Pitt to mention to him these circumstances, and to ask him how far he thought the Bank might venture to go on paying cash, and when he would think it necessary TO INTERFERE before our cash was so reduced as might be detrimental to the immediate service of the State. Mr. Pitt said, this was a matter of great importance, and that he must be prepared with some resolutions to bring forward in the Council, for a Proclamation to stop the issue of cash from the Bank, and to give the security of parliament to the notes of the Bank. In consequence of which he should think it might be proper to appoint a Secret Committee of the House of Commons, to look into the state of the Bank-affairs; which they assured him the Bank were well prepared for, and would produce to such a Committee. Mr. Pitt also observed that he should have no objection to propose to Parliament, in case of a Proclamation, to give parliamentary security for Bank-notes. The Governor and Deputy Governor this day waited on Mr. Pitt, to mention to him, that it would in the present circumstances be highly requisite that some *general meeting of the bankers and chief merchants of London* should be held in order *to bring on some resolution* for the support of the public credit in this alarming crisis; and they took the liberty to recommend to Mr. Pitt, to *have a private meeting* of some of the *chief bankers at his house* to-morrow, at three o'clock, in which *the plan* for a more general meeting on Tuesday or Wednesday next might be laid, in the propriety of which Mr. Pitt agreed, and said he would *summon a previous meeting for to-morrow accordingly.* This was communicated by the Governor to the Committee.

Thus, you see, Gentlemen, the Stoppage-measure clearly *originated in the representation of the Bank Directors*; and, which is very well worthy of your marked attention, Mr. BOSANQUET was one of the persons deputed to wait upon Mr. PITT on this last mentioned occasion. The shuffle of saying, that the Bank Directors were afraid that the drain might injure the "*public service*" is too paltry, in any view of the matter, to have any weight; for, whose claim upon the Bank could be so good as that of the *holders of the Promissory notes?* And who were "the public" but the holders of these notes? But, as if it had been resolved to leave no room even for this miserable attempt at excuse, the Minute of the Directors of the 24th of February expressly says, that it was "*alarm for the safety of the* HOUSE" that sent the deputation to ask for the *interference* of Mr. Pitt; alarm for the safety of the HOUSE, and not any motive at all connected with the public service or the public good.

Having now pulled aside the curtain; having laid the whole thing bare to your view; having placed the application to Parliament in its true light; I shall, in my next, lay before you an account of the *measures*, which the Parliament adopted, and which have, under one pretence or another, been continued in force to this day.

In the meanwhile, I remain,

Gentlemen,

Your faithful Friend,

WM. COBBETT.

State Prison, Newgate, Thursday, October 25th 1810.

LETTER XIV.

"The question for the people to ask, and the only question, is this: whether the quantity of Bank Notes, "payable on demand, which the Bank has issued, be greater than the Bank can pay off in Gold and "Silver."——*Paine.*

The Measures adopted by Parliament, in consequence of the Bank Stoppage—Names of the Bank Directors in 1797.—King's Message—Mr. Pitt's Motion for a Secret Committee—Mr. Fox and other Members wished for an Inquiry into the Cause of the Stoppage—Mr. Pitt's Motion carried by a great Majority—List of the Minority—Necessity of a Parliamentary Reform---Manner of appointing the Secret Committee---Names of the Committee---Restricted Powers of the Committee---Reports from the Committee---Not a Word said about the Quantity of Gold and Silver in the Bank---Mr. Paine's Assertion about the Inability of the Bank to pay in Gold and Silver-- No Attempt made to disprove this Assertion---Mr. Pitt's, Sir John Mitford's, and Lord Hawkesbury's Assertions--Mr. Grey not satisfied with the Evidence produced before the Committee---Mr. Sheridan's Answer to Lord Hawkesbury.

GENTLEMEN,

I HAVE now to beg your attention to a very important part of our subject; namely, the *measures*, which, by way of *remedy*, were adopted by the Parliament, in consequence of the run upon the Bank and the Stoppage of Gold and Silver payments there.

The Letter immediately preceding this put you in possession of a thorough knowledge of the way, in which the Bank Directors and the Minister had gone to work, in order to prepare the way for the *Parliamentary* Measures which were to follow. You were there placed behind the curtain; you saw all the actors in their natural-persons;* all the paints, patches, cloaks and visors; all the trap-doors, pullies, pegs and wires. You not only saw the *Resolving* and *Subscribing* show acted, but you saw it got up; you saw the Showman and all his people busy in making their preparations; and, after that, you were let in to the rehearsal.

In Letter XII, at page 155, you have seen how the matter was first brought before the Parliament, on Monday the 27th of February 1797, in the form of a Message from the King; † and, you have seen, that the Minister, the hitherto-bragging Minister, being upon that occasion pressed by Mr. Combe and others for an answer to the question as to *what he meant to do*, had no answer to give.

On the 27th Pitt gave notice of a motion, to be made next day, for the appointment of a Committee to inquire into the *ability* of the Bank to pay the demands upon it; and also to inquire and make report as to the necessity of *continuing of the measure* adopted by the Council, that is to say, *continuing the refusal of money-payments at the Bank*.‡

We shall have to speak more fully about this Committee by-and-by; but we must stop here a moment, and take a brief sketch of the *debate* that ensued upon Pitt's motion. Mr. Fox and those who were with him said, that they had no objection to the appointment of a Committee, provided it was appointed fairly; but, they insisted, that it would discover a shameful disregard of their duty, if the House moved an inch further without inquiring into the *causes* which produced that alledged *necessity*, upon which the Order of Council, sanctioning a violation of the law, was *founded*. They said, here is the

---

* Truth and Justice demand, that, as far as possible, the NAMES of all the persons who took an active part, upon this memorable occasion, should be recorded. Parliament may yet *revise* the measures of that day; and, then, the names of all the parties, immediately concerned, ought to be known, and must be known.—From this opinion it is, that I insert here the names of the persons who were the Directors of the Bank of England, at the time when the Stoppage took place, and amongst them we find our friend, Brook Watson, who was, as we have seen, in the Chair at the Mansion-House Meeting.

Thomas Raikes,—*Governor*.
Samuel Thornton,—*Deputy Governor*.

T. Boddington.	Job Mathew.
S. Bosanquet.	Sir R. Neave.
Alex. Champion.	Joseph Nutt.
Edward Darell.	John Pearse.
Thomas Dea.	George Peters.
George Dorrien.	Charles Pole.
N. Bogle French.	John Puget.
Daniel Giles.	James Reed.
Jeremiah Harman.	P. I. Thellusson.
Thomas Lewis.	Godfrey Thornton.
Beeston Long.	Brook Watson.
William Manning.	John Whitmore.

† GEORGE R.

His Majesty thinks it proper to communicate to the House of Commons, without delay, the measure adopted to obviate the effects which might be occasioned by the unusual demand of specie lately made from different parts of the country and the metropolis.—The peculiar nature and exigency of the case appeared to require, in the first instance, the measure contained in the Order of Council which his Majesty has directed to be laid before the House. In recommending this important subject to the immediate and serious attention of the House of Commons, his Majesty relies with the utmost confidence on the experienced wisdom and firmness of his Parliament for taking such measures as may be best calculated to meet any temporary pressure, and to call forth, in the most effectual manner, the extensive resources of his kingdoms in support of their public and commercial credit, and in defence of their dearest interests. G. R.

‡ "That a SECRET COMMITTEE, be "appointed to ascertain the total amount "of the out-standing demands on the Bank "of England, and likewise of the funds "for discharging the same; and that they "do also report their opinion of the *necessity* of providing for the *confirmation and continuance of the measures*, taken in pursuance of the minute of Council on the 26th "instant."

Entered at Stationers' Hall.
Printed by Wm. Molineux, 5, Bream's Buildings, Chancery Lane; Published by Wm. Cobbett, Jun. No. 8, Catherine Street, Strand; and Retailed at 192, Strand.

minister calling upon you still to confide in him, in him, under whom the Bank has been compelled to stop paying its notes. Ought you not to inquire, first of all, into his measures? Ought you not to inquire into the *causes*, of the fatal and disgraceful necessity of this Stoppage? Here is a minister, who has had a majority of your votes for years; he has had your unlimited and blind confidence; he had the absolute command of all the resources of the nation; he has done what he pleased for years past; he has *within these very few weeks*, told you himself, and advised the King to tell you, in the most solemn manner, that your pecuniary affairs were in the most flourishing state, and rested upon the most solid foundation; and this same man now comes and tells you, that *necessity*, that *urgency*, that *something* had compelled him to issue an *Order to sanction the Stoppage of Cash payments at the Bank*, and to *oblige* the public creditor, contrary to law, to receive his dividends in paper instead of the Gold and Silver coin, which the law gave him a right to demand.

This, said Mr. Fox and his friends, is what this Minister now tells you; and, will you not, before you proceed to inquire into the propriety of *continuing* the Stoppage, inquire into the *cause* of the imperious necessity, which is said to have produced it? Will you attempt an expedient, will you attempt a remedy, without inquiring into the *cause* of the evil? Will you do that, which, even now, after all that you have seen and felt, shall prove to the world that your confidence is as blind as ever? "Have "any three months, in the course of "this war," said Mr. Fox, "past "without the minister's producing "some new expedient? and have not "all his expedients proved errone "ous? Year after year he has been "amusing us with predictions with "respect to France, which was now "on the verge and now in the gulf of "bankruptcy; the *assignats* and the "*mandats* could not possibly continue, "he said; which was very true, but "while he was thus amusing us, he "led us to the very same verge, aye, "into the very same gulf." Mr. Hobhouse said, "that the assur- "ances of the minister would never "beat down this plain dictate of "common sense, that by his conduct "the Bank had been obliged to com- "mit an act of insolvency, by re- "fusing specie for its paper, and, "therefore he wished for a full in- "quiry into his conduct." Mr. Sheridan, in a most admirable speech, laid the whole matter open, completely exposed the motive of the proposed committee, and moved to Mr. Pitt's motion an amendment, in the following words, "That the Com- "mittee should inquire into the causes "which produced the Order in Coun- "cil."

In spite, however, of these speeches; in spite of all the arguments made use of on this side, and none of which met with even an attempt at an answer from any one but Mr. Pitt himself; in spite of all this, the House decided, by a majority of 244 to 88, against Mr. Sheridan's amendment, that is to say, against in-

W. MOLINEUX, Printer, Bream's Buildings, Chancery Lane.

quiring into the *cause* of the alledged necessity which induced the Privy Council to issue an order, sanctioning a refusal, on the part of the Bank, to pay their promissory notes in Gold and Silver. The men, who voted upon this occasion, should be known. We have only the names of the *Minority* recorded. Those you will keep in mind, Gentlemen, and, before we have finished the subject, we shall come at the names of the *Majority;* or, at least, we can get the names of all the members *besides the minority.** Mr. Fox renewed the subject, on the 1st of March, by a motion for the appointment of a separate Committee "to inquire into the causes, which "produced the Order in Council of "the 26th of February," for the Stoppage of cash payments at the Bank; and he was *left in a similar Minority.*

Here it is, Gentlemen, that you see the real cause of all the calamities that have fallen upon our country, and of all the dangers that now threaten it, and these are dangers that will not be frowned out of countenance, that will not be made to hide their head, at the sound of the voice of men in power; dangers that are not to be *talked* or *voted* away. You have seen these dangers creep on upon us by slow degrees, but you have seen their pace to be steady. They have never stopped. They keep gathering about us; and he is a very foolish man, who expects any remedy, 'till the great cause of the evil be removed; that is to say, until there shall take place a radical Reform of the Commons' House of Parliament, agreeably to the principles of the English Constitution, which Reform, to use the words of the Kent Petition, is *now* more than ever necessary to the safety of both the people and the throne.

The motions for a full inquiry being rejected, the minister proceeded in his work of getting a SECRET COMMITTEE, who were to inquire into the *affairs of the Bank,* and to report their opinion relative to the necessity of *continuing,* by Act of Parliament

---

List of the Minority, on Mr. Sheridan's Amendment, on the 28th of February 1797.

Aubrey, Sir J.
Baker, J.
Bampfylde, J. C.
Barclay, G.
Bastard, J. P.
Beauclerk, C.
Biddulph, R.
Baker, W.
Bunbury, Sir C.
Bird, W. W.
Burdett, Sir F.
Bouveric, Hon. E.
Brogden, J.
Burch, J. R.
Byng, J.
Clarke, E.
Coke, F.
Combe, H. C.
Courtenay, J.
Crewe, J.
Curwen, J. C.
Copley, Sir L.
Dolben, Sir W.
Dashwood, Sir H. W.
Denison, W. J.
Dundas, C.
Fitzpatrick, General
Fletcher, Sir H.
Folkes, Sir R.
Fox, Right Hon. C. J.
Galway, Viscount
Greene, J.
Hare, J.
Harrison, J.
Hobhouse, B.
Hussey, W.
Jefferys, N.
Jervoise, C. J.
Keene, W.
Kemp, T.
Knight, R. P.
Langston, J.
Langston, W. G.
Lemon, Sir W.
Lloyd, J. M.
Miller, Sir W.
Nicholls, J.
North, D.
Northey, W.
Pierse, H.
Palk, L.
Phillips, J. G.
Plumer, W.
Pollen, G. A.
Porter, G.
Pulteney, Sir W.
Rawdon, Hon. J.
Rawdon, Hon. G.
Ridley, Sir M.
Richardson, J.
Robson, R. B.
Russell, Lord J.
Russell, Lord W
St. John, St. A
Scudamore, J.
Sheridan, R. B.
Shum, G. C.
Shuckburgh, Sir G.
Sinclair, Sir J.
Smith, W.
Spencer, Lord R.
Stanley, Lord,
Sturt, C.
Tarleton, General
Taylor, C. W.
Tyrwhitt, T.
Townsend, Lord J
Tufton, Hon. H.
Vane, Sir F.
Vyner, R.
Walwyn, J.
Walpole, Colonel
Western, C. C.
Wilkins, W.
Winnington, Sir F
Wycombe, Earl of

TELLERS.

Charles Grey *and* Samuel Whitbread.

the refusal of coin at the Bank. And now, Gentlemen, I beg you to observe well the *manner* of appointing this Committee. It was to consist of *fifteen* members; every member of the House, who was present, might put *fifteen* names into a box; and, when all the names were taken out, the fifteen persons whose names appeared *oftenest* upon the tickets put in, were the Committee. Of course that side which had a *majority of tickets to put in* would choose the members of the Committee. The custom, indeed, is, upon such occasions, to make out a *List* and send it round amongst the members, and of course, all those, who are on the side of the Minister, will take the Ministerial List; so that, in fact, whoever has a majority in the House, *chooses the Committee*. Upon the particular occasion before us, Mr. SHERIDAN, *before* the Report of *who were* the Committee was made to the House, *read the names of them out loud in the House*; and, when the report came to be made, it appeared, that *his List was perfectly correct*.* Indeed, he had got hold of one of the Ministerial Lists, and of course, he could not be in error in this respect.

But, even a Committee, thus formed; a *Secret* Committee *chosen by the Minister's own party*; even this Committee were, Mr. PITT said (See Debates, 28th February) "by no "means called upon to *push their in*"*quiries*, into circumstances, the dis"closure of which would be attended "with *temporary injury to the credit* "*of the country*, and with permanent "*embarrassment to the operations of* "*the Bank*." Mr. PITT said, that his principal object in appointing such a Committee was to have it ascertained, that the *affairs of the Bank were in a prosperous state*; that the Bank had abundant means to *answer all the demands upon it*; and that, therefore, the holders of Bank Notes ought to look upon them as being equally good with gold and silver. Now, the way, and the only way, to produce this so-much-wished-for conviction was, one would have thought, to let the Committee ascertain that the *quantity of Gold and Silver in the Bank* was sufficient for paying off the Notes; or, at any rate, was in a due proportion to the Notes. But, so far from this being done, the Committee did not make *any inquiries at all* relative to the *quantity of Gold and Silver* in the Bank. They merely inquired into the state of the books at the Bank, setting their *Bank-notes* on one side and their Stock on the other side. The Bank said: We owe the *holders* the amount of our Notes, but the *Government* owes us still more; and not a word was said about *Gold and Silver*, though one would have thought, that this was the great, and indeed, the *only* thing to make inquiry about; especially as Mr. PAINE, in his pamphlet, published the year before, had made statements, whence he had drawn a conclusion, that the Bank, if put to the test, "had not "money to pay *half a crown in the* "*pound*."

This was a charge, which, one would have thought, it would be the grand object of the Minister and the Bank to do away. But, no such thing

* *List of the Secret Committee.—William Hussey; William Plumer;* Thomas Powys; Thomas Grenville; William Wilberforce; John Blackburne; Thomas Berney Brampston; Charles Bragge; Sir John Mitford (Solicitor General); William Wilberforce Bird; John Fane; Isaac Hawkins Browne; Sir John Scott (Attorney General); John William Anderson.

The *three first* had, as will be seen by a reference to the List, voted with Mr. Fox for a full inquiry; but all the rest belonged to the party of Mr. Pitt.

was even attempted, and the two Reports of the Committee,* did ac-accordingly not at all tend to the restoration of *that sort* of confidence, which would have enabled the Bank to open its doors to the applicants for *Guineas*. It was in vain that Mr. PITT told the House, that the reports of the Secret Committee were highly *consoling;* that the affairs of the Bank were in a most prosperous state; that persons most conversant (alluding to the Mansion House Resolvers) believed in the solidity of its means; that the public had nothing to do with the internal economy of the Bank; that it was sufficient for the public to know, that the corporation was a rich corporation; that the solidity of the Bank was asserted in the report of the Secret Committee then on the table; that that report left *no doubt* upon the subject; that it was an important consolation, that there were funds *amply sufficient* for the ultimate security of those who could not have their demands satisfied for a time; and that as to what was due from the Government to the Bank, it rested upon the *best possible* security, because it rested upon the *aggregate powers of the country*. (See Debates 9th March 1797). In vain did Lord Hawkesbury, in answer to Mr. Fox,

---

* FIRST REPORT, March 3, 1797.—The Committee appointed to examine and state the total amount of out-standing demands on the Bank of England, and likewise of the Funds for discharging the same; and to report the result thereof to the House, together with their opinion on the necessity of providing for the confirmation and continuance, for a time to be limited, of measures taken in pursuance of the minute of Council on the 26th of February last; and who are empowered to report their proceedings from time to time to the House; have, pursuant to the order of the Honse, proceeded to examine into the several matters referred to their consideration, and have unanimously agreed upon the following Report, viz.—Your Committee have examined the total amount of outstanding demands on the Bank of England, and likewise of the Funds for discharging the same; and think it their duty, without loss of time, to state those total amounts, and to report the result thereof to the House.—Your Committee find, upon such examination, that the total amount of out-standing demands on the Bank, on the 25th of February last (to which day the accounts could be completely made up) was £.13,770,390; and that the total amount of the Funds for discharging those demands (not including the permanent debt due from Government of £.11,686,800, which bears an interest of three per cent.) was on the same 25th day of February last £.17,597,280; and that the result is, that there was, on the 25th day of February last, a surplus of effects belonging to the Bank beyond the amount of their debts, amounting to the sum of £.3,826,890 exclusive of the above-mentioned permanent debt of £.11,686,800 due from Government. And your Committee farther represent, that since the 25th of February last considerable issues have been made by the Bank in bank-notes, both upon Government securities and in discounting bills, the particulars of which could not immediately be made up; but as those issues appear to your Committee to have been made upon corresponding securities, taken with the usual care and attention, the actual balance in favour of the Bank did not appear to your Committee to have been thereby diminished.

SECOND REPORT, Tuesday, 7th March.—Mr. Brampston brought up the following Report:

The Committee appointed to examine and state the total amount of outstanding demands on the Bank of England, and likewise of the Funds for discharging the same; and to report the result thereof to the House, together with their opinion on the necessity of providing for the confirmation and continuance, for a time to be limited, of measures taken in pursuance of the Minute of Council on the 26th of February last; and who were empowered to report their proceedings from time to time to the House; have farther examined into the several matters referred to their consideration; and have agreed to report to the House;—That, in their opinion, *it is necessary to provide for the confirmation and continuance, for a time to be limited, of the measures taken in pursuance of the Order of Council on the 26th of February last;* submitting to the wisdom of parliament to determine for what limited time it may be necessary that those measures should be continued.

deny that the term *Bankruptcy* applied to the situation of the Bank or the Government. He said, what was very true, that the embarrassments of the Bank were imputed to the scarcity or *want of specie.* But, in vain did he question the truth of this proposition; in vain did he say that a *scarcity of guineas* might rise from an *increase of trade*, and not from the *the excess of paper;* (Debate 9th March 1797) in vain did Sir John Mitford, then Solicitor General (same Debate) say that no man, however rich, would be able to stand a run; that it was unfair to call the stoppage a Bankruptcy; that the Bank was solvent, although at this time unable to pay in cash; that the refusal to pay in cash could not be called a fraud, *because the public knew that such an event might happen;* that the stoppage at the Bank was like that which might be enforced by the door keepers of a theatre, upon a false alarm of fire, in order to prevent the people from rushing out all at once, to their destruction or injury; that if nothing had been done to put a stop to the run upon the Bank, the Bank must have been totally ruined; that there were other public creditors besides the Stock-holders, the *army* and the *navy;* that they were as much *public creditors* as the holders of Bank-notes could be, and that they required payment in cash more so than any other description of men in this country.

In vain was all this said. Mr. GREY (now Earl Grey), said that the evidence brought before the Committee had not satisfied him; and the satisfaction to the public was evidently not greater; for, if it had been satisfactory, or if the report of the Secret Committee had been satisfactory, there could have been no occasion whatever for continuing the power of the Bank to refuse payment in specie. This was told them by Mr. FOX and Mr. SHERIDAN, who asked: if the Bank be in so prosperous a situation as you say it is, why do you wish to pass a law to protect them against the demands of the holders of their notes? If the Bank be so rich as you say it is, what need has it of your assistance? You tell us, said Mr. SHERIDAN (alluding to the speech of Lord Hawkesbury) that paper " is not only a cleaner, neater, " and more portable medium to re- " present property; but that it is the " very essence of wealth itself, and " that the flourishing state of our " commerce is the cause of this in- " ability to produce specie to answer "demands upon the Bank of Eng- " land." See Debate of 9th March, where these observations are followed up by an inimitable instance of what is called by logicians the *reductio ad absurdum.* You tell us, said he, that the public are of your opinion, and that they reject our opinion; you tell us that the public are satisfied with the report of the Committee; you tell us that the public like Bank notes as well as guineas. But, with these assertions, upon your lips, you pass a *law* to protect the Bank against the demands of that public; you pass a law to *compel* that public to receive paper at the Bank, instead of that gold, which you say they like no better than that paper.

The truth is, Gentlemen, the public, generally speaking, knew nothing at all about the transactions between the Government and the Bank; they knew nothing at all about the trade or the property of the Bank; they knew that they held promissory notes issued by the Bank, payable to the bearer on demand, and they looked upon these notes as being equally valuable with gold, because, until now, they could, at any time, carry them to the Bank, and receive gold in exchange for them. Nothing, therefore, could have the smallest tendency to convince them of the solidity of the Bank, unless it, at the same time, tended to convince them, that there was *gold in the Bank,* sufficient to answer the demands of those, who presented notes for payment, or who chose to demand gold in payment of their dividends, or interest upon their Stock. And, not a particle of conviction, in this way, were the reports of the Secret Committee calculated to produce.

Mr. SHERIDAN (see Debate 28th February 1797) said that he was "convinced that if the Bank was not "able to resume its payments immediately, he foresaw it *never would* "*be able afterwards* to defray its "outstanding engagements in cash." And the reason he gave was that the suspension of cash payments would produce the issue of a greater quantity of paper. This reason was so manifest, that it was impossible that the truth of it should not be *felt*, though owing to the prejudices of the times, there were few persons amongst the Merchants and Bankers, by whom it would be acknowledged. The same was said, by Mr. NICHOLLS and Mr. HOBHOUSE, in whose speeches, together with those of Mr. FOX and Mr. SHERIDAN, will be found predictions of all the consequences, which have already flowed, and which are likely to flow from the stoppage of gold and silver payments at the Bank.

We have now seen enough of the measures which were adopted as forerunners of the *Acts of Parliament* relating to the Bank Stoppage; and, in my next Letter, I shall, I flatter myself, be able to present you with a complete, though a very concise, view of those Acts, with which every man in this country ought to be thoroughly acquainted. In the mean while, I remain,

Gentlemen,

Your faithful friend,

WM. COBBETT.

State Prison, Newgate, Thursday, November 1st, 1810.

LETTER XV.

"When the situation of the Bank of England was under the consideration of the two Houses of Parliament "in the year 1797, it was my opinion and that of many others, that *the extent to which Paper currency had been carried, was the first and principal*, though not the sole cause of the many difficulties, "to which that corporate body was then, and had of late years from time to time, been exposed, in supplying the Cash occasionally necessary for the commerce of the Kingdom; for the Bank of England being at "the head of all circulation, and *the great repository of unemployed cash*, it necessarily happens, that "whenever a sudden increased supply of Coin becomes indispensable, in consequence of private failures "or general discredit, by which Notes of the before mentioned description are driven out of circulation, "the *Bank of England can alone furnish the Coins which are required to make up this deficiency*, "and this corporate body is thereby rendered *responsible*, not only for the value *of its own notes*, which "it may have issued, but, in a certain degree, for such as may be issued *by every private Banker in the* "*Kingdom*, let the substance, credit, or discretion of such a Banker be what it may."—— LATE EARL OF LIVERPOOL. Letter to the King. Published in 1805.

"The Quantity of Cash in the Bank can never, on the evidence of these circumstances, be so much as two "millions; most probably not more than one million; and on this slender twig hangs the whole funding "system of four hundred millions, besides many millions Bank Notes. The sum in the Bank, if Mr. "Chalmers be correct, is not sufficient to pay one fourth of only one year's interest of the national debt, "were the creditors to demand payment in Cash, or to demand Cash for the Bank Notes in which the "interest is paid. A circumstance always liable to happen."——PAINE. Decline and Fall of the English "*System of Finance*. *Published in* 1795.

A more minute View of the Affairs of the Bank necessary—State of the Case between the Bank and the People—The Property of the Bank—The Statement of Debts and Credits in the Report of the Secret Committee—The Bank renders its own Account—The more detailed Statement published by Mr. Allerdyce—The Property of the Bank is in Paper and not in Specie—Amount of the Bank Notes compared with the Cash—The great Question was, what Cash and Bullion there was in the Bank—Mr. Paine's Opinion founded upon the Estimate of Mr. Eden and Mr. Chalmers—Error in supposing that the Minister took Specie out the Bank to send it abroad—Mr. Pitt's Answer to Mr. Hobhouse and Mr. Hussey—Mr. Pitt's Argument verifying the Opinion of Mr. Paine—The whole become a System of Paper.

Gentlemen,

In the foregoing Letter (at pages 191 and 192), we have seen the Reports of the Secret Committee of the House of Commons, relative, first, to the state of the Bank's Affairs; and, second, relative to the continuance of refusal of refusal of Cash Payments at the Bank. We shall next take a view of the Acts, passed by the Parliament, upon this memorable occasion; not, however, 'till we have looked a little more minutely into the state of the Bank's Affairs.

It was before observed, that the Committee, that even a *Secret* Committee, and that Committee; appointed, too, in the manner that we have seen (at page 189); that even a Committee like this were not permitted (to use the phrase of Pitt) to "push their inquiries into circumstances, the disclosure of which would be attended with injury to public credit." Accordingly, not a word do this Committee say about *the quantity of Gold and Silver in the Bank*, though the great, and, indeed, the *only* cause of the Stoppage, and of the whole of these proceedings, was, the alarm felt by the Directors at the daily decrease in their Gold and Silver. The question, and the only question of any importance to the peple, that is to say, to the holders of the Bank Notes, was: "Is there a quantity of real money in the Bank sufficient to pay us the amount of our notes, when we may choose to present them for payment." This was the question, to which the people wanted an answer; but with nothing relating to this question, were the Committee to meddle. This question was, with assurance unparalleled, said to belong wholly to the "*private economy* of the Bank, with which *the public had nothing at all to do.*"

Surely nothing ever was heard so impudent as this. The holders of the Bank Notes, the creditors of the Bank Company, the creditors of this Company of Merchants, carry their notes and demand payment; the Company of Merchants apply to the Minister, and he obtains from the Privy Council an Order to authorize the Company *to refuse to pay the just and lawful demands of their creditors*, and then the Minister, when he comes to the Parliament for an Act to sanction and to continue this refusal, tells the House of Commons, that even a Secret Committee of them, though chosen as we have seen, are *not to push their inquiries into circumstances*, the disclosure of which might injure the *credit of the Bank;* and yet he has the face to say, at the same time, that the report of this Committee cannot fail to *satisfy* the country of the *ability* of the Bank to pay all its outstanding demands.

Gentlemen, we will now look a little more minutely into that report. It states, that the *Government owes the Bank Company* £.11,686,800, which bears an interest of *three per cent;* that is to say, that the Bank Company, like our neighbour Grizzle Greenhorn, is a Stock-holder and has its name writtten in the GREAT BOOK; which Great Book, you will bear in mind, is kept *at* the Bank itself, and the interest upon the said stock is paid *by* the Bank Company *to* the Bank Company and *in bank-notes* made *at the order of* the Bank Company! This was all very fine, to be sure; but, it certainly did not go one inch towards convincing the holder of a bank-note, that the Bank was *able to pay him in Gold or Silver.* The Committee next state the means and the Debts of the Bank as follows:

Total amount of the Funds of the Bank (exclusive of debt due to it from the Government of £.11,686,8000) on the 25th of Feb. 1797	£.17,597,280
Total amount of outstanding demands upon the Bank on the 25th of February 1797	13,770,390
Surplus in favour of the Bank	3,826,890

This was all very fine again; but what was it to the *public?* What was it to the holders of the bank notes, who wanted *Gold* for them? Besides, *whence* came the *evidence* of the *truth* of this? The proofs of a trader's solvency is not, I believe, generally left to *himself.* The Bank Company had stopped payment, and, when an inquiry was taking place into the state of its affairs, and especially with regard to its *ability to pay,* how comes it that the inquirers were content with *its own statement and its own story?* This is not the way that inquiries are made into the affairs of other traders, when they stop payment. Mr. GREY, as we have seen before (See Debate of 9th March 1797), said that, though one of the Secret Committee the *evidence* had *not satisfied him;* and, indeed, what was this report more or less than the Bank's presentation of the state of its own affairs?

But, supposing the statement to be correct, still what was there to satisfy the people of the country; what to satisfy the holders of the notes, that the Bank was able to *pay those notes,* that is to say, to *give gold and silver for them.* For, as to *payment* in any other way, it is nonsense to talk of it. What was there, in this Report, then, to cause it to be believed, that the Bank was able to *pay* its notes? Here is very big talk; high-sounding words, and more high-sounding figures; but, if we put them to the scrutiny we find nothing at all in them: we find not the smallest circumstance to induce any holder of a bank note to suppose, that the Bank is, or ever will be, able to pay that note off, agreeably to the promise, expressed upon the face of it.

The statement, however, from which it appears, the Secret Committee made up their Report, was more in detail. This statement was afterwards given to the public by Mr. ALLERDYCE, a member of the then Parliament, and a person who constantly voted with the Minister. The statement thus given was as follows:

STATE OF THE FINANCES OF THE BANK OF ENGLAND, FEB. 25, 1797.

Particulars of Debt Account.		*Particulars of Credit Account.*	
Drawing Account	£.2,389,600	Bills and Notes discounted—Cash and Bullion	4,176,080
Exchequer Bills	1,676,000		
Unpaid Dividends	983,730	Exchequer Bills	8,228,000
Do. in Bank Stock	45,150	Lands and Tenements	65,000
Do. in India annuities	10,210	Money lent to India Company	700,000
Sundries unclaimed	1,330	Stamps	1,510
Due from Cash on the loan of 1797	17,060	Navy and Victualling Bills	15,890
		American Debentures	54,150
Unpaid Irish dividend	1,460	Petty Cash in House	5,320
Do. on Imperial loan	5,600	Sundry articles	24,150
		5 per Cent. annuities	795,800
	5,130,140	5 per Cents 1797	1,000,000
Bank notes in circulation	8,640,250	Treasury bills paid for the Government	1,512,270
	13,770,390	Loan to Government	376,000
		Bills discounted unpaid	88,120
Balance	3,826,890	Treasury and Exchequer fees	740
		Interest due on different Loans advanced to Government	554,250
	17,597,280		17,597,280

Now, what is all this? Why, it is, with the exception of *three of the items*, a mere account of *paper* between the *Government* and the *Bank*, and in which the people, who *held the bank notes*, could have no interest whatever. The Bank held Exchequer Bills, and Navy and Victualling Bills, and had lent money (that is to say bank notes) to the East India Company and had five per cent. stock and Treasury Bills and had interest due upon loans; all which might be very well for the Bank, but what was it to a man, who held a bank note and who could not get payment for it when he presented it to the Bank? These fine articles of credit were very good for the Bank Company; but what good were they to 'SQUIRE GULL, who, being alarmed at the prospect of a Jacobin invasion, wished, in spite of his loyalty, to turn his bank notes into guineas? What use were they to our neighbour GRIZZLE GREENHORN, who now wished, of course, to put by a few guineas, and who, of course, wished *to receive her dividends in gold*, to prevent her from doing which by *law* this very report was a *preliminary step?* What consolation was Grizzle to draw from this account of debts due from the Government to the Bank, especially when it was clear, that if the Government ever paid the Bank, it must *pay it in bank notes*, seeing that in bank notes *the taxes* were now paid?

The *three items* to which the people would look, were those expressing on one side, the *amount of the bank notes in circulation;* and, on the other, the amount of the *cash, or coin, and bullion in the Bank Company's House*, commonly called the Bank. According to the above statement these were on the 25th of February 1797, as follows:

Amount of Bank Notes in circulation	£8,640,250
Bills and Notes discounted, Cash and Bullion	4,176,080
Petty Cash in the House	5,320
	4,181,400
Difference	4,458,850

But, who is to say how much the Bills and Notes *discounted* amounted to? Who is to answer, that they did not make one half; who is to say, that they did not make *nine tenths* of the sum of £4,176,080? Why was the amount of the *cash* and *bullion* huddled up in one sum along with the amount of Bills and Notes discounted! Why were things so different in their nature confounded together? If GRIZZLE GREENHORN wanted her bank notes payed at the Bank, she would not take *discounted bills* in payment. What the nation wanted to see, was, how much the Bank had of *that sort of thing, in which bank notes could be payed;* how much it had of that sort of thing, the value of which *no invasion or revolution would destroy:* how much it had of that sort of thing, in which it had *promised to pay upon demand the bearers of its notes;* how much, in short, it had of MONEY, and not of *bills and notes discounted*, with which the people had nothing at all to do, there being no man of common sense, who could care a straw about how much of its paper the Bank gave to others for their paper, so that he got guineas for his bank notes; and, if he could not get this, what consolation was it to him to know, that the Bank had lent but little of its paper to the merchants?

As to the exact quantity of *cash and bullion* in the Bank, when the Stoppage took place, MR. ALLERDYCE gives a table, shewing the amount at stated periods, for several years, according to which Table, the total amount of the cash and bullion in the Bank, at the time of the Stoppage, was £.1,272,000. Aye, ONE MILLION, TWO HUNDRED AND SEVENTY-TWO THOUSAND POUNDS. He comes at this sum thus. The Bank of England have *Numbers*, to denote their quantity of *cash and bullion*. When they submitted their accounts to Parliament, in 1797, it was thought necessary to keep the amount of the *cash and bullion* a secret from Parliament and the public. They, therefore, only gave the *Numbers* for distinct periods in several years, in order to shew the proportionate increase or diminution of the cash and bullion. From these *Numbers*, however, a discovery was, it is said, made, and the sum above-named, ascertained to be the amount of the cash and bullion in the Bank at the time of the Stoppage. But, upon this, I wish to place no *reliance;* nor do I care, whether the statement above given, of cash and bullion and discounted bills be correct, or not. These are things of inferior consequence compared with the great and well-known facts; namely, that no proof was produced, or attempted to be produced, that the Bank Company had gold or silver, or both together, sufficient to pay its promissory notes; and that no account was rendered to the Parliament of the amount of the cash and bullion in the Bank.

Mr. PAINE had, only the year before, said, in the words of my motto, that the quantity of cash in the Bank could never, on the evidence of circumstances, be so much as *two millions*, and most probably, *not more than one million;* that, on this slender twig, always liable to be broken, hung the whole funding system of four hundred millions, besides many millions in bank notes; that the sum in the Bank was not sufficient to pay one fourth of only one year's interest of the National Debt, were the creditors to demand payment in cash, or to demand cash for the bank notes in which the interest is paid: a circumstance always liable to happen. Mr. PAINE founded this opinion upon a statement of Mr. EDEN (now Lord AUCKLAND) and Mr. CHALMERS, Clerk to the Board of Trade, who had given an account, or, rather an estimate, of the gold coin circulating in the kingdom; and, it is truly surprising to observe how near Mr. PAINE was to the exact truth as to this point, though at the time when his pamphlet was published, its calculations and predictions were treated with scorn, and the work itself was ascribed to a malicious desire to cause the *ruin* of England; just as if it were in the power of PAINE, or of any one else, to injure the credit of a *nation;* or, as if any thing but the want, the real want of the gold and bullion could shake the faith of the public in such an establishment as that of the Bank. PAINE might have written 'till this time without persuading any one that *a guinea* was a thing not to be relied upon. He never would have written people out of their belief in the goodness of *guineas*. And, if the Bank had stood a run for only *one week*, he might have written his pen to the stump, but would not have shaken the people's confidence. Credit that has a *solid* foundation need fear no assaults.

At the time, when this subject was under discussion in the House of Commons, the Minister was charged, by the Opposition, with having *taken the Money from the Bank* and sent it abroad *in subsidies*. This was certainly a very great *error*, or, it was made use of for the purpose of *annoying the Minister* at the expence of truth. I am, however, disposed to attribute it to error; for, it was urged in such a manner, and by such persons, as to obviate all suspicion of its being a mere party weapon. Mr. HOBHOUSE (Debate 28th February 1797), said, that he suspected that the money had been buried in *Ger-*

many, and not by the people of England, in dread of invasion. And Mr. HUSSEY said, that the Minister "had *laid his rapacious hands upon* "*the sums destined for the payment* "*of the public* creditor. He knew "that the public creditors had been "refused their just demands. He "had witnessed the truth of this woe"ful circumstance himself. He had "been told by a person who had ap"plied for payment, that, in payment "of a sum of *twenty-three* pounds, "*three pounds* in cash had been of"fered, and the rest only in notes. "Such a melancholy day as this for "England he had hoped never to live "to see. Let the Chancellor of the "Exchequer *pay the ten millions* "*Government owed the Bank, and* "*then it would be able to fulfil all its* "*engagements*. It was not that the "Bank was unable to satisfy its cre"ditors, but it was the *continued de*"*mand of money to feed the expences* "*of this ruinous and disastrous war*, "which rendered it unjust to those "who depended upon its credit."

Mr. PITT, who seemed to have avoided this point with all his care, and who, as I once heard Mr. WINDHAM describe him, was so dextrous in the selection and use of words as to be able "to speak a king's speech "off-hand," could not remain longer silent under this attack. He had been told nearly the same by Mr. SHERIDAN; but he seemed to be willing to take the chance of that being ascribed to *party* motives. When, however, he heard the same, seriously urged by Mr. HUSSEY, and saw that the notion was making its way amongst the public, and of course, that the whole of the calamity would be ascribed to him and his Anti-Jacobin war, he could no longer refrain from declaring what was the *nature of the property of the Bank*, and to avow, that the whole of its transactions with Government, or nearly so, were transactions of *paper*, a fact of which the country had, till that moment, been in complete ignorance.

He said that Mr. HUSSEY was wholly in error to suppose that the Bank made advances to the Government in *specie*; he said, that the advances were made in *notes*, and paid in the *same* manner; that, if the Government were to raise money and pay the Bank, the Bank would *not thereby be supplied with an additional guinea in cash*; that the taxes were *not paid in specie*; that loans were advanced without any expectation of *re-payment in specie*; that the Bank never had it in contemplation that every quarterly dividend was to be paid *in cash*; that the receipt of the revenue was *in paper*, and that the whole of Mr. HUSSEY's observations were intirely founded in mistake.

Mr. SHERIDAN, in answer to this, said, that the deficiency, or inability at the Bank arose not merely from the positive want of cash, but from the disproportion between the quantity of cash and the quantity of paper; and, of course, that, if their lent paper was returned to them, they would find themselves at liberty *to issue more of their specie*. This would have been true in a state of things where the *difference* between the quantity of specie and the quantity of paper was less; but, in the present case, it was too great for confidence to be restored, and, of course, for the Bank to return to its payments in cash. Mr. PITT's answer was complete. It was the plain truth, which he was obliged to bring out, in order to divide the blame with the Bank. He was told to *borrow* and to pay the Bank what he owed them. What good will that do, said he, when my loan will consist of Bank notes, and I must pay the Bank in those notes? He was told to raise the sum in *taxes* and so pay the Bank. What good will that do, said he, when my taxes will consist of Bank notes, and I must pay the Bank in those notes. The answer was complete towards his adversaries in debate, and not less complete as a demolisher of his own reputation as a Minister of Finance. He now said precisely what Mr. PAINE had said the year before; he now confirmed, with his own lips, what PAINE had been so abused for saying.* He appears clearly to have perceived his dilemma; but, to extricate him from it was beyond the power even of his dexterity. He was obliged to acknowledge, that the whole was become a *system of paper*, or, that *he had taken the gold from the Bank*, and, of the two evils he chose that, which would expose him to the least share of public odium.

This view of the State of the Bank's Affairs has led me further than I expected; but it was quite necessary as an introduction to that of the Acts of Parliament, which will be the subject of my next.

I am, in the meanwhile,

Gentlemen,

Your faithful friend,

WM. COBBETT.

State Prison, Newgate, Monday, November 5th, 1810.

LETTER XVI.

"It is admitted that a paper medium, under the form of bank notes or Government securities, is circulated "in France, England, and most other commercial countries; but nobody is compelled by law to receive "the payment of any debt in such money: hence it is, that the paper of those countries bears no "resemblance to ours, except in name. Every man receives a bank note or refuses it at pleasure. "When he receives it, he knows that on the next hour he may have it changed for gold or silver, as the "Bank is obliged to make such payments on demand. For this reason, bank-notes being portable, are "frequently preferred to coin of the weighty metals."——SYLVIUS, on the American paper-money, 1787

Introduction of the Bank Restriction Act into the House of Commons—The Origin of this Measure—The Bill moved for by Mr. Pitt—Suspension of the Two Acts Prohibiting Small Promissory Notes—The Title and Preambles of those Acts—The Principles of those Acts—Title and Preamble of the Bank Restriction Act—View of the Provisions of that Act—The Legal Tender—The Meaning and Application of the Word Restriction.

GENTLEMEN,

We have now to take a view of the *Acts of Parliament*, passed in consequence of the Stoppage of cash payments at the Bank of England; then to see what was, at the passing of these Acts, said by the advocates of them, respecting their *duration*; and this will enable us to form a pretty correct judgement as to the statesman-like wisdom of those advocates, and also as to the probability of the Acts

---

* I speak here of those writings merely of Mr. PAINE, which relate to *Finance*, without wishing to convey any commendation of some of his other writings, the subjects of which, are in no-wise, connected with this subject. In the principles of finance he was deeply skilled; and, to his very great and rare talents as a writer, he added an uncommon degree of experience in the concerns of paper-money, the rise and fall of which he had witnessed in the American States and in France. Truth is truth, come from whom it may; and there is no greater folly than that of rejecting it, that of shutting one's eyes and ears against it, merely because it proceeds from persons, of whose conduct, in other respects, one may disapprove. The writings of LORD BACON are held, and justly held, in great estimation; though he was, as our elegant and virtuous poet describes him, "the meanest of mankind." The late Lord Liverpool, Mr. Pitt, Mr. Fox, Mr. Sheridan, Mr. Nicholls, Mr. Hobhouse and others, and as we shall see by-and-by, a Committee of the House of Commons, have since acknowledged the truth of the principles of Mr Paine's work. Events have proved the truth of them, and, to point out the fact, is no more than an act of justice, due to his talents, and an act the more particularly due at my hands, I having been one of his most violent assailants. Any man may fall into *error*, but a fool or a knave will seldom *acknowledge* it.

ever being hereafter removed, except by a total annihilation of the paper-money.

Until the time at which the Bank Stoppage took place; until the 26th day of February 1797, the Notes of the Bank Company were considered as good as real money, because, if the holder chose it, he could, at any moment, demand and receive real money in exchange for them. But, when the Bank, in the manner that we have seen, refused payment upon demand, the nature of the notes was wholly changed. They were no longer equal in value to real money; and nothing but a species of *compulsion* would, of course, induce the people to receive them in payment of any debt theretofore contracted.

Now, then, came the pinch. Now came forth the fact, that it was beyond all the powers of hypocrisy, trick, and confusing verbosity any longer to disguise: forth came the fact, that Bank Notes were to be, in reality, *forced* upon the people; that the man, who had a debt due to him, must take them in payment, or if he refused them, be unable to arrest his creditor: forth came the fact, aye, forth it came, after all the railing against French assignats; forth came the fact, that no man who held a Bank note; that no man who held a note of that Company of Traders, payable on demand, could compel them to pay him, except *in other such notes.* Forth came this fact, and yet those who had brought the finances of the country into such a state, were still kept in power; to their management were the nation's affairs still left: to their promises did the credulous and affrighted people still listen; and of their measures has the nation ever since been feeling, and will, it is to be feared, long feel, the consequences.

The Order of the Privy Council (See it in Letter XI, page 149) required the Bank Company *to stop paying their notes in money.* The words are "to *forbear* issuing any "cash in payment." I beseech you, Gentlemen, to consider well the nature of this transaction. Look back at the origin of the Bank. Consider it, as it really was, a mere Company of Traders. Then view the holders of the Notes, who were so many legal creditors, so many persons having a just and legal claim to be paid upon demand. See all these creditors at once deprived of their legal rights of payment by *an Order of the Privy Council,* of which the Minister himself was a member. See here a Company of Traders, having promissory notes out to the amount of many millions, *required* by the Privy Council "to "*forbear*" to pay off the said notes; and above all things, observe, and NEVER FORGET, that this order, or *request,* was made in consequence, as we have seen from the official documents, of *representations made by this Company of Traders themselves,* who, as is stated in those documents (Letter XIII, page 172), made such representations in consequence of the drain upon their cash and of the alarm they therefore felt for the *safety of their House.*

This was a fine spectacle to behold: it was a fine thing to be held forth to the world by a Minister, whose boasting about his financial resources and about his support of public credit had been incessant from the day he first vaulted into the saddle of power. If this could be done with regard to one Company of Traders, why not with regard to any other Company of Traders, or any other single Trader, in the kingdom? If the Privy Council, avowedly upon the representation of the Minister, were to protect this Company of Traders against the lawful demands of their creditors; what reason was there that other Traders, that other Debtors, should not be protected in the same way, if they should "feel "*alarm* for the *safety of their House?*" We must never lose sight of this fact, that the Order in Council arose from a representation of the Minister; that representation arose from one *made to the Minister by the Bank Company*; and this latter representation arose (See Letter XIII, p. 179) from the drain of cash at the Bank, and from the alarm which the Bank Company felt for the safety of their House. This should be constantly kept in view. We should never, for one moment, lose sight of the fact, that the whole of this measure of protection to the Bank had its *origin* in representations *made by the Bank Company itself*. And, if we keep this fact steadily in view, we shall be in no danger at coming at a proper conclusion.

Thus far then, we have seen the transaction going no further than the Privy Council. We have seen it originate with the Bank Company, the demands of whose lawful creditors had given them alarm. We have seen the Bank Company calling upon the Minister to know when he would *interfere*. And, we have seen the Minister, after saying, on the 24th, that *he would prepare a resolution of Council*, go to the Council, on the 26th, and obtained the Resolution and Order that we have seen. Thus the Privy Council became a party to the transaction; and we are now about to see how the Parliament put the finishing stroke to it by giving to the Order of Council the sanction of law; we are now about to take a view of the Legislative Acts, by which, to use the expression of the late Lord Liverpool, *paper-credit* was exchanged for *paper-currency*, by which *bank-notes* were moulded into *paper-money*.

In Letter XII, page 164, we have seen how the minister first introduced to the House of Commons the project of passing *a law* to sanction the Order in Council; that is to say, to sanction the refusal of the Bank Company to pay their promissory notes. We have seen, that, upon being asked by Mr. ALDERMAN COMBE, whether he meant to make the bank-notes a *legal tender*, he knew not what to answer; that he twisted and writhed in great apparent embarrassment of mind: but, that he knew not what to answer. We have also seen, that, before the House met the next day (28th of February 1797) the meeting at the Mansion-House had taken place, having been, as we have seen, previously contrived, in private, with the Minister. We have seen an account of the other Meetings through the country; and we have seen, in Letter XIV, the manner of forming the SECRET COMMITTEE, from whom came Reports (Letter XIV, p. 189), declaring the affairs of the Bank to be in a most *flourishing* way, and that the Company were possessed of a great *surplus* of means.

Thus prepared, and perceiving, by this time, that his adherents were resolved to stand by him (See Letter XIV, p. 194) the Minister, on the 9th of March, 1797, moved for leave to "bring in a *bill* to *confirm* and "*continue* the Order in Council of "the 26th of February, for a time to "be limited." This was the first motion towards making of the *law* for authorising the Bank to refuse to pay its creditors their just demands; that law, which has filled the kingdom with banks and with paper-money, and which, as we shall by-and-by see, has produced no small share of our present dangers and distress. But, before we proceed any further in the history of this ACT, which, you will bear in mind, is the Act, which the Bullion Committee have proposed to repeal in two years from this time; before we proceed any further in the history of this Act, we must shortly notice two other Acts, which were passed before it, and which, though of inferior importance, were the *first-born* of the Bank Stoppage.

The refusal of the Bank Company to pay their notes was, as every one must naturally suppose, productive of the consequence of driving all the gold coin out of circulation; for, under such circumstances, the moment a guinea or a half guinea got into the hands of a person *able to keep it*, and not an ideot, it would remain very quiet in the chest of that person; and, as the smallest notes then in circulation, were notes for *five pounds*, the difficulty in making payments would necessarily be very great. The distress, arising from this cause, was so great, that on the 1st of March, it was resolved by the House of Commons to bring in a bill to legalize the issuing of *small notes* by private persons; and, on the same day a bill was read a second time for enabling the Bank of England to issue notes *under five pounds*.

The reason for passing these Acts was this: there were in existence two Acts of Parliament, which prohibited the negociating of promissory notes and other paper of an amount under *five pounds*. These Acts are, upon this occasion worthy of our particular attention; because they were passed upon the principle, that *small paper promises* were *injurious to the community*. The first of these Acts was passed in the year 1775, and, as will be seen from the Title and Preamble, which I beg of you to read,* *small paper currency* was, at that time, declared *by law* to be of "*great prejudice to trade and public credit.*" There were in 1775, as we have already seen, no bank-notes for sums less than TEN POUNDS, and, it was then supposed, that smaller notes would be an injury. In two years after the above Act was passed the effect of it having been found good, another Act was passed carrying the prohibition to any sum under *five pounds*. And, Gentlemen, I beg you to pay particular attention to the language of these Acts. The first says, that the circulation of notes for very small sums, *in lieu of cash*, is to the great prejudice of *trade* and *public credit*; and, after the Parliament have had two years' experience of the effects of this Act, they pass another, in which, after declaring that the effects of the former Act have been "*very salutary*," they extend the provisions of it from the sum of *twenty shillings* to the sum of *five pounds*.† Thus, then, small paper currency was proved to have been an evil; it was proved, by experience, to have been injurious *to trade* and to *public credit*; and, therefore, while there were no bank notes for sums less than

* FIFTEENTH GEO. III. Chap. LI.—An Act to restrain the negociation of promissory notes and inland bills of exchange under a limited sum, within that part of Great Britain called England.—Whereas various notes, bills of exchange, and draughts for money, for *very small sums*, have for some time past, been *circulated* or negociated in *lieu of cash*, within that part of Great Britain called England; *to the great prejudice of trade and public credit; &c. &c.* Be it, therefore, enacted by the King's most excellent Majesty, by, and with the advice and consent of the Lords Spiritual and Temporal, and Commons, in this present Parliament assembled, and by the authority of the same. That all promissory or other notes, bills of exchange, or drafts, or undertakings, in writing, being negociable or transferable for the payment of any sum or sums of money, *less than the sum of twenty shillings* in the whole, which shall be made or issued at any time from and after the twenty-fourth day of June, one thousand seven hundred and seventy-five, shall be, and the same are hereby declared to be, absolutely void and of no effect, any law, statute, usage, or custom to the contrary, therefore in any wise notwithstanding.

† SEVENTEENTH, GEO. III. Cap. XXX.—An Act for further restraining the negociation of promissory notes, and inland bills, of exchange, under a limited sum, within that part of Great Britain called England.—Whereas by a certain Act of Parliament passed in the fifteenth year of the reign of his present Majesty (intituled an Act to restrain the negociation of promissory notes and inland bills of exchange under a limited sum, within that part of Great Britain called England, all negociable promissory or other notes, bills of exchange, or draughts, or undertakings in writing, for any sum of money *less than the sum of twenty shillings* in the whole, &c. &c. and whereas *the said Act hath been attended with very salutary effects*, and in case the provisions therein contained *were extended to a further sum, the good purpose of the said Act would be further advanced*. Be it, therefore, enacted, &c. And the Act extends the prohibition to any sum under *five pounds*.

ten pounds, the law forbade that there should be any other *circulating* or *negociable* notes, under five pounds.

Thus, as to paper-currency, stood the law in 1797, when the Bank Stoppage took place; and as we have already seen, in the former part of this Letter, the country was, in consequence of the Stoppage, thrown into the greatest distress for the want of something to represent small sums. The manufacturers, and, indeed, all the journeymen and labourers, throughout the kingdom, could not be paid in the usual manner. The *coin* had *disappeared*, as it naturally would the moment a bank-note would not fetch its amount in guineas at the Bank; and, the guineas and half guineas having gone out of sight, which they did instantly, there were no means of paying small sums. Therefore, the very first thing to be done, was to provide something to supply the place of the guineas and half-guineas, and, indeed, the whole of the coin, except the hammered-out shillings and sixpences, such as we now see current.

For this purpose, it was necessary to pass an Act to *repeal*, or, at least, to *suspend*, the two Acts, of which we have just taken a view, and, accordingly a *suspension* Act was passed on the 10th of March 1797, the title and preamble of which Act are here inserted as worthy of attention, and as matter for future remark.* This Act, by which the suspension was to be continued only till the first day of the then ensuing month of May; that is to say, for *forty days* only, was, as we shall by-and-by see, afterwards extended in its duration, and has continued in force till this day.

But, this was nothing without giving a power of making small notes to the Bank of England. The Bank had dividends to pay; and, of course, all the sums, or parts of sums, under *five pounds* (there being, as yet, no notes under that sum) they were still compelled to pay in cash, which was what they *did not like*, and, in fact, what they were not, perhaps, able to do. It was, therefore, necessary, above all things, to give them a power of making small notes. There was a *doubt* whether the two Acts of the 15th and 17th of George the Third, above-mentioned, applied to bank notes; and, it was thought by some persons, that they did not so apply; but, an Act of Parliament, the great cure for all doubts and difficulties, was passed to remove this *doubt;* and such was the *haste* in doing this, that the Act was *passed* on the *3rd of March*, though the bill was brought in only on the *28th of February*. This Act authorized the Bank to issue notes for sums *under five pounds;* and, accordingly, *two* and *one* pound notes were immediately issued.†

Now, Gentlemen, I beg you to stop here for a moment, and take

* THIRTY SEVENTH Geo. III, Chap. XXXII.——An Act to suspend for a limited time, the operation of two Acts of the fifteenth and seventeenth years of the reign of his present Majesty for restraining the negociation of promissory notes, and inland bills of exchange, under a limited sum, within that part of Great Britain called England.——Whereas an Act of Parliament was past in the fifteenth year of the reign of his present Majesty, intituled an Act to restrain the negociation of promissory notes, and inland bills of exchange, under a limited sum, within that part of Great Britain called England: And whereas another Act was passed in the seventeenth year of the reign of his present Majesty, intituled, an Act for further restraining the negociation of promissory notes, and inland bills of exchange under a limited sum, within that part of Great Britain called England; and whereas IT IS EXPEDIENT that the said Acts *should be suspended for a certain time*, so far as the same may relate to any notes, draughts, or undertakings made payable on demand: &c. &c. &c. The Act then suspends those laws until the first day of *May* 1797.

† THIRTY-SEVENTH Geo. III. Chap. XXVIII.——An Act to remove doubts respecting Pro-

Entered at Stationers' Hall.

Printed by W. MOLINEUX, 5, Bream's Buildings, Chancery Lane; Published by W. COBBETT, Jun. No. 8, Catherine Street, Strand: and Retailed at No. 192, Strand.

another look at the language of these Acts of parliament, these solemn declarations of the Legislature. In the year 1775, they say, that the circulation of small notes, in lieu of cash, is of "great *prejudice* to *trade* and "*public credit.*" In 1777, they declare, upon the evidence of two years of experience, that their having lessened the quantity of small notes had produced "*very salutary effects.*" And in 1797, under the ministry of PITT, whose *debts* the public have paid, and for whom they are to pay for a monument; aye, under the ministry of this man, the parliament were brought to declare, that to make small notes, that to do just the contrary of what the above two acts were intended to effect, was "*expedi nt* for the *public service*, and "for the *convenience of commerce.*" In 1775 and 1777 it was enacted, that small promissory notes, in lieu of cash, were "a great *prejudice* to "*trade* and *public* CREDIT." In 1797 it was enacted, that small promissory notes, in lieu of cash, were "*expedient* for the *public service* and "for the *convenience of commerce.*" Gentlemen, when you have paid due attention to this, you will hardly want any thing more to enable you to answer those, who have yet the folly or the impudence to attempt a defence of the ministry of PITT, who, as it has been well observed, in reply to one of his eulogists, found the country *gold*, and left it *paper*.

But, the grand measure was yet to come. There was, as yet, no *law* to sanction the deed of refusing to pay the bearers of the Bank's promissory notes. This was a thing that the people had yet to receive at the hands of those, who had plunged them into the Anti-jacobin war, and who had fed them with the hopes of beating France through her finances. Yes, the people of England, the "most *thinking* peo-"ple," had yet to swallow this; they had yet to gulp this bolus from the hands of those, who had buoyed them up for so many years, by comparisons of the *flourishing* state of the English finances compared with those of France, which last nation they still believed to be, as PITT told them, "in the very gulph of bankruptcy."

This measure was, as we have seen, introduced into the House of Commons, in form, on the 9th of March, 1797, in a motion made by PITT, for leave to bring in a Bill for continuing, for a limited time, what he called the RESTRICTION (pray mark the word) upon the Bank, relative to its issue of specie. This Bill, after undergoing the discussions, some of which I shall have to notice more particularly by-and-by, became a *Law*, on the 3rd of May, 1797.*

missory Notes of the Governor and Company of the Bank of England, for payment of sums of money under five pounds.——Whereas it is *expedient* for the *public service*, and for the *convenience of commercial circulation*, that the Governor and Company of the Bank of England should issue Promissory notes, payable to bearer, for sums of money *under five pounds*; &c. &c.

* THIRTY-SEVENTH Geo. III. Chap. XLV. ——An Act for confirming and continuing for a limited time the *Restriction* contained in the minute of council of the twenty-sixth of February, one thousand seven hundred and ninety-seven, on payments of cash by the Bank.——Whereas, by minute of his Majesty's Privy Council, made on the twenty-sixth day of February, one thousand seven hundred and ninety-seven, upon the representation of the Chancellor of the Exchequer, stating, that from the result of the information which he had received, and the inquiries which it had been his duty to make respecting the effect of the unusual demands for specie, that have been made upon the metropolis, in consequence of ill-founded or exaggerated alarms in different parts of the country, it appeared, that unless some measure was immediately taken, there might be reason to apprehend a want of sufficient supply of cash to answer the exigencies of the public service; it was declared to be the unanimous opinion of the board, that it was indispensably necessary for the public service, that the directors of the Bank of England should forbear issuing any cash in payment, until the sense of Parliament could be taken on that subject, and the proper measures adopted thereupon for maintaining the means of circulation, and supporting the public and

W. Molineux, Printer, Bream's Buildings, Chancery Lane.

When you have read the Title and Preamble of this Act, you will accompany me in a brief sketch of its provisions, which you will find not only curious and interesting, as an object of public attention, but useful also to each of you as *individuals*, who will hence learn, how far you are *compelled* to receive payment in Bank-notes, and in what way your previous contracts have been affected by this Act.

The Preamble of the Act having repeated what was contained in the *Order of Council*, and having declared that to *confirm* and *continue* the refusal to pay in Gold and Silver, though such refusal was *not warranted by law;* having acknowledged the *illegality* of the things done, and declared the necessity of *continuing to do* them; having made this beginning, the Act next proceeds, SECTION I. to *indemnify* the Bank Directors, and all other persons for having done these illegal things; that is to say, to protect all such persons against any *appeal to the law*, that any suffering party might be inclined to make. So that, whatever loss or hindrance or injury any man might have suffered from the non-payment of the promissory notes of the Bank-Company, such sufferer was, by this Act, at once deprived of all legal means of obtaining redress. The Act next provides, in SECTION II. that the Bank should be liable to no prosecution for the non-payment of any of their notes, that they might be willing to *exchange for other notes*, and, that in case the Bank were sued by any one for the non-payment of their notes, they might apply to *the Court* to *stop proceedings in such actions*, who might stop them accordingly, and without costs to the plaintiff in any action brought against the Bank for non-payment of its notes, unless *the Court* should think the action *necessary*. SECTION III. *Permits* the Bank to issue cash in payment of any sum *under twenty shillings*, or where less than twenty shillings should be a fractional part of a sum to be paid by the Bank. This was a very gracious *permission!* The same Section *allows* them to issue cash for the service of the *Army*, the *Navy*, or the *Ordnance*, in pursuance of an order of the Privy Council. SECTION IV. Specifies that the Bank, during the restriction or stoppage, shall not advance to the Government any cash or notes exceeding in amount 600,000 pounds. SECTION V. Permits the Bank to repay cash to *those persons that may choose to lodge cash in the Bank*. But, the Section permits the Bank to repay *in cash* only three fourths of the amount of what shall be so lodged with them.

SECTIONS VI. and VII. Permit the Bank to advance the sum of 125,000 pounds to the Bankers of London and Scotland. SECTION VIII. Treats of payments between private individuals, and it provides, that all payments which have been made, or which shall be made during the continuance of this Act, in Bank of England notes, shall be deemed payments in cash, if accepted as such. SECTION IX. Contains the great alteration made in the law between debtor and creditor. We have seen, that by the 2nd Section, the Bank notes were made to be *quite equal to cash* in the case of all demands, made upon *the Bank* for payment of its notes, which therefore, made the notes of the Bank, as far as related to debts due from the Bank, on account

commercial credit of the kingom at this important conjuncture; and it was ordered, that a copy of the said minute should be transmitted to the directors of the Bank of England, and they were hereby required, on the grounds of the exigency of the case, to conform thereto until the sense of Parliament could be taken as aforesaid: And whereas, in pursuance of the minute, the said governor and company of the Bank of England, have, since the said twenty-sixth day of February, one thousand seven hundred and ninety-seven, *forborne* to issue cash in payments, except for purposes for which the issue of cash *was deemed unavoidable*; it is necessary that the *Restriction* in the said of its notes, a LEGAL TENDER, which words mean such money or currency as the law regards as good in the payment of debts. Guineas, for instance, are a LEGAL TENDER, because, the tender or offering of them in payment is sufficient to prevent any action or proceeding at *law* being entertained against the person, who may have offered them in payment, in quantity equal to the amount of the debt. But, Bank-notes were not made a legal tender, and they are not now a legal tender, between *private individuals*. If a man owe me money, I can still demand *coin* in payment; and the only difference is, that I cannot, if my debtor tender me the amount of the debt in Bank of England notes, cause him to be *arrested and held to special bail*, as I might have done, if this Act had not been passed. This part of the Act every one should read, and, therefore, I have put the 9th Section in a note*, SECTION X. Provides that the collectors of the public revenue shall accept payment in Bank of England notes. SECTION XI. Permits the Bank to issue cash, in certain cases, upon giving five days' notice to the Speaker of the House of Commons. SECTIONS XII. and XIII. Provide for the continuance of the Act to the 24th of June (a duration of only *fifty-two days*), and for the repealing or altering of it during the then present session of parliament.

This, Gentlemen, is what is called the Bank-RESTRICTION Act, a very convenient phrase, calculated to convey the notion, that the Bank is *able* and *willing* to pay; but, that it is *not permitted* to do it. I beg you to bear along with you the meaning of the word *Restriction*, which implies an act done by one party to prevent another party from doing *what he would do if not prevented*. To *restrict* is to *limit*, or *confine*. I am *restricted*,

---

minute, although *not warranted by Law*, should be *confirmed*, and should be *continued* for a limited time, by the authority of Parliament: Be it therefore enacted, &c. &c. &c.

* SECTION IX.——And be it further enacted by the authority aforesaid, That during the continuance of the restriction on payments by the said governor and company in cash, imposed by this Act, no person shall be held to special bail upon any process issuing out of any court, unless the affidavit which shall be made for that purpose according to the provisions in the Act of the twelfth year of the reign of his late Majesty King George the First, for preventing frivolous and vexatious arrests, shall not only contain the several matters required by the said Act, but also that no offer has been made to pay the sum of money in such affidavit mentioned, and therein sworn to, for the purpose of holding any person to special bail, in notes of the said governor and company, expressed to be payable on demand (fractional parts of the sum of twenty shillings only excepted;) and if any process shall be issued against any person, upon which such person might have been held to special bail before the passing of this Act, and no affidavit shall be made as aforesaid, that no such offer of payment in notes of the governor and company had been made as aforesaid, such person shall not be arrested on such process, but proceedings shall be had against such person in the same manner as if no affidavit had been made for the purpose of holding such persons to special bail, under the provisions of the said Act of his said late Majesty King George the First; and all provisions in such Act, or in any other Act of Parliament, for preventing frivolous and vexatious arrests, shall be applied to the provisions in this Act contained, so far as the same are capable of being so applied: Provided always, that if affidavit shall be made upon which any person or persons might have been held to special bail upon any such process as aforesaid, before the passing of this Act, and it shall be likewise sworn in such affidavit, that such offer of payment has been made as aforesaid, so that the person or persons who might have been arrested and held to special bail upon such process, if this Act had not been made, cannot, by reason of such offer and of the provisions in this act contained, be so arrested and held to special bail, it shall be lawful for the court out of which such process shall issue, or for any judge of such court, in a summary way, to order the defendant or defendants in the action in which such process shall issue, and who might have so held to special bail as aforesaid, if this Act had not been made, to cause notes of the said governor and company, expressed to be payable on demand to the amount of the sum of money for which such person or persons might have been so held to special bail, if this Act had not been made, to be deposited in such manner as

for instance, from going out of Newgate. I am here in a state of *restriction.* I should go home to my farm and my family, if it were not for this restriction; and so "the *most thinking* people of Europe" think, of course, that the Bank Company would pay their notes in Gold and Silver, if they were not *restricted* in the same manner. But, of this we shall see more in the next Letter, when we come to speak of the *duration* of this restricting Act; and, in the mean while, I remain,

Gentlemen,

Your faithful friend,

WM. COBBETT.

State Prison, Newgate, Monday, November 12, 1810.

LETTER XVII.

"Nothing but a law, declaring bank-notes to be a *legal tender* of payment, can relieve the bankers and "the trading part of the community from the hardships to which they are now liable; and yet, the "remedy must, in the end, be worse than the evil."——*Mr. Hobhouse.* Speech in the House of "Commons, 27th March, 1797.

The Legal Tender—Gold is the only Legal Tender for any Sum above 25 Pounds—Acts of the 14th and 39th of Geo. III.—Mr. Huskisson's Remark upon the Legal Tender—The Effects of a Legal Tender in Paper—Illustrated by the Case of New Jersey—Act against Legal Tender in Paper, 4th Geo. III. chap. 34—Mr. Huskisson's Misstatement as to the Notions entertained respecting the Legal Tender at the passing of the Act of 1797—Mr. SHERIDAN's Prediction when the Act was moved for---Sir F. Baring proposes to make the Notes a Legal Tender---Mr. Pitt declines it for the present---The Mansion House and other Meetings had, in some sort the effect of Law---The Law as it now stands as to the Legal Tender of the Bank of England Notes---Country Bankers may be compelled to pay their Notes in Gold.

GENTLEMEN,

BEFORE we proceed in our inquiries as to the DURATION of the Act, which was the subject of the foregoing Letter, and by which the Bank of England was protected against the *cash demands* of the holders of their promissory notes; before we proceed in these inquiries, which will discover matter not a little curious in itself, and, very interesting as connected with *what is now going on;* before we thus proceed, I must beg your attention to a few more words upon the subject of the LEGAL TENDER.

The truth is, that *gold* and gold *only* is a legal tender, in this kingdom, for any sum above 25 pounds, unless the silver be tendered in *weight.* This was settled by an Act, passed in 1774 (14 Geo. III. Chap. 42), which Act provided, that no tender in payment of money made in the *Silver* Coin exceeding the sum of 25 pounds, should be deemed a legal tender for more than its value by weight, at the

---

such Court or Judges shall direct, to answer the demands of the plaintiff or plaintiffs in such action; and if such deposit shall not be made within the time limited by such order, after such notice thereof as shall thereby be directed to be given, it shall be lawful, upon affidavit duly made and filed, that such deposit has not been made according to such order, to arrest such defendant or defendants, and hold him, her, or them to special bail, in such and the same manner as if the said Act had not been made.

rate of 5*s.* 2*d.* for each ounce of Silver. This Act continued in force for two years, when it expired; but it was again revived in the year 1799, and made perpetual. Thus, you see, that even Silver *coin* was not, except in small sums, a legal tender, and is not a legal tender to this day.

But, though the Bank of England notes were not by the *Restriction*, or *Stoppage* Act, made a legal tender, *to all intents and purposes*, they were made so to a certain extent; for, by the tender of them in lieu of money, *any* debtor could escape *arrest* and also escape the giving of *special bail*; and, as to the Bank of England, the Act not only protected it against the demands of its creditors; that is, against the holders of its notes, but by the same Act, the Bank was to *pay to the public*, any thing due from the former to the latter, in its notes, and not to be compellable to pay in gold or Silver. This was going some way, at least, in making bank-notes a *legal tender*, and this seems to have been overlooked by Mr. HUSKISSON, (a Gentleman of whom we shall have much to say by-and-by,) who in speaking of the *change* created by the Act of 1797, in our money system, observes, that that Act did not repeal any of the former regulations relating to the *coin*, and that it did not alter the Act of the 39th of the King. "It "did not," says he, "alter in any "respect the existing state of the law, "either as to the weight or the fine-"ness of the gold coin; or the Act of "the 39th of the King." I have quoted this Gentleman's own words, because I am not quite sure that I clearly understand them. Mr. HUSKISSON is a member of parliament, and a pensioner, and such people are apt to talk in a style that common men cannot comprehend. Whether he means, here, that the *weight* and the *fineness* of the Act of the 39th of the King remained unaltered; or, that the *existing state of the law* as to the Act of the 39th of the King remained unaltered; or, that the Act of the 39th of the King did *itself remain unaltered;* which of these may be his meaning, I cannot positively say; but, of this I am sure, that, in all the three suppositions, it was quite unnecessary to express such meaning, seeing that the Act, which he so positively and carefully assures us was not *altered* by the Act of 1797, was not in existence at the time, and was not passed till two years afterwards.

The mischievousness of *forcing* paper-money upon a people are very well known. It has been most severely felt in all the countries where it has been resorted to, and it has never failed, sooner or later, to annihilate the whole of the paper, attempted so to be forced upon the people. This was the case in all the States of North America, every one of which has, first or last, had a *public debt*, a *paper-money*, a *legal tender in paper*, and a *state bankruptcy*. The last of the States, I believe, that clung to a legal tender in paper, was NEW JERSEY; and, the consequence was, that, even in the year 1792, when I first went to the United States, that part of the Union was still suffering from the disreputation brought on it by the *legal tender*, which, before it was put an end to, had not only produced a total stagnation of trade, and had brought ruin upon thousands of people, but it had begun to drive the people out of the State; and, had it not been put an end to, the State would long ago, have been *wholly depopulated.*

But we need not go *abroad* for any thing to convince us of the settled opinions of statesmen and politicians as to the effects of a *legal tender in paper.* We have only to look into our own Statute-Book, where we shall find the thing sufficiently reprobated, as in the Act passed in the year 1763, which declares such a *tender* to be *discouraging and prejudicial to trade and commerce*, and the cause of *confusion in dealings and a lessening of credit*, in the Provinces where it was in use; and, having declared this; having laid down these as principles, the Act goes on to forbid the issuing of any more such paper; it makes void all Acts of Assembly thereafter passed to establish or keep up such tender; and it inflicts a fine of 1,000 pounds (with immediate dismission, and future incapacity to fill any public office or place of trust) on any Governor, who shall give his assent to such Act of Legal Tender.*

Mr. HUSKISSON, who was one of the *Bullion Committee*, of the labours of which we shall soon see a good deal; Mr. HUSKISSON, who enjoys a large *pension*, paid out of the taxes raised upon the people, and who, therefore, ought to understand something of such matters; this Mr. HUSKISSON (of whom I shall have to tell you a great deal before we have done) has just *published a pamphlet*, under the title of, "The Question concerning the Depreciation of our Currency stated and examined;" to the doing of which he was, it would seem, like Rosa Matilda, *reluctantly forced by the pressing partiality of friends*. This Mr. Huskisson, in his pamphlet, which is, apparently, intended to justify his conduct as a member of the Bullion Committee, has said, that "if "it had been proposed, at once to "make bank-notes a legal tender and, "in direct terms, to enact, that every "man should thenceforward be obliged "to receive them as *equivalent to the "gold coin* of the realm, *such a pro-"position would have excited universal "alarm*, and would have forcibly "drawn the attention of the legisla-"ture and the public to the nature of "our circulation and to the conse-"sequences of such an innovation. "But, certainly, *nothing of the sort "was in the contemplation of any "man* when first the suspension-act "was passed." But, is this *true*, Mr. Huskisson? Your *memory* fails you, I hope; for, not only was it in the *contemplation* of many persons; but several persons said, that, *in effect*, the bank-notes would become a *legal tender*, and that, they would, of course, depreciate.

Gentlemen, it is at all times right, that the *truth* should be known, respecting the conduct and the characters of men in any-wise entrusted with the management of the public affairs; and, at *this time*, and especially as relating to this most important subject it is right that no part of the truth should be hidden. With this conviction in my mind, I shall be rather minute in my references to what was said at the time when the Act of 1797, which protected the Bank against the demands of the note-holders, was under discussion.

The bill, as was stated in my last, was moved for by MR. PITT on the 9th of March; and during the debate of that very day, Mr. FOX contended, that, if the bill passed, the property of the Stock-holder must, at once, be

* FOURTH YEAR, Geo. III. Chap. 34. An Act to prevent Paper Bills of Credit, hereafter to be issued in any of his Majesty's Colonies or Plantations, in America, from being declared to be *a legal tender* in Payments of Money; and to prevent the legal tender of such bills as are now subsisting from being *prolonged* beyond the periods limited for calling in and sinking the same. ——Whereas great quantities of Paper Bills of Credit have been created and issued in his Majesty's Colonies or Plantations in America, by virtue of Acts, Orders, Resolutions, or Votes of Assembly, making and declaring such Bills of Credit to be legal Tender in payments of Money. And whereas such Bills of Credit have *greatly depreciated in their value*, by means whereof *Debts have been discharged with a much less Value than was contracted for*, to the great *discouragement and prejudice* of the *Trade and Commerce* of his Majesty's Subjects, by occasioning *Confusion in Dealings*, and *lessening Credit* in the said Colonies or Plantations:——The Act then proceeds as above described.

depreciated in value; and, Mr. SHERIDAN said, that "he believed we "should not long be able, after the "inundation of paper to which this "system gave birth, to stop them "from making bank-notes *a legal* "*tender*, and then adieu to the ap- "pearance of specie at the Bank, "and soon afterwards to the *real* "*value* of the Bank note." When the bill was under discussion on the 27th *of March*, Mr. PITT having said, that the clause, respecting the bar to arrests for debt, did not go the length of making Bank Notes a legal tender, nor to take away the power of the creditor to pursue the debtor *in the usual course of law*, in order to obtain payment in *cash*. Sir FRANCIS BARING said, that he saw no means of avoiding the evil to be apprehended by bankers and merchants but that of making Bank Notes a *legal tender*; and Mr. DENT was for making Bank Notes *a legal tender* during the suspension of cash payments. Now, what did Mr. PITT say, in answer to this suggestion from his *friends?* He said, that "as to "making Bank Notes a *legal tender*, "he thought, that, if *it was possible*, to "meet the present difficulty without it, "it ought to be met without it; that, "upon a subject of so much difficulty "and uncertainty, *no man could speak* "*with confidence;* but, that *as long* "as the circulation rested upon paper "taken by consent, he thought it "would not be *adviseable* to have it "taken *by compulsion*."

Upon this ground, the Act was passed; and, it is very clear, that one of the objects of the short duration of the first Act, which was passed for only 51 days, was, to see whether people were inclined to have recourse to the law to compel *payments in cash* for debts due from private individuals to other private individuals. Every means, as we have seen, had been taken to prevent this. A planned Meeting of Bankers and Merchants had been held at the Mansion House in London, and its resolutions for taking and circulating Bank Notes had been issued under the sanction of the then LORD MAYOR. Similar resolutions had been issued from the several benches of *Justices* at the quarter sessions, in all the counties; and, indeed, as these resolutions were signed by the Clerks of the Peace, and had about them all the air of acts of authority, the effect upon the farmers and tradesmen in general was nearly the same as that of an Act of Parliament, making Bank Notes a *legal tender*. If these means had failed, however, there can, I think, be very little doubt, that the measure of making Bank Notes a *legal tender* would have been adopted; for, the only reason which Pitt offers, as we see above, for not doing it at once, is, that the people seemed, *at present*, to be disposed to take the Bank Notes as cash *without compulsion*; and, he very clearly meant, that, if the people refused to consider them as cash, *compulsion* must and would be resorted to.

And yet, after all this, and with these facts recorded in the Parliamentary Proceedings of the time, Mr. HUSKISSON, who was actually in office under PITT or DUNDAS when the measure was discussed; with all this before his eyes, this Gentleman tells the public, that neither the making Bank Notes a *legal tender* nor *any thing of the sort* was in the *contemplation of any man* at the time when the Act for the suspension of cash payments was passed; and that any *proposition* of the kind would have *excited universal alarm*, and would have forcibly drawn the attention of the legislature and the public to the possible consequences of such an innovation!

Here, Gentlemen, we have an instance either of the *incorrectness*, I might say, the *ignorance*, or the *insincerity*, of Mr. Huskisson, who, to say the truth, is not without his temptations, as we shall by-and-by see, to draw a veil over the origin and the conduct of the originators of the measure of protecting the Bank against the demands of the note-holders; to do which it was absolutely necessary either to make Bank Notes a *legal tender*, or to do something that should answer the same purpose. To make them a *legal tender* by law, at once, would, indeed, have been a thing so shameful as not to be endured, in the face of the principles laid down by the Parliament, in the Act of the 4th year of Geo. III. above quoted. To pass a law making English Bank Notes a legal tender, putting English Bank Notes upon a level with the colonial paper mentioned in that Act; to make Bank Notes the degraded thing there described, was what could not be thought of, until all the means of avoiding it had been tried; but, it is, nevertheless, very clear, that if the circulating; if the promulgating (with all the appearance of official authority) of the resolutions from the Mansion House and from the benches of county Justices; it is very clear, that if these had failed in giving currency to the Bank Notes, these notes would have been made a *legal tender* in all cases, and to all intents and purposes whatever. They are a legal tender *from the Bank itself.* They are a legal tender to the Stock-holder in payment of his *dividends.* No man can sue the Bank Company on account of their refusing to give him gold for any of their promissory notes of which he may be the holder; nor can any Stockholder sue the Bank Company on account of a refusal to pay him the amount of his dividends in cash.

They are certainly *not a legal tender* between man and man, any farther than as far as relates to the barring of an *arrest* and of the necessity of *special bail.* You cannot arrest, or demand special bail from the debtor, who tenders you the amount of your debt in Bank of England notes; but you may sue him in the other way. The tender of Bank Notes secures the debtor from arrest and from being obliged to give special bail, in the first instance; but, it does not protect him against being *finally* compelled to *pay in cash.* If, for instance, GRIZZLE GREENHORN owes either of you a hundred pounds; or, which is better illustration, perhaps if you have in your hands a hundred and five pounds in amount of the notes of Messrs. PAPERKITE & Co. Country Bankers, and you have a mind to have gold for those notes, looking forward to a time when you may want them, and having a greater attachment to the king's picture than to the arms and crests of Paperkite & Co. In such a case, you go to Paperkite with his notes, and demand *payment* of them. He tenders you, as a matter of course, Bank of England notes to the amount of those of his own which you present for payment; but you, in pursuance of your design to be possessed of a hundred of the King's pictures, demand *gold*, and stick to that demand. If he cannot, or will not, pay you in gold, you cannot *arrest* him or compel him to put in *special bail*, but, you can bring the ordinary action of debt against him, the decision of which is *sure* to be in your favour with the usual costs, and, while the action is going on, he is obliged to *deposit the Bank of England notes in court,* as the ground of being protected in the meanwhile against arrest and against the demand of special bail; and, if he does not make this deposit, you can even *arrest* him, as in any other case of refusal or inability to pay.

Thus, Gentlemen, stands the law, with regard to the legality of a tender of Bank of England notes. The Tax-gatherer cannot refuse them in payment of taxes; the Stockholder cannot refuse them in payment of his dividends; and the note-holder cannot demand *coin* for them of the Bank Company or of any body else, of whom he has once *received* them in payment; but, any private individual may *refuse* them in payment of money due to him from any body but the Bank Company; and, may proceed to recover payment in real money, in the way above described.

Thinking it desirable to keep this subject of the *Legal Tender* distinct from that of the *Duration* of the Act of 1797, and having necessarily a good deal to say upon the latter subject, and much interesting matter to develope, I shall not enter thereon till my next Letter; and, in the mean while, I remain,

Gentlemen,

Your faithful friend,

WM. COBBETT.

State Prison, Newgate, Monday, November 91th, 1810.

LETTER XVIII.

"He hoped gentlemen would direct their most serious attention to the subject. The bill was of the utmost "importance; if a paper currency were once established, how could it be got rid of? If gold and silver "were once driven out of circulation, how were they to be recovered? The sure consequences of a paper "currency would be a debt so enormous, that it would never be removed. The old debts and the new would "vanish together, and the funded property would sink with them. A revolution in property might produce "a revolution in Government, and all those scenes of blood which had disgraced France."—MR. "NICHOLLS. Debate, 27th March 1797. On the Bank Restriction Bill.

Duration of the Bank Stoppage or Restriction Act—Recapitulation of the Dates of the principal Occurences leading to the Act—Apparent Reluctance with which the Bank Company submitted to the Restriction—They now discover that they have no Objection to be restrained—Mr. Huskisson says that the Duration could not have been foreseen—The probable Reason of this—Mr. Huskisson's Places and Pensions—Such a Person ought to have foreseen these Consequences of the Act—Others did forsee them.

GENTLEMEN,

WE now come to that subject which naturally connects the proceedings and measures of 1797, with the Report of the Bullion Committee, namely, the DURATION of the Act of 1797, that Act, which was made for the purpose of protecting the Bank Company against the legal demands of the holders of its promissory notes, and which Act, as you will not fail to bear in mind, arose out of an alarm felt by the Bank Company *for the safety of their House.* It is very material to keep constantly in view the progress which ended in the passing of this Act, which, as you will have already perceived, did, in fact, decide the fate of the paper-money in England; and, therefore, I will here again place before you a recapitulation of the dates of the principal occurrences.

February 21st, 1797, the Directors of the Bank, "observed "with *great uneasiness* the large "and constant *decrease in their* "*cash*," a deputation of them went to the Minister (Pitt) to make him acquainted therewith; and, as they attributed the run to the alarm of invasion, they begged of the Minister to say something in Parliament, "in "order to *ease the public mind* "upon that score."

February 24th. At a meeting of the Directors, it appeared that the "loss of cash yesterday was "above £ and that about "£ * were already drawn

* There were *no sums* inserted. The statement of sums was left *in blank* as it is here.

"out this day, which gave *such "an alarm, for the safety of the "House,"* that a deputation was sent to Mr. Pitt, to ask him when he would think it necessary to *interfere*. At this meeting with the Minister it was agreed, that a resolution should be by him prepared to bring before the Council for stopping payments in cash; also that a general meeting of Bankers and Merchants should be contrived in order to pass resolutions to support public credit; and the Minister, *at the recommendation of the Deputation*, agreed to get a *private* meeting of the chief bankers at *his house* the next day, in order then to lay the *plan* for a general meeting.

February 26. The Order of Council was issued, stating, that the Minister had given the Council such information relating to a run upon the Bank, as induced the Council to *require*, and they therefore did *require*, the Bank Company to *forbear issuing any cash in payments*, until the sense of Parliament should be taken upon the subject.

February 27th. An immense crowd of people assembled early in the morning at the doors of the Bank and in Threadneedle-street, in order to get gold for the notes they held; but, instead of gold they received a notification, that they might have *bank-notes* lent to them in discounts, and that the *dividends*, or interests upon stock, would be *paid in the same manner*. Whereupon they retired, shaking their long ears, and consoling themselves with the hope, that they would get gold in a week or two.

On he very same day (27th Feb.) the general Meeting of Bankers and Merchants, *which had been proposed to the Minister by the Bank Directors*, was held at the Mansion House in London; that is to say, the State House of Lord Mayor (Brook Watson) the *Chief Magistrate* of the City, who was Chairman of the Meeting, and who signed the Resolutions, to which, therefore, the air of *authority* was given.

February 28th. The Privy Council, including all the Ministers, of course, had a Meeting, and signed an agreement to take and give bank-notes in the same way as the Bankers and Merchants who had signed their resolutions.

March 2nd. The Magistrates met at the Quarter Sessions for the County of Surrey, signed an agreement of the same sort, which was promulgated "*by Order of the Court*," and was signed, like any other *magisterial act*, by the *Clerk of the Peace*. The like was done in all the other counties.

March 3rd. At a meeting of the Bank Company, consisting of the Bank Proprietors in general, was passed an unanimous *vote of thanks* to the Directors for having *obeyed* the order in Council and for having *refused to pay in cash*. From this Meeting it was promulgated, that *no application* had been made by the Bank Directors for the Order to withhold cash; that the measure was *not adopted at the instance of those concerned in the direction of the Bank;* that they *complied* with the order, *understanding* it to have been dictated by *national policy*, and meant to operate only for *a short* time; that their affairs were in a state of the *greatest affluence*, and that they *earnestly* hoped they would soon be **PERMITTED** to *pay their notes in cash* in the same manner as they had formerly done.

March 9th. The Ministers moved in the House of Commons, for

leave to bring in a Bill to sanction what had been done by the Privy Council and by the Bank Directors; to protect both against any legal proceedings for having done an unlawful act; and to authorize the Bank Company to CONTINUE to refuse to pay their notes in cash, for a certain time to be named.

May 3rd. This Bill became a *law;* and by it the Bank Company were authorized to refuse to pay their promissory notes in cash, until the *24th of June* in that same year; that is to say for *fifty two days.*

Such, Gentleman, was the progress which ended in the passing of the *Cash Stopping* Act, which is generally called the BANK RESTRICTION Act, and which, to those, from whom the above facts have been kept hidden, would, from this name as well as from the language of the Act itself, appear to have been made without any *application* for such a measure on the part of the Bank Company, and even *against the wishes* of that Company, who would, from outward appearances, be looked upon as being *compelled* against their will, to refuse cash-payments of their promissory notes, and to yield to this compulsion without remonstrating, merely from their sense of loyalty and public spirit.

These outward appearances, however, have nearly lost their effect; and, it certainly would be something very wonderful indeed if they had not, seeing that the advocates of the Bank now *complain,* not of the "*restriction,*" but of the Bullion Committee, who have proposed to *remove the restriction* at the end of two years! Oh! this is delightful. This is, perhaps, the finest instance of putting professions to the test that ever was heard of in the world. Here are the Bank Company *restrained;* they are *restrained from paying their promissory notes* in the current coin of the kingdom; there is, which seems very hard, a *law* to *prevent* them from paying in gold; they would seem to have been so eager to do it, that it was absolutely necessary to pass *a law* to hold in their hands. Well. You have, say the Bullion Committee, endured this *restraint* for thirteen long years, which is long enough in all conscience, and therefore we will *remove* this *restraint;* we will *permit* you to pay in gold. This kind proposition, however, instead of calling forth expressions of joy and gratitude, throws the advocates of the Bank Company into the utmost *consternation* and *dismay,* and they abuse the Bullion Committee as men who have aimed a blow at the very vitals of public credit. Alas! what, then, the Bank Company were not so uneasy as we thought under this restraint? They did not *complain* and *moan,* in secret, as we suppose they did at being *restrained* from paying their promissory notes? Nay, by all that is wonderful, it would seem that they *like* to be *restrained?*

To return from this digression, into which I was drawn by this strange perversity of taste in the Bank Company, let us now, after having refreshed our memories as to the pogress which led to the passing of the Cash Stopping, or Bank Restriction Act, see by what means, and *upon what grounds,* it has been *continued* in force from the 3rd of May, 1797, to this day; and, here, Gentlemen, you will find the most curious and most valuable part of this most curious and most valuable history.

One of the objects which we ought to have in view, is, to ascertain, and not only to ascertain, but to put safely upon record, so that they may be turned to at any moment, the *names* of as many as possible of those, who *had a hand,* who really aided and abetted, the measure of what is called the *Bank Restriction,* that is to say, the Act to bear the Bank Company harmless in refusing payment of its promissory notes. The Bullion Committee has described the consequences of that measure; they have plainly told us what mischiefs have arisen from it; they have told us how very injuriously it has operated towards *creditors* of all descriptions, but they have been wholly silent as to the parties by whom the fatal measure was promoted and brought about, as well as to the parties by whom it was opposed; and, they, have also been quite silent as to the *grounds*, upon which the Act authorizing the refusal of cash has, from time to time, been *continued* from May 3rd, 1797, to the present day. Nay, Mr. HUSKISSON, one of the members of the Bullion Committee, who, not content with the share he took in the labours of the Committee, has, as we saw in Letter XVII, published a pamphlet upon the subject, has not only avoided to say *who* it was that was the *cause* of the Act, but would seem to wish his readers to believe, that those who caused that Act to be passed could have no idea of its being *continued* so long, and, the inference he leaves to be drawn is, that, THOSE PERSONS *have not been the cause of such continuance.*

To explain satisfactorily the probable reason why Mr. HUSKISSON endeavours to give this turn to the thing, it might, perhaps, be sufficient to tell you, that he himself has been steadily on the side of the minister at the time when the first Act was passed, in 1797, and also at every renewal of that Act. This might suffice in explanation of this part of Mr. HUSKISSON'S conduct; but, I must not omit this opportunity of introducing this gentleman to you in form. He is one of the men, whom you help to *pay;* and, it is possible, that you will have to pay him as long as he lives. Therefore, you have a perfect right to know *who* and *what* he is; what he has *done*, and what he is likely *to do*, for the people of England.

Mr. WILLIAM HUSKISSON, the author of the pamphlet mentioned in my last, owes what he has got not to any *family* connection, but solely to his own personal exertions, having, in his early days, been, according to some, an Apothecary, and, according to others, a Banker. He did not waste the precious days of his youth at schools and colleges, learning Latin and laziness. Like you and I, Gentlemen, he owes nothing to pedagogues or to pedigree; and though he does not belong to that class of men whom PAINE calls the *Nobles of Nature* yet, were Nature to give titles, she would certainly dubb Mr. Huskisson a *Knight*. This gentleman was in France at the breaking out of the ANTI JACOBIN war; that is to say the war which begun in 1793, and which, as we have seen, produced such effects upon the bank-note system. He appears, from a French pamphlet which I have in my possession, to have been a very ardent friend of the French revolution, at the outset, and, a speech of his, delivered in a club at Paris, upon *funds* and *tythes*, it would do your hearts good to hear. From Paris, however, Mr. Huskisson returned to England in 1793, having come away upon the recall of our ambassador, Lord Gower, now Marquis of Stafford, to whom, it is said, he had been useful at Paris and who is said, in return to have recommended him to the notice of those two worthy associates in power, and never to-be-forgotten ministers, PITT and DUNDAS. They found him *useful;* and, though his out-set was low, he found himself, at the end of less than seven years, an *Under Secretary of State* in the Colonial Department, and a *Member of Parliament.* In the winter of 1801, when PITT and DUNDAS went out of office, Mr. HUSKISSON followed them, but not without taking care to cast a look behind him; and by the advice of Mr ADDINGTON, the successor of Mr. PITT, our author had conferred on him a PENSION, for life, to be paid out of the taxes raised on the people, to the amount of 1,200 a year; and afterwards, a pension, to be paid from the same source, was settled upon his wife, Mrs. ELIZA EMILY HUSKISSON, to the amount of 615 pounds a year for her life, to commence at her husband's death. What a nice comfortable way this is, Gentlemen, to make provision for one's wife and family! Mr. HUSKISSON'S pension was to be *suspended* whenever he should be in possession of an office of the annual value of 2,000 a year, or upwards, and, when he quitted such office, he was again to receive the pension. So that he made *sure* of 1,200*l.* a year for life, and of 615 pounds a year for the life of his wife, if she should out-live him. This shewed not only a very *provident* but a very *affectionate* disposition. But, our author did not stop here; for he obtained the *Agentship* of the Island of *Ceylon*, acknowledged by himself to be worth 700 pounds a year, and this he still held along with the office of Secretary of the Treasury which he got in 1804, and which at 4,000 pounds a year salary, he held, with an interval of about fifteen months, 'till about October, 1809. So that, while *in office* he got 4,700 pounds a year; and while out of office, 1,900 pounds a year, 1,200 pounds of which he has *for life*, with a provision of 615 pounds a year for the life of his wife, if she should out-live him.

Such, Gentlemen, is the history of the public life of the author of the pamphlet, of which I am about to speak. He is now one of the Members of Parliament for *Harwich*; he was one of the members of the BULLION COMMITTEE, and his pamphlet, the title of which was mentioned in my last Letter, has been published for the purpose of explaining some parts and defending other parts of the famous and immortal Report of that Committee.

But as perfection is not to be expected in any thing human, this Report omits to say any thing about the *grounds* of the continuance, or *duration* of the *Cash Stopping*, or Bank-*restricting* Act; and Mr. HUSKISSON seems to think it incumbent upon him to say some little matter upon that subject. He put himself in a ticklish predicament, when he took up his pen upon such a subject; for, we have seen, that he was in office; we have seen that he was in the receipt of the public money from the year 1793 to the time when he became a member of the Bullion Committee; we have seen, that, from 1804 to the end nearly of 1809 (with the exception of about fifteen months) he was a Secretary of the Treasury, and it is perfectly notorious, that he was what was called the Minister PITT'S right-hand man; that he had, in fact, the chief actual management of the pecuniary affairs of the Exchequer and Treasury; that he was so closely intimate with Mr. PITT, that he was one of the few persons with him when he died; and that he was one of the witnesses of his will and one of his *creditors*.

A person thus situated ought to have had *some knowledge* of the financial affairs of the kingdom. A person thus situated ought to have known pretty well the nature and tendency of a measure like the Cash-Stopping, or Bank-restricting Act. A person, to whom the people of England pay 4,700 pounds a year while he is in office, and 1,900 a year when he is out of office. A person, to whom, at the very least, we are to pay, out of the taxes, 1,200 pounds a year for his life, with a contingent 615 pounds a year for the life of his wife. Such a person, Gentlemen, ought to have a mind capable of extending its inquiries and conclusions beyond the present moment; and, in a case like that of the Stopping or Restricting Act, to be able to foresee the consequences that will result. In short, the man, be he who he may, that receives from the people such pay, ought, if his department be that of the Treasury, to be ashamed to plead *ignorance* as to any principle or point connected with the subject before us.

Yet, what does Mr. HUSKISSON say as to the *duration* of the Stoppage, or Restriction Act? He is in a dilemma. To pass over the matter in silence, will not do, because he is compelled to speak of the injuries arising from the *long duration* of the Act; and, to censure the *passing* of the Act will not do, because it is so well known that he was in office when it was first passed, and also when it was twice or three times renewed. In this difficulty, he has recourse to a plea, which he does not appear to conceive makes against himself. He wishes his reader to gather from what is said, *that those who were the cause of the Act originally* never could dream of its being *continued in force so long*. He says, that that Act was, when first passed, "*considered* and proposed, as an expedient that should be of *short duration*, the course of the proceedings of parliament abundantly indicates; but, *if*, in the year 1797, *it had been foreseen*, that this temporary expedient, would be attempted to be converted into a system for an *indefinite number of years*, and that, under this system, in the year 1810, every creditor, public or private, subject or alien, to whom the law, as it then stood, and as it now stands, had secured the payment of a pound weight of standard gold for every £46 14*s*. 6*d*. of his just demand, would be obliged to accept, in full satisfaction, about 10¼ ounces, or not more than *seventeen shillings in the pound;* with a prospect of a *still further reduction in every subsequent year:*—it is impossible to conceive *that the attention and feelings of parliament would not have been alive* to all the individual injustice, and ultimate public calamities, incident to such a state of things; and that they would *not have provided for the termination of the restriction*, before it should have wrought so much mischief, and laid the foundation of so much confusion in all the dealings and transactions of the community."

Here are two questions; that of the *duration* of the Act, and that of *depreciation of the Bank notes.* The latter will form the subject of a subsequent Letter. As to the former, Mr. Huskisson would evidently have us believe, the *continuation* of the Act for any length of time was *not foreseen*, either by *him*, or by *any body else*. HISTORY, TRUTH, JUSTICE; justice to the living and the dead; but especially to the dead, demand the proof of the contrary; demand that you, Gentlemen, and that the whole of the people of England should know, that if PITT and his colleagues; that, if those to whom we have paid so many many thousands and hundreds of pounds, in salaries, pensions, allowances, and fees; that, if they did not foresee the consequences of the Act of May 3, 1797, there were others, who *did foresee* those consequences, though, unfortunately for the country, the parliament were deaf to their predictions, and still supported Mr. Pitt and his system.

It is now more than THIRTEEN YEARS since this Act was passed, since this deed was done; since the blow, under which credit is now staggering, was struck; but, it is not only necessary to *justice* towards individuals but to *public safety* to shew, *who* it was that did that deed, and who it was that had endeavoured to prevent the measures which produced it and foretold its fatal consequences. It is now the practice of the PITT school, when they speak of the Stoppage, or Restriction Act, to speak of it as of a thing that *nobody could help;* as men speak of a flood, or thunder-storm, or any other calamity, in the causing or the preventing of which it is well known that mankind can have nothing to do. But, we must not, Gentlemen, suffer them thus to get off. They have had the sway in the country for the last *twenty-six years*, fifteen months excepted. They have followed their own plans. They have constantly insisted that theirs were the wisest plans. They have made people feel that it was full as safe to leave their plans unattacked. Well. We have now the result before us. PITT and his admirers and adherents have possessed the places and the powers of the state for *twenty-six years*; and we now see what are the consequences. Those who like the consequences; those who think the present state of things *a good one*, will of course, be thankful that we have had such men in power; but, those, who, like Mr. HUSKISSON, are able to discover some grounds for apprehension, must excuse me, if I point out those to whom we owe the danger; or, if, in the words of the old maxim, "I clap "the saddle upon the right horse."

This task must, however, be reserved for my next; and in the mean while, I remain, Gentlemen,

Your faithful friend,

WM. COBBETT.

State Prison, Newgate, Thursday, November 26, 1810.

LETTER XIX.

"Thus, the measure of non-payment originated with the persons bound to pay."——*Mr. Tierney's Speech, in the House of Commons, Nov. 22, 1797.*

The Reason for the Stoppage, or Restriction, Act—Mr. Pitt and his Adherents represent it as of short Duration—Mr. Fox and others foretell that it will never be repealed—The Dates of the several Renewals of the Act—Pretence for the first Renewal—Resolution of the Bank Directors—Report of the Secret Committee—Pretence for the second Renewal—Exposure of this by Mr. Hobhouse—Miserable Answer of the Minister—Mr. Tierney's Exposure of the whole Thing—The Measure traced to the End of the last War.

GENTLEMEN,

THE task first to be performed, agreeably to the conclusion of my last letter, is, to point out to you, and I flatter myself, to your children's children, those persons, who bore a distinguished part in the discussions of the Stoppage, or Restriction, Act; and, especially to show you, that that Act was not a thing that came like a flood or like thunder, as Mr. Huskisson appears to wish us to believe; and that its *duration* was a circumstance which was not only foreseen but distinctly foretold by several of those persons, who, by the party to which Mr. Huskisson belonged, were represented as the enemies of their country. The Bill was, as we have seen, brought into the House of Commons on the 9th of March, and became a law on the 3rd of May. Between these days there were several debates upon the subject; and, you will now see, whether, as Mr. HUSKISSON would have the public believe, there was nobody that could *foresee* or *dream* of, this *long continuation* of the non-payment of cash at the Bank. Justice to the dead as well as to the living, as was before observed, demands that the truth of this fact should be well known; but, besides that, the knowledge of the truth here will be of great utility in the guiding of our judgment for the future. I shall, therefore, give the very words of the several speakers upon the subject, just as they stand in the Reports of the Parliamentary Debates of that time; and, that any one may, when he pleases, examine into the correctness of my statements, I shall give the *date* of the Debate from which I make my quotations.

Mr. PITT and his adherents held a language of great confidence in the solvency, and even in the *wealth of* the Bank Company. You have seen, that the first Act of Stoppage, or, as it is called, of Restriction, was to last for only *fifty-two days*, which, of itself, amounted to a declaration, that the Bank would be able to resume their payments in a short time; and, during the debates upon the bill, in its several stages, every thing was said, that could be thought of by the Minister and his adherents, to cause the public to believe, that the suspension of cash-payments would be very short indeed. In the debate of the 23rd of March, Mr. WILBERFORCE said, that, "Gentlemen did not consider how much "of this distress arose from the very "nature of our commercial dealings. "The credit we gave was one year, "eighteen months, or two years, "while we paid at six months; so that "in the *progressive increase of trade* "it was some time before the balance "flowed in. *The bad effects were* "*passed, the good were yet to come.*" On the 24th of March, Mr. PITT said, that, "as to the *exact period*, he could "make no positive conjecture: for he "felt it difficult to say, whether "*one month*, or *two*, or *three*, would "be better. But when he reflected, "that it must require some time for "money *to circulate back from the* "*country* to the Bank, and also to be "*refunded from abroad*, and from *all* "*the other sources*, from which its "wealth may be derived, he could "not entertain a firm hope that the "restoration of the Bank could be "other than gradual, he would, *there-* "*fore*, limit the operation of the present clause to the 24th of June "1797." On the 29th of March, Mr. LUBBOCK said, that "if *no particular day was fixed*, and th Bank "began to pay specie without such "notice, all would go on gradually "and smoothly; that he was con- "vinced, with a very little assistance, "that the Bank might go on as usual "*immediately*, and discount freely; "if £3,000,000 were added to their "capital, it would enable the Bank to "discount to a much larger amount, "which would more than accommo- "date the commercial world; and *he* "*would venture to be d—d*, if such a "sum would not be subscribed in "twenty-four hours; this would *put* "*all to rights*." On the 31st of March Mr. PITT said, "Leave the Bank and "them to exercise a discretion con- "cerning it, which, at all events, "could do no injury, and might, more "than probably would, lead to the at- "tainment of that which the right ho- "nourable gentleman himself seemed "so anxious for, namely, *the restora-* "*tion of cash payments at the Bank*." And, again, on the same day he said: "Probably then the cash in the Bank "on the 25th of February was no "yet diminished — then if more "cash came in, it would gradually "*enable the Bank to open again and* "*resume its operations by those slow* "*and successive steps which would* "*make a resumption safe*."—On the same day, Mr. SAMUEL THORNTON one of the Bank Directors, said, in speaking of the clause, which invites people to carry gold to *deposit in the Bank*, that, "on the whole he con- "sidered it as a most important mea- "sure, and that *it would enable the* "*Bank to resume its usual gene-* "*ral payments long antecedent to the* "*period fixed for its recovery*." Thus, all of them spoke either of a *gradual* or a *speedy* return to cash-payments; and this last gentleman, a most firm adherent of the Minister, and a Bank Director expressed his opinion, that the Bank would be able to pay ever *before* the expiration of the *fifty-two days*, for which the Act was made.

Entered at Stationers' Hall.
Printed by W. MOLINEUX, 5, Bream's Buildings, Chancery Lane; Published by W. COBBETT, Jun. No. 8, Catherine Street, Strand: and Retailed at No. 192, Strand.

' Now, Gentlemen, hear the other side. You have heard the Minister PITT and his adherents. Now hear Mr. Fox and those who stood with him. But, above all things mark the words of Mr. Fox. Look at his *predictions;* and, I need not point out to you, how exactly they have been accomplished *thus far*, and how manifest it is that the rest are in the way of speedy accomplishment. Mr. Fox is no more; but his words will never die. The evils he foretold, and that he laboured to prevent, have all come upon us, or now menace us with horrid aspect.

In the debate of the 7th of March, Mr. HOBHOUSE said: "But we are "told that this bill is to exist for *a* "*short time only*. Has the right "honourable Chancellor of the Ex-"chequer considered what is likely "to take place when this bill shall ex-"pire? Will not the holders of Bank "of England notes, the very moment "that the suspension of payment in "specie is at an end, *rush in large* "*bodies to the Bank and demand* "*specie?* Having been once deluded, "will they ever expose themselves to "the risque of being deluded a *second* "*time;* having once lost the opportu-"nity of converting their notes into "specie by a sudden and unexpected "Order of Council, *will they ever* "*voluntarily become holders of such* "*notes again?* The least wound "given to public credit is not easily "healed; public confidence once lost, "is not easily recovered." What Mr. NICHOLLS said, in the debate of the 22nd of March, we have seen in the Motto to Letter XVIII. In the same debate Mr. Fox said that, "He "knew not what the duration of the "bill was intended to be, whether for "three weeks or for three or six "months; but this he knew, that the "longer the duration, the *greater our* "*difficulty would be;* and he must "be a sanguine man indeed, if he "thought the country would not be "ruined in its credit, if this bill con-"tinued for six or eight months.— "There were some persons who con-"fessed that this evil could not be "removed *during the war: he agreed* "*with them;* but he doubted whether "it could be removed EVEN IN "PEACE, unless that desirable event "should take place *very soon*. Every "hour that it was delayed diminished "our chance of removing the cala-"mity. If we had not peace in the "spring of 1797, what should we say "in the autumn? This was a question "which did not depend on the taking "of a town or a fortress. An enume-"ration of many successes in that re-"spect would be of no avail. This "was a time in which we should not "conceal any thing from the public. "A new loan of several millions was "speedily wanted, which certainly "would not tend to improve the situa-"tion of paper credit. He could not "bring himself *to state the circum-*"*stances of this country without the* "*most painful anxiety*. The House "ought to consider that this country "was now on the brink of a dreadful "precipice, and that one false step "might *throw it into a gulph out of* "*which it never could rise.*" In the same debate, in answer to a remark of Mr. PITT "that an *increase of* "*Bank notes* would *hasten the period* "*of cash payments,*" Mr. Fox said,

I

W. MOLINEUX, Printer, Bream's Buildings Chancery Lane.

that "to say that paper differed from "the nature of every thing else, and "that it was *valuable in proportion as* "*it was plentiful*, and not as it was "*rare;* and that the abundance of "paper would incline people *not to* "*hoard guineas*, but would induce "them to *carry them to the Bank*, "were propositions so inconsistent "with sound reasoning, that he was "ashamed of calling up principles so "merely elementary, and which were "as clear as the simplest proposi-"tions of mathematics." In the same debate, Mr. SHERIDAN said, that "There would be *no end to the bill*, "should it be carried into effect. He "would repeat, therefore, what he "had said before, that it would be "better to suspend the proceeding "altogether, than to hazard the evils "which its enactment, *without the* "*prospect of a limitation*, would pro-"duce." In the same debate, Sir WILLIAM PULTENEY said: "Does "any man, in his senses, imagine, "that if this stoppage of payment in "specie is to be of *long duration*, "that the merchant will not advance "the price of his foreign articles?— "This appears to me to be a great "evil; and I have no idea of assenting "to any bill of this kind, *unless the* "*duration be fixed*, and *irrevocably* "*limited to a short period*." In the debate of the 24th of March, the same gentleman, Sir WILLIAM PULTENEY, said, that "he was of opinion "that the longer the period was, the "heavier would our difficulties grow. "It was useless to say, that cash "might *flow back from the country* "*and from abroad;* for, while we "were waiting for that reflux of "specie, our destruction must ensue; "it was impossible to restore the "Bank by the balance of trade to "which the right honourable gentle-"man, Mr. PITT, alluded. The "theory was false, and nothing solid "could be expected from it. Three "weeks had already been given to "the Bank, and, he was willing to "grant it one month more; if, then, "it could not pay, we must *look for* "*some other remedy:* for that now "proposed would be found of no "avail. We should be *only compelled* "*to prolong the restriction from one* "*period to another*, till our paper met "*the fate of the French assignats*."

Such, Gentlemen, were the opinions expressed, upon this part of the subject, when the cash-stopping bill was first before the House of Commons. You see, then, that, while Mr. PITT and his adherents were full of confidence of the Bank being able to return to its payments in cash; while they saw no danger at all from this measure; while they thought that the invitation contained in the Act for people to bring money into the Bank Shop would again fill the Shop with real treasure; while they, and especially Mr. WILBERFORCE, described the Stoppage of cash-payments rather as a sign of *prosperity* and riches than the contrary; while *they* did not, as Mr. HUSKISSON says, *dream* of the Act being *continued for a length of time;* while *their* opinions, or, at least, their declarations, were of this sort, the declarations on the other side of the House, the declarations of those whom this "*most thinking*" nation *would not believe*, the declarations of those whom this "most think-"ing" nation were persuaded to look upon as its enemies and as the friends of France, were just the contrary. Mr. FOX and his party not only foresaw, but they *foretold*, what has since come to pass. They said, that, if the Act was once passed, it must go on; and they gave *reasons*, for their opinion; reasons that were not attempted to be overset by other *reasons*, and that were opposed by nothing but *abuse* or *foul insinuation*.

Having, now, as far as relates to this point, done justice to the parties who took a part in the debates upon the occasion referred to; having shewn that Mr. HUSKISSON has not fairly represented the matter; having shewn that Mr. PITT and his adherents either meant to deceive the nation as to the ability and willingness of the Bank to return to payments in cash, or were themselves ignorant of the natural consequences of the measure, and that they had either *less sincerity* or *less knowledge* than their opponents; having placed this important part of the subject beyond the power of future misrepresentation, we will now trace this famous Act of Parliament through its several renewals, from its first passing to the present day. In the whole, there have been *Six Acts* passed; the original Act, of which the several clauses are mentioned in Letter XVI, page 214, and *Five Acts of Renewal.* There are, in some of these *five,* trifling deviations from the original Act; but, these are very unimportant. The great provisions about stopping cash-payments, about protecting the Bank Company against the demands of their creditors, and about the protection from arrests in individual cases, are all preserved, are now in full force, and, therefore, the alterations of no material consequence.

We have seen the *title* and *preamble* of the Act before, at page 215, and it will be best, before I offer you any observations upon the *reasons,* which at the different renewals, were stated *in justification* of the measure, to furnish you with the *dates* of the six Acts, that you may, if your affairs should require it, and opportunity enable you to do it, refer to these Acts yourselves.

THE FIRST was passed in the 37th year of the reign of George III, and is, of the Statutes of that year, Chapter 45. The date, according to the common way of dating, is 1797, and on the 23d of May. To continue in force to the 24th of June 1797; that is to say, for only *fifty-two* days.

THE SECOND: 37 year George III, Chapter 91. That is, in 1797; and the day when the Act passed was the 22nd of June; to continue in force *'till one month after the commencement of the then next Session of Parliament!* Mark this. See what a leap was taken. But you will see a greater presently.

THE THIRD: 38th year George III, Chapter 1. That is, 1797; and the day when the Act was passed was the 30th of November; to continue in force *'till one month after the conclusion of the then war by a difinitive treaty of peace!* Bravo! See how it gains stre gth as it goes. "Give "them an *inch,* and they'll take an "*ell,*" says the old proverb. But, we have not yet seen the boldest leap. This Act, mind, was to protect the Bank *'till the end of the war;* and the reasons for that we shall see by-and-by.

THE FOURTH *(Peace was now come,* observe): 42nd year George III, Chapter 42. That is, 1802; and the Act was passed on the 30th of April; to continue in force *(though peace was made)* till the *1st of March,* 1803. We shall by-and-by, see the *reasons* that were given for this.—These *reasons* are the interesting matter.

THE FIFTH *(Peace still continuing): 43rd* year George III, Chapter 18. That is, 1803; and the Act was passed on the 28th of February; to continue in force till *six weeks after the commencement of the then next Session of Parliament.* This was the *second* renewal after the end of the war. The second renewal *during peace.*

THE SIXTH (War was now *begun again) :* 44th year George III, Chapter . That is, 1803; and the Act was passed on the 15th of December; to continue in force till *six* MONTHS *after a conclusion of a difinitive treaty of peace!*

This last, Gentlemen, is the Act which is now in force. This is the Act, which now protects the Bank Company against the demands of the holders of their promissory notes.—This is the Act, which the BULLION

COMMITTEE recommended to be *repealed* in such a way that the Bank Company shall be compelled to pay again in cash in *two years from this time.* You will now be so good as to recall to your minds, that the main question for us to determine is, whether, if such a law were passed, it is likely that it could be executed: in other words; *whether it be likely that the Bank Company will ever again be able to pay their notes in money.* This is the main question for our determination, because upon that question hangs the whole paper system; and, in order the better to enable ourselves to determine that question, and also to complete the *history* of the Bank Company and the Bank Stoppage, or Restriction, as they call it, we must now take a view of the REASONS, which, at the several renewals of the Stoppage, or Restriction Act, were urged *in justification* of the measure.

The FIRST Act was, as we have seen, proposed to the Parliament by the Minister, and defended by him and his adherents upon the ground of *necessity.* The drain of cash was said to have been *sudden* and *unusual,* arising from *false alarms of invasion.* The emergence was said to be *temporary.* The stoppage was acknowledged to be a *great evil;* but, it was maintained, that it was absolutely necessary, as the only means of avoiding a *greater evil.* It was, particularly by the then Attorney-General (now Lord Eldon), and by the then Solicitor-General (now Lord Redesdale), urged, that the measure was necessary to the safety of the public creditor, or Stock-holder; because, if the run upon the Bank had not been checked by force of law, the Bank would have been totally ruined, and, of course, that the Stock-holder would have lost his all.

But (and I beg you to mark it well) when the SECOND Act came under discussion, in June 1797, the Minister and his adherents began to hold a different sort of language, and to speak of the Act, not as the less of *two evils,* but rather as a measure adopted from *choice* and not from *necessity.* This Act, which was the *first act of renewal,* had for its forerunner, a correspondence between the minister and the Bank Directors. His letter to them was dated on the twelfth of June, and their answer on the 13th. These letters having been prepared, he, the minister himself, moved, in the House of Commons, on the 15th of June, that the said letters should be laid before the House, which was done. And, what do you think, Gentlemen, that these letters contained? Why, the minister's letter told the Bank Directors, that *he did not think that it was expedient,* that they should begin again to pay in cash, at the time specified in the first Act of Parliament; and they, very submissively, *acquiesced in the minister's opinion!* Now, pray do not laugh, Gentlemen; for, you will find in the end, it is no laughing matter.

These two Letters, and nothing in the world besides, were made the ground of a legislative proceeding; made the ground, and the sole ground for continuing, for five months longer, an Act of Parliament, which protected the Bank Company against the demands of their numerous creditors, the holders of their notes. In the course of his speech, the Minister, the "*heaven-born* Minister," said, "that "he had the *satisfaction* to say, that "there was in the affairs of the Bank, "with regard to the means of pay "ment in cash, an *improvement* that "was *highly consoling,* and that the "*apprehension* of their not recovering "their ability to pay in the accustomed "manner had been *greatly exagge-* "*rated,* when the subject first came "before the House." He said, in another part of his speech that "he "was still anxious to come to the ter- "mination of the restriction; and, al- "though that could not be on the day "appointed, yet it was a *satisfaction* "to the public to find, that the *incon-* "*venience* of the measure was much "*less* than had been foretold; and that, "indeed, the consequence of the mea- "sure had been the *reverse* of what "had been predicted by its oppo- "nents."

Without more ado the bill was brought in, and was passed, as we have seen, in seven days afterwards, without any further debate about the matter. Four fifths of the House of Commons were still at the back of the Minister; he appears to have lost not a single vote in consequence of the state to which it was now manifest he had brought the affairs of the nation; there were still the same majorities for him in the House, and there was still the same shouting for him at Lloyd's; the majority of the nation, partly from folly, partly from fear, partly from the influence of the paper system, were still as loud in his praises as ever, and Mr. Fox, apparently wearied with exertions which afforded no hope of success, left the people to feel the effects of their infatuation.

But, when the THIRD Act came to be passed, in November 1797, a little more preparation was necessary; and it was also necessary to find out *new reasons*, a quite *new doctrine*, in justification of it; or, to acknowledge, at once that the Bank was *unable to pay*. The refusal to pay their notes in cash had now lasted for *nine months*; the *alarm of invasion was over*; and, it appeared difficult to conceive any reason whatever for the continuation of the Stoppage, or Restriction Act, other than that of the *inability* of the Bank Company to pay their notes in money. *Other reasons* were, however, found out; but, by way of preparation another SECRET COMMITTEE was now appointed in the House of Commons, which Committee were, as we shall see, the vehicle through which the *new doctrines* first made their way into that House.

This Committee, by the hands of Mr. CHARLES BRAGGE (now Bragge Bathurst, and Member for Bristol), made their Report to the House on the 17th of November 1797; and, I will venture to say, that a more curious document never was produced in the world. Every syllable of it is worthy of your attention; and I beg of you to go carefully through it before you proceed any further. The Report was, in part, grounded upon a Copy of a *Resolution of the Bank Directors*, which had been passed some time before, and which was laid before this Committee of Secrecy. I shall insert this Resolution first; and I must again beseech you to read every word of both documents with attention; for, you may be well assured, that the whole world never saw such documents before.*

---

* *Resolution of the Court of Directors of the Bank.*

At a Court of Directors, at the Bank, on Thursday the 26th October 1797.

RESOLVED.—That it is the opinion of this Court, That the Governor and Company of the Bank of England *are enabled to issue specie*, in any manner that may be deemed necessary for the accommodation of the public; and the Court have no hesitation to declare, *that the affairs of the Bank are in such a state, that it can with safety resume its accustomed functions, if the political circumstances of the country do not render it inexpedient*; but the Directors deeming it *foreign to their province to judge of these points*, wish to *submit to the wisdom of Parliament*, whether as it has been ONCE JUDGED PROPER TO LAY A RESTRICTION on the payments of the Bank in cash, it may, or may not, be *prudent to continue the same.*

The Committee of Secrecy, appointed to enquire whether it may be expedient further to continue the Restriction, contained in two Acts, made in the last Session of Parliament, respecting payments in Cash by the Bank; have enquired accordingly, and agreed upon the following Report; viz.

Your Committee have, in the first place, examined the total amount of out-standing demands on the Bank of England, and of the funds for discharging the same; and find, from the examination of the Governor and Deputy Governor of the Bank, and the documents produced by them, that the total amount of out-standing demands on the Bank was, on the 11th day of this instant November, 17,578,910*l.*; and that the total amount of the funds for discharging the same (without including the permanent debt

This Report, this matchless, this immortal Report, having been laid before the House, having been submitted "to the Wisdom of Par-"liament," the "*heaven-born* Minister" rose to move, at once, without any time for printing the Report, to bring in a bill to extend the duration of the Act of Stoppage, or Restriction, as it is called. He said, that he would, however, move for the printing of the Report, "in order that all the Mem-"bers might have the *satisfaction* of "informing themselves, *in detail*, of "statements *so very pleasing* and *im-"portant;* those gentlemen, he said, "who had now heard the report read, "would think with him that after the "*full examination* the subject had un-"dergone *in the Committee;* after "the *clear* and *decided opinion* that "Committee had pronounced upon "it; and after the *distinct statement* "not only of them *but of the Bank* "*Directors;* it would be unnecessary "to detain the business merely on "account of the printing; and that it "would be proper to proceed without "delay to the object of that Report; "and move for leave to bring in a bill

---

due from Government, of 11,686,800*l*, which bears an interest of three per cent.) was, on the same day, 21,418,460*l*.; leaving a balance of surplus in favour of the Bank (exclusive of the above mentioned debt from Government) of 3,839,550.

Your Committee next proceeded to examine the principal articles of which the above mentioned sum of 21,418,460*l*., being the credit side of account, is made up, with a view of ascertaining how far the Bank might be enabled to resume its accustomed payments in cash, in case the restriction at present subsisting should be removed: and your Committee find, that the advances to Government have, on the one hand, been so much reduced, since the 25th of February last, as to amount, on the said 11th day of this instant November, to no more than the sum of 4,258,140*l*. while, on the other hand, *the cash and bullion in the Bank have increased to an amount more than five times the value of that at which they stood on the same 25th of February last*, and much above that at which they have stood at any time since the beginning of September 1795.—Your Committee farther find, that the course of exchange with Hamburgh is, at present, *unusually favourable to this country*, and that, from the situation of our trade, there is *good reason to imagine it will so continue*, unless political circumstances should occur to affect it.—Your Committee next proceeded to examine the Governor and Deputy Governor of the Bank, as to their opinion of the *inconvenience* which may have arisen from the restriction imposed on the Bank from making payment in cash, and of the *expediency of continuing such restriction:* and your Committee find, that they are *not aware of any such inconvenience*, and that they are supported in that idea, by knowing that the bankers and traders of London who had a right by the Act of Parliament to demand three-fourths of any deposit in cash which they had made in the Bank, of 500*l* or upwards, *have only claimed about one sixteenth:* and your Committee find, that the Court of Directors of the Bank did, on the 26th of October, 1797, come to a resolution, a copy of which is subjoined to this Report.—Your Committee having farther examined the Governor and Deputy Governor, as to what may be meant by the political circumstances mentioned in that resolution, find, that they understand by them, *the state of hostility in which the nation is still involved*, and particularly such apprehensions as may be entertained of invasion, either in Ireland or this country, together with the possibility there may be of advances being to be made from this country to Ireland; and that *from those circumstances so explained*, and from the *nature of the* war, and the *avowed purpose of the enemy to attack this country by means of its public credit*, and to *distress it in its financial operations*, they are led to think that it will be expedient to continue the restriction now subsisting, with the reserve for partial issues of cash, at the discretion of the Bank, of the nature of that contained in the present Acts; and that it may be so continued, *without injury to the credit of the Bank, without an advantage to the nation.*—Your Committee, therefore, having taken into consideration, the general situation of the country, are of opinion, that notwithstanding the affairs of the Bank, both with respect to the general balance of its accounts, and its capacity of making payments in specie *are in such a state that it might with safety resume its accustomed functions*, UNDER A DIFFERENT STATE OF PUBLIC AFFAIRS, yet, that it will be expedient to continue the restriction now subsisting on such payments, for such time, and under such limitations, as to the wisdom of Parliament may seem fit.

"for that purpose." He further said, that it was necessary to continue the restriction *during the war* to defeat the object of the enemy, which was *to destroy our credit;* that the further continuation of the restriction could not reasonably produce any *alarm* or *apprehension,* since they had now *indisputable evidence* before them, that, so far from the *gloomy* predictions of the opponents of the measure having been verified, the national *credit* had rapidly risen to the *high condition of prosperity* which had just been exhibited. At the end of this harangue, he moved for leave to bring in a bill for continuing the Stoppage of cash-payments, at the Bank, *till a month after the conclusion of a definitive treaty of peace;* which, by the Representatives of "the *most thinking* people in the world," was agreed to *without a single dissenting voice!*

When, however, the subject came to be discussed again on the 22nd of November, the thing was not suffered to pass off in silence. Mr. HOBHOUSE observed upon the *new doctrine* which was now brought forward in defence of the measure: "He reminded the "House, that he had said on a former "occasion that this would be the case; "and now the Minister was making "good his predictions, alledging as a "reason for so doing, that the nature "of the contest in which we are engaged demanded it, *though this was "no part of the grounds for the former "restriction, and though in comparing "the war now with its nature at that "time, it did not appear there was "any material difference.* Why the "nature of the war, then, made a "restriction of six months only necessary, and its nature now made a "restriction during the contest necessary, he could not discover; to him "it appeared absurd and irreconcileable to common sense and sound "policy." What *answer* was given to this by the Minister? What answer *could* he give? He had, in fact, nothing to say. He repeated all the former assertions about the *riches* of the Bank, though those assertions evidently made against him; and, as to the main argument, what did he do, but rely solely upon *the opinion of the Secret Committee,* a Committee, who had, in fact, been *chosen by his own adherents.* He said: "As to the "plan of continuing the restriction "for the whole term of the war, the "reasons for it being stated distinctly "in the Report of the Committee, it "was unnecessary for him to say a "word more upon the subject; it "would be found there distinctly set "out that the Bank was in a state "which in ordinary times would "enable it to resume its cash payments and operations on the accustomed scale. But that the *avowal "of the enemy to attack us through our "finances, and to ruin our public "credit,* was the motive (he presumed "a sufficiently cogent motive) to make "an additional term of restriction; "and when it was remembered that "*no injury* nor *even inconvenience,* "had been sustained by the restriction hitherto, the House could not "but think it a sufficient encouragement to adopt that now called for." In a subsequent stage of the bill, the next day, he said: "*We were contending with an enemy whose object "was to attack* the *credit of the "country, and to embarrass its financial operations.* It was necessary "to meet these attacks in a manner "that would defeat the object of the "enemy. The House should take "every measure to ward off the "danger, and the present was, in his "opinion, the best that could possibly "be adopted. Mr. HUSSEY having pressed him closely upon this point, he further said, that, "It was necessary to hold out to the enemy, that "the country was *prepared to meet all "its efforts of desperation;* but it did "not follow that the restriction would "be continued during the whole of the "the war. While, however, it was "pursued in its *present shape,* he cer-

" tainly considered the restriction as " absolutely necessary."

These miserable reasons; these most pitiful pretences, Mr. TIERNEY exposed, in his speech of the 22d of November, in a manner so complete, that one is shocked at the thought of the House afterwards suffering the measure to proceed; one cannot help wondering, that the Minister was able to sit and hear him; and, it is impossible to feel any compassion for the people who still supported and *extolled* him; and who richly merit all that could, or can, befall them from that cause, they having supported him with their eyes open, and against the clearly and loudly expressed dictates of *reason* and *truth*. Mr. TIERNEY said: "that the enemy would aim a " blow at our credit and finances, all " would agree, for all modern wars " have been without exception car- " ried on upon that principle. Mo- " dern wars are made upon resources " rather than blood; but was this the " way to prevent the enemy from suc- " ceeding?—*most whimsical expedient!* " —In *order to leave to the enemy no* " *credit to attack, they destroy credit* " *themselves*. But at last they speak " plainly, at last it comes out it will " distress *the financial operations* of " the country; and then they delibe- " rately weigh and find that it will be " expedient to continue the restric- " tion with the reserve of partial is- " sues of cash at the discretion of the " Bank, and that it may be so conti- " nued with *advantage to the nation*, " and *without injury to the credit of* " *the Bank*. This was the result of " the examination of the Governor " and Deputy Governor of the Bank " of England. This was *their advice*. " This precious plan, which first ori- " ginated in the diabolical, but fer- " tile mind of that monster Rober- " spierre."

Mr. TIERNEY, in this speech, which was one of the best made upon the occasion, and to which I do not pretend to do full justice, then shewed how clear it was, that the Bank Company and the Minister went hand in hand through the whole of the transaction; that their operations were intended *to screen one another*; that the Bank Company called upon the Minister for protection; and the Minister made that the pretext for his propositions to Parliament. He observed that the principal reason for continuing to protect the Bank from paying their notes, *came from the Bank Directors themselves*, who even before the meeting of Parliament had come to a resolution, that they were *able* to pay *if the political circumstances of the country did not render it inexpedient*, but that the stoppage of payments in cash having been ONCE judged proper, they *submitted to the wisdom of Parliament*, whether it would not be proper to *continue* the same. "Thus," said Mr. TIERNEY, "the measure of nonpayment *originated* with the persons *bound to pay*;" and who, from the language of the Act, the world would believe were *restrained* against their will from paying.

From the Report of the Secret Committee, you will have perceived, that the Bank Company of Traders, were the chief source of the Committee's information; for the Committee say, that, having asked them what they meant by those "*political circumstances* of the country," mentioned in their Resolution, the Bank people told them, that they alluded to *the war* in which the country was engaged? Upon this; aye upon this ground, suggested by the Bank Company themselves, did the Committee report, that it would not be safe for that Company to pay its notes during the war; and upon the same ground did the House of Commons come to a like determination.

Gentlemen, were not these facts fresh in our memories; were they not capable of proof by living witnesses; nay, were they not proved by the existence of the Act of Parliament, of which we are speaking, would they, could they be believed? Could they be believed to have taken place in any nation upon earth; and, especially amongst a people, calling themselves "the *most thinking* people in the world?"

Thus have we traced down this Act of Stoppage, or Restriction, as it is called, to *the end of the last war*. We have seen that its continuation was at last justified upon the ground of its being dangerous for the Bank to return to money payments DURING THE WAR. And now we have to see what *reasons* were given for continuing the restriction, or refusal to pay, AFTER THE WAR WAS OVER. But, this, by no means the least interesting part of the subject, must be reserved for another Letter.

In the mean while, I remain,

Gentlemen,

Your faithful friend,

WM. COBBETT.

State Prison, Newgate, Thursday,
December 4th 1810.

LETTER XX.

"The English are a sober, THINKING people, and are more *intelligent* and more *solid* than any people "I ever had the fortune to see."—LORD STORMONT'S SPEECH in the House of Lords, 1st Feb. 1792.

The War being now over, Mr. Pitt's Reasons ceased of course—The Peace brings no golden Payments at the Bank---Mr. Addington becomes Minister---Gives Notice of an Intention to continue the Act of 1797---Mr. Robson calls for Papers, which are refused ---He compares Bank-Notes to Assignats, and is himself called to Order—Mr. Addington's Reasons for renewing the Act in April 1802---His Reasons for another Continuation of the Bill in February 1803---Mr. Tierney calls for Inquiry---the Act renewed again, in Dec. 1803, till six Months after Peace.

GENTLEMEN,

IN Letter XIX, page 246, we traced the Bank Stoppage or Restriction Act, down to the end of the last war, in the year 1802. We saw it introduced under pretence of the absolute *necessity* of a *temporary* purpose; we saw it passed, at first, for only *fifty-two days;* and with every expectation held forth, that it would be repealed before the expiration even of that time; we then saw, that it not only lived for the fifty-two days, but, at the expiration of that time, was prolonged for *five months*; and, when the end of that five months came, we saw it prolonged for the *duration of the war,* upon the ground, that the enemy had *openly avowed his determination to effect the destruction of our public credit,* and that, therefore, it was necessary to keep upon the *defensive.* This was the precise ground stated by the Minister himself. The enemy had avowed his determination to *destroy* our *credit,* and *therefore* the Bank was to be *protected from paying its promissory notes,* agreeably to the conditions on which these notes had been received in payment. The enemy had avowed his determination to blast the credit of England, and, *therefore,* the Bank of England was to *stop payment with impunity, as long as the war should last.*

Such were the *reasons,* such the *doctrine,* to which was at last driven the "Grand financier," Mr. PITT, who had begun his career by bespeaking a column to his memory, on which the words "PUBLIC CREDIT" should be inscribed; such was now the doctrine of the "heaven-born minister;" "the "Pilot that weathered the storm;" "the "great statesman now no more." He weathered the storm so ably, that, at the end of only four years of his war against the Republicans of France, during which four years he had, perhaps, forty times foretold that France would sink beneath the weight of *bankruptcy,* he himself comes into that same House of Commons where his promises to ruin France had been so often heard, and there he calls upon the members to protect the Bank of England in non-payment of its notes; he calls upon them for a law to compel the Public Creditor to take his dividends in a paper not convertible into gold; and, his reason for this is, that the French, that those same French, that the *bankrupt* French, that the beggared French *threatened to make war upon our finances!* Aye, he, the boaster, who had made so many, so many scores, of triumphant comparisons between the situation of England and France; who had so many scores, I might say hundreds of times (for he frequently did it several times in one speech), represented England as so highly blessed in wealth and credit, while France was sunk into the lowest abyss of poverty and threatened with all the evils attendant upon a debased paper-money; he, this very same man; the identical "heaven-born minister," now asked for a law to protect the Bank against the demands of the holders of its notes, and to compel the Public Creditor to receive his dividends in that same sort of notes or not at all; and, all this he did, because those same poor, ruined, beggared, and beaten French, had *avowed their intention of making war upon our finances.*

But, at any rate, this reason held good only *during the war.* The "heaven-born man," as we have seen in the last Letter, expressly stated, that the measure was a mere *war* measure, intended to *meet* the hostility of the enemy; "to meet his efforts of "*desperation.*" But, it did not follow, he said, that the non-payment of cash would continue during the *whole* of the war; but merely while the enemy pursued the war in its then "*present shape.*" So that, at all events, it was believed, or, it was intended to make this "*most thinking* people in the world" believe that the measure would last only for the war at longest, and that when peace returned, they would once more get guineas for their notes, and that those of them who had dividends to receive, would receive them in gold if they chose, as they formerly used to do; and, this was one of the reasons why the nation so anxiously wished for *peace.*

Well, in 1802, *Peace came!* But, alas! it brought no guineas in payments at the Bank. It brought with it no golden payments to the Stockholder, or *Public Creditor,* as some people call him. Peace brought no repeal of the Bank Stoppage, or Restriction Act. On the contrary, it did, as we have seen at page 254, bring an extension of the duration of that Act from the 30th of April, 1802, to the first of March, 1803. And thus it was that the promise was kept. Thus it was that "the *most* "*thinking* people in the world" saw their "heaven-born Minister's" doctrines verified.

But, what was *now* the *pretence* for continuing this Act? The war was over. The shoutings and the bonfirings and the bell-ringings for *peace* had taken place. Mr. ADDINGTON, the prime minister, and LORD HAWKESBURY, the negociator, had been praised in all manner of ways for the "blessings of peace." What, then, could be the pretence for continuing the Stoppage Act? You shall hear, Gentlemen; for it is impossible to do justice to the reason except in the words of the Minister himself and of those who supported him.

You must remember, Gentlemen that *just before the peace was begun to be negociated,* the "heaven-born and some others went out of office, and that MR. HENRY ADDINGTON, now **Lord Viscount Sidmouth**, succeeded him, as prime minister. To *his* lot, therefore, it fell to propose the continuation of the Stoppage Act, *in peace;* but, you should bear in mind, that this was, in fact, no *change of ministry;* it was merely a change of *a very few of the men* in power. All those who had voted for Pitt, continued to vote for his successor, as did also Mr. Pitt himself. So that the continuation of the Stoppage Act is not to be ascribed, in anywise, to this *change of men*, the people still in power being the same people who supported all the measures of the minister, Pitt, and who, indeed, brought him back into power again in the year 1804.

It was on the 9th of April 1802, that the continuation was proposed by Mr. Addington; but, notice of his intention having been before given, Mr. Robson, on the 2nd of April, moved for certain papers, shewing the nature of the affairs of the Bank, which was *opposed* by the Minister, Addington, who, without more ado, moved the *previous question* upon it. Whereupon Mr. Robson said, that this was using him and those who thought with him very ill. Notice had been given, he said, by the minister, of his intention to bring in a bill to continue the Act, which protected the Bank from paying in gold and silver, and, he wished to know how the affairs of the Bank stood, that he might be able judge whether he ought to consent to such a measure or not. "He maintained that "all Europe was contemplating the "payments of specie by the Bank, as "the criterion of the credit of the "Country. If the Bank continued "to issue paper, country banks would "do the same without controul; they "would issue their notes *without* "*mercy*. It was, in his opinion, "THE COMMENCEMENT OF "A COURSE OF ASSIGNATS. *(Order! order! and question! was* "*called from every part of the* "*House.*")

The question being put, it was carried against Mr. Robson, without a division. He was not allowed to have the papers he wanted. It was unnecessary, he was told; and, when he ventured to compare bank notes to assignats, he was *called to order*. He was called to order for speaking *irreverently* of those notes, those promissory notes, which were by law rendered not payable agreeably to promise, and which law it was now proposed to continue.

Now we come to the Minister, Addington's *reasons* for continuing this Act *after the end of the war;* and to those reasons we must pay particular attention. He prefaced his proposition, as his predecessor always used to do, by very high language about the *ability* of the Bank to pay in coin. He said, in the debate of the 9th of April, "I have the satisfaction of "being convinced, that the measure "cannot furnish *a pretence to the* "*most timid man in the House, to* "*suppose the Bank does not possess* "*within itself the most ample means* "*of satisfying the full extent of the* "*demands which may be made upon* "*it, by the payment of its notes in* "*specie.*" In the debate of the 21st of April, he said, that "on the *soli-*"*dity* of the Bank, he was *entitled* to "*say* and *assume*, there was *now no* "*question*, either in that House or "elsewhere. On the DISPOSI-"TION of the Bank to make pay-"ments in specie, he was also en-"titled to *assume*, nay he owed it to "the Bank to ASSERT, they had "*manifested a readiness to do so.* It "was, however, thought necessary to "continue this restriction *for a* "*while.*" Having said this, he said, that it was, *of course*, quite unnecessary to enter into any *inquiry* as to the state of the Bank's affairs; and, accordingly, it only remained for him to state the *grounds*, upon which he proposed the continuation of the measure. But, Gentlemen, pray bear in mind, that this Minister gave the country to understand, that the Bank Company had, even at that time, "*manifested a readiness to make payments in specie*," and this was now nearly nine years ago. Yet, Mr. RANDLE JACKSON now bestows something very much like abuse upon the Bullion Committee, because they recommend to the House to make the Bank Company *begin* to pay in specie in *two years* from this time. What should make the Bank Company angry with the Committee, if it was true, that they *wished to pay in money so long as eight years and nine months ago?*

The *grounds* which the Minister, ADDINGTON, stated for the continuation were as follows. In the debate of the 9th of April, he said: "The grounds on which I shall rest "the proposition I have to make to "the House are notorious; and it "will be for the sober and dispassionate reflection of the House, "whether the measure I shall submit "does not necessarily result from "facts and circumstances too well "known even to require a particular "statement of them. It cannot be "necessary for me to inform the "House, *that the rate of exchange "beween this country and foreign "parts is disadvantageous to ourselves*....... It cannot be necessary for me to prove, that *while "the rate of exchange is disadvantageous to us, an augmentation of "the circulating cash would create a "trade highly injurious to the interest and commerce of this country.* "It is well known, that for several "months past there has been a trade "carrying on in *purchasing guineas "with a view to the exportation of "them*........ In addition to these "reasons, the House will reflect upon "the inconvenience which would unavoidably result from *letting loose* "such a proportion of the coin of the "country as would be circulated by "taking off the restriction. I am not "aware of *any inconvenience* that "can *possibly arise* from continuing "it. We have had the *satisfaction*, "arising from the experience of three "or four years of difficulty? We have "had experience, that during such "period, *the credit of the Bank has "undergone no diminution whatever.* "Bank notes have maintained their "reputation, and have been every "where received *cheerfully* and *readily*. . . . . Some Gentlemen are "desirous that the Bank should pay "in cash for notes of small denomination; but till there is a full and "abundant supply of cash by opening the Bank entirely, it is *extremely convenient* to afford circulation to £.1 and £.2 notes. By "the payment of them in specie, a "*general anxiety* would be introduced *of obtaining cash at the Bank.* "Notes of £.1,000 and £.500 would "be changed for notes of £.1 and £.2 "*in order that they might be immediately changed again for cash.* If "a restraint was to be imposed with "respect to the number of notes of "small denomination, they would be "driven out of circulation altogether; "and there would be no small notes "but those issued by Bankers."

There, Gentlemen, you have now before you the reasons why this Act was continued *after the war.* The Minister, Mr. PITT, told the nation, that it was necessary during the war, in order to prevent the enemy from executing his vow of *destroying our credit;* and the Minister, Addington, told the nation, that it was necessary *after the war was over,* because the rate of exchange was against us, because people were exporting guineas when they could lay hold of them, because to repeal the Act would let coin loose, because the experience of years had shewn that the stoppage of cash payments had done no harm to the credit of the Bank whose notes were every where received cheerfully and readily, and finally, because (pray mark!) if a part of the notes were to be paid in specie, *that would give rise to a general anxiety to obtain cash at the Bank,* and that people would change large notes into small ones, *in order immediately to change these latter for cash.*

So, then, Mr. ADDINGTON, the people did, even in your time, like gold better than the notes? Though you could not perceive, not you, any *inconvenience* from the continuation of the Act; though you had seen with *satisfaction* the experience of the years of suspension; though the *credit* of the Bank had undergone *no diminution* whatever;" though the Bank notes had *maintained their reputation* and had been every where received cheerfully and readily: yet, notwithstanding all this, you object to make the small notes payable in gold, lest the holders of them should *run to the Bank and get cash for them;* lest this taste for the sweets of gold should excite *a general anxiety of obtaining cash at the Bank;* and lest large notes should be changed into small ones for the purpose of again changing these latter *into cash.* But, why was this to be feared? The Bank Directors were surely, the best judges of this; and, you say, not only that they are *able* to pay; but that they have manifested a *readiness* to pay their notes in specie. Now, *this being the case,* what danger was there of a *run* upon the Bank; And, if there had been a run, what danger was there in that; seeing that there were means amply sufficient to meet such run?

Mr. ROBSON, whom we have seen called to order for speaking so irreverently of Bank notes, opposed the bill in its subsequent stages: he pointed out the advantages which the Bank derived from the Act; he *foretold* what the Bullion Committee have now declared *to have come to pass;* in short he did all that it was in his power to do to prevent the continuation of a measure, which a Committee of that same House of Commons have now declared to have produced such fearful consequences; and this Mr. ROBSON, did while Mr. HUSKISSON, who now tells us that *no one foresaw* the evil, not only suffered the measure to pass in silence, but was one of the majority of the Minister by whom the measure was proposed and put in execution.

Well, but, after all, the Act was to last *only* ten months; *only* till the first of March 1803; it was only, as the Minister's brother, Mr. HILEY ADDINGTON, called it, "a *temporary provision,* 'till the *effects of the peace* should have *begun to operate.*" Only this. Nothing more. Yet did they, when the 1st of March, 1803, came, renew the Act again. Again did they pass a law to protect the able-and-willing-to-pay Bank against the demands of the note-holders! Again did they pass an Act, to continue in force till six weeks after the commencement of the then next session of Parliament, the measure for preventing payments in cash, though peace had been made *a whole year,* and though they said, that the Bank was *able* and *ready* to pay.

Let us see, then, Gentlemen, what were the *reasons* given *now.* "The "*most thinking* people in the world," were, as we have seen, told the last time, that the Act of renewal was "a *temporary provision,* 'till the effects of peace should have begun to operate;" and, as peace had now lasted a whole year, what reason, what pretence, what excuse, what apology was now to be found? This is what we ought to keep our eye upon. We know well, that they renewed the Act; but, in order to be able to judge of what will be done *in future,* we must take care to keep in view the *reasons,* which, at the different renewals, were given for the measure.

When he came to propose the *second* renewal *after the war was over,* it must be confessed, that Mr. AD-

DINGTON did appear to perceive the light in which he stood. He did appear sensible of his situation; and, doubtless, this was amongst the things, for which, as it was asserted by a pamphleteer soon afterwards, Mr. PITT was *under obligations* to his successor. It was on the 7th of February, 1803, that he moved for leave to bring in this bill. He begun by saying "that "it was with the *utmost reluctance* "that he submitted the proposition to "the House, but the reasons which "suggested it were too strong, and "and the *necessity* too *urgent*, to be "resisted; that necessity, however, "*he hoped, would soon disappear;* "and, he *anxiously and impatiently* "looked forward to the day, which "he trusted was not far removed, "when the Bank would be *at liberty* "to resume its payments in specie." The *grounds* for proposing this measure he stated to be, that the *course of exchange* was still against this country, and, as the House "last "year, considered that a sufficient ar-"gument for the measure, he would "appeal to the candour and good "sense of the House whether it would "be expedient to allow the restric-"tion to cease." He also said, "that a "sudden issue of cash from the Bank "would produce a run upon the coun-"try banks, and a consequent run "upon the Bank of England, which "might be productive of most serious "consequences." He further observ-ed "that the exchange being against "us had arisen from the circumstance "of *scarcity of coin*, which, of late "years had caused so much Bul-"lion to be sent out of the country, "and that it was obvious, that we "should wait the operations of a flou-"rishing commerce to bring back "some proportion of this vast amount "of Bullion, before we attempted to "permit the Bank to issue specie."

The whole world never, in my opinion, heard any thing like this before. Were it not upon record, in a manner not to be disputed, it would not, it could not, be believed. Mr. TIERNEY, and Mr. FOX, spoke against the motion, and particularly wished for an inquiry previous to the passing of such a bill. Mr. Tierney said "ac-"cording to the report of the Com-"mittee of 1797, the proportion of "cash and Bullion in the Bank "*amounted to* ONE MILLION, "when the Order of Council was "issued; and some short time after-"wards *this sum was increased to* "SIX MILLIONS. Was it not "now a fit object of inquiry; What "*had become* of their six millions? if "it was forthcoming to meet any ex-"igency? and if it was, why should "the Bank hesitate to resume their "operation? They could not be "afraid of a run upon them, for who "could now think of any material "advantage from hoarding gold?" Nevertheless, the bill passed; and thus was the Bank protected against demands upon them for cash, until six weeks after the commencement of the then next Session of Parliament, which Session began in November 1803.*

After what we have now seen, we can hardly expect to hear of any more *reasons*. It would, I think, have been utterly impossible to invent any pretext that Mr. ADDINGTON would have made use of; but, most fortunately for him, before Parliament met, and of course, before the Act expired, WAR had begun again. That was quite enough; and, without any scruple, hesitation, or ceremony, the Minister brought in a bill to prolong the Stoppage, or Restriction, till the *war should be over*, and until *six months after a definitive treaty of peace should be concluded.* He said, that "though "doubts had been entertained as to

* The whole of this debate is very important, and also a subsequent one of the 11th of February, 1803. They will be found at full length, and very accurately given, in the POLITICAL REGISTER, Vol. III. pages 1243 and 1347.

"the propriety of the measure, during "a period of peace. Under the impression, therefore, that no doubts "existed on the subject, he should "take it for granted that no objection "would be made, in the present instance, to a renewal of the measure. "It was satisfactory to know that the "credit of the Bank had remained "firm and unshaken, during the past "experience of the measure, and that "its *sufficiency to make good its engagements, both was*, and is, *unaffected by even the slightest suspicion*."*

This was all. There was very little more said about the matter. All the *anxiety* that he expressed upon the former occasion, for the happy day of cash-payments to come, was now forgotten; or he had got an entirely new view of the matter. There were some very interesting debates upon the subject, in the House of Lords, in which LORD KING and LORD GRENVILLE took a part, and in which they shewed, that they were duly impressed with the dangerous consequences of continuing this Act in force;† but, what they said was of no avail. The Act was passed; it is, as you well know, Gentlemen, in force to this day; and, the proposition of the Bullion Committee is, that it shall be in *force*, to its present extent, at least, *only* two years longer.

When we take a review of the *reasons* for the passing of this Act, at the several times at which it has been passed; when we see how those reasons have *varied;* when we see how many times the expectation of a return to cash-payments has been disappointed; but, especially when we look well into the part which the *Bank Company themselves* have borne in these transactions; when we look at what passed between the Minister and the Bank Company *previous* to the Stoppage; when we look behind the curtain and see the *plan* laid for a private Meeting of the principal Bankers to settle upon the scheme for a general meeting; when we afterwards hear the Minister, in Parliament, talking of that Meeting as of a thing in which he had had nothing to do, and citing it as a mark of the *public confidence in the Bank Paper;* when we take this view, Gentlemen, it is not, I think, possible, that any of us can ever again be deceived by *professions, promises*, and *outward appearance*, as far, at least, as relates to the subject of *Bank notes*.

I have now gone through the whole history of the Stoppage of money-payments at the Bank of England, which history, though it has, Gentlemen, taken up a good deal of time, will, I trust, be found well worth both our time and our labour. Without a knowledge of this history, it is impossible for any one to form so correct an opinion, as to the *future*, as he will be able to do with this history fairly imprinted on his mind. In this history he has before him the experience of thirteen years; and, from what has been, he will easily form his opinion as to what, under the operation of similar circumstances, is likely to be. We have, by toiling through this history, furnished ourselves with all the knowledge (of any real *use* here) possessed by the members of the Bullion Committee; and, perhaps, a little more; so that, we shall now enter into an examination of their production without any dread of difficulty in the progress, or of error in the conclusion.

I am, Gentlemen,
Your faithful Friend,
WM. COBBETT.

State Prison, Newgate, Monday,
10th December, 1810.

* See Parliamentary Debates, Vol. I, page 52. Where the reader will find Mr. ADDINGTON's grave ideas respecting *hoarding money*.

† See Parliamentary Debates, Vol. I, page 152 to 156. And page 304 to 319. These two debates are of great importance. There is scarcely any thing to be found in the Bullion Report, as touching the main points, which will not be found to have been said, upon this occasion, by one or the other of these two Noblemen.

LETTER XXI.

Appointment of the Bullion Committee—Names of the Members—Quantity of Bank-Notes, compared with the Quantity of Real Money—Amount of Bank of England Notes in 1797, and at this Time—Number of Country Banks—Probable Amount of their Notes—Amount of Real Money in the Bank of England—Probable Amount of Real Money in the Hands of the Country Bankers.

GENTLEMEN,

WE have now arrived at a point whence we can see to the end of our discussion. We have seen how the Bank and the Stocks and the Bank Notes arose; we have seen that they all grew up with the National Debt and the Taxes; we have seen, that, at last, the Bank Notes became so large in amount that they could no longer be paid in money at the Bank Shop in Threadneedle Street; we have seen the means that have, in the several stages, been resorted to, in order to protect the Bank Company against the demands of its creditors, the holders of its notes; and we have had a pretty fair view of the conduct of all the parties concerned in these transactions. With the EVIL and with the causes of the Evil we are now well acquainted: it only remains for us to obtain as good information with respect to a REMEDY.

To discover and point out a REMEDY were the objects of the BULLION COMMITTEE, of whom I must speak here a little more fully than I hitherto have done. This Committee, consisting of the members, whose names you will find below,* was, as I stated in Letter I, appointed by the House of Commons, during the last Session of Parliament, "to "inquire into the cause of the *high* "*price of Gold Bullion*, and to take "into consideration the *state of the* "*circulating medium*, &c. &c. and to "report the same to the House." They did so; and their Report was, by the House of Commons, ordered to be printed on the 8th of June last.

This Report, after shewing that the Bank Notes have depreciated; after giving very clear proofs of this fact, and also of the fact that the depreciation must continue to *increase*, unless put a stop to by some means or other; after this, the Report recommends, as a *remedy*, that the Bank Company shall be, by law, *compelled to pay their notes in cash*, as formerly, *in two years from this time;* and, therefore, the only great object which remains for our consideration, is, whether this proposed remedy be *practicable*, or, whether it be one that *cannot be put in practice*.

In order to arrive at a correct conclusion as to this great question, upon which, as you must already have perceived, the very existence, not only of

* Mr. Horner, Mr. Davies Giddy, Mr. Henry Thornton, Mr. Abercrombie, Mr. Sharp, Mr. Baring, Mr. Huskisson, Mr. Foster, Mr. Tierney, Mr. Sheridan, Mr. Grenfell, Lord Temple, Mr. Parnell, Mr. Perceval, Mr. Brand, Mr. Long, Mr. George Johnstone, Mr. Thompson, Mr. Dickenson, Mr. Manning, Mr. Magens

Entered at Stationers' Hall.
Printed by W. MOLINEUX, 5, Bream's Buildings, Chancery Lane; Published by W. COBBETT Jun. No. 8, Catherine Street Strand; and Retailed at No. 192, Strand.

the paper-money system, but also of the Stocks or Funds, entirely depends, we must, 1st, take a view of the *quantity of paper-money now afloat*, compared with the quantity of real money and bullion in the hands of the Bank Company and in those of the Country Bankers; 2d, we must inquire into the *rate of the depreciation of the paper-money*; 3rd, we must inquire into the *means which the Bank Company would have of obtaining real money*, wherewith to redeem, or pay off, their notes, or any considerable part of them, and, if we shall find, that for them to do this would be impossible, our conclusion must be, that the Bank Company cannot return to their payments in gold and silver.

The discussion of these matters I shall divide into three Letters, in this first of which I shall take a view of the *quantity of paper-money now afloat*, compared with the quantity of *real money* in the *hands of the Bank Company* and in those of *the Country Bankers*.

The amount of *Bank of England* notes in circulation before the Stoppage of payments in Gold and Silver, in the year 1797, was, as the Committee state, between 10 and 11 millions of pounds. But, as it was natural to expect, when the Bank Company was protected by Act of Parliament against the demands of their creditors, they immediately began to *increase* the quantity of their notes; and, let me ask, what lover of gain would not do the same? Where shall we find a private person of that description, who would not increase the issues of his promissory notes as long as any one would take them, if there were an Act of Parliament to protect him against the demands of the holders of those promissory notes?

That the consequence, which was naturally to be expected, did take place, was very well known, and had been clearly shewn in the Register, and much commented upon therein, long before, several years before, the Bullion Committee existed, the readers of the Register need not be told. But, the Bullion Committee have *verified* the facts and opinions given, in this respect, in the Register; they have published to the world, through the channel of the House of Commons, that, what had been before published in the Register, relating to this matter, was *sound* and *true*.

They state, with regard to the amount of the Bank of England notes, that, previous to the Stoppage of cash payments, in 1797, and the consequent Act of protection to the Bank, the amount of these notes "was between TEN and ELEVEN "millions, hardly ever falling below "NINE, and not often exceeding "ELEVEN;" and that in May 1810, the amount was upwards of TWENTY ONE millions.

Gentlemen, you have so recently felt the effects of a paper-money, not convertible into gold and silver, look at this. You see, that the amount of the Bank of England notes has been doubled in the course of 13 years, even according to the account *given in by the Bank Company themselves.* It is not my intention to insinuate, that this account is not a true one; but, it is right that we should know, that this statement has been made by the Bullion Committee from an account made out and presented to the Committee by the Bank Company themselves; and that, therefore, we may rest perfectly satisfied, that the amount of the increase in their notes has not been stated too high.

But, as yet, we have seen only one limb, and, perhaps the least fruitful of this paper-money tree. The other the *Country Banks*, has been, according to all appearance, much more prolific. It appears from the Report, that, before the Stoppage, or Restriction law was passed, there were TWO HUNDRED AND THIRTY

W. Molineux, Printer, Bream's Buildings, Chancery Lane.

Country Banks, and that, in April last, they had increased to SEVEN HUNDRED AND TWENTY ONE; which is an increase more than threefold as to the *number of Banks*, and, if we allow, as it is reasonable to do, that the notes of the old banks also increased in quantity, the addition in the whole amount must have been prodigious. No wonder that gold, and crown-pieces, disappeared; for how were they to be expected to remain in circulation along with such masses of paper?

As to the *amount* of the *Country* Notes at either of the periods beforementioned, or, at any period at all, the Bullion Committee say, that they are unable to *ascertain it* with any degree of precision; but, from certain returns obtained by them from the stamp office, they shew, that, after making all allowances, and taking the matter in the most favourable point of view, there was, during the year 1809, *in the 5 and 10 pound notes alone*, an INCREASE to the amount of more than THREE MILLIONS; and, from the other notes which appear to have been stamped in that year, there could not be an increase of less than TWO MILLIONS more in the Country notes for other sums. In that same year there was an increase of a MILLION AND A HALF in the amount of the Bank of England notes; so that, in the year 1809, the total amount of the increase of the Notes of all sorts could not be less than *six millions and a half*. And yet "the *most thinking* people" seem to be quite astonished, that they no longer see any guineas; that guineas are bought up and sent abroad; and that people in trade purchase, at a premium, with Bank Notes, the things called shillings and sixpences, *from the keepers of the Turnpike Gates*.

The amount of the Country notes, though it has not been ascertained by the Bullion Committee, and though they were unable to ascertain it, may be computed with a tolerable degree of accuracy, seeing that they have ascertained and stated, that there was, in the 5 and 10 pound notes alone, an increase to the amount of *three millions* of pounds in the year 1809, and in the whole of the Bank of England notes to the amount of *a million and a half*; for, unless any one can see, which I cannot, any reason for a greater proportionate increase in the Country Bank paper than in the London Bank paper, the question is nothing more than a very plain one in the Rule of Three (if one ought, in such a case, to be permitted to use the *Golden* Rule,) and which question would thus present itself; if 1,500,000, of increase require a total amount of issues of 21,249,980, what total amount of issues will be required by an increase of 3,095,340. The Answer will be 43,000,000 and upwards. And if we make our computation upon the increase of 5,000,000, we shall find the whole amount of Country Bank notes, in 1809, to have been 70,000,000 and upwards, which, there being 721 Country Banks, is less than 100,000 for each; and, it is well known, that many of them have half a million of notes out. Your great Bank, at Salisbury, had, I believe, notes out to the amount of 600,000 pounds.

Now, I am not aware of any thing that can be said against this mode of computation. I am, for my own part, fully persuaded that it is fair, and, that the result of it is not very far from the truth. But, in order to leave no room for cavil, let us suppose the amount of the Country notes to be only one half what it is here computed at. Even in that case there must be now in circulation paper promises to the amount of 56 millions of pounds and upwards.

This, then, is the sum against which we have to set the *coin* and *bullion*, the gold and silver *in the hands of the London Bank Company*, and *in those of the Country Bankers*.

What is the exact amount of this no one can tell, but every one must suppose, that comparatively, it is *very small indeed;* for if this had not been the case with regard to the Bank Company, even in 1797, why did they not state the amount of their real money? Why were they so shy upon that score? And, indeed, if their stock of real money had not been *very good indeed*, why did they apply to the Minister to know when he would *interfere?* If they could have stood a run of a week, they would have needed no Act of Parliament to protect them against the demands of the note-holders. But this they could not stand; and there needs no other proof of the smallness of the quantity of their cash.

In Letter XV, page 202, we have seen, that the whole amount of their *Cash* and *Bullion* and *Bills discounted* was only 4,176,080 pounds, on the 25th of February, 1797. As was there asked, who is to say how much of this consisted of *Bills discounted?* If more than one *half* had consisted of cash and bullion they would not have been jumbled together with *Bills discounted*. Indeed, the cash, at that time, in possession of the Bank Company, was computed at 1,272,000 pounds, and, in a speech of Mr. TIERNEY, quoted in Letter XX, page 276, it is stated at 1,000,000 of pounds. There is no *certainty* in this, to be sure; but, Gentlemen, we are quite certain of one thing, and that is, that when men, whether single, or in companies, have plenty of pecuniary means, they never are very cautious to *disguise* the fact.

Is it probable then, that the quantity of cash in the hands of the London Bank Company has *increased* since 1797? Is it likely that, if they had but about *a million before* they were protected against the demands of the note-holders, they have *increased* the quantity *since?* Will "the "*most thinking*" people believe this? If they will there is certainly no doubt but they are prepared for the verification of the old proverb about believing that the "moon is made of "green cheese."

And, as to the Country Banks, to suppose that they contain any thing worthy of notice, in *gold* or *bullion*, would be too absurd to be treated seriously. The *moon-raking* adventure, which has been ascribed to a *Wiltshire-man*, was thus applied by DEAN SWIFT at the memorable time of the South-Sea Bubble, when so many thousands and tens of thousands of families were ruined by jobbers and dealers in Funds and Stocks:

> One night a fool into a brook
> *Thus* from a hillock looking down,
> The *Golden stars* for *guineas* took,
> And *Silver Cynthia* for a *crown*.
>
> The point he could no longer doubt,
> He ran, he leap'd into the flood,
> There sprawl'd a while, and scarce got out,
> All cover'd o'er with slime and mud.

But, Gentlemen, foolish as our poor countryman was, in this case, he was not half so worthy of ridicule as we should be, if we, with all the information we now possess, or have, at least, had the means of possessing, were still to believe, that Country Bankers have, or ever will have, gold or silver sufficient to pay off a thousandth part of the notes that they have issued.

After taking this view of the matter; after comparing the amount of the Bank notes with the amount of the Cash and Bullion, in the hands of those by whom the notes have been issued, ought we to wonder, that those persons and all their friends, deprecate the notion of paying again in cash? You have seen, Gentlemen, in the course of these Letters, that the Bank Company have been represented, upon several occasions, as being perfectly *ready* to pay again in cash, and that they have, upon *all* occasions, been represented as *able* to pay again in cash. You have, all along, heard the Stoppage spoken of as a *temporary* measure; as a measure to last only *for a time;* the pretences were lame, to be sure, but still there were pretences. Now, all this is thrown aside, and they say, in plain terms, that not to pay in cash is a very good *permanent system.*

With such a mass of paper and so little coin and bullion, it was not to be expected that the paper would not *depreciate* or fall in value: but, as I wish to make this depreciation the subject of a separate Letter, I shall here conclude by subscribing myself

Your faithful friend,

Wm. COBBETT.

State Prison, Newgate, Monday, December 17th, 1810.

LETTER XXII.

"Legal Tenders have been the cause of the overthrow of every financial system into which they have been "introduced."—*Essay on American Paper-money.*

The Question of Legal Tender in Bank of England Notes—Two Letters received from Correspondents as to the true Constitution and Practice of the Act of 1797—How far the Bank of England Notes are a Legal Tender—They are so far as relates to Debts due from the Bank of England including the Dividends—Not so with regard to Debts and Contracts between man and man—Any holder of a Country Bank Note may compel the Payment of it in the Coin of the Kingdom—This proved by the Decision in the Case of Grigby against Oakes—The Opinions of the four Judges in that Case—The Justice of this Decision—The Reason why People have not hitherto compelled the Country Bankers to pay their Notes in Coin.

GENTLEMEN,

THE proposed subject of this Letter, was, an inquiry into *the rate of the depreciation of paper-money;* but, two letters, which I have received, in the last six days, the one from *Glasgow,* and the other from the neighbourhood of *Exeter,* induce me to devote this present Letter to the answering of them, they being upon the very importent subject of the *legal tender.*

The writer of the first letter expresses his *doubts* as to the *correctness* of my exposition of the Bank Stoppage, or Restriction Act, (See Letter XVI, page 219,) and his wishes that I would give him my opinion again, after having taken time to revise what I before said upon this part of the subject. My correspondent near Exeter, who tells me that he is *a farmer,* thanks me for the useful information that he is so good as to say he has received from this series of Letters, and begs me, in a very earnest manner, to tell him, whether I am *quite sure,* that I was correct, when I said, that any holder of *country* bank-notes might *compel the payment of them in gold and silver.* Both these gentlemen have put their names to their letters; but, as the same doubts and uncertainties may have occurred to others of my readers, I shall give my answer in this public manner, and, after having so done, there will, I trust, remain no doubt or uncertainty at all.

I stated to you, Gentlemen, in Letter XVI, that, as far as related to *debts due from the Bank of England,* the notes of *that* Bank were, by the Act of 1797, called the Bank Stoppage, or Restriction Act, made a *legal tender;* that is to say, that the creditor was compelled to take those notes in payment, or to go without any payment at all. If, for instance, any one of you has a Bank of England note of *ten* pounds, and carry it to Threadneedle Street for payment, the Bank Company may compel you to take other of their notes in payment, or they may, if you refuse such notes in payment, refuse you payment in any thing else.

It is the same with regard to the payment of the *dividends*, that is to say, the *interest* of the *Stocks* or *Funds*. If, for instance, our neighbour, GRIZZLE GREENHORN, when she goes to receive her half-year's interest upon her Stock, which, you know, is paid her by the Bank Company, were to say: "pay me in good "gold and silver," would, or might, receive for answer, an assertion, that the law, the Act of 1797, protected the Bank Company against such an *unreasonable* demand. In a word, the Bank Company might refuse, absolutely refuse to pay her her interest in any thing but their own promissory notes; and, then, if she tendered them those promissory notes for payment, they might refuse to pay them in any thing but *other* of their own notes; that is to say, they would be ready to give her *fresh promises to pay* in lieu of the promises to pay which they had given her before; but, she could not compel them to give her one shilling's worth of gold or silver, except there might be due to her, in the way of interest, any *fractional part of a pound.*

Thus far, then, the Bank Company's notes are a *legal tender*. And, in the affairs between man and man, if such notes be once *accepted* and *received* in payment of any debt whatever, they are, *after* such acceptance and receipt, to be considered as a legal payment in that case. If, for instance, I owe my neighbour a hundred pounds, and tender him Bank of England notes in payment, and he *receive* them in payment to the amount of the sum due to him, he is paid, I am acquitted of my debt; he cannot afterwards sue me for the debt, upon the ground, that I have not paid him *money*, as he might do in the case of other promissory notes, if there were no particular agreement to bar him.

But, here the legal tender of Bank of England notes stops. They are not *yet*, in any other case, put upon a footing with money. As to all the transactions between man and man, except in the above circumstances, which can occur only where the Bank of England itself is a party, no person is obliged to take Bank of England notes in payment of any debt, or legal demand. And this is a thing well worthy of the attention of all those, who have it in contemplation to enter into contracts which are to have *a future operation;* for, if the value of gold and silver, compared with that of Bank notes, should continue to increase, those who now make contracts for payments to be made some years hence, should bear it constantly in mind, that the party to whom they will have to make such payment, will, at all times, have it in his power *to insist upon gold coin in payment.*

If this be the law, without any other exceptions than those above named, it follows, of course, that I can have not the least hesitation in telling my Devonshire correspondent, that I am *quite sure*, that any holder of a *Country* Bank note has it, at all times, in his power to *compel the payment of it in gold or silver coin from the King's mint, and of full weight and due fineness.* I know, that a different notion has prevailed; and, I have heard it said, or seen it stated in print, that this *compulsion* cannot be effected; because, it has been said, if you were to bring your action of debt against Paperkite and Co. they would *pay the amount into Court in Bank of England notes;* and that, upon proof of their having done this being produced, the Court would stop the proceedings, or at least, throw all the costs thereafter incurred *upon you*.

This would, indeed, make the Bank of England notes a legal tender *in fact*, though not *in law*; or, in other words, it would make an Act of Parliament a mere delusion, a shuffle, a cheat, a base premeditated fraud. But, this is all a mistake; it is not founded in fact; the Courts would attempt to do no such thing; for, if one could in any case, suppose the inclination to exist in the mind of a Judge, he would not do it, nor think of it, in the face of what has already been done.

The question has been *decided*, and that, too, with all possible solemnity, as will appear from the case which I am now about to lay before you, and the perusal of which will remove all doubts whatever upon the subject.—There appears to have been no doubt about the *letter* of the law, in the mind of either of my correspondents; but they both doubt of *its interpretation in the Courts*; and the last-mentioned gentleman says, that, though upon the *face* of the Act, there is nothing to warrant the supposition, that a holder of a *Country* Bank note could not compel the payment of it in gold and silver, yet he thinks, that such holder would, by the judicial construction of the Act, be defeated in any attempt to compel such payment; and, he seems to think, that this is pretty clearly demonstrated in the fact (as he supposes it to be), that no one has ever yet attempted to compel *Country* Bankers to pay their notes in gold and silver.

He will, doubtless, be surprised to find, that the attempt has not only been *made*, but that it fully *succeeded*. In the year 1801, four years after the Bank Stoppage, or Restriction Act was passed, a Mr. Grigby, in the county of Suffolk, went to the Bank Shop of Messrs. Oakes and Co. of St. Edmunds Bury, and in presenting them one of their own Five Guinea notes for payment, demanded *money*. The Bankers tendered him *a five pound Bank of England note*, and *five shillings*, which he refused to receive, saying, that the five pound Bank of England note was *not money*, and that he would not take it. The Bankers told him, that if he wanted specie for his *accommodation*, they would let him have it. He declined to receive it in that way; he said that he stood in no need of it as an *accommodation*; that he demanded it as a *right*; and that, unless they paid him in the *coin* of the kingdom, he would bring an action of debt against them. Upon this ground they refused him payment in coin, whereupon he brought his action and obtained a verdict in his favour *at the Assizes*; but the question *of law* was, upon the motion of the Defendant's counsel, reserved for decision by the Judges; and the following is the Report of the Case, as argued before, and determined by the four Judges, of the Court of Common Pleas, on the 19th of November 1801.

Grigby against Oakes and Another—"This was an action on a promissory note; the Defendants as to "all but five guineas pleaded *non assumpserunt*, and as to the remaining five guineas they pleaded *a tender*. The cause came on to be "tried at the Summer Assizes for "Suffolk, before Mr. Baron Hotham, "when a verdict was found for the "Plaintiff, with one shilling damages, "subject to the opinion of the Court "upon the following case. The Defendants are Bankers at Bury St. "Edmunds, and issued the note in "question for five guineas, payable on "demand to the bearer. On the 31st "of January last, the Plaintiff carried "several notes to the shop of the Defendant, and demanded payment. "He first presented other notes, to "the amount of 50 guineas, for which "he received payment, partly in "Bank of England notes and partly "in cash, the cash being ten pounds, "and being the proportion of money "they usually pay. He then presented the note in question, for which the Defendants tendered in payment a five pound Bank of England note and five shillings in in silver. This the Plaintiff refused on the ground that the tender was partly in a Bank of England note, objecting to such note, and insisted on being paid wholly in money. The Plaintiff did not at the time say he wanted money for his own particular accommodation, but stated that he came on purpose to have cash for the note, or to bring an action if payment in money was refused.

"The question for the opinion of the Court was, Whether under the circumstances before stated, the Plaintiff was entitled to recover?

"*Serjeant* SHEPHERD, for the Defendants, urged, that though unquestionably previous to the passing of the 37 Geo. 3, c. 45, commonly called the Bank Act, a bank-note would not have been a legal tender, yet that, since the passing of the above Act such notes must be considered as cash, for that the necessary consequence of the above Act being to absorb a vast proportion of the actual cash of the country, the Legislature must have intended to give a new character to Bank notes by way of substitute; that they had specifically declared them to be a good tender so as to prevent an arrest, and yet if the same spirit which actuated the present Plaintiff in the commencement of this action was to continue to influence his conduct, and that of others also, a Defendant, though exempted from arrest might ultimately be taken in execution, though ready to pay in Bank notes, since he might possibly be unable to satisfy the judgment obtained against him altogether in money: because even if a sale of his goods took place, the Sheriff might not be able to avoid receiving a large proportion of bank-notes from the purchasers; that, indeed, in some respects, bank-notes were privileged by the 37 Geo. 3, c. 45, beyond cash, inasmuch as a tender of them in satisfaction of a debt operated to discharge a party from arrest, which was not the case with a tender of money, which must be pleaded in bar; and that no contrary inference could be drawn from the 8th section of the Act, which declared payments in bank-notes to be equivalent to payments in cash, if made and accepted as such, because that must have been the case before the passing of the Act, and therefore that clause must be deemed nugatory.

"*Serjeant* SELLON, on the other side, was stopped by the Court.

"LORD ALVANLEY, *(Chief Justice)*.—The question for the Court to decide is a mere question of law, arising, as it has been contended, out of the provisions of the 37 Geo. 3, c. 45. In fact we are called upon to say whether it follows as a necessary consequence from that Act, that a tender in bank-notes is equivalent to a tender in money? It may be very true that individuals may be occasionally subjected to great inconveniences from the operation of that Act; but are we therefore to say that the Legislature has enacted that which the provisions of the Act do not warrant? If we were at liberty to refer to our own private knowledge of the language that was held in Parliament while this Act was pending, no doubt could be entertained upon the subject. We know that it was very much canvassed at that time, Whether or not the Legislature ought to go the length of declaring bank-notes a good legal tender? If, therefore, it had been intended by the Legislature so to make them, that intention would have been expressed in such clear terms that no question could have arisen upon the subject. Indeed, it is expressly provided, in the 2nd section of the Act; that if the Gover-

"nor and Company of the Bank of "England shall be sued on any of "their notes, or for any sum of mo- "ney, payment of which in their notes "the party suing refuses to accept, "they may apply to the Court in "which such proceedings are insti- "tuted, to stay proceedings during "such time as they are restricted "from paying in cash. But with re- "spect to individuals it was not intend- "ed to prevent any creditor, who "should be so disposed, from capti- "ously demanding a payment in mo- "ney, though such a creditor is de- "prived of the benefit of arresting his "debtor. Thank God, few such cre- "ditors as the present Plaintiff have "been found since the passing of the "act! But yet, whatever inconveni- "ences may arise, and to whatever "length they may go, Parliament and "not this Court must be applied to for "a remedy. Inconvenience arising "from the operation of an act of Par- "liament, can be no ground of argu- "ment in a Court of Law; and even if "it were, still I should entertain no "doubt, that it was the intention of "the Legislature to make bank-notes "a legal payment only in certain cases "by them expressed, and that in all "other cases they should remain upon "the same footing upon which they "stood before the act, except as to "the exemption from arrest, which "they afford to the party tendering "them in payment. The 8th section "of the act, which has been treated "as nugatory in the argument, how- "ever it may enact nothing new, still "appears to me pregnant with the in- "tentions of Parliament, and to speak "loudly the resolution not to alter the "character of bank-notes, but in those "cases which are specially provided "for. Without however referring to "any of those specific clauses, and ar- "guing from them as to the intent of "the Legislature, I should be clearly "of opinion, that the present Plaintiff "is entitled to our judgment in his fa- "vour.

"*Judge* HEATH. I am of the "same opinion. The question for us "to decide is, whether a tender in "bank-notes is a good legal tender? "Now the 37 Geo. 3, c. 45. appears "to me to negative that question; for "the several provisions of the act "making them a good and legal tender "in certain excepted cases, excludes "the idea of their being so generally "in cases not provided for by the act. "It has been argued, however that "the operation of the act will in many "cases be very injurious, unless we "determine it to be a necessary infer- "ence from the act that bank-notes "were intended by the Legislature "to be put upon the same footing as "cash. But whatever inconvenien- "ces may arise, the Courts of Law "cannot apply a remedy. I think, "indeed, the Legislature acted wisely, "having the recent example of France "before their eyes, to avoid making "bank-notes a legal tender; for in "France we know that legislative pro- "visions of that kind in favour of "paper currency only tended to de- "preciate the paper it was designed "to protect, and were ultimately re- "pealed, as injurious in their nature.

"*Judge* ROOKE. I am of the "same opinion.

"*Judge* CHAMBRE. This case ap- "pears to me almost too plain for "argument. It has been thought "that the Courts went a great way "in holding a tender in bank-notes to "be a good tender, if not objected to "at the time. Certainly that was an "innovation; though perhaps a bene- "ficial one. But the act upon which "the present question arises affords "nothing but arguments against the "inference attempted to be drawn "by it. Surely the observation that "in some respects the Legislature "have put bank-notes on a more fa- "vourable footing than cash, leads to "a conclusion directly contrary to "that which it was intended to sup- "port. If the Legislature have not "gone far enough, it is for them, "not for us, to remedy the defect. "Indeed, by making bank-notes a "good tender in certain cases, specifically provided for, they appear to "me to have negatived the construction we are now desired to put upon "the act."

It will hardly be doubted, that I have copied this report with great care. I have, indeed, given every word of it; but, for the satisfaction of my correspondents, to whom I am really obliged for their inquiries, I will add, that the report is taken from a well known law-book, entitled, "Bosanquet's and Puller's Reports of "Cases argued and determined in the "Court of Common Pleas and Exchequer Chamber and in the House "of Lords, from Michaelmas Term, "in the 40th year of the reign of "George III. (1799) to Michaelmas "Term, in the 42nd Year of the same "reign (1801,) both inclusive."

After reading this report, there cannot remain, in the mind of any man, the smallest doubt upon this subject. Here is the fact, in practice as well as in theory, clearly established, that any holder of a *Country* bank-note, payable to bearer on demand, or the holder of any such note, except of the Bank of England, may, at any time, when he pleases, demand payment of such note in the gold and silver coin issued from the King's mint, that coin being of legal *weight* and *fineness*. And, if such payment be refused, *upon demand*, the holder of such note may immediately proceed to sue for such payment, which, if the party sued has the means, he must finally pay in coin, together with full costs of suit.*

And, indeed, if this was not the law, the Bank of England notes would be *a legal tender* to all intents and purposes; for, the issuers of these notes being protected by law against the holders of *them*, the holder of a *Country* Bank note would have no claim upon the Country Banker, or upon any body else, for *coin*. The man who chooses to take a Bank of England note, does it *knowing* that he cannot force any one to pay him its nominal amount in coin; and, therefore if he choose to take it, he has no reason to complain. Persons, who buy Stock, *know* that they are to be paid their interest in Bank of England notes; and, therefore, they have no reason to complain. But, if either of you sell your corn or your wool, and take a *Country* Bank note for it, that is to say, the promissory note of your neighbour, you expect to have the *real* worth of your corn, or your wool; and, of course, you expect to be paid by your neighbour in the *real money of the kingdom*, which money, as I have now shewn you, you have a *legal*, as well as a *moral*, right to demand.

Lest any one should raise a doubt upon the circumstance of Mr. GRIGBY's demand having been founded upon a note given for *guineas* instead of *pounds*, I beg you to observe, that this circumstance was not even alluded to by either of the Judges, or by the Counsel who argued against Mr. GRIGBY. You will perceive, besides, that the Judges speak generally of *all debts*, except those only due from the Bank of England itself. The decision is founded upon the broad principle, that Bank of England notes may be refused *in all cases*, except only those wherein *the Bank of England itself is the debtor*, including the dividends upon the National Debt, and there *the Bank* is regarded as the debtor to the Stock-holder.

It is also worthy of your observation, that, though the Chief Justice seemed to think, that it might become necessary to make the Bank of England notes a *legal tender* in *all cases*

* The *shilling damages*, mentioned in the first part of the above Report, is merely the *nominal* damages, which it is the custom to lay, in cases where the object, as in this case, is to ascertain the question of *right*. But, the Plaintiff had his *costs of suit* in this case, as every other plaintiff must have, who brings an action in a similar way, and on similar grounds.

another of the Judges expressed himself as decidedly of opinion, that such a measure would be both unjust and impolitic; and, indeed, that it would be, in part, at least, to imitate the measures of ROBESPIERRE, who compelled the people of France to take paper-money upon *pain of death*.

If it should be asked, why other persons have not done as Mr. GRIGBY did, the answer is, that the people of this country, generally speaking, have really thought, that, by the Act of 1797, the Bank of England notes were made, to all intents and purposes, a *legal tender*, and, of course, that, if a man refused to take them in payment, he had not the means of forcing the debtor to pay him in any other sort of thing. Nor is this generally prevailing error to be much wondered at, seeing what were the *means* made use of at the time of the Bank Stoppage. When you reflect upon the famous *meeting* and *resolutions* at the *Mansion-House* in London, the secret history of which I have given you. When you reflect upon the effect of these RESOLUTIONS, issued under the signature of the LORD MAYOR; followed, as they immediately were by Resolutions, of a similar purport, from the PRIVY COUNCIL, and from the Justices *assembled in Quarter Sessions*, in the several counties. When you reflect on the *official* manner, and the *authoritative air* of all these promulgations, you will cease to wonder, that the Resolutions to take and pay the paper of the Bank of England were, by the mass of the people, regarded as having the *force of law*.

Now, however, you know the true value of those Resolutions; you know what is, and what is not, the law, relating to this important matter, in which every man of you is so deeply interested, and on your judgment and discretion with respect to which may depend the permanent welfare of yourselves and your families, to assist in the advancement of which welfare has always been, and always will be, a principal object of the labours of

Your faithful friend,

WM. COBBETT.

State Prison, Newgate, Monday, December 24th, 1810.

LETTER XXIII.

"It is in the *last twenty years* of the Funding System, that all the *great shocks* begin to operate."—*Paine.*

Events since the Date of the foregoing Letter—Bank Notice about the Dollar—Various Reports of the Effect of that Measure—Proposals in Parliament respecting the Bullion Report.

GENTLEMEN,

In reviving my correspondence with you, it will be necessary for me to revert for a moment to the point, at which I broke off, which was at Letter XXII, in which, as you will recollect, it was shewn, for the satisfaction of two correspondents in the country, that any man, having country bank-notes in his possession, had (and he still has, of course) the power of compelling the drawer of such notes *to pay him in gold or silver*, the lawful coin of the realm.

But, that Letter was a digression from the main track of our subject, which, at the close of Letter XXI, was leading us into the great question as to the *depreciation*, that is to say, *fall*, of the Bank of England notes; a question, which has caused more discussion than any other that has been agitated for many years past, and which, I think, we may now look upon as completely decided, seeing that, while the dispute was going on, the Bank Company themselves have done an act which can, in the mind of no man out of a mad-house, leave the smallest doubt upon the subject.

Nevertheless, as I wish that this series of letters should contain *the whole* of what I have thought, and still think, relating to this interesting matter; I shall treat of the question here spoken of, after I have recorded the *events*, which have taken place *since I last addressed you;* and which events are important to a degree, that few persons, comparatively speaking, appear to imagine.

When, on the 24th of December, I wrote my last Letter to you, I did expect, that the winter would not pass over our heads without some striking change as to the circulating currency of the country. It appeared to me, as I had, upon former occasions, told my readers, quite impossible, that things could go on much longer without events that would strike the impudent partizans of the paper system dumb. The guinea had, for some time, been a marketable commodity; and under such circumstances, the paper will not continue much longer without being openly at a discount in all transactions. The coin of every denomination grew daily more and more scarce; till at last, change for a pound note was with difficulty obtained; and, as these difficulties increased, people, of course, felt an increased inclination to hoard the coin.

As a *remedy* for this evil, the Bank Company issued a *Notice*, raising the Dollar (which was in circulation at the rate of 5*s*.) to 5*s*. 6*d*. and it was afterwards found, that this Notice had been issued with the advice and approbation of the PRIVY COUNCIL, or, at least, of a Committee of the Privy Council, appointed to watch over the affairs of Coin.* This Notice, which was first published on the 18th of March, not only failed to produce the intended effect; but, it produced an effect *precisely the opposite* of that, which was intended by the Privy Counsellors and the Bank Directors. The few Dollars that were in circulation immediately disappeared, and the distress for *change* became so great, that people were obliged to take ten shillings worth or 15 shillings worth of *halfpence* in changing a pound note, which halfpence were, for the most part, mere *raps*, not worth a tenth part of their nominal value.

Many of the shop-keepers in London, in order to procure the means of carrying on their business, notified, by bills put in their windows, that they would receive the Dollar (the real value of which, is *less* than 4*s*. 6*d*.) at 5*s*. 9*d*. and some of them notified, that they would receive it at 6*s*. The same continues to be done now; and, that man must be blind indeed, who does not perceive, that *two prices* have to a certain extent, already taken place.

The inconvenience arising from the want of money *under a pound note* was felt very severely by the Bankers, whose customers drawing upon them for any sums that they might happen to want, frequently, of course, drew for *parts of a pound*. These the Bankers were unable to supply; and, on the 9th of April, a circular paragraph appeared in the London newspapers, exhorting people to draw for whole pounds. On the same day it was stated, that, in the shops, markets,

---

* The *Notice*, and the *Minute* of these Privy Counsellors will be found in the Appendix (C).

and public offices, people gave *written acknowledgments* for the parts of a pound, and left them thus unpaid. On the 11th of April, Mr. MANNING, the Deputy Governor of the Bank, and who is also a Member of Parliament, informed the House, that the Bank were about to issue a large quantity of Dollars; and he observed, that those persons who were hoarding them, in the expectation that they would rise in price, would be disappointed.——Some days before this (on the 4th of April) the Bank thought it necessary to publish an advertisement, that the report of great quantities of their notes having been forged, and that the plates from which the said notes had been taken, had been stolen, was wholly false; and, it seems, that this report was spread very widely through the country; the object being to excite suspicion of the Bank of England notes, and thereby to insure a preference for the Country bank-notes.——On the 19th of April, it was stated in the public prints, that a person had a promissory note dishonoured because he could not produce to the person, who had to receive the payment, the change of 18s. 3*d.*——On the 23rd of April a prisoner, confined for debt in the Marshalsea Prison, obtained his release, because his creditor in paying him his maintenance money, gave him a piece of foreign coin instead of a sixpence.——On the same day, it was stated in the public prints, that at some of the public offices, change was not only refused, but that certain of the *Clerks* in those offices, were dealers in the article, and *supplied the bankers with silver at 3 per cent.*——On the same day, 23rd of April, JAMES KING, a Guard to a coach, was taken before the Lord Mayor, upon a charge of having *bought guineas*, and was *held to bail.*——On the 26th of April, there was a paragraph, published in all the London daily prints, stating, that the *Chinese* had just discovered that gold and silver were too abundant with them, and, it was added, that they were going *to send great quantities of it hither*, some of which might be speedily expected. In the public prints of the 27th, 29th and 30th of April, it was stated, that *ten thousand pounds* in gold had been seized on board of a ship, about to carry it abroad. Many statements of this sort had appeared before, but this one was worthy of particular attention.——Also that a riot, attended with acts of violence and killing, had taken place at Sampford, in consequence of the scarcity of change.—A circular paragraph appeared at this time reprobating the practice of hoarding, and hinting that it would be proper to *punish* it as a *crime.*——At the same time another circular paragraph appeared advising people *not to hoard the change*, for that a new silver coinage was just coming out that would sink the value of the present coin.——At the same time *Mock bank-notes* were circulated from the *King's Bench and Fleet Prisons*, by the means of which some unwary persons were cheated. An account of gold lawfully exported during one week was published at this time, from which it was manifest, that the gold and silver were going to France and her dominions as fast as possible. It was now announced that the Bank had issued more Dollars, and that £.300 worth had been sent to each of the Banking Houses in London.

Such, Gentlemen, were the symptoms of the effect of raising the nominal value of the dollar; and on the 8th of May, it was stated in the public prints, that another seizure of guineas had been made on board a ship sent into Dover. The words of the statement were these:——"*Four thousand and* "*fifty more guineas* have been found "on board the ship sent into Dover "last week. It is supposed she will "be *pulled to pieces*, as her very *iron* "*ballast is hollowed to receive gold.* "She is called the New Union of "London." They may pull her to pieces and burn her; they may do what they like with her; but, Gentlemen, as long as this paper-money exists in England, the gold and silver will continue to go out of it in some way or other. The Government may be ingenious, and we know it is able to employ great numbers of artful men; but, all their art put together; and all the powers of the government, not excepting the power of life and death, will never make gold and silver circulate at par with a depreciated paper.

I have thus filled up the history of the time since I last addressed you. That time is hardly *five months*, and yet, what events are here! What a *change* is here, in so short a space of time! And, can you be made to believe, that the thing will *stop where it is?* Is it possible that you can be persuaded to believe, that the Bank Notes will now, or will ever, *revive?* The grand effort now, with all those who wish to deceive the people, and to profit from their credulity, is to persuade them, that it is not the Bank Note that has *fallen*; but, the gold and silver that have *risen*. This seems to be the last trick in the budget; but, what I have to say upon this head I must reserve till I come to my intended Letter upon the subject of depreciation.

In the mean while we must see what has been passing *in Parliament*, relating to this matter; so that, before we proceed upon the remainder of our inquiries, we may have the whole history of the paper-money before us, down to the very day when we shall come to our conclusion. In the foregoing Letters, there will be found, I am convinced, the most complete history of our Paper Money that has ever yet appeared in print. We have there traced it from its very outset to the day when the people of Salisbury became, all in a moment, destitute of the means of getting a dinner. In this Letter its history has been brought down to *last Saturday*; and all that we have now to do is to give, in as few words as possible, the history of the BULLION DEBATE, which, perhaps, would be unnecessary for *our present* purposes; but, this is a subject every fact belonging to which ought to be so recorded as to be capable of being hereafter referred to; and ought, if possible, to be made known in every part of the world.

The Report of the Bullion Committee, which was printed last year, was laid before the House of Commons but a short time previous to its rising. It was ordered to be printed on the 8th of June, and I must say, that it gives me great pleasure to reflect, that it issued from the press *on the very day that I was sent to jail!* I shall always remember this with satisfaction. It will be a source of delight to me as long as I have breath in my body; aye, and it will be borne in mind, too, long after the bank-notes and all, yea *all*, that thereon *depend*, shall have come to their true level; their proper state.

The time being so short, the House could not take the Report into consideration, during the last Session; therefore, this part of the business was to be performed during this Session. The Chairman of the Committee, Mr. FRANCIS HORNER, was to propose some measure to be adopted in consequence of the Report; but, he being a *lawyer* and a *placeman* at the same time; having to go the Western circuit and to manage the Nabob of Arcot's Debts, he, of course, could hardly find time for this Bullion affair. After many appointments and disappointments, however, he, at last, brought the matter forward on Monday last, the 6th instant, when a Debate ensued, which lasted during four successive *nights*; it being the custom in this Assembly to carry on the greater part of their works after it is dark.

Previous, however, to this Debate Mr. HORNER had laid upon the table of the House a string of PROPOSI-

TIONS, expressive of his opinions as to the state of the coin and paper-money of the country, and also as to the remedy to be applied. In a few days after these had been before the house, Mr. NICHOLAS VANSITTART, who took the other side of the question, laid before the House a set of *opposing* PROPOSITIONS; which he soon afterwards followed by a set of Propositions being the former set amended; and these were followed by another paper from Mr. HORNER, containing Propositions in the form of *amendments* upon his brother lawyer's Propositions, both of the gentlemen being "learned friends."

The way being thus prepared, all the preliminary steps having been taken, the discussion was entered upon on the day before-mentioned, at the end of *one year, two months, and fourteen days* from the time that the Committee commenced its labours. I have began inserting this Debate, and I shall insert all the principal speeches before I have done; and I do it, because I wish to afford all my readers, and you, Gentlemen, in particular, an opportunity of perusing, at your leisure, what these persons have said upon this important subject; and, besides, my wish is to place these speeches where they may be, at all times, *conveniently referred to*, seeing that my conviction is, that *events* are now hastening on apace; events that will set all low cunning, all chicanery, all trick, at defiance; and that, of course, will put the opinions, contained in these speeches, to the test. My conviction is, that the time is not far distant, when it will be impossible to deceive the people of England; when *truth* will reign; and, at that time, it will be of great advantage for us to know what have been the opinions of men who have taken a part in these discussions, and to what point, whether good or evil, their endeavours have tended*.

What *we* have to discuss is the question of *depreciation*, or *fall*, in the value of the Bank Notes; and, after that, the *remedy* proposed by Mr. HORNER and those who side with him. I shall, I trust, go to work in a way very different indeed from that of these gentlemen; and, when I have written my opinion, there the matter will rest, and the truth of our several opinions will be tried by *Time*, which tries all things.

I remain,

Gentlemen,

Your friend,

WM. COBBETT.

State Prison, Newgate, Friday, May, 10th, 1811.

---

* Appendix D.

LETTER XXIV.

"Sauce for the Goose is sauce for the Gander"—*Old Proverb.*

Injury to Commerce by Buonaparté—He is said to have caused the Gold to leave England—The Fault is with our Government—Our Appeals to the French People absurd—Forged Bank Notes sent into Kent from France—Forged Assignats—Decision in the Court of King's Bench

GENTLEMEN,

WE have now to discuss the question of *Depreciation*. We have now to inquire, whether the Bank of England Notes have, or have not, *depreciated*; that is to say, *fallen in value*.

After what we have seen in the former Letters, and particularly in that immediately preceding, it is, indeed, nearly useless to *put* this question to any man of sense, and much more so to make it a subject of serious discussion. Nevertheless, it will be right so to do; seeing that these Letters are intended to treat of every part of this great subject, and to put upon record all the material facts and arguments appertaining to it.

In the House of Commons, during the Debate on the Bullion Report and on the Resolutions thereon proposed, by Mr. FRANCIS HORNER on the one side, and Mr. NICHOLAS VANSITTART on the other, it was contended, by those who were for Mr. VANSITTART, that is to say, by the MINISTRY, and their adherents; by this part of the House it was contended, that the Bank paper had *not depreciated*, or *fallen* in value; and, being asked, how they then accounted for the fact, that a guinea was worth 26*s.* or 27*s.* they answered, that it was very true, that Gold and Silver had *risen*; but, that the Bank paper had *not fallen*.

They were then asked, how, since they would insist upon it that it was a *rise* of Gold and Silver, it had come to pass at this time above all others. Allowing, for argument's sake, that it was a *rise* in the value of *the guinea*, they were asked how the value of the guinea came to rise. Their answer to this was, *that it was owing chiefly to the injury done to our commerce by the extraordinary, the cruel, the savage measures of the inexorable tyrant Buonaparté*, whom they designated by every appellation characteristic of a despot, and even a fiend,

Gentlemen, we will stop here and make a few observations upon these charges against the Emperor of France; for, it would be very foolish in us, who call ourselves "the *most* "*thinking* people in the world," to suffer ourselves to be amused with charges against Napoleon, when we should be considering of the real cause of the mischief that is now come upon us, and of the greater mischief that is still coming, and will come with most dreadful effect, unless we take timely measures for preventing that effect; this would be selling ourselves to laughter indeed, making ourselves an object for the contempt of Europe, not excepting the Dutch and those other nations, whom, with empty insolence, our hireling writers and others affect to *pity*.

We call upon the Bank for Gold and Silver in payment of their promissory notes. They have no Gold or Silver to give us; or, at least, none do they give. They are protected by law against our demands. Some persons propose to remove this impediment to our demands. The men in power and a great majority of the House of Commons say, *no*; and, they, in objecting to the proposition, say, that the Bank *have not the gold and silver*; that *they cannot get it*; and, that it is, therefore, *impossible to make them pay*. This is a sorry answer enough; but, when we complain, we are told, that the *fault* is not with the Government or with the Bank, and that it is wholly with Buonaparté, by the means of whose laws, edicts, and workings of one sort or another, the Gold and Silver have been drawn out of England.

What should we think, Gentlemen, what should we "*thinking* people" think of a General, who was to write home word, that he had been beaten and routed and lost half his army; but, that the fault was none of his, and that it was wholly the fault of the enemy's General, who had adopted against him a series of extraordinary, cruel, and savage measures? What should we thinking people say to such a general? What would Mr. QUIN, the editor of the Traveller news-paper, in his sublime orations, in the Common Council, say to such a general? Would he vote him thanks and a sword? I do not say that he would not; but, I think, that you will agree with me, that such a general would, amongst most men, meet with but a cold reception; and, that he would be told, that it was the *business* of the enemy to beat him, to rout him, to break him up, to ruin him; and that it was *his business* to prevent the enemy from so doing, and also to beat and break up and ruin the enemy.

Just such, must, if we have a grain of sense left, be our answer to the ministers and their adherents, when they blame Buonaparté for having deprived us of our Gold and Silver. It was *their business* to prevent him from doing us this mischief. It was their business to protect the country against the fatal effects of the enemy's measures; and, if they found themselves unequal to the task, they should have said so; and, I warrant them, there would not have been wanting others to take the labour off their hands. These ministers and their predecessors, for the last twenty years, have had the complete command of all the means, all the resources, of this kingdom, of every sort. They have carried all the measures that they proposed. They have found out the way of putting down all opposition, or, at least, of rendering all opposition quite inefficient; and, therefore, to them, and to them alone, the nation is to look for responsibility for whatever mischiefs exist, or are likely to exist. If, indeed, all be well; if there be nothing to complain of; if the nation be in no danger; if there be no evil; then, they have nothing to be blamed for; but, if there be any thing in our situation, the existence of which we have cause to lament, to whom are we to look for responsibility but *to them?*

But, to take another view of the matter, what, let me ask, has Napoleon done against our commerce and our currency, for which he will not easily find a justification in *our example?* Have we neglected any means in our power to injure the commerce and the finances of France? Did not Pitt, from the very outset of the war against the French Jacobins and Levellers, call it *a war of finance?* And, were not all our efforts bent down towards the beating of France through her finances? This is notoriously the fact; and, as to her commerce, it must be well known to every one, that we risked a war with the American States for the purpose of intercepting *provisions* in their way to the people of France, *when they were menaced with famine.* Was this fair and honourable warfare? I shall be told that it was. I will not discuss the point. But, if it was so, what reason have we to complain now, when France prevents us, *not from receiving corn from her dominions;* but, merely from *sending our products to those dominions.* This is the utmost that Napoleon does, or that he can do; and, I put it, then, to any reasonable man, whether we have real cause of complaint. We may be *sorry* for what Napoleon is doing; and we must be sorry for the individuals who suffer from his measures, but, can we complain *of him* for not receiving our goods *now,* when we recollect, that we would not suffer the people of France to receive *flour* from America when we thought them in the midst of famine, and when we further recollect, that we openly avowed the *wish* and the *endeavour* to prevent their receiving *Jesuit's Bark,* a drug so necessary, in many cases, to the preservation of life? This was *fair* in us, I shall be told. Very well. That I am not questioning; but, if this was fair; if a state of war tolerated this, have *we,* I ask

Entered at Stationers' Hall.

London:—Printed by Wm. Molineux, Bream's Buildings, Chancery Lane.

again, any reason to complain of him, any reason to call him *tyrant* (as GEORGE ROSE did) because he will not now permit any part of his people to receive goods which are our produce or our property?

Oh, no! We must expect that the people of France have the same sort of feelings that we have; and, Gentlemen, *mark it well,* I pray you, we intercepted the flour on its way to France long before Napoleon's name was known to us. We, or at least, our venal writers, now affect a vast deal of *compassion* for the *people* of France. These writers appear to lament that the French *people* are subjected to so terrible a despotism. But, either the people of France hear what our writers say, or they do not: if they do not hear it, then it cannot possibly produce any effect upon them; and, if they do hear it, they cannot fail to call to mind, that *we have been at war against them through all their forms of government;* and, that while they were under a *republican* form, or *name,* our hostility was much more decided and bitter than at this moment; for, we then declared war against the principles of their constitution; we declared that no relations of peace were to be maintained with them; and, now that they are under a *monarchy* (for that means a government by the will of *one* person), we affect to feel a great deal of *pity* for them; we sigh to see them *free;* and call upon them, as loudly as our venal writers can, to rise against their *tyrant.* Had we begun war with them only when their revolution had worked itself into a monarchy, then, indeed, our appeals to them against their ruler might have been of some avail; but, how is it possible for them to believe, that we are now desirous of seeing them free, when they recollect our conduct at the outset of the war; and for many years, during its continuance? All our appeals, therefore, from Napoleon to the *people* of France are absurd; and only bespeak the desperateness of our situation.

To return more closely to our subject; it appears from the report of the Bullion Debate, that Lord CASTLEREAGH said, that the tyrant of the Continent had, thus far, been defeated in all his attempts against us; that he at first attempted *invasion,* that he next endeavoured to excite *rebellion,* that he then assailed our *commerce;* and, that having failed in all these, he was now endeavouring to ruin our *currency.*

Now, how far this statement was true, I shall not pretend to say; and, indeed, except as to the last point, it is beside my purpose to make any remark upon what is reported to have been said by this Lord. That that part of the statement is true, there can, however, be little doubt; for, it has been stated in the public prints, that there have been great quantities of forged Notes, purporting to be Notes of the Bank of England, *sent into this country from France and Holland.* This interesting fact has been very carefully kept out of the London daily papers; but the country papers have been less cautious, owing, I suppose, to their being at too great a distance from *good advice* and *powerful arguments.* The following article, which I take from the OXFORD MERCURY of the 4th instant, will be quite sufficient to explain the nature of what is going on in Kent. "We are sorry "to learn that a vast number of "forged notes, purporting to be those "of *the Bank of England,* are in cir- "culation, particularly on this coast, "to an alarming extent; we have "heard to the amount of 200,000*l.* "having been *recently imported into this county* from France and Hol- "land, where it is said they are ma- "nufactured! We know not to what "extent the evil may extend. Several "5*l.* 10*l.* and even 20*l.* of those notes "*have already been detected;* and "numerous 1*l.* of the same description "are in circulation; indeed, at Folk- "stone, and some other places, the "notes of the Bank of England are "almost generally refused in pay- "ment from this circumstance; and "we hope some steps will be imme- "diately adopted to put a stop to "them. Two 5*l.* were recently *passed* "*through the Dover Union Bank;* "and a 20*l.* note was remitted to "town by a respectable tradesman "in Dover, a few days since, which "proved to be a forgery. We should "recommend every person to keep "the number of the notes which pass "through their hands, or have them "previously indorsed by the person "who passes them; we look upon "this to be a very necessary precau- "tion, as it is a matter of the most "serious consequence to tradespeople "in general; for if the Bank of Eng- "land notes can be so readily imi- "tated, how easy must it be to forge "the Provincial Notes of this and "other counties."

This is a *war of finance* with a vengeance! But, even this I am not disposed to call an *unfair* and *dishonourable* species of warfare. I am not disposed to call this a cheating, swindling, base and cowardly mode of attacking a nation: indeed, I should not dare to call it so, if I were disposed to it, seeing that *we did the same towards the French when they had a paper-money.* It is well known to us, but, it ought also to be known to *our children* (some of whom will, I dare say, read these Letters); that, in the year 1791, the French people made a revolution in their government; that they chose representatives to frame a new constitution for them; that they changed their absolute monarchy, or despotism, into a limited monarchy; that they declared freedom to be their birthright; that the nobility, not pleased with the change, left the country; that the princes of the blood did the same; that the fugitives met with protection and encouragement from foreign Governments; that these Governments afterwards made war against the French; that England joined in that war; that, sometime after this war began, the French put their King and Queen to death, and declared their country a republic; that the French had, at that time, a paper-money, called *Assignats;* that upon this paper-money, it was thought, depended the fate of the French revolution; that, from the Speeches in the English Parliament, it will clearly appear, that the Government of England looked upon the debasement of those *Assignats* as the sure means of subverting the new order of things in France. All this should be known to our children as well as to ourselves; and, when they have a thorough knowledge of these facts, they should be told, that *false Assignats*, that *forged Assignats*, that *counterfeit French paper-money;* that these things were fabricated in England in quantities immense. They were intended, of course, to be sent into France, there to undermine the French finances, and to produce the overthrow of the Republican government. The former of these objects they did effect; or at least, assisted to effect; and, they, in all probability, contributed towards those causes, which finally led to the re-erection of the absolute monarchy in the person of Napoleon.

I was always, after hearing of these forged *Assignats*, very desirous of seeing one of them; and, some time ago, a gentleman gave me nine or ten, which, with many others, were given to him at the time that the fabrication was going on. He gave me an *Assignat* for 90 Livres, one for 50

Livres, one for 10 Livres, and several for 5 Livres. We cannot have this fact too strongly imprinted upon our minds, and cannot make the impression too strong upon those of our children. It is a great point, not only in the history of paper-money, but also in the political history of the world. I will, therefore, give here, as nearly as I can, a copy of one of these forged *Assignats*, but not of so large a size as the original, from which I take it.

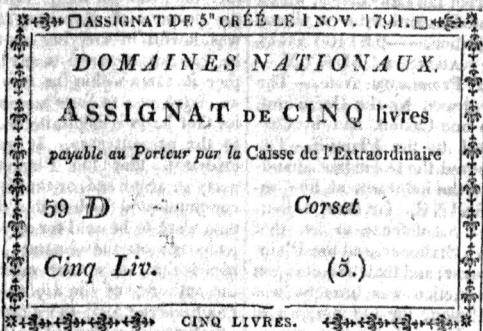

ASSIGNAT DE 5" CRÉÉ LE 1 NOV. 1791.

DOMAINES NATIONAUX.

ASSIGNAT DE CINQ livres

payable au Porteur par la Caisse de l'Extraordinaire

59 *D* *Corset*

Cinq Liv. (5.)

CINQ LIVRES.

The translation of this, is: "Assignat of 5 Livres, created 1 Nov. "1791.——National domains.—— "Assignat of Five Livres, payable to "the bearer by the Extraordinary "Chest." And the word "CORSET" was the name of the Cashier, I suppose, who signed the Assignats in France.

Such were the means, which *we* made use of *towards the French nation*; and, therefore, I trust, we shall not now hear of any *complaints* against *them* for their endeavouring to send *us* an ample supply of Bank notes. "Sauce for the goose is sauce for the gander," all the world over.

But, was this; do I *know* that this was, the work of Government? That it was actually done by the order of "the *great statesman* now no more," and *paid for out of the people's taxes.* It was not a trifling sum that these *Assignats* cost in the forging. They were wrought with great care in France. There was a very ingeniously contrived *dry stamp* upon them. The engraving was of most exquisite workmanship. To have effected the imitation the most ingenious artists in England must have used their talents. But, how do I *know,* that this forging work was carried on under the authority of the Government? Suppose it was not? What do we, the nation, get by that in the argument? If it was not the Government who ordered the thing to be done, it was *the people of England* who did it themselves; and, therefore, they have, in that case, still less reason, if possible, to complain of the French for sending over forged Bank Notes to England at this time.

Whether, however, it was, or was not the act of the English Minister and Government, you, Gentlemen, shall now have a fair opportunity of judging for yourselves. I could here relate to you what I have heard many persons say upon this subject; I could state to you names and transactions upon what I deem, and upon what you would, I dare say, deem very good authority; but, as to matters of this sort, I always love to deal in *undeniable evidence;* proof positive; facts that leave no room for shuffle. So I shall do here.

It happened, some time after this

forging work had been going on, that there was a *law-suit* between two of the parties engaged in it. Law-suits are apt to lead to exposures. So it happened now, as you will see by the following Report, which I copy, word for word, from the Law-Books, which are daily cited as authorities in all our courts of justice.——"STRONGI'TH'ARM AGAINST LUKYN.—*Case on a Promissory Note.*—The Note was drawn by the Defendant, payable to one Caslon, and by Caslon indorsed to the Plaintiff.—The Plaintiff proved the Defendant's handwriting and the indorsement by Caslon.—ERSKINE, for the Defendant, stated his defence to be, that Lukyn was a Stationer, and the Plaintiff an Engraver; and that the Note upon which the Action was brought was given to Caslon, for the purpose of paying the Plaintiff for the engraving of Copper plates upon which FRENCH ASSIGNATS were to be FORGED; and contended, that as the consideration of the Note was *fraud,* that it contaminated the whole transaction, and rendered the Note not recoverable by law.—Caslon, the indorser, was called as the witness. He proved that Lukyn, the Defendant, having it in contemplation to strike off impressions of a considerable quantity of Assignats, to be issued abroad, had applied to him for the purpose of recommending an engraver for the purpose of engraving the necessary plates; and that Lukyn represented to him that they were *for the Duke of York's army.* He said that he applied to Strong'ith'arm, the Plaintiff, who at first declined the business totally; but that, being assured by the witness that it was *sanctioned by Government,* and was for the use of the Duke of York's army, he then consented. The witness further denied that it was ever communicated to the Plaintiff that they were to be circulated for any other purpose than as he had represented.—LORD KENYON said, that if the present transaction was grounded on a fraud, or contrary to the laws of nations, or of good faith, he should have held the Notes to be void; but that it did not appear that there was any fraud in the case, or any violation of positive law. Whether the issuing of these Assignats, for the purpose of *distressing the enemy,* was lawful in carrying on the war? he was not prepared to say; or whether it came within the rule *an dolus an virtus quis in hoste requisit?* But let that be as it might, it did not apply to the present case. It was not in evidence, that the Plaintiff was a party in any fraud, or that it was ever communicated to him that the Assignats were to be used for any improper purpose: on the contrary, he supposed that they were circulated by the authority of the *higher powers of this country;* and, therefore, did not question the propriety *or legality of the measure.*—His Lordship declared his opinion, therefore to be, that the consideration was not impeached, and that the Plaintiff was entitled to recover.—The jury found *a verdict for the Plaintiff.*—MINGAY and MARRYAT for the Plaintiff.—ERSKINE and LAW for the Defendant.*——Having read this document, Gentlemen, you will want nothing from me to enable you to decide *who* it was that *caused* the Assignats to be forged; nor will you want any one to assist you in forming a correct opinion as to the conduct of either the *Plaintiff,* the *Defendant,* or the *Judge.* The thing is before you; and it speaks for itself much too plainly to be misunderstood.

Well, now, after this; with this before our eyes; knowing that the world is well acquainted with this fact, is it not a little too impudent in us to pretend to find fault with the French for supplying our coast with Bank Notes? I do not know any thing tha is more disgusting than this species of injustice, which proceeds from self-

* See Espinasse's Reports; Mich. Term, 36 Geo. III. 1795.

conceit. It is the worst kind of insolence, and whoever has paid attention to its effects, must have perceived, that it never fails to excite contempt in men of sense. What, I should be glad to know, is there in us that we should be justified in forging French paper-money any more than the French should be justified in forging English paper-money? Upon what ground is it that we claim the *exclusive* right of forging the paper-money of our neighbours?

After what we have seen above, you will, I am persuaded, agree with me, that it is *childish* in the extreme, to say the least of it, for us to *complain* of the Emperor of France for having, as LORD CASTLEREAGH said, set about a scheme for the *ruin of our currency*. And, it is equally childish in us to suppose, that he will not *now*, when we have proclaimed the effects, persevere in his hostility to our *commerce*. He is now told, by a majority in the House of Commons, that it is *his* system, which has *produced all our pecuniary distress*. We now say that it is he who has filled the Gazette with the names of Bankrupts; which has made one of the two "pillars of "the Stock Exchange" blow his brains out; which has raised the paper price of the Dollar ten per centum at a slap; and which now makes the fund-holder tremble. He is now told this by our Minister of finance; aye, and by the vote of a majority, and a very great majority too, of the Honourable House, upon whose Journals it now stands declared and recorded, that the commercial system of Napoleon has produced the very effects that he intended, and that he vowed, it should produce. And, yet, there are men amongst us to call Napoleon a *madman!*

I have taken up too much of your time to enter now upon the subject of *Depreciation*, which, therefore, I must postpone till my next, begging you, with reference to the above related facts, always to bear in mind, that, at the *outset of our war* against the Jacobins of France, we had plenty of gold and *the French* had nothing but paper, and that *now the French* have plenty of gold and *we* have nothing but paper.

I am,

Gentlemen,

Your friend,

WM. COBBETT.

State Prison, Newgate, Friday,
17th May, 1811.

LETTER XXV.

"Nothing is more certain than death, and nothing more uncertain than the time of dying; yet, we can "always fix a period beyond which man cannot live, and within some moment of which he will die. We "are enabled to do this, not by any spirit of prophecy, but by observation of what has happened in all "cases of human or animal existence. If, then, any other subject, such, for instance, as a system of finance, "exhibits, in its progress, a series of symptoms indicating decay, its final dissolution is certain, and, "from those symptoms we may calculate the period of that dissolution."——*Paine*, Decline and Fall of the British System of Finance, published in 1796.

The Subject of Depreciation discussed—Lord Stanhope's Bill—Lord King's Notice to his Tenants.

GENTLEMEN,

THE foregoing Letter we began with proposing to discuss the question of *depreciation*, but were stopped by the desire of shewing how childish, and, indeed, how unjust it was in our Government to complain of the endeavours said to be used by the French for destroying our paper-money, seeing the endeavours which were used here to destroy the *Assignats* in France. We will now resume the subject of *depreciation*, and see whether the paper money of England be, or be not, *actually depreciated*; and, if we find that it is, we will inquire whether it can be restored to its former value by any of the means, called *remedies*, that have been pointed out by any of those who are our rulers, or lawgivers.

To *depreciate* means *to lower in value*; and the word *depreciation* is used to signify that state, in which any thing is, when it is *lowered*, or has *fallen*, from its former value. Hence the term *depreciation*, as applied to Bank Notes; and, when we thus apply it, accompanied with the affirmative of the proposition, we say, that Bank Notes have *fallen in value*, and, of course, that any given sum in such notes is *not worth so much as it formerly was*.

Much puzzling has, upon this subject, arisen from a very natural cause: namely, that the note always retains its *nominal* value; that is to say, always goes by the *same name*; a *pound* note still is called a *pound* note, whether it be *worth* as much as it formerly was, or not. But, to this point we shall come more fully bye-and-bye, after we have spoken of the way in which a depreciation of money, or the lowering of the value of money, takes place.

Money, of whatever sort, is, like every thing else, lowered in its value in proportion as it becomes *abundant* or *plenty*. As I said upon a former occasion, when apples are *plenty* apples are *cheap*; and cheap means *low in price*. The use of money is to serve men as a sign of the amount of the value of things that pass from man to man in the way of purchase and sale. It is *plenty*, or *scarce*, in proportion as its quantity is great or small compared with the quantity of things purchased and sold in the community; and, whenever it becomes, from any cause, plenty, it *depreciates*, or sinks in value. Suppose, for instance, that there is a community of *ten men*, who make amongst them 100 purchases in a year, each purchase amounting to 1 pound. The community, in that case, would possess, we will suppose, 10 pounds; and no more, because, the same money might, and naturally would, go backwards and forwards, and because, except under peculiar circumstances, men do not hoard. Now, suppose, that the money in possession of this community is doubled in quantity, without any other alteration taking place, the quantity of goods and chattels and the quantity of things, including services, purchased, and the number of purchases all continuing the same. Suppose this; and, we are here speaking of money of *any sort*. No matter what sort. Suppose it to be gold, and that its quantity is thus *doubled*. The consequence would be, of course, that at each of the hundred purchases, *double the sum would be given that was given before*; because, if this were not the case, part of the money must be kept idle, which, upon a *general scale*, can never be, there being no motive for it. Suppose that one of the hundred purchases was that of a horse. The purchase, which was made with 1 pound before the doubling of the quantity of money, would require 2 pounds after that doubling took place; and so on through the whole; and, in such a state of things people would say, that *prices had risen*, that commodities had *doubled in price*, that every thing *was twice as dear* as it used to be. But, the fact would be, that *money* was become *plenty*, and, like every thing else, *cheap* in proportion to its abundance. It would be, that money had *fallen* or had been depreciated, and not that things had *risen*; the *loaf*, for instance, having a *real* value in its utility in supporting man, and the money having only an *imaginary value*.

Prices in England have been *rising*, as it is commonly called, for hundreds of years; things have been getting *dearer* and *dearer*. The cause of which, until the Bank note system began, was the increase of gold and silver in Europe, in consequence of the discovery of South America and the subsequent working of the mines. But the increase of the quantity of gold and silver was slow. "Nature," as PAINE observes, "gives those materials out "with a sparing hand;" they came, as they still come, in regular annual quantities from the mines; and that portion of them which found its way to this country was obtained by the sale of things of real value, being the product of our soil or of our labour. Therefore, the quantity of money increased very slowly; it did increase, and prices gradually rose, but the increase and the rise were so slow as not to be strikingly perceptible. During the average life of man the rise in prices was so small as hardly to attract any thing like general attention. Curious men observed it, and some of them recorded the progress of prices; but, as there was no sensible difference in prices in the average life of man, the rise never became an object of general interest, as long as *gold* and *silver* were the only currency of the country.

But, when the *funding system* began, and paper became, in many cases, a substitute for gold and silver; when the increase of the quantity of money in the country was no longer dependent upon the mines; when the check which nature had provided was removed; then money, or its substitute, paper, increased at a rate much greater than before, and *prices* took a *proportionate rise*, as they naturally would. The nature of the FUNDING SYSTEM has been fully explained before; we have also seen how it would naturally cause the paper-money to go on increasing. We have seen, that the Government, as soon as it began to make loans, was compelled to establish a Bank, or a something, in order *to get the means of paying the interest upon the loans.* The amount of the loans would naturally go on increasing in order to meet the rise in prices, and thus the increase of the paper would continue causing rise after rise in the prices, and the rise in the prices would continue causing addition upon addition to the quantity of the paper. This was the natural progress, and it was that which actually took place.

Still, however, the paper passed *in company* with the gold and silver. Money was more *plenty;* it was of *less value;* and, of course, any given quantity of it would purchase less bread, for instance, than formerly; but, still there was no difference in the *quality* of the two sorts of money; *metal* and *paper* both not only passed at the sums that they had usually passed at; but people liked the one just as well as the other; and, it was a matter of *perfect indifference* to any man, whether he took a hundred guineas in gold, or one hundred and five pounds in paper. And, the reason of this indifference was, that the holder of a bank-note could, at any moment, go to the Bank, and there demand and receive payment in guineas. This was the reason why the paper passed in society with the gold. But, it was impossible that this society should long continue after the paper increased to a very great amount, and especially after the notes became so low in nominal value as 5 pounds; for, then, it was evident, that all the taxes would be paid in paper; that the Government would receive nothing but paper; that the Bank could get nothing but paper from the Government; that whatever gold went out of the Bank would never return to it; and, of course, that the Bank would, in a short time, be unable to pay its notes in gold, if called on for that purpose to any great extent.

A call of this sort was made upon it in 1797; and, as we have seen, and now feel, the Bank was unable to pay. Its creditors, that is to say, the holders of its notes, demanded their money; the Bank flew to the minister Pitt for protection; the minister, by an Order of Council, authorized the Bank to refuse to pay its creditors; the Bank did refuse; the Parliament passed an Act to shelter the Minister and the Bank Directors and all who had been guilty of this violation of law, and, at the same time enacted, that, for the future, the Bank should not be compellable to pay its notes in gold or silver. After this memorable transaction, the full and true history of which I have recorded in the foregoing Letters; after this, the whole concern assumed a new face and indeed a new nature. The holder of a bank-note could no longer go and demand payment of it in guineas; it was impossible, therefore, that he should look upon 105*l.* in notes as quite equal in value to 100 guineas. Still, however, in consequence of the Meetings and Combinations of the rich, and of the enormous influence of the Government, to which may be added the dread in every man of being marked out as a Jacobin and Leveller; in consequence of all these, and of the necessity of having something to serve as money, the notes continued to circulate; and, as the alarm subsided, the guinea returned and circulated in company with them; but, not with that cordiality that it used to do. It became much less frequent in its appearance in company with the notes; it held itself aloof; seemed to demand a preference; but not appearing to like to assume this superiority over an old and familiar associate, and yet unwilling to pass for so much less than its worth, it soon began to keep away altogether, retiring to the chests of the hoarders, or going upon its travels into foreign parts, until such time as it found itself duly estimated in England, which would naturally be when people began to make openly a *distinction* between paper and coin.

That time arrived about two years ago; but, no sooner was the distinction thus made, and acted upon, than the Government began to prosecute the actors, and commenced, I believe, in the well known case of DE YONGE, who, under laws passed about two hundred years before such things as bank notes were ever heard of, was convicted, about a year ago, of the crime of exchanging guineas for more than their nominal value in bank notes.* DE YONGE moved for an *arrest of judgment*; the case has been since argued before the judges, and their decision thereon has recently been promulgated. Other persons have been prosecuted in the same way and upon the same ground, the effect of which naturally has been to deter people from openly purchasing and selling guineas, and also from tendering them generally in payment for more than their nominal value in paper. But, it is very notorious that the distinction is, nevertheless, made, and that, in payments, men do take gold at *its worth* in comparison with the paper. *Two prices* are not yet openly and generally made; but, they exist partially, and the extent of them is daily increasing.

To this point, then, we are now arrived, and here we see proof, not of a depreciation of money of *all sorts*, arising merely from that general *plenty* of money spoken of above; but arising from the abundance, or plenty, of *paper*, that is to say, the great quantity of the paper compared with that of the coin. Hence we say, that they bank notes have depreciated, or fallen in value; and, that there should be found any human being to assert the contrary, or to believe, or affect to believe, the contrary, is something that, were not the fact before our eyes, no man could think possible; but, we live in times when wonder no longer seems to form a feeling of the mind.

This state of things it was easy to foresee; but, the nation has been de-

* The report of this Trial, together with observations thereon, will be found in the appendix, (B.)

luded by the specious argument of the *equal powers of gold and paper in purchases.* "Go to market," we have been told, "and see whether *the* "*pound note and a shilling* will not "bring you as much meat or cloth as "*a guinea.*" This was conclusive with unreflecting minds, and it quieted, or assisted to quiet, all those, who, though they were capable of discerning, dared not look the fearful truth in the face. I looked it in the face rather more than eight years ago, and strenuously laboured to prepare my countrymen for what has now come, and what is now coming to pass. Upon one occasion, this standing delusive argument was made use of in answer to me: whereupon I made the following remarks:——"The objection of my "other correspondent has more plausibility. These are his words: "I "think the argument, that Bank "paper is depreciated, drawn from "the difference between the sterling "and the current value of a dollar, "if it prove any thing, proves too "much. That *guineas* are depre- "ciated you will hardly insist, yet "I would sturdily maintain, from "your premises, that they are, since "a guinea will not purchase so "many dollars as it formerly "would."—Yes, but I do insist "though, that guineas *are depreciated:* "not in their intrinsic value, but in "their value *as currency,* that is to say, "in their power of purchasing commodities in this country. When "there is a depreciating paper in any "country, the current coin of that "country depreciates in its powers "along with the paper, because it has "a fixed nominal value, and it can "pass currently for no more than an "equal nominal value in paper, until "the paper is at an open discount. "The metal is degraded by the society "of the paper; but, there comes a "time when it will bear this degradation no longer; it then rises above "its nominal value, or, in other words, "the paper is at a discount."

This was published so long ago as the 14th April, 1804. "*There comes a time!*" Aye, and that time is now come. But, let me not be guilty of robbery, and especially of the *Dead,* and more especially of one whose writings, and upon this very subject too, as well as other subjects, I formerly, through ignorance condemned. I allude to the writings of PAINE, the abused, the reprobated, the anathematized, TOM PAINE. In his work from which I have taken the perspicuous and impressive passage that serves me as a *motto* to this Letter, and the equal of which has seldom dropped from the pen of any man; in that work, PAINE thus exposes the delusive argument of which I have just been speaking; "It is said in England, that the value of paper keeps "*equal pace* with the value of gold "and silver. But the case is not "rightly stated: for, the fact is, that "the paper has *pulled down* the value "of gold and silver to its own level. "Gold and silver will not purchase "so much of any purchasable article "at this day (March, 1796) as they "would have purchased if no paper "had appeared, nor so much as they "will in any country of Europe, "where there is no paper. How "long this *hanging together* of paper "and money will continue makes a "new case; because it daily exposes "the system to sudden death, independant of the *natural death* it "would otherwise suffer." Here he lays down the principle; and, if, instead of reviling his writings, the Government of England had lent a patient ear to him, and taken a lesson from his superior understanding and experience, how different would have been our situation at this day! He proceeds thus: "I have just mention- "ed that paper in England has *pulled* "*down* the value of gold and silver to "level with itself; and that this *pull-* "*ing down* of gold and silver "money has created the appearance "of paper money *keeping up.* The "same thing, and the same mistake, "took place in America and in France, "and continued for a considerable "time after the commencement of "their system of paper; and the "actual depreciation of money was "hidden under that mistake. It was "said in America, at that time, that "every thing was becoming *dear;* "but gold and silver could *then* buy "those articles no cheaper than paper "could; and therefore it was not "called *depreciation.* The idea of "*dearness* established itself for the "idea of depreciation. The same "was the case in France. Though "every thing rose in price soon after "*assignats* appeared, yet those dear "articles could be purchased no "cheaper with gold and silver, than "with paper, and it was only said that "things were *dear,* The same is *still* "*the language in England.* They "call it *dearness.* But they will soon "find that it is *an actual depreciation,* "and that this depreciation is the "effect of the funding system; which "by crowding such a continually-"increasing mass of paper into cir-"culation, *carries down the value of* "*gold and silver with it.* But gold "and silver will, in the *long-run,* "revolt against depreciation, and "*separate from the value of paper;* "for the progress of all such systems "appears to be, that the paper will "take the command in the *beginning,* "and gold and silver in the *end.*"

How well is this expressed, and how clearly the truth of it is now verified! Yes: we talk about *dearness;* we talk of *high prices;* we talk of things *rising in value;* but, the fact is, that the change has been in the *money* and not in the articles bought and sold; the articles remain the same in value, but the money, from its abundance, has *fallen in value.* This has till of late been imperceptible to the mass of the people, who were convinced of the non-depreciation by the argument built on the circumstance of the guinea and the paper being upon an equal footing at market. They did not perceive, that the paper had *pulled down* the gold and silver along with it; they did not perceive that the coin was sliding by degrees out of the society of the paper; they did not perceive that, in time, the coin would disappear altogether; they did not perceive that an open contest would, at last, take place between the guineas and the paper, and that, if the *law* came to the assistance of the paper, the coin would *quit the country.* Now, however, they do perceive this; the facts have all now been established in a way that seems, at last, to have produced conviction even in the minds of this "*most thinking* people;" but, there is reason to fear, that this conviction will have come *too late.* How happy would it have been for this nation, if the opinions of Mr. PAINE, touching this subject, had produced, at the time, their wished-for effect! No man in England dared to publish his work. Any man who had published or sold it would have been punished as a *seditious libeller.* Yet, in my opinion, does that work; that little work, in the space of *twenty-five pages,* convey more useful knowledge upon this subject, and discover infinitely greater depth of thought and general powers of mind, than are to be found in all the pamphlets of the *three-score and two* financiers, who, in this country, have, since I came into this jail, favoured the world with their opinions upon the state of our money system. The writings of these people would make *twenty-five thick octavo volumes;* and in all of them there is not so much power of mind discovered as in PAINE's *twenty-five pages.* Yet, no man would dare to publish this little work in England. By accident I possess a copy that I brought from America, but which I never read till after my return to England. In 1803, when there was much apprehension of invasion, and when great complaints were made of the *scarcity of change,* I began to read some books upon the subject; and, after reading several without coming to any thing like a clear notion of the real state of our currency, I took up the little essay of PAINE. Here I saw to the bottom at once. Here was no bubble, no mud to obstruct my view: the stream was clear and strong: I saw the whole matter in its true light, and neither pamphleteers nor speech-makers were, after that, able to raise even a momentary puzzle in my mind. PAINE not only told me what would come to pass, but shewed me, gave me convincing reasons, *why it must come to pass;* and he convinced me also, that it was my duty to endeavour to open the eyes of my countrymen to the truths which I myself had learnt from him; because his reasoning taught me, that, the longer those truths remained hidden from their view, the more fatal must be the consequences. The occasion of this work of PAINE is worthy of notice. One of the motives of writing it was, as he says, at the close, to *retaliate* upon PITT, who, in speaking of the French Republic, had said, that she was "*on the verge, nay, even in the gulph of Bankruptcy.*" PAINE said, that England would soon be in a worse situation than France as to her finances; and, in less than twelve months after he wrote his work, the Bank became unable to pay its notes in cash.

To return to the subject of *depreciation,* the fact has now been established in all sorts of ways. Gold coin has been, and is, sold at a premium; a guinea will sell for 27 shillings, and the other coins of the realm in the same proportion; many persons in London have written upon their shop windows notifications that they will take the coin at a higher than the nominal value; in numerous cases a distinction is made in prices paid in coin and prices paid in paper. If these are not proofs of an *actual depression of the paper*, what, I should be glad to know, will ever be admitted as proof of that fact? Indeed, there is no longer any doubt remaining upon the subject; and, therefore we will now proceed to take a view of the REMEDIES that have been proposed by our Rulers and Lawgivers, who, if they had followed the advice given in PAINE's Second Part of the "RIGHTS OF MAN," instead of prosecuting the author, would not, I am convinced, have had to lament the present state of our finances.

As to REMEDIES, Gentlemen, I, in the first of this series of Letters, stated to you, that the Bullion Committee had recommended to the House of Commons to pass a law to compel the Bank to pay their notes in gold and silver *at the end of two years.* This same proposition has been since made in the House; but the House have resolved, that *no such measure is necessary.* Those who *opposed* the proposition said, that the Bank had not the gold, and could not get it, and that, therefore, they could not pay in gold. This was a very sufficient reason: and, I must confess, that I was and am, as far as this goes, exactly of the opinion of these gentlemen. For, to what end pass such a law, if the gold was not to be had? There were several sensible men belonging to the Bullion Committee, and the gentleman who brought the measure forward in the House, is looked upon as a person of good understanding. It, therefore, appeared astonishing to me, that they should propose such a measure, seeing that I have never been able to discover any way whatever, by which gold could possibly return to the Bank and remain there in quantity sufficient to enable that Company to pay their notes in gold upon demand. To resume payments in gold would, indeed, be a *complete remedy;* but, to do this, in my opinion, and, for many years past, has been, utterly impossible. By what means are the Bank Company to get the gold? We are told, that *there is gold enough* if the Bank

Company will but purchase it? What are they to give for it? Why *their paper*, to be sure; and, as it would require 27 shillings in their paper to purchase a guinea, this would be a most charming way of obtaining the means of paying off the paper with guineas. Let us take an instance. Suppose the Bank Company, by way of preparing for cash payments, to be purchasing all the guineas they can find, and, in such case, they would, of course, apply to our old friend, Mrs. DE YONGE, to whom, by the by, I here present my congratulations on the late decision of the judges in favour of her husband; the Bank Company would, I say, naturally apply to this good Lady, who, it being now decided that the old biting law does not forbid the buying and selling of bank notes and guineas, would drive with them as good a bargain as she could. Suppose them to buy 100 guineas of her at the present price, 27 shillings each, they would, of course, give her for them 135 pounds in their notes. And, thus they must go on with other people. Having, at last, got a good lot of guineas together, they begin paying their notes in guineas. It is pretty evident that the vast increase of paper occasioned by the purchase of the guineas would have caused a new and great depreciation of the paper, and that, therefore, the moment the Bank was open to demands in coin, people would crowd to it in all directions. I can fancy the eager crowd now before me, pressing in from every quarter and corner; and, amongst the very foremost and most eager, I think I see our friend Mrs. DE YONGE. "What "do *you* do here, Madam," I think I hear a dejected Director say, "what "do *you* do here, *you* who *sold* us "guineas but the other day?" "Aye, "Sir," says the lady, "and for these "very guineas I am come again, and "mean to take them away too, with "105 pounds of the 135 that you "gave me for them."

Need I say any more upon this subject? Is it not something monstrous to suppose, that it would be possible for the Bank Company to *buy* gold in quantity sufficient to be able to pay their notes in it? "Well," say others, "but the Bank may *lessen* "*the quantity of its paper by narrow-* "*ing its discounts*." To be sure they "might; and the only consequence of "that would be, that *the taxes would* "*not be paid*, and, of course, that "the soldiers, the judges, and all other persons paid by the public would have to go without pay. The *discounts* make a part of the system; and, if it be put a stop to, that is neither more nor less than one of the ways of totally destroying the system. To *lessen* the quantity of the paper is, therefore, impossible without producing ruin amongst all persons in trade, and without disabling the country to pay the taxes, at their present nominal amount.

But, suppose all other difficulties were got over, did these gentlemen of the Bullion Committee ever reflect upon the consequences of *raising* the value of money to what it was before the Bank Stoppage? Sir FRANCIS BURDETT, in his speech, during the Bullion Debate, told them of these consequences. He observed, and very justly, that, if money were, by any means, to be restored to the value it bore in the year 1796, the interest of the national Debt never could be paid by the people; that interest, he observed, was now 35,000,000*l*. a year; and, if the value of money was brought back to the standard of 1796, this interest would instantly swell to 43,000,000*l* of money at the present value. All the grants, pensions, fixed emoluments, pay of soldiers, judges, chancellors, clerks, commissioners, and the rest would be raised, in point of real amount, in the same proportion; so that, it would be utterly impossible for taxes to such an amount to be raised. And, if it were possible, it would be frequently unjust; for, observe, all the money (making nearly one half of the national Debt) that has been borrowed since the Bank Company stopped paying in gold and silver; all the money borrowed since that time; all the loans made in the name of the public since that time; all the money lent to the public, as it is called, has been lent in *depreciated paper;* and, that which has been so lent this year has, if guineas are at 27 shillings, been lent in paper 27 *shillings of which are worth no more than a guinea.* And, are the people to be called upon to pay interest upon this money in a currency of which 21 *shillings are worth a guinea?* This would be so abominably unjust, that I wonder now any man like Mr. HORNER ever came to think of it. He expressly stated, that the paper was now worth only 15*s.* 10*d.* in the pound; of course he must have known, that this was the sort of thing of which the loans, for some years past, consisted; and yet, he would have had a law passed, the effect of which would have been to make the people pay interest for this money at the rate of *twenty shillings in the pound.* This is what never could have been submitted to: not because the people would have *resisted;* that is not what I mean; but, it is what could not have been carried into effect, and for the same reason that the man could not have two skins from the carcass of the same cat. If the quantity of the Bank paper were diminished, its value would rise; and, if its value rose, the value of the interest upon the National Debt, would rise also; therefore to enable the people to continue to pay the interest upon the Debt, the amount of the interest must be *lessened,* and what would that be but a *partial sponge.* So that, turn and twist the thing, whatever way you will, you still find it the same; you still find, that the system must go on in all its parts, or be put a stop to altogether.

In most other cases, when men talk of a *remedy,* they advert to the *cause of the evil.* If I find that my health is injured by drinking brandy, the first thing I ought to do, in order to recover my health, would naturally be to leave off drinking brandy. What a fool, what worse than ideot, must that man be, who, feeling the fire burn his shins, still retains his seat. Yet, in this important national concern, never do you find any of our writers or legislators dwelling upon the *cause* of the evil, of which they appear so anxious to get rid. They tell us, indeed, that the *depreciation* of the paper is occasioned by its *excessive quantity;* but here they stop; they never go back to the *cause* of that excessive quantity of paper; or, if they do, they only speak of the *interests of the Bank Company.* If they did go back to the real cause, they would find it in the *increase of the national Debt,* to pay the interest of which, commonly called dividends, has *required,* has rendered *absolutely necessary,* the present quantity of paper. Indeed, one engenders the other. Every loan occasions a fresh batch of paper to pay the interest upon it; that fresh batch of paper causes a new depreciation and a new demand for paper again to make up in the quantity what has been lost in the quality. So that to talk of *lessening* the quantity of the paper, while the national Debt *remains undiminished,* does really seem to me something too absurd to be attributed to any man of sense. What, then, must it be to talk of *lessening* the quantity of paper, while the national Debt is *increasing* at an enormous rate, and while it is notorious that that Debt has been nearly doubled in amount during the last fourteen years; aye, while it is notorious, that, during the last fourteen years, that Debt has increased as much as the whole amount of it was before; or in other words, that, since 1796 as much money has been borrowed by the Government as was borrowed in the whole *hundred years* preceding? What must it be, then, to talk of *lessening* the quantity of the paper, while the national Debt, which was, and is, *the cause of the paper*, keeps on in this manner *increasing?* One really would think that such a proposition could have originated only in Bedlam. In 1798, the next year after the stoppage, the amount of Bank of England Notes in circulation was, 13,334,752*l.*; and the amount of the interest upon the national Debt, in that year, was, 17,750,402. In 1809, the amount of the Bank of England Notes in circulation was, 21,249,980*l.*; and the amount of the interest upon the national Debt in that year was, 30,093,447*l.* (exclusive of Irish loans.) Now let this be tried by the Rule of Three, and you will see with what exactness the amount of the Bank Notes keeps pace with the amount of the interest upon the national Debt, commonly called the *Dividends*, which many poor creatures in the country look upon, or, rather, used to look upon, as something of a nature almost divine. Let us put this down a little more distinctly.

In 1798, the Dividends amounted to	£.17,750,402
The Bank Notes out in circulation	13,334,752
In 1809, the Dividends amounted to	30,093,447
The Bank Notes in circulation	21,249,980

Here we have the real cause visibly before us. What folly, what madness, is it, then, to talk of *lessening* the amount of the notes while we are continually *augmenting* the amount of the Dividends, which are the *cause* of the notes? Here we have before our eyes proof that the Dividends (by the use of which word I mean to include all the annual charges upon the Debt) and the Bank Notes have *gone on increasing for the last ten years*, and I had before shewn that they had done so theretofore; and, with this fact before our eyes, we, the people of this "*most thinking* nation," hear some of our legislators propose to *lessen* the amount of the *paper*, while not a man of them seems to dream of lessening the amount of the *Debt*. We hear them propose to narrow the stream, while they say not a word about narrowing the spring whence it flows. They have seen, or *you*, at least, have seen, Gentlemen, that the bank-paper arose out of the national Debt; you have seen that the Bank was created in a short time after the Debt began; you have seen the increase of the paper keep an exact pace with the increase of the Debt; and, is it not, then, to war against facts, against a century of experience, against the nature of things, to propose to narrow the issues of the paper without previously narrowing the bounds of the Debt and its Dividends? If the authors of this proposition had read the work of Paine, they would never have offered such a proposition. *Read* this work they may, but they have not duly considered its arguments, or they have shut their eyes against the clear conviction that it is calculated to produce. He pointed out in his Second Part of the Rights of Man, the means of saving England in the way of finance. That work was written in 1791. So early as that he foresaw and foretold what we have now before our eyes, and what we have daily to expect. He there pointed out the sure and certain means of effectually puting a stop to further increase of the Debt, of insuring a real diminution of it, and, at the same time of doing ample justice to the fund-holders. For this pamphlet he was prosecuted, and having gone out of the country, he was *outlawed*. A Royal Proclamation was issued principally for the purpose of suppressing his work, scores of pamphlets having been written in *answer* to him in vain. He was burnt in effigy in most parts of this his native country; and his works were suppressed by the arm of the law. Well, our Government had its way; it followed its own counsel and rejected that of PAINE; he was overcome by it, and driven from the country; those who endeavoured to cause his principles to have effect were punished or silenced, or both: and, *what is the result?* That result is now before us, and fast approaching us; and, in a short time, in all human probability, events will enable us to form a perfect correct decision upon the respective merits and demerits of the then conflicting parties.

Now, Gentlemen, if you have attentively read the Letters, of which I now address to you the XXVth, you will have no doubt at all, that the cause of the influx of paper and of the consequent depreciation of all money first, and then of the paper itself alone as compared to the money; you will have no doubt that the real cause of all this, is, the increase of the national Debt; and, yet, in all the parliamentary debates upon the subject, you have heard of scarcely any man who ventured to mention this cause. It was a thing too tender to touch. It was what we call a *sore place;* and, the old proverb about the galled horse applied too aptly. If the depreciation had been traced to the national Debt, as Mr. HORNE TOOKE once traced it while he was in Parliament; for, *he* then foresaw and foretold what was now come to pass, and told the House, that, if they continued the then expenditure, the fundholder would not get, in a few years, a *quartern loaf* for the Dividend upon a hundred pounds of stock; if the depreciation had thus been traced back to its real efficient cause, it would have awakened reflections of an unpleasant tendency; it would have set men to consider what was the cause of the increase of the Debt; to look back and inquire whither the money was gone; for what purpose it had been borrowed; *who were the persons that had profited, from that borrowing;* who, in short, it was that had swallowed all that money the interest of which the nation was paying, and had so long been paying. These reflections it was not the desire of either party to awaken; but, they belong to the subject, they naturally present themselves to every one who looks only a little beneath the surface, and I venture to say, that, in the end, they will become familiar to every man in the kingdom. If this *real cause* of the evil had been acknowledged, it would have saved a great deal of time; for, then, men would not have amused themselves with talking about such REMEDIES as that of Mr. HORNER; and all the talk about the *narrowing of discounts* and the *purchasing of gold* and the *improving of the exchange* would have been heard like the twice told tale of an ideot. The short and the only question would have been this: *can we, by any means, diminish the amount of the Dividends?* And, if that question had been answered in the negative, there was no course, for those who wished to support the Pitt system, to pursue but that of letting things take their own course, and aid the paper with their *wishes*.

So much for the REMEDY of the Bullion Committee; but, our attention is now called to another, founded on more imperious circumstances. I allude to the proposition of EARL STANHOPE, which was, on the 27th of June, brought forward in the shape of a Bill, and which is, in that shape, now actually before the House of Lords, where it has undergone a second reading. Compared with this proposition, all that has been said and done before is mere child's play. This Bill brings the matter home to the public mind; it shews the most credulous that even those, on whose stoutnesss they rested their faith, begin to quiver. It cries, a truce with all *pretensions.* It puts the sense and the sincerity of every disputant to the test. The minister told us, that he wished the debate on the Bullion Report to come on, that the matter might be *set at rest.* Set at *rest!* Mercy on us! Set at rest! And so said OLD GEORGE ROSE too. But, what did they mean by setting the matter at *rest?* Is it possible, that they could imagine, that this matter was to be set at rest; that this great question of paper-money; that this subject in which every human creature in the country is so deeply interested; is it possible that they thought this matter would be completely set at rest by a vote for their majority? No, no! This is one of the things that that House cannot do. They can do a great deal; they can do more than I dare to trus myself to describe; but, they cannot set this matter at rest, nor have they, and all the branches of the Government united, the power to stay the progress of the paper-money only for one single hour. The Minister and his people have now seen what *rest* they insured for the subject! I always said, that the "first "man of landed property who openly "made a distinction between paper "and gold, would put the whole "system to its trumps, and compel "the Bank notes to sue for the "power of the Government for their "protection." This has now been verified, and the remainder of my prediction, which I need not here repeat, is not far from its accomplishment.

The grounds of LORD STANHOPE's proposition were stated by himself very explicitly, in moving, the 2nd instant, the second reading of his Bill. He said, that he had long thought upon the subject and had long entertained the opinion, that some legislative measure was necessary to preserve the bank note system from total ruin; that a notice recently given by LORD KING to his tenants, signifying that he would no longer receive his rents but in gold or in a quantity of paper equivalent in powers of purchase to gold,* had convinced him that there was no time to be lost, and that the measure in contemplation ought to be adopted before the Parliament rose. He said that the Ministers having declared, that their only objection to the measure arose from an opinion, that they thought no measure of the kind necessary, being persuaded that nobody would be found to follow

---

* "By Lease, dated 1802, you have contracted to pay the annual rent of £47 5s. "in good and lawful money of Great Britain. In consequence of the late great "depreciation of paper money, I can no "longer accept any Bank notes, at their "nominal value, in payment or satisfaction "of an *old contract.* I must therefore desire you to provide for the payment of "your rent in the legal gold coin of the "realm. At the same time, having no "other object than to secure payment of "the real intrinsic value of the sum stipulated by agreement, and being desirous "to avoid giving you any unnecessary "trouble, I shall be willing to receive payment in either of the manners following "according to your option.—1st, By payment in Guineas;—2nd, If Guineas cannot be procured, by a payment in Portugal Gold coin, equal in weight to the "numbers of Guineas requisite to discharge "the rent;—3rd, By a payment in Bank-paper of a sum sufficient to purchase (at "the present market price) the weight of "standard Gold requisite to discharge the "rent.—The alteration of the value of the "Paper-money is estimated in this manner, "the price of Gold in 1802, the year of "your agreement, was £.4 an ounce. The "present market price is £.4 14s. arising "from the diminished value of Paper; in "that proportion an addition of £.17 10s. "per cent. in Paper-money will be required "as the equivalent, for the payment of "rent in paper."

Entered at Stationers' Hall.

LONDON:—Printed by WM. MOLINEUX, Bream's Buildings, Chancery Lane.

the example of Lord King, it was only necessary for him to shew them that there were others to follow that example, in order to convince the ministers, that the Bill was entitled to their support. Having made these preliminary observations, he said, that he had a bundle of instances of this sort, and he only wished that a great many other persons would declare their intentions at once, and then the House would proceed to prevent the evil. He then produced a number of letters, from which he read extracts. One person wrote, that his landlord had said, "what *one* landlord can do, "*all* can do, and if Lord King suc-"ceed, I will do the same." Another letter related a recent transaction in Hampshire, where a man bought an estate for 400*l.* and paid down 100*l.* of the money, and afterwards laid out several hundreds of pounds upon the premises, and when the time of payment came, the seller insisted upon having payment in guineas, which the buyer could not obtain, the seller, however, would have it, or have his land back again, and the only consolation left to the buyer was an intimation from a friend of the seller that he could inform him where he might obtain the guineas at 27 shillings each. Another letter stated that a Lady, who was a Land-owner, had insisted upon her rent in gold, and that the tenant apprehended a seizure of his goods, and was ready to verify the facts if called on. Another informed him, on the part of an Attorney, that the practice was become very common to sell guineas and then pay debts with the paper.

These were the grounds, stated by LORD STANHOPE, of the measure that he proposed; and, upon his stating these grounds, the Ministers, who had, at the first reading, said that they did not see any necessity for the measure, or any measure of the kind, allowed that there was such necessity, and supported the second reading accordingly.

Now, Gentlemen, before I offer you any observations upon this measure itself, or upon the conduct of LORD KING, whose notice to his tenants seems to have given rise to it, it may not be amiss for me to say, that, from all that has ever come to my knowledge, there is not a more disinterested man, or a truer friend to freedom and to his country, breathing, than LORD STANHOPE, whom I trace through the parliamentary proceedings of the last twenty years, always standing nobly forward in the cause of justice, liberty, and humanity, and, but too often standing forward *alone*. His protest against the Anti-Jacobin war, which began in 1793, and which has finally led to our present calamities, will live when we shall all be in our graves. He there pointed out all, yea *all*, that has now come to pass. That protest, every sentence of which is full of wisdom and of just sentiment, has these remarkable words: "Because war "with France is, at present, most im-"politic, *extremely dangerous to our* "*allies the Dutch*, hazardous with "respect to the internal peace and "external power of this country, and "is likely to be *highly injurious to* "*our commerce*......The war may, "therefore, prove to be a war "against our commerce and manufac-"tures, *against the proprietors of the* "*funds*, against *our paper-currency*, "and *against every description of* "*property in this country*." How completely has all this been verified! LORD STANHOPE was abused: he was called a *jacobin* and a *leveller*, and *now* the nation is tasting the bitter fruit of the spirit that dictated that abuse. Every where was he to be found, in those horrible days, where liberty was assailed. Not an act, which he deemed injurious to the rights of Englishmen, escaped his strenuous opposition. In short, were I called upon to name the peer, whom I thought to have acted the best and truest part in those times, and for the whole course of the last twenty awful years, I should certainly name this very nobleman.

You will, therefore, Gentlemen, believe that, if I dissent from the measure which he has now proposed, that dissent proceeds from my conviction, that the measure itself is not calculated to produce that good, which I am certain its author wishes it to produce.

The detail of the Bill I will not attempt to discuss. Its principles are what have struck me, and these I gather from its chief provisions, which are, that, in future, the gold coins shall not be tendered or taken for *more* than their nominal value, and that the bank paper shall not be tendered or taken for *less* than its nominal value. This is LORD STANHOPE'S REMEDY; and this he appears to think will prevent the possibility of a further depreciation of the paper. We have seen the cause and the progress of that depreciation; we have seen how the paper *pulled down* the coin along with it, 'till the coin could no longer endure the society; we have seen the time and the manner of their *separation*; but, LORD STANHOPE appears to think, that, by the means of this Bill, he shall be able not only to restore that harmony which formerly existed between them; but that he shall be able to chain them together for ever after; to bind them as it were in the bonds of marriage, and to render the ties indissoluble. If he do this, he will do what never was done before in the world; he will destroy all the settled maxims of political economy as far as they relate to finance; his achievement will be a triumph not only over the opinions and experience of mankind, but over the very nature of man, which incessantly impels him to seek his own interest, and, at the very least, to use all the means in his power to provide for his own preservation.

After having said this I shall naturally be supposed to be convinced, that the Bill would be utterly inefficient for the purposes it contemplates. Indeed, such is my decided opinion, and the reasons for that opinion, I will now proceed to submit to you. A guinea is not to pass for more than 21*s*. There must be some *penalty* to prevent the passing of it for more. Lord STANHOPE will propose nothing *cruel*; but, for arguments' sake, let the penalty be death. What, then? Why need any one risk any penalty, as far as *ready money* transaction goes? One of you go to market with a pig for sale. "What do you ask for that "pig, farmer?" Answer: "*Twenty "seven shillings*." "I'll give you a "guinea." "You shall have him." Where is the possibility, then, of enforcing such a law? The parties, in any case, have only to settle, before they deal, in what sort of currency payment shall be made, and then they will, of course, make the price accordingly. As to *debts*, indeed, whether book debts, or debts arising from contract, in the payment of them, the gold and notes must, if this Bill pass, be taken at their nominal value; that is to say, the paper must; for, as to gold, who will be fool enough to tender gold in payment at its *nominal amount*, when it is notorious that it will fetch a premium of six shillings upon the guinea? If the Bill become a law, therefore, any tenant who has rent to pay, and who has guineas in his purse, will first go and purchase paper-money with his guineas, and with the paper-money, he will go and pay his rent. This rent, for instance, is 105*l*. a year, and he has a hundred guineas in his chest. But, he will not be fool enough to carry these to his landlord. He will go and buy 105 pounds worth of paper-money with *seventy eight* of his guineas; and will then go and pay his rent, and will return home with 28 of his guineas still in his pocket. So that, as far as the Bill will have effect, it appears to me that it will bear almost exclusively upon landlords.

I shall be told, perhaps, that, though guineas may *now* be bought and sold, in consequence of the decision of the judges, which, in the case of DE YONGE, has been promulgated since I began this Letter,* yet, we are not to suppose, that the present Bill will not *provide against such traffic* by making it penal to be concerned in it. But, as I have shewn above, men may go on with all *ready money* transactions, and with perfect safety, make a *distinction* between paper and coin, which amounts to the same thing as *buying* and *selling* the coin or the paper. It will require but very little ingenuity to discover the means of so managing the matter that the landlord shall never see a shilling's worth of coin from the hands of the tenant.

But, suppose that the coin should not be permitted to be bought and sold; does any one believe, that any law will prevent a private traffic in the article? And, if that could be done, is any one mad enough to suppose, that the guinea *will still circulate at par with the paper?* Pass this Bill, or any Bill, that shall prevent men from passing the guinea for more than its nominal worth, and the consequence will be, that a *guinea will never again be seen in circulation.* Those who have them will keep them in their chests, waiting an occasion to export them, or more patiently waiting till circumstances have produced the repeal of the law which has driven the guinea into the hoard. The cause that we see no guineas now in *common circulation*, is, as I said before, that they cannot obtain their fair value. They would have been openly sold long enough ago, had there not been an opinion, that the traffic was punishable by law. Now that obstacle is removed; but, in all likelihood, another will be erected by the present Bill. In that case the guineas will *all* either be hoarded or sent out of the country, and paper must and will be made to supply their place. The Dollars, the new things of three shillings and eighteen pence, now coming out from the Bank, will also be hoarded, and to notes for shillings

---

* The following is the Report of this DECISION, as given by the Chief Judge, Lord Ellenborough, in the Court of King's Bench, on the 3rd instant.——"THE KING "*against* DE YONGE.--Lord ELLENBOROUGH "communicated the Judgment of the Court "in this case, which along with another "case, the King v. Wright, coming from "the Assizes for the County of Bucking-"ham, had been reserved for he opinion "of the 12 Judges, on a point of law. "Both causes had been fully and ably "argued before the Judges in the Court of "Exchequer Chamber, and the argument "had occupied a number of days. The "question arising in the present case was, "the Defendant having been convicted of "purchasing 52 Guineas at the rate, in "Bank Notes, of 22*s.* 6*d.* per Guinea, "whether, in so doing, he had been guilty "of an offence punishable under the Act of "the 5th and 6th of Edward VI. which "prohibited the exchanging of coined gold "for coined silver, or for gold and silver, "the party giving or receiving more in "value than the same was current for at "the time? All the Judges, except three, "were present at the whole of these arguments, and at the last of them the whole "of the Judges were present. The Court "had no opportunity of knowing what was "the opinion of the absent Judges on that "part of the case at the argument on which "they were not present, but they had no "reason to presume that they dissented "from the opinion of the other Judges who "were present, all of whom concurred in "opinion that the Defendant in this case "was not liable under the Act of the 5th "and 6th of Edward VI. The Judgment "therefore, fell to be *arrested;* and the "Judgment *was arrested accordingly.*" Thus, then, this case is decided as I always said it *must* be, unless all semblance of *law* was banished from the land. Many people thought and said, that the conviction would be confirmed; but, I never thought so for a moment. Oh, no! The Judges knew a great deal better than to do that!

and sixpences, we must come, I am convinced, in the course of the year, if this Bill pass; so that the Bill, while it will be wholly inefficient for the purpose of arresting the progress of depreciation, will be efficient enough in producing a contrary effect.

The Bill does not, the author of it says, make bank notes a *legal tender.* It does not do it in *words*, but it appears to me to endeavour to do it in *effect*; and that being once done, all the usual consequences of a *legal tender* must follow. It was easy to see that the system would come to this pitch; there is nothing in the state to which we are come, that ought to *surprize* any one; what has happened was to be expected, and was, indeed, long ago *foretold;* but, what might reasonably surprize one, is, to hear this measure represented by the ministers as necessary to the *protection* of the *fund-holder;* Can they be serious! Is it possible, that they can be serious when they say this? If they are, nothing that they say or do can ever be a subject of wonder. Men, who are capable of believing that the Bill of Lord Stanhope will operate as a *protection to the fund-holder*, are capable................... but, really, I want words to answer my purpose. Imagination can frame nothing that such men are not capable of in the way of belief. That the paper would, at last, become a *legal tender*, or *forced circulation*, it was easy to see. I did, indeed, for my own part, expect this state of the paper to be apparent long ago. The faith of this "*most thinking* people" I knew to be almost passing conception; but, still I did not think it adequate to the supporting of this paper-money for 14 years after the issuers had ceased to pay in cash and after they were protected by law against the demands of their creditors. It was, however, certain, that the thing must come to this point at last; it was certain, that, if the national Debt and the taxes continued to increase, the time must come when landlords would see that they must either starve, or demand their rents in coin; and, whenever this time came, it was, as I have many times said, impossible to keep up the paper only for six months without making that paper a legal tender, which might eke out its existence, perhaps for a year or two, but which, in the end, must ensure its total destruction. I have several times been asked, what reason there was why landlords should not demand their rents in gold and silver; or in bank notes to the amount of the gold and silver; and, my answer has always been, that there was no reason at all against it *now*, but that there soon would be; for that the moment such demand was made, Bank notes would be made a *legal tender.* This was natural, and, therefore, the ministers are now doing just what I always expected they would do, whenever any land-holder did what Lord King has now done; but, to hear them speak of it as a measure calculated to afford protection to the *fund-holder* is what I never could have expected. They will see what sort of *protection* it will give him; and he will *feel* it! What will be his fate I shall not pretend to say; but, I hope, there is *justice* enough yet in the country, *real* justice enough to prevent him from perishing, while there exist the means of such prevention. I trust, that his claims will meet with serious and patient consideration; that the question of *what is due* to him and *to whom he ought to look for payment* will be settled upon sound principles of equity. I am for giving real protection to the fund-holder; but, to hear the Ministers say, that he is to meet with protection from a measure such as that now before Parliament, a measure that must inevitably accelerate the depreciation of the paper, is, surely, sufficient to fill one with surprize and dismay, if, at this day, and after all that we have seen, any thing ought to produce such an effect in our minds.

On the 2nd of July, a protest was entered, in the House of Lords, against LORD STANHOPE's Bill, which protest I here insert. "Dissentient, —Because We think it the duty of "this House to mark in the first instance with the most decided reprobation, a Bill, which in our judgment manifestly leads to the introduction of laws, imposing upon the "country the *compulsory circulation* "*of a Paper Currency;* a measure "fraught with injustice, destructive "of all confidence in the legal security of contracts, and, as invariable "experience has shewn, necessarily "productive of the most fatal calamities:

GRENVILLE, LANSDOWNE,
ESSEX, COWPER,
JERSEY, KING,
GREY, LAUDERDALE.

"For the reason assigned on the "other side, and because the repeal "of the law for suspending Bank "Payments in Cash is in my judgment *the only measure which can* "*cure the inconveniences already felt,* "and avert the yet greater calamities "which are impending from the present state of the circulation of the "country. VASSALL HOLLAND."

In the protest of the eight peers I heartily concur; but I do not agree with LORD HOLLAND in his addition to it, if his lordship means to say, that it is *possible to resume cash payments at the Bank.* To pay the notes in gold upon demand, agreeably to the promise upon the face of the notes, is certainly the only cure for the inconveniences already felt and the calamities now impending; but that it is utterly impossible to adopt this cure is, to my mind, not less certain. His Lordship proceeds upon the notion of Mr. HORNER and the Bullion Committee, namely, that the cause of the depreciation consists in *an excessive issue of paper,* which is very true, if you compare the quantity of the paper with that of the gold, or of the real transactions of purchase and sale, between man and man; but, which is not true, if you compare the quantity of paper with the amount of *the Dividends payable on the National Debt;* and, I would beg leave to put, with sincere respect, this question to LORD HOLLAND: "If cash payments were "restored, and money, as must be "the case, were restored to its former value, *where* does your Lordship think would be found the *means* "*of paying the Dividends?*"

It is impossible! The thing never can go *back;* no, not an inch; nay, and it must keep *advancing.* This very measure, by hastening the depreciation, will cause a new addition and still larger than former additions, to the National Debt, and of course to the Dividends. Those additional Dividends must be paid in an additional quantity of bank notes; and thus the system *must go on,* as PAINE foretold, with an *accelerated velocity,* until it can go on no longer. Having this opinion so firmly fixed in my mind, I was quite surprised to see the Marquis of LANSDOWNE endeavour to *mend* the Bill of LORD STANHOPE by the introduction of a clause for *prohibiting the Bank Company from augmenting the quantity of their paper after the passing of the Bill.* This shews, that his Lordship has, what I deem to be, and which, I think, I have proved to be, a most erroneous view of the real cause of the depreciation. If he thought with me, that the cause is in the increase of the National Debt and of the Dividends, he would have proposed no such amendment as this.

As to the conduct of LORD KING nothing could be more fair or more laudable. He wished to take *no advantages* of his tenants; he only wanted a fulfilment of his contract with them; and, as the spirit of the contract was more favourable to them than the letter, he abandoned the letter, and only required them to hold to the spirit. To hear him, therefore, charged with *oppression,* and by......! But, it is as well to keep ourselves cool. Let others chafe and foam. And, if the House of

Lords do choose thus to determine why, all that I can say about the matter, is, that they are the best judges whether they stand in need of their rents, and, if they do not, I really do not see much harm in their giving them to their tenants; and, this act will be the more generous as they are about to do it by a *law*, so that the tenants will keep the rents without having to give the landlords even *thanks* in return. That such will be amongst the effects of the Bill, if it pass, there can be no doubt; and, as far as it operates in this way, a most popular Bill it will be. It will act as a *distributor* of wealth; of money, lands and tenements; for, to suppose, that, in many cases, the *tenants* will not soon become the *proprietors*, is to discover but very little *thought* on the subject, and that, I am sure, would be a shame in a body of HEREDITARY LEGISLATORS in the "*most thinking* nation in the world." What a change this will make! Happy is the man who is a *tenant!* Much better off is he than the man who tills his *own* land; because the former has given nothing at all for his, whereas the latter has paid, at some time or other, *purchase money* for what he possesses. The letting of *long leaess* is out of fashion; but, in general, the lands of great proprietors are held upon lease, and these leases are not, upon an average, for less than *seven years* at the lowest. Some of these leases are nearly expired, of course, but, others will naturally be but just commenced. So that, the average time, for which the land is now let, I shall take at *three years and a half.* All the Duke of Bedford's estates, for instance, are let, then, *for three years and a half yet to come.* Now, if the paper depreciate three or four times as fast as it has hitherto done, the tenants of the Duke of Bedford will have a brave time of it for these three years and a half. But, if the Bill, which is now before Parliament, should send down the paper to the state of the French assignats in 1794, *what will, in that case, be the situation of the Duke of Bedford?* There are many landlords, who cannot *hold out* for three years and a half, and who, therefore, must sell, in whole or in part; but, there will, indeed, be this convenience, that they will every where find a purchaser ready at hand in their tenant, and one, too, who will not only know the real value of the property, but who will have the money ready to pay for it. This is nothing in the way of a *joke.* I am in earnest; it is what I am convinced will take place, if the Bill of Lord Stanhope pass into a law; but, as I said before, if the Lords like it, nobody else can possibly have a right to interfere. They may, surely, do what they please with their own property. All that I wish to stipulate for is, that we Jacobins and Levellers shall never be accused of this act of distributing the lands and houses of the rich amongst those who are not rich; that we shall not be accused of this great act of *pulling down* and *raising up.* Hume remarked that the funding system, *in the space of 500 years,* would cause the posterity of those now in the coaches, and of those upon the boxes, to change places; but, if this Bill of LORD STANHOPE pass, this change will be a thing of much quicker operation.

I shall be told, that *Lord King's example* would have operated even more quickly than this measure in *destroying the paper.* Granted. It would there is no doubt, have produced, in a very short time, that which must have *totally destroyed the paper system, root and branch,* namely, TWO PRICES, against which, openly and generally adopted, no paper-money ever did, or ever can, stand for any length of time. That that *example* would have been generally, nay universally, followed, there can be no doubt at all, for, no man voluntarily gives away his rents, or, rather, lets another withhold them from him. Some persons would have been a little shy at first; but, when they found that others did it, they would have got over their shyness, and the demand would have been universally made. Thus, then, the TWO PRICES would have been established; and the gold and silver, finding that they could pass current for their real worth, would have come forth from their hiding places, some, while the rest would have hastened back from abroad. "Surely!" say you: "why then, are the Government "alarmed at the effect of Lord "King's example, if it would bring "back gold and silver into circulation?" Oh! there is good reason for their alarm; for, observe, THE TAXES WOULD CONTINUE TO BE PAID IN PAPER! When the tax-gatherer came to the door of one of you, for instance, you would, if you had only gold or silver in the house, beg him to call the next morning, or to sit down a bit, while you, with your gold, would go and purchase paper-money sufficient to pay him th amount of his demand! There needs no more to convince you that the Government has *good reason for alarm* at the prospect of seeing Lord King's example followed, as it assuredly would be, if there were no law to prevent it. In short, that example would annihilate the paper system in a year.

The next Letter will close the series. In the mean while,

I remain,

Gentlemen,

Your friend,

WM. COBBETT.

State Prison, Newgate, Friday,
5th July, 1811.

LETTER XXVI.

"It is not that the *money* which the Public Creditor receives, as interest for his capital, is *less* than it used "to be; it is that the *quantity of goods* he receives for his money is *less*; and he will be still receiving "less and less, while your taxes will be rising more and more. If the next Administration" (Addington was "just at this time coming into power in place of Pitt) "mean to go on like the last, it would be a good "thing for the country if no man would lend them a groat. Let them take three fourths of a man's "interest, or property, from him, and take off the taxes, and the people would be doubly gainers. If you "*reduce the National Debt*, we may laugh and sing at home and bid defiance to all the world; *if you do* "*not reduce it*, the consequence will be, that, instead of paying the National Creditor 120 *quartern loaves* "for a year's interest of his £.100 you will go on, till you only pay him 2 *or* 3 *quartern loaves*. Depend "upon it that it will be the fate of the National Creditor."——Mr. *Horne Tooke's* Speech, in the House of "Commons, 2nd *March*, 1801.

Mr. Horne Tooke and the Reformers—Effect of Lord King's Example—Two Prices—How these would affect the Government, the Generals, the Judges, the Sinecure Placemen and Pensioners—Lord Mornington's Speech in 1794—Progress of the Assignats in France—Mr. Perceval's Speech in the House of Commons, 9th July, 1811.

GENTLEMEN,

LOOK at the *motto!* Look at the motto; and, especially, if any of you should unfortunately be *fund-holders;* in that case, let me beseech you, to look at the motto. They are the words of a very wise man. They were spoken, you see, rather more than ten years ago. The speaker was *laughed at* by some, and *railed at* by others; but, I imagine, that, at this time, those, who then laughed, are more disposed to cry, though I by no means suppose, that the *railers* have ceased, or ever will cease their railing, as long as they have tongues or pens wherewith to rail. The House of Commons passed an Act which, for the future excluded Mr. Tooke, soon after he made this speech. They did so upon the ground of his being a *Clergyman in Holy Orders*.

No matter: they got rid of him for the future; but, they have *not got rid of the event that he foretold.* Oh, no! that is coming upon them in spite of all their triumphs over Mr. TOOKE and Mr. PAINE and Messrs. MUIR, PALMER, MARGAROT, GERALD, WINTERBOTTOM, GILBERT WAKEFIELD, and many others. The Government beat all these reformers; they not only put them down; they not only ruined the greater part of them; but they succeeded in making the nation believe that such ruin was just. Well! The Government and the nation will now, of course, not pretend, that the *present* events have sprung from the Jacobins and Reformers. Mr. TOOKE told them to reduce the National Debt. They rejected his advise. They despised his warning. The kept him, for the future, out of Parliament. Well. Let them, then, not blame him for what has since happened, and what is now coming to pass.

I beg you, Gentlemen, to reflect well on those observations; for, such reflection will be very useful in preventing you from being deceived in future, and will enable you, when the utmost of the evil comes, to ascertain who are the men who have been THE AUTHORS OF THE EVIL, and to whom, accordingly, you ought to look for a just RESPONSIBILITY. But, upon this *vital* part of the subject I have some hints to offer to you hereafter: at present I must return, for a while, to the point where I broke off in my last Letter, namely, the *reason for the alarm of the Government* at the prospect of seeing Lord King's example followed.

I spoke of the TWO PRICES before; but, let me say a few more words upon that very interesting part of our subject. *Two Prices* have always proved the death of paper money. In this case it would have been the same, and, in the *end*, it will still be the same; for, the Bill of Lord Stanhope can do no more than *retard* the event of six or nine months, and mind, I tell you this with as much confidence as I would venture to foretel the arrival of Christmas day. I do not say, that the event will come in six or nine months; but I say, that *this Bill* will not keep it off for a greater length of time than that. If TWO PRICES were generally made, we should see the gold and silver back into circulation immediately; but, *none of it could get to the Bank*, because no man would pay his TAXES in gold and silver. Consequently the *fund-holder* and the *Government* would be paid in paper while gold and silver would be circulating amongst all the rest of the community. As soon as there are two prices, the paper must depreciate at an enormous rate; and, as the Government would have to pay its contractors and others whose pay was not fixed, in this depreciated paper, it must have *a greater quantity of that paper*, and it must come from the Bank. It is so easy to see how this must work; how rapidly it must go on; how soon it must render the paper worth little more than its weight in rags; all this is so easy to see, that I will not suppose any one of you so very dull as not to perceive it.

The Government, with nothing but paper at its command, would soon begin to feel somewhat like a person who has taken a powerful emetic. The big round drops of sweat would stand upon its forehead; its knees would knock together; it would look pale as a ghost; an universal feebleness would seize it. That is to say, all this would take place, if the Government persevered in the Pitt system, and that it would do so, who can doubt after what we have seen during the last twenty years. If the TWO PRICES were openly made, and became general, as they, in all probability, would, in the course of six or eight months, the paper would fall so low as that *5, or, perhaps,* 10 *shillings would be required to purchase a quartern loaf.* How, then, would the Government, who would get nothing but paper, make shift to pay its way; The Generals and Judges and others, having a *fixed* pay, would, indeed, still be paid as they were before, and, of course, the Government would lose nothing by taking paper as far as this description of expence went; for, you will observe, that I hold it to be impossible, that the parties I have just mentioned, namely, the Generals, the Judges, the Tax-Commissioners, and the like; I hold it to be impossible, that these men should not all of them be excessively happy to take the paper-money, though at a hundred for one, seeing that the greater the degree of depreciation, the finer the opportunity for them to give proofs of their devotion to public credit. But, though my Lords the Judges and Lord Arden and Lord Buckinghamshire and Lord Liverpool and Lord Bathurst and the Marquis of Buckingham and Lord Camden and Old George Rose and Mr. Canning and my neighbour the Apothecary General and Lord Kenyon and Lady Louisa Paget, and, indeed, the hundreds of those who have *fixed* sums paid them by the Government out of money raised upon the people, whether in the shape of salary, sinecure or pension; though all these persons would, I dare say, from motives of public spirit, cheerfully continue to take the paper till a pound of it would not purchase a pinch of snuff; still, there would be some things and some *services* that must be paid for in money, or they would not be obtained. Beef and Pork and Biscuit could not be bought without real money These are commodities that do not move without an equivalent. Whether the *soldiers* would be paid, under such circumstances, in paper so much reduced in value, I shall not pretend to say, and will leave the point to be settled by those who have lately said so much about this useful and numerous class of active citizens. But, one thing is certain: that THEY must be paid in a kind of money that will purchase eatables. They have bargained to receive a certain sum *per day*; and, if the same should not purchase half so much beer or beef as it does now, the bargain will not be so good an one as it is now; though, observe, I am not supposing, that there would not be found public spirit enough amongst the soldiers to make them take the paper in preference to gold. At any rate, this is a matter which belongs exclusively to those who have the management of our affairs, and who are paid very well for such management.

It would be useless to extend our remarks here. It is as clear as day-light, that, whenever TWO PRICES shall be generally established, the death of the paper is at hand, and, indeed, *the death of the funding system;* because, owing to the rapidity of the depreciation, the fund-holders, our poor friend GRIZZLE GREENHORN and all the rest of them, would soon be in the situation described by Mr. HORNE TOOKE, in the passage taken for my motto; that is to say, a hundred pounds of their stock would yield them a couple or three quartern loaves in the year; and, it is within the compass of *possibility*, that many persons, who are now enabled to ride in their coaches by incomes derived from the funds, may end their days as paupers or beggars. In short, it is quite impossible for any man of common sense not to perceive, that the establishment of TWO PRICES would put an end, in a short time, not only to the property of the fund-holders, but to the *sinecures* and *pensions*, and *also to great numbers of other emoluments derived from the public revenue.* Put an end to all *for a time* at least, and subjecting them to an *after revision.*

If we are of opinion, that *this effect*

would have been produced by the example of Lord King being followed, there is, I think, little room for wonder, that the ministers were *alarmed* at the prospect. I know it will be said, and with perfect truth, that, in time, the same effect will be produced by Lord Stanhope's Bill; but, supposing it to be produced full *as soon* by the Bill, it does not follow, that the ministers *perceive* that. On the contrary, it would seem, that they do not perceive it at all; and, it is evident, that they have a sort of vague notion, that the Bill will *stay* the depreciation. I am convinced, that it will not; I am convinced, that it will hasten the depreciation, and though not quite so fast as the example of Lord King would, still that, in the end, the effect will be the same. But, the ministers could, in the one case, see the effect: in the other they appear not to have seen it; and, this is quite sufficient to account for their giving their support to the Bill.

I said before, Gentlemen, that this Bill was the *first of a series* of measures, the object of which would be to keep up the paper by *the force of law*. This seems to be the opinion of all those who have opposed it in the House of Peers: that it is merely a step in the old beaten path of keeping up by the arm of power a depreciated paper-currency. This course has been before pursued, in other countries, and it has, in every part of the world, led to the same end; the total destruction of the paper. Each of the Colonies, now moulded into an united nation in America, had its *debt*, its *paper-money*, its *legal tenders*, and its *public bankruptcy*, before their separation from England, and even before the revolutionary quarrel began. But, it was *in France*, where the thing was performed upon a grand scale; and, by taking a view somewhat more close than we have hitherto done, of the progress of the measures in France, we shall be able more correctly to judge of the tendency of what is now going on here.

There are divers histories of what was done in France, relative to the *assignats*; but I choose to take for my authority one of the present Ministers, the Marquis WELLESLEY, when he was Lord MORNINGTON, made a speech in the House of Commons, which was afterwards published in a pamphlet, or rather *book*, in which he gave an account of all the pranks played with the assignats in France, up to the time of his making the speech, which was on the 21st of January, 1794, just three years and a month before the then ministry, whom he supported, issued an Order in Council to protect the Bank of England against the demands of cash for their notes.

In this memorable speech, manifestly drawn up for the purpose of exciting horror in the people of England at the wickedness of the French Rulers relative to the assignats, and also to make the people believe, that the state of the assignats must prove the overthrow of France; in this memorable speech, not only facts are stated, but principles and maxims of finance are laid down. We will take a cursory view of them all; for *time*, which tries every thing, has now brought us into a state to judge correctly of those facts, principles, and maxims.

Lord Wellesley told the House of Commons, that the rulers of France were very *wicked*, but that they were not less *foolish* than wicked; that their ignorance was, at least, equal to their villainy, though the latter was surprisingly great. He said, that "the "French Revolutionary Government, in order to supply an "extravagant expenditure, had recourse, at first, to *increasing the* "*mass of paper-money*; and, that they "declared, that they had *no other* "*means of sustaining the pressure of* "*the war*, than by the creation of *an* "*additional quantity of assignats*."

There is, then, nothing *original* in the declarations of Lord Liverpool and Perceval and Rose. Nothing *new* in their recent assertions, that it was the paper-money that enabled them to provide for the defence of the kingdom, to make such great exertions against the "enemy of the human "race," to gain such *victories* in Spain and Portugal, and to add such *glories* to the English name! This was all very fine and full of comfort; but, as you now see, Gentlemen, there was nothing *new* in it. The same thing had been said before by the revolutionary rulers of France; the same thing had been said by Danton and Robespierre and their associates in praise of the revolutionary money of France.

The ministers have frequently denied that the *coin* of the country is, or ought to be the standard of value. Rose and Lord Westmoreland and several others of them have denied, that the Bank notes ought to be looked upon as depreciated, merely because they would not go for the same quantity of gold as formerly; and the hireling writers have taken infinite pains to *decry* and *run down* the gold and silver coin. One of them calls *guineas an incumbrance;* another says that gold and silver are merely *articles of traffic*, and that the Bank notes are the only money fitting the country; another has said, that, were it not for the *National Debt*, the *patronage*, and the *paper-money*, the *Government could have no existence*, and that the Bank notes offer to the government a most indestructible support, because they *make the daily bread of every individual depend upon the Government;* and, another has said, that Bank paper is the best bond of individual and public security, and the *only medium of currency to suit and exert the energies of an insular and commercial people!*

What a similarity between this language and the language of the Rulers of France in favour of their *assignats!* They called them, as Lord Wellesley said in his speech, *revolutionary money;* their Chancellor of the Exchequer said that it was a happy thing for the people to have *Republican assignats* instead of *pieces of metal bearing the effigy of tyrants;* that the whole nation *despised the corrupting metals*, and that he would soon find a way of driving back the vile dung into the bowels of the earth. In another part of his speech, Lord Wellesley tells us, that people were *imprisoned* and *punished* for their *contempt of assignats.*

Nevertheless, the people of France had, it seems, still an unnatural hankering after gold and silver in preference to assignats; and, they did in fact, make TWO PRICES; the consequence of which was an enormous rise in the price of all the necessaries of life, the proprietors of which were reviled as enemies of the country, and, as such, many hundreds of them were put to death. This, however, was not sufficient to put a stop to the rise of prices, and, indeed, did not check it at all. Then came the law of MAXIMUM (as it will in England if the present course be pursued), fixing the highest price at which any of the necessaries of life should be sold. and at which men should *work* and *render services*. This terrible law, Lord Wellesley tells us, had nearly starved the whole nation; for the farmers would not bring their produce to market, and tradesmen kept their goods locked up. Then, he tells us, that these persons were pursued as monopolists; and thus, said Lord Wellesley, "every "*farmer* whose barns and granaries "are not empty; every merchant and "*tradesman* whose warehouse or shop "is not entirely unprovided with "goods, must be subject to the charge "of monopoly. This *crime* is punished differently, according to the enormity of the case; but, most frequently the punishment is *death*." So that it is time for farmers and tradesmen to look about them, and especially the farmers; who, if they do not already see the danger of their landlord's property being withheld from him, will, perhaps, be more clear-sighted when their own natural fate is pointed out. They hear LORD KING accused of *black malignity;* they hear him charged with selfishness; they hear him classed along with *pedlars and Jews.* This was, as Lord Wellesley tells us, precisely the language which Danton and Robespierre and their underlings made use of towards the people of property in France, who had a "*contempt* for assignats." They were accused of *incivism;* they were called *egotists,* and were, in almost the very words in which LORD KING is now arraigned by the COURIER, told that they "committed a robbery against the "RIGHTS OF SOCIETY!" And, this is what the people of England are told, observe, after eighteen years of war, after eighteen years of blood and taxation, in order, as they were promised, to preserve their country from what they saw going on in France!

"But, our paper is *at par,*" say some of the PITTITES still; "Our "paper *is not depreciated.*" So they said in France. Yes, said Lord WELLESLEY, "the French minister "of Finance has boasted, that his "assignats are *at par;* but, the laws "which have been passed for punish-"ing with *long imprisonment* any "person who takes, gives, or offers "assignats *under par,* sufficiently ac-"count for this circumstance." Good God! It would really seem, that every saying is to come home to us! that upon our devoted heads are to be visited all that was felt, and, which is more, perhaps, all that was, by our rulers, said to be felt by the people of France: aye, it really would seem, that all, that *all,* to the very letter, is now to *come home to the people of England,* who were led to build their hopes of success and of safety upon the ruin of the people, or at least, the Government of France! This very Bill now under discussion, will impose a *penalty,* whether of *imprisonment* or not I do not yet know, upon any person, who takes, or gives, or offers, bank notes, *under par.* The prohibition was made in the Lords, and the Minister has said, that he means to add the *penalty!*

Let us now look, then, at the *contrast* which Lord WELLESLEY drew, upon that memorable occasion, between the situation of England and that of France. "From this dis-"gusting scene," said he, "let us "turn our eyes to *our own situation.* "Here the contrast is striking in all "its parts. Here we see nothing of "the character and genius of ARBI-"TRARY FINANCE; none of "the bold frauds of bankrupt power; "none of the wild struggles and "plunges of despotism in distress; "no lopping off from the capital of "the debt; *no suspension of interest;* "no robbery under the name of loan, "NO RAISING THE VALUE, "no DEBASING THE SUB-"STANCE of THE COIN. Here "we beheld public credit, of every "description, rising under all the "disadvantages of a general war; "an ample revenue, flowing *freely* "and *copiously* from the opulence of "a *contented* people."

Gentlemen, read this with attention; and, when you have so done, draw yourselves the contrast which the situation of England *now* presents with that of France! It is a fact perfectly notorious, that there is no such thing as paper money in France; it is also notorious, that not only does France abound in gold coin, but that the coin of this country, the guineas of England, are now gone and are daily going to France; aye, to that same country, which was to be ruined and overcome and subdued by the failure of its finance! This speech of Lord Wellesley, and all the numerous other speeches of the same description, were intended for the purpose of gaining the people's concurrence to *the prosecution of the Antijacobin war*, which war, by adding *five hundred millions sterling to our Debt*, has produced the fruit of which we are now about to taste. Year after year the same means were made use of for the same purpose, and with similar success. At the opening of the Session of Parliament, in October, 1796, PITT himself told the Honourable House, that, *in his conscience*, he believed, that, with finances so dilapidated, the French would *not be able to stand out another campaign!*" "This DE-"PRECIATION of the Assignats," said he, "is so severely felt, that it "has been repeatedly admitted, that "means must be found to employ "resources less wasteful. This principle has been recognized by every "financier or statesman. Even at "the period when the depreciation "was only one half, it was declared, "that unless some immediate remedy "was applied, they would be unable "to maintain their armies. Months "have since elapsed, and no substitute has been employed. *Resources "thus strained to their utmost pitch*, "and *incapable of any renovation*, "must have in themselves the *seeds "of decay*, and the cause of *inevitable dissolution*."

This, Gentlemen, was PITT's reasoning as applied to France. Little did that presumptuous and shallow man dream, that, in *less than four months* from that very day, he was doomed to come into that same House of Commons, and from the same spot where he then stood, announce that the Bank of England was no longer able to pay its notes in the coin of the realm, and that he had been guilty of a violation of the law in issuing an Order of Council to guarantee the Bank Company against the consequences of refusing to pay the debts due to their creditors! But, as if this were not enough, he must, in the speech just referred to, comment upon certain *metallic money* then, it was said, about to be issued in France "Metallic pieces," said he, are, it "seems, to be put in circulation; but "it is not said, whether these are "to be of the DENOMINATED "VALUE: if *not so*, they are only "METALLIC ASSIGNATS!"— Yet this same minister, who has been impudently called "the *great "Statesman* now no more," had, in a short time afterwards, to propose to this same House of Commons, to sanction the issuing of Dollars at 4*s*. and 9*d*. the real value of which was 4*s*. 4½*d*.; he lived long enough to propose to the same House of Commons, to give its sanction to an issue of dollars at 5*s*.; if he had lived till now, (I always regret that he did not!) he would have seen the Dollar at 5*s*. 6*d*. And, what he would have seen it at, if he had lived till *a few years hence*, I must leave TIME, the *trier* of all things, the rewarder of all good deeds, and the *avenger of all injuries*, to say.

You will now be able to judge how far our situation, in respect to paper-money, *resembles that of France* at the time when the revolutionary rulers of that country were endeavouring to keep up the Assignats by the arm of the law, by the terrors of the jail and the guillotine. Mr. PERCEVAL says that there is *no resemblance whatever* between the bank notes and the assignats. I shall show you, that Mr. Perceval is deceived; that he does not understand this matter; and that, if he had read the works of PAINE, at the time when his colleague Lord Eldon (then Attorney General) was prosecuting the author, he would not have hazarded any such assertion.

But, we must now take a look at the whole of this speech of Mr. Perceval. I mean his speech in the House of Commons, on Tuesday last, the 9th instant, upon the first reading of Lord Stanhope's Bill in the House of Commons. This speech will be a memorable one. The child yet unborn will have cause to think of this speech, and of the series of measures, of which, as appears to me, it is the necessary forerunner.

Mr. Perceval (I have the report of his speech as given in the COURIER) began by stating his reasons for having come round to the support of Lord Stanhope's Bill after having, at first, disapproved of it. He says, that he, at first, thought it *unnecessary*, because he did not think, that any body would follow the example of Lord King; but, that finding that it was likely, that the example would be followed, he then thought it necessary to support the Bill. Thus, then, at any rate, it has been *one individual* who has caused this Bill; the Bill is made for the purpose of preventing that individual and others from obtaining in payment of rent what the law now authorizes them to demand; it is a Bill, in fact, which, against the will of one of the parties at least, *alters contracts* made years ago. Yes, says Mr. Perceval, it does so; but, *the same was done in* 1797! That is the *answer*. Because the thing was done by Pitt, he may do it! He said, that, until now, this preference for coin before paper had been shewn by none but *Pedlars, Jews*, and *Smugglers;* and, in speaking, afterwards, about the possibility of the Bill being inefficient, and a legal tender being necessary, he said that "he did, however, "*hope*, that the ODIUM attaching to "the conduct which gave rise to "this Bill, WOULD PREVENT "OTHERS FROM FOLLOW-"ING THE EXAMPLE." These are memorable words, especially considering from whom they came.—Aye, aye! I know well what workings of mind there must have been before they were uttered. I would not have such workings in my mind for ten times the worth of the *reversion* of Lord Arden's sinecure. Oh! a time is coming, when all these things will be seen and felt as they ought to be.

But, let us return to this memorable expression. "the ODIUM!"—A man, then, is it seems, to incur *odium* if he demand his *due;* his *due* in *equity* as well as in *law!* Gentlemen, you are, for the most part, *tenants;* but, take care how you suffer yourselves to be led to wish for any advantage from this Bill, which will most assuredly operate, in the end, to your injury, and perhaps, to your utter ruin. Let me explain to you, a little more fully than I have hitherto done, the nature of Lord King's demand upon his tenants. He let a farm, for instance, in 1802, to JOHN STILES for £.100 a year, *in good and lawful money of the realm*. He has until now, continued to take the £.100 a year in bank notes; but now he finds, that those notes are so far from being good and lawful money of the realm, that they have sunk in value 20 per centum, and that, instead of £.100 he would, in effect, get only £.80. If, however, the thing was likely *to stop* where it is, he might possibly go on receiving paper to the end of the present leases, when he would take care to raise his rent of course; but, the thing is not likely to stop; it goes regularly on; gold is purchased up; a guinea sells for 27*s*. 6*d*. And is it not, then, time for Lord King to begin to protect himself against this depreciation? JOHN STILES, you see, suffers no hardship in this, because he *raises the price of his corn and cattle* to meet the effects of the depreciation. Suppose, for instance, that the paper has depreciated 20 per centum, or five pounds in every twenty, since 1802; and suppose, that wheat is now 25 pounds a load; consequently, it will require only *four loads* of wheat to pay £.100 now, but it must have required *five loads* to pay £.100 in 1802. But, is it not just and fair, that JOHN STILES should give Lord King as much wheat for his rent in 1811 as he contracted to give him in 1802? If he does not do this, and if the paper go on depreciating, may it not come to pass, that JOHN STILES wi not give Lord King more than *a bushel of wheat in a year*? Aye, may it; and a *great deal sooner* too than many persons seem to imagine. And, because Lord King wishes to avoid this ruin is he to be lumped along with jews, pedlars, and smugglers, and are we to be told of the *odium* attaching to his conduct?—However, upon this head, I shall always say, for my part, that the Lords are the best judges of whether they or their tenants are likely to make the best use of the rents; and, if they like to give the rents to the tenants, I know of no one who has any right to find fault with them.—They and the other great land-owners appear to have abundant confidence in Mr. Perceval, in the Bank, and in the East India Company; and the *Clergy* appear to have equal confidence in them. Well, then; I really see no good reason that we, the people in general, have to find fault with what is going on. The matter seems, I think, to lie wholly between the land-owners and this little sharp gentleman and his colleagues; and to them I will leave it, being quite satisfied, that the former are now about enjoying the just reward of their conduct for the last twenty-six years.

Mr. Perceval said, that those who supported the Bank Restriction Act in 1797, were inconsistent in not supporting this Bill; and he talked a great deal about the inconsistency of those who proposed, the other day, to continue the Restriction for two years longer. With these matters, Gentlemen, WE have nothing to do. The affair is all *their own*. THEY made the war that produced the *loans* that produced the *paper* that produced the *run* that produced the *stoppage of cash payments* that produced the *depreciation* that produced the *sale of guineas and the hoarding and exportation of them*. THEIR work the whole of it is, and which set of them were first at it, or which last, is of no consequence to us. They have it all among them. They chose the grounds of war, and the time for beginning; they put down all those who opposed them; they have been, for 26 years, the rulers of the country and the masters of all its resources. One set, therefore, is, and ought to be, just the same as the other in the eyes of the people. Let them settle the matter of precedence between them; let them bait one another as long as they please; but let not us be, by such baiting, amused and drawn away from the great points at issue.

The "*object of the Bill*," Mr. Perceval said, "was *to prevent the establishment of TWO PRICES* which "must be the case if Lord King's example were generally followed."—Now, you will be so good as to bear in mind, Gentlemen, that this is, Mr. Perceval says, *the object of the Bill*; and, I beg you also to bear in mind, that I say, that *in this object the Bill will fail*. Here we are, then, I and the Minister, foot to foot in opposition. I say his scheme will not prevent the TWO PRICES. I say it will not: he says that such is its object: we shall see who is right. He ought to be; for, I am sure, he is paid money enough for thinking for *this most thinking people* in the world. He did, however, confess, that it was *possible*, that this Bill might not be *efficient*; and, what was then to be done? Why, the bank notes, he said must in that case, be made *a legal tender!* Bravo! Come: to't again! Once more, and then comes the *maximum!* I always said, that it would be thus. I always said, that the moment any one put the paper-money to the test, the paper-money would be made a legal tender. This Bill it was (but I do not believe it now is) believed would have the same effect; but, if it fail of that effect, then the legal tender is, it seems, to come.

Mr. Perceval says, that this may become *necessary*. For *what*, Mr Perceval? *What* may it become necessary for? Necessary *to do what*, thou Minister of Finance? Why, you will say, I suppose, to prevent TWO PRICES, and to PROTECT THE FUNDHOLDER. And, dost thou really think; dost thou, a disciple of the great statesman now no more, think, in good earnest, that a legal tender law would *prevent two prices* and *protect the fundholder?* Forgive me, but, it is impossible for me to refrain from laughing at the idea. You will say, I suppose, that it is "no laughing matter." Cry then, if you like, but I will not; nor will any one belonging to me. But, how is the *legal tender* to prevent TWO PRICES being made? An Act of Parliament, making the bank-notes a legal tender, would cause *debts* to be paid in paper; but, it could not make the butcher or the baker give their meat or bread for bank-notes. They would and they must and they will have two prices; a money price and a paper price; and this will become general in spite of every thing that can be done to oppose it. What *protection*, then, will the fundholder, or "*public creditor*," as he is called, derive from measures like these? Mr. Perceval supposes a case (of which I will say more by-and-bye) in which the fundholder of £.6,000 capital rents a house of £.300 a year, and says that it would be *extremely hard*, if this man, who is obliged to receive his £.300 a year from the Government *in paper*, were to be left exposed to the compulsion of paying his £.300 a year rent in gold. Where is the *hardship*, if bank-notes are as *good as gold?* Where is the hardship, if the notes have *not depreciated?* And these assertions are daily and hourly made. But, to return to the baker and butcher, for these are the lads that it will be most difficult to manage; what will this fundholder do with *them?* How will Mr. Perceval *protect him against them?* Why, to be sure, he will, and indeed, consistently, he must, have recourse to *maximum*. And, it may not be amiss here to explain to you *farmers* and *tradesmen* what a *maximum* means; for, you will find it a matter, in which *you* are very deeply interested.

They had a *maximum* in France, in the times of depreciated paper-money. The rulers of that day, finding the assignats depreciate very fast, passed a law to put a stop to the depreciation, which only made them depreciate the faster; and, as the assignats were *bought* and *sold*, as our bank paper now is, they passed another law to prevent the gold from passing for *more* than its nominal worth and to prevent the paper to pass for *less* than its nominal worth. This object, though attempted to be accomplished by the means of very severe penalties, was not accomplished. There was still a *money price* and a *paper price*; for, when a man went to market, he pulled out his paper, or his coin; and, the article was *high* or *low* priced accordingly. If the thing to be bought was a quarter of mutton, for instance, *a crown piece* in silver might be the price; but, if the payment was to be made with paper, then the price might be *ten pounds* or *fifty pounds*, perhaps. The next thing, therefere, was to *prohibit the use of coin* altogether. But, this did not answer the purpose. The assignats still kept depreciating, and the rate of depreciation kept on increasing, till, at last, it required *a hundred pounds to purchase a pair of common shoes*; and, this was not at all wonderful; for, when once a paper money is got into an acknowledged

Entered at Stationers' Hall.
Printed by W. Molineux, 5, Bream's Buildings, Chancery Lane; Published by W. Cobbett, Jun. No. 8, Catherine Street, Strand: and Retailed at No. 192, Strand.

and notorious depreciation, it always goes on *with accelerated velocity.* Well, what was now to be done? If it took a hundred pounds to purchase a pair of common shoes, what was the use of *collecting taxes* in such money? And what was to become of those whose incomes, founded on former contracts, were paid them in such money? What was the Government to do? Why, to fix a *price upon all the necessaries of life,* and to *compel people to sell their goods at those prices.* This was done, and all farmers, bakers, butchers, and others, were compelled to sell their commodities at the same price, in assignats, as they used to sell them at in money, before any assignats were made. The consequence of this was, that those who had corn or meat or other necessaries, did not bring them to market; the shopkeepers shut up their shops, or hid their goods. To counteract this, a law was passed to punish *monopolists,* and every man, who kept more corn, meat, or necessaries of any sort, in his house, than was absolutely necessary for the use of his own family, became a *monopolist,* and, in many cases, such persons were punished with *death!* This was the last of that series of measures, which was adopted in France during the reign of terror and blood. The guillotine was continually at work to enforce this last measure. The market place in every considerable town reeked with human blood. Hundreds of thousands of innocent country people and shop-keepers perished upon the scaffold and in prison in consequence of the laws made for the *purpose of sustaining a depreciated paper-money in France;* and, wherever a similar project is attempted to be forced into execution, similar consequences will follow.

At last, however, the people of France, unable to endure so hellish a system any longer, put an end to it and to its authors. The paper-money was *totally annihilated,* and, in a short time, gold and silver came back into circulation. But, in the mean while, what *protection* did any of these measures give to the man of *fixed income,* who might be compared to our fund-holder? How did he get any *protection* from any of these measures? Yet, he got full as much as the fund-holder in England will get from this measure of Mr. Perceval, who, though he may, in part, ruin the land-owner, will not, thereby, do the fund-holder the smallest good. The *rent of the fund-holder's house* is the least article of his yearly expences. His servants, his upholsterer, his butcher, his baker, his haberdasher, his draper, his brewer, his wine-merchant, &c. &c. will all be paid in gold, or in paper upon the principle of TWO PRICES. There is, therefore, no means of protecting the fund-holder against these gentlemen, except the *maximum.* It is useless to talk about it, and for people to attempt to buoy themselves up with a sort of vague notion of the impossibility that an English ministry should ever do what was done by Robespierre. I hope they never will, indeed; but, this I am sure of, that, without doing what was done by Robespierre, they cannot make the fund-holder's income equal in value to gold and silver. This is what Mr. Perceval wishes to do; this is what he calls *protecting* the fund-holder, and this would be protecting him; but this, I tell him, he cannot do, nor can all the powers on earth do it. To stop where we are is within the scope of *possibility.* By an immediate stop to the increase of the National Debt and the Dividends; by an immediate stop to all Loans and issues of Exchequer Bills; by an immediate reduction of the Taxes; by

W. MOLINEUX, Printer, Bream's Buildings, Chancery Lane

such means; *immediately* adopted, we might stop where we are; but, to *restore* is impossible. To make the dividends worth their nominal amount in gold and silver is no more possible than it is to bring back yesterday.

When I closed my last Letter, I thought that, in this, I should have been able to conclude the discussion; but, the debate in the House of Commons has created new matter, and, as I wish to see the event of the Bill now before that House, before I take my leave of the subject, I must defer the conclusion till next week.

I remain, Gentlemen,

Your Friend,

WM. COBBETT.

State Prison, Newgate, Friday, 12th July, 1811.

LETTER XXVII.

"I maintain, that all Europe is contemplating the payment in specie at the Bank as the criterion of the "credit of the country. If the Bank continue to issue paper *without controul*, the Country Banks will "do the same. They will pour out their notes upon us without mercy; and we are now BEGINNING "A COURSE OF ASSIGNATS. ...... Loud cries of *Order! Order! Question, Question, Question*, from "*every part of the House*."——Mr. ROBSON's Speech, in the Honourable House, 2nd April, 1802.

"By these WISE and provident measures (the measures relating to the Bank Stoppage) all the apprehensions "that were entertained are vanished: the credit of the Bank is as high, both at home and abroad, as it "ever was; and, *not the slightest inconvenience possible* is, or has been, experienced from its not paying "in cash."OLD GEORGE ROSE.——Brief Examination of the Finances, published first in 1799, and republished in 1806.

Mr Robson's Proposition—George Rose's "Blessed Comforts"—The Nature and Extent of these Comforts—Great Use of ascertaining them—Necessity of discovering who has got the Money that has been borrowed on Account of the Public—Case of De Yonge.

GENTLEMEN,

BEFORE I resume the thread of our discussion, which was rather abruptly broken off at the close of my last Letter, give me leave to beg your attention to the two passages, which I have, upon this occasion, taken as MOTTOS.

You see, that Mr. ROBSON was called to *Order;* that he was run down *by all parts* of the Honourable House; that he was hooted out of countenance, and, you may see in the history of that day's proceedings, that he was obliged *to sit down and to hold his tongue*. And yet, what did he say? What was the *folly* he was guilty of? Why, foretelling precisely what has now come to pass. And, I beg you to observe, that he recommended upon the occasion here referred to a *controul* as to the quantity of paper to be issued by the Bank, a measure now recommended by the *whole of one party* in the Honourable House and by *part of the other party*; and, though I am not one of those who think that it would have been possible to save the paper by the means of any such controul; still, the proposition is now put forward as the *only* one that can restore the paper to its former value. Yet did the members of the Honourable House hoot Mr. ROBSON down; they coughed and laughed and hallooed him off his legs. Ah! but those times were very different from the present. The enemies of the truth were then strong. They had not as yet seen the guinea at a premium, and the bank-note at a discount.

Faith! They have a great deal more to see yet: what they have to see they can scarcely guess at. Much good may it do them. They hooted down Mr. Robson; they had their own way; and, therefore, let them not complain when the days of their humiliation shall arrive.

The second motto calls to our minds the means that were, and that, all along, have been made use of to deceive the people as to the finances in general, and especially as to the state of the paper-money, in which work this GEORGE ROSE has borne a principal part. He was, for many years, Secretary to the Treasury under PITT, by whose authority this publication was made in the name of ROSE. In short, he has been a great actor in the drama, which is now drawing to a close; and he is one of the men, of whose past conduct it will, hereafter, be necessary, absolutely, necessary, to give the history. "*Not* "*the slightest inconvenience.*" No, not to George Rose, perhaps; but, could the rest of the nation say so? Could they say so, out of whose taxes George Rose was getting about *ten thousand pounds a year?* But, there is another passage in this same publication of GEORGE ROSE, to which I must beg leave to solicit your attention, of which it is well worthy.

"There is *a time* for all things," and now is the time for reminding the people of England of the means by which they have been deluded. It was in vain to endeavour to open their eyes before; but, *now*, perhaps, they may be induced to make use of their senses. The following is a specimen of the means employed to delude them, at once to *wheedle* and to *scare* them into a *quiet surrender of their money.* I beg you to read it with *attention*; and you will, I hope, be ashamed at having been deceived by lies and hypocrisy so glaring. "As "the *amount of the debt*, which will "be incurred in this and every sub-"sequent year of the war, will be so "*reduced* by the application of the "money coming in from the tax on in-"come (after ten millions shall have "been raised for the service of each "current year), as that the perma-"nent debt, which will be left as an "addition to the antecedent one, "will not exceed the annual amount "of the whole produce of the sink-"ing fund. This is A TRUTH "so important, that it cannot be too "often or in too many shapes exhi-"bited for the *satisfaction of our* "*country*, for the *conviction of our* "*enemies*, and for the information of "Europe. If France has built hopes "(founded on *ignorant or visionary* "*calculations*), on the expected over-"throw of our financial system, and "has trusted to the failure of "our resources, she may now per-"ceive what means, after so many "years of this arduous struggle, Great "Britain still possesses for maintain-"ing it. It would be a slander to the "sense and virtue of the people, to "suppose an *abatement of that spirit* "*which has enabled Government to* "*call forth those resources.* The "prosperous state of the empire "which affords the power, furnishes "all the motive, for continuing the "contest; a contest, the support of "which to a successful issue is *to se-*"*cure us in the enjoyment of every* "*national advantage*, and to protect "us from *the infliction of every na-*"*tional calamity.* The imperious and "awful necessity of the present crisis "unavoidably subjects us to heavy "burdens. It has been said that "they ought to be considered as a "SALVAGE for the remaining part "of our property. In the consider-"ation of property, to which it was "applied, the figure is sufficiently "striking; but, in other respects, the "metaphor, though just, is *inade-*"*quate.* What Tariff shall settle the "difference between *national inde-*"*pendence* and *inexorable tyranny?* "between *personal liberty* and *requi-*"*sitions, prisons,* and *murder?* be-

"tween the BLESSED COMFORTS OF RELIGION, and "the gloomy despair of Atheism?"

Well said, Old GEORGE ROSE! This was the sort of language by which the nation was led on in the former war. The cant does, indeed, no longer take. It has not the powers that it possessed ten years ago; but, still there is cant in the nation, and we ought to be constantly upon our guard against it. "Between the *blessed comforts of religion*, and the "*gloomy despair of Atheism!*" Why this, Gentlemen! What had the blessed comforts of religion to do with the matter? How, if any of you had had the spirit to put the question to him; how were the blessed comforts of religion to be *taken from* you by the French Republicans? How were those blessed comforts to be *secured to you* by a bloody war against those Republicans? In short, what had religion or atheism to do with the matter? What an impudent thing to tell you, that, if you did not part freely with your money, you would be plunged into the gloomy despair of Atheism! What an impudent thing was this! But, let us see what GEORGE ROSE really meant, when he was talking about the *blessed comforts of religion* and the *salvage* upon your property. He says "salvage upon OUR property;" but, we shall soon see what sort of salvage *he* paid. You were to pay *salvage*, but he did not tell you to *whom*. He did not tell the "*thinking* people," that *he himself* was one of the great receivers and pocketers of the said salvage. Yet, at the time when he wrote he and his sons were, and they *now are*, in the receipt annually of public money to the following amount:

OLD GEORGE ROSE, as Treasurer of the Navy ...	£. 4,324
OLD GEORGE ROSE, as Clerk of the Parliaments, which is a sinecure, and is for his *life*, and is granted also *for the life of his eldest son* YOUNG GEORGE ROSE	3,278
OLD GEORGE ROSE— Keeper of Records in the Exchequer, another sinecure place	400
WILLIAM STEWART ROSE, second son of Old George Rose, as Clerk of the Exchequer Pleas, which is also a sinecure place............	2,137
	£. 10,139

Such was the sum which "the "blessed comforts of religion" yielded to this man: no wonder, then, that he felt an uncommon degree of horror at the thought of seeing those blessings supplanted by the "gloomy "despair of atheism," which of course being interpreted, meant the loss of this ten thousand pounds a year! So you, the people of England, yea, "this *most thinking* people of Eu-"rope," as Lord STORMONT (who, by-the-by, had a fat sinecure) called them, were to pay George Rose and his sons ten thousand pounds a year in part of the means of preserving themselves from the gloomy despair of atheism! But, observe, Gentlemen, OLD GEORGE ROSE has been for nearly thirty years in the receipt of large sums annually of the people's money. His salary as Secretary of the Treasury he had before he was Treasurer of the Navy, and that was 4,000*l.* a year. It is *sixteen* years, at least, since he got the grant of the office of Clerk of the Parliaments, at 3,278*l* a year, which is just so much money for doing nothing at all, the office being what is called a sinecure. How long he has possessed the 400*l.* a year as keeper of the Exchequer Records I do not know; but, I believe, *twenty* years if not more. So that, I think, we shall not be far from the mark, if we suppose him to have possessed the *whole* for twenty years past. What *other* emoluments he may have had, how much more of the public money he may have received, I do not know. His son

GEORGE is, I believe, to have *a large pension for life* for his trip to America; where he did not remain a year, I believe, altogether. But these will be matters for *another day's reckoning*. For the present let us see what the above sum amounts to in the course of twenty years. The principal money is 202,780*l*. In words, *two hundred and two thousand, seven hundred and eighty pounds*; and if, we add the *interest*, the amount is about 323,000*l*. in words, THREE HUNDRED AND TWENTY THREE THOUSAND POUNDS, nearly two thirds of which has been received for *sinecure places*, that is to say, for *doing nothing*.

Here are "*blessed comforts of religion!*" The thinking people, "the *most* thinking people in the world" were desired to believe, that unless they paid this and other such sums, they would lose all the "blessed comforts of religion," and would be plunged into the gloomy despair of *atheism*; that, in short, if they did not continue to pay these sums of money, they would all go to hell as sure as they were born. Oh, "*most thinking* people!"

But, Gentlemen, now let us apply what has here been seen to the subject before us. I observed to you, before, and, indeed, *proved* to you, the measure of Lord King was rendered necessary by the difference between the value of paper and that of coin, that that difference has arisen from the depreciation of the paper, that that depreciation has arisen from the abundance of the paper compared with the quantity of gold in circulation, that that abundance has arisen from the stoppage of the payments of cash at the Bank, that that stoppage arose from the vast *increase in the amount of the National Debt and the Dividends*: all this I have before *proved* to you, and in a manner, I trust, that you clearly understand; but, there is still one stage further to go back, and that is, to the CAUSE *of the increase of the National Debt!* Mark well; what I say here, Gentlemen. Mark this well; for this is now, or, at least, it very soon must be, the great, and indeed, the only object, connected with the paper system, worthy of our attention.

In the common concerns of life, in the affairs of individuals, where interest induces men to do the best they can for the prosperity of the concern, we always find, that, in the case of embarrassment, arising from debt, the *cause* of such debt is looked well into by those who wish to retrieve the affairs of the concern; and, if they find, that the debt has been incurred by this or by that species of extravagance, they set to work to put a stop to such extravagance, and, in cases calling for it, they inquire who it is that has derived *gain* from the creation of the Debt. And, why should *we* do this? Why should not *we*, in our present state, inquire *who* have, if any persons have gained by this increase of debt; or, in other words, whether there be any persons who have been receiving, for the last twenty or thirty years (we may stop there,) large sums of money *out of the loans*, which loans have added to the Debt? Why, in short, should not we look with this sort of eye into our affairs? The nation, this "*most thinking* nation," seems here again to be deluded. The public were getting into motion; it was impossible to keep them perfectly quiet any longer: but, it was easy to throw them off upon a *wrong scent*; and, for this purpose, the halloo against Lord KING was set up. But, "*steady*" men of England! "*Solid*" men of England! Thinking, "most *thinking* "people" of England! Do not, thus, to the last, expose yourselves to the ridicule and contempt of the world! Let me beseech you not to be dupes and gulls to the last moment!

What, considering us as rational men; considering us as intellectual beings; considering us as creatures having souls in our bodies; considering us as something superior to the beasts that perish: considering ourselves in this light, what, I ask, have we to do with the manner in which LORD KING, one of the land-owners, wishes to settle with his tenants for their rent? Let him, in the name of common sense, manage his affairs in any way that he likes best; and let us endeavour to retrieve our affairs. With this laudable determination in our minds, and being convinced that all our embarrassments arise from our Debts, let us look back into our books for the last twenty or thirty years, and see how we have got rid of our money. We have always had a *large income*, and yet our AGENT, for the time being, has been *borrowing money for us*. This may possibly have been necessary; but, at least, let us not act the part of careless men in common life, who, in in spite of circumstances enough to awaken suspicion in credulity itself, still confide in a plundering sharper. Let us look into our *books*; let us look back into our *old accounts*, and see what our AGENTS, in succession, have done with our money. Our income they have expended, they have made prodigious loans in our name, and have charged us with interest upon them: let us see, then, to *whom* and for *what* they have paid away all this money; for, if we should find, that they have taken any part of the money *to themselves* or *given it away*, that opens to us a most interesting view of the matter.

Well, then, in looking over the account books of the nation for the last twenty or thirty years, I find several large sums paid to OLD GEORGE ROSE and his sons, and I find, too, that the far greater part of it has been paid them for *sinecure* offices, that is to say *nothing-to-do-Offices*. I put these sums together, I calculate the interest upon them, and I find them, together with the interest, amount to £.323,000 or thereabouts. So! say I, here I have, then, discovered the *cause*, in part, of this embarrassment in our affairs. If this money had not been given to the ROSES, the nation would not, of course, have been so much in Debt, the Dividends upon the interest of the Debt would not have been so large, the Bank Company need not have made so much paper to pay the Dividends with, the run upon the Bank would not have taken place so soon, the stoppage of cash payments would not have been called for at so early a period, the depreciation would not have come on so fast, the gold would have been longer in arriving at a premium, and LORD KING would not as yet, at least, have given the notice, which has led to the Bill now before parliament.

I shall be asked, perhaps, what signifies £.323,000 when the whole of the Debt amounts to £.800,000,000. My answer is that *millions* are composed of *ones*; and that no sums are so large as those which grow out of many small ones. But *is* this a *small* sum? Look at it! *It is a 2,500th part of the whole of the National Debt.* Think of that! I may have had an error in my estimate: the Roses may not have had this income for so long a time; and I may have committed an error in computing the amount of the interest; but, if I am right, as I think I am, and under the mark instead of over the mark, then have these persons, this one family, and, indeed, one member of it chiefly, received, from the nation, in principal and interest, a 2,500th part of the whole of the National Debt at this day in existence.

Here we are upon the TRUE SCENT, Gentlemen; and I am quite satisfied, that all the hallooing and hooting and doubling and luring in the world will never, in the end, prevent us from having success in the chace. A 2,500th part of the *whole* Debt mind; but, of the Debt created within the last twenty or thirty years, it will make about 1,800th part. So that, if my calculations be correct, George

Rose and his Son (without including the value of the *reversionary grant* or of the *Envoy's* pension) have, during the last twenty or thirty years, received, in principal and interest, a sum of money from the people *equal to* a 1,800*th part of all that portion of the National Debt, which has been created during the last thirty years*!

When sinecures and pensions have been talked of, you have observed certain persons set up an affected horse laugh, as if the amount was a mere *trifle*, a thing to *laugh at*; but, you see, Gentlemen, that these are not trifles; that they are things worth looking into; and there are few persons, I believe, who have ever had to do with embarrassed pecuniary affairs, who will not think with me, that *the sooner we look into these things the better*. For, if we were, for instance, to find out, in searching the Nation's old accounts, 1,800 persons, each of whom has received of the public money, in the last thirty years, a sum in amount equal to that received by GEORGE ROSE, then the thing is made clear at once. There is no more difficulty. We, at once, see the cause of the increase of the national Debt; or, at least, we see the means that might have been employed to prevent the stoppage of the Bank cash payments, and the consequent depreciation of the paper-money.

I shall be told, may be, by some persons, that I forget the *services* which GEORGE ROSE has rendered to the country. That is a point upon which men may differ in opinion; but, then, that claim has been satisfied by the *Salaries* as Secretary of the Treasury and Treasurer of the Navy; so that, at any rate, there are more than *six tenths* of the whole sum to be kept to the sinecure amount; and, as I said before, there may have been many and large emoluments of which I have, and can have, no knowledge. There is, indeed, the other claim, mentioned in the early part of this letter, namely, the preserving to us, the "*most thinking* people in the world," the "BLESSED COMFORTS of religion;" and really I must confess, that, against those who thought that paying taxes and creating national Debts were necessary to prevent them from being made Atheists by French Republicans, this claim is good. Those who could be made believe that must be of so stupid and so base a nature as to make them wholly unworthy the attention of him, whose object is happy and free; because such people must have been fashioned by nature to be slaves. What a degrading idea! Pay money to prevent myself from being made an Atheist! Pay taxes; suffer in silence my estate to be taken from me by piece-meal, and sit quiet while I am told, that this is necessary in order that the French may not take from me "the BLESSED COMFORTS of religion!" Talk of credulity, indeed! Talk of the pilgrims who used to go and make their offerings at the shrine of Thomas à Becket! Talk of the Priest-craft and gullibility of three centuries back! I defy any man to produce me, from the annals of superstition, from any of the records of human credulity or human cowardice, any thing which to the character of man is so degrading as this is.

Yet, this was the sort of language made use of by the partizans of Pitt, during the whole course of the Anti-jacobin war. There were many tricks played off; but the grand, the master trick, the never failing fraud, was the alarm at the danger of seeing *atheism* introduced instead of the *Christian Religion*; the "gloomy despair of Atheism," says GEORGE ROSE, instead of "the BLESSED COMFORTS of religion!" What would I give to have seen GEORGE just at the moment of his finishing that sentence! I should like to have watched his looks, and, if possible, to have heard his soliloquy! "BLESSED COMFORTS of religion!" He seems totally to have forgotten the *ten thousand pound a year;* but, I trust, that the time is not far distant, when that and all other matters of the kind will be well and scrupulously attended to.

Upon a future occasion, Gentlemen, I intend entering more at large into an inquiry as to *what has become of the money borrowed* during the last twenty or thirty years; but, this I must defer till another opportunity. In my next I intend closing this series of letters, when I shall have seen the discussions upon the Bill, now before the Parliament, brought to an end. That will be a natural point for me and you, Gentlemen, to rest at, until something new and important shall arise, and that that will soon be the case I am pretty certain. In the mean while I beg leave to subjoin a a few remarks on the case of DE YONGE, together with a Letter from himself to LORD VISCOUNT FOLKESTONE, and remain,

Your faithful friend,

WM. COBBETT.

State Prison, Newgate, Thursday, 18th July, 1811.

THE Case of DE YONGE, the Jew, who, in the month of August last year, was tried for selling Guineas for more than their nominal value in Bank Notes, has proved what I then said it would be, "one of the "most important that had taken place "for many years."——I said, and published, at the time, my opinion, that, notwithstanding the prosecution had been ordered and carried on by the *Attorney General* (Gibbs), and though the man had been found guilty by a *Special Jury* and in coincidence with the direction of the *Judge* (Ellenborough;) notwithstanding all this, I gave it as *my* decided opinion, and maintained that opinion by argument, that the Jew had been guilty of *no crime* in the eye of the law of England. The case, as we have before seen, has since been argued before the *Twelve Judges*, and they have pronounced, that what the man was charged with was *not a crime*.——It is a long time since this man's prosecution *began*. Notice will be found of it in the Register *a year and a half ago*. It was manifest, that the poor man must have greatly suffered in purse as well as in mind; and, when the Judges had declared him guilty of *no crime*, LORD FOLKESTONE, who had before interested himself greatly in the man's fate, and had given notice, that if the case was not speedily decided upon by the Judges, *he would bring it before Parliament;* when the Judges had decided, his lordship complained, in the House of Commons, that the poor man had suffered greatly, and *ought to have compensation made him*. The ATTORNEY GENERAL answered, that *every man* was liable to the same sort of inconvenience and injury. To be sure, said his lordship, every man is liable to have a false accusation preferred against him; every man is liable to be prosecuted without sufficient grounds; but, this was a singular case: the prosecution was ordered *by the King's own Attorney General;* and, what is more, the *crime*, as it was called, was, by the government Solicitor, *procured to be committed;* so that the man was *prevailed* upon by the prosecutors to commit what they deemed a great crime; they tempted him to commit the crime; they, in fact, *made* the crime, or the supposed crime, that they intended to prosecute, and that they actually did prosecute. This is by no means a *common case;* it is by no means one of those vexatious and groundless prosecutions to which any man is liable from the malice or mistake of others. This was a prosecution *by the law officers of the Crown*, and by the *Attorney General* in particular; and, all the sufferings of DE YONGE have arisen from the Attorney General's *not knowing the law upon this point*. It is no crime, to be sure, to be ignorant of the law upon any point; nor is it to be supposed that Attorney Generals are conjurors any more than other men; but, when they *seek to get the grounds* of a prosecution; when they get a man to commit a crime (or when those under them do it), they may have an opportunity of prosecuting it; when this is the case, there can be no doubt, I think, that they *ought to know the law* before they proceed. And, I am quite sure, that, in all such cases, where there is an acquittal at last, the suffering party ought to be indemnified for his sufferings and losses. For, if this be not so, *what* man is safe from utter ruin? *Who* may not be ruined? What De Yonge has suffered we shall now see, in a Letter, which he has had the gratitude to address to Lord Folkestone, and which, as being a very clear and modest statement of his case, and as a document connected with the great subject of which we are treating, I here insert.—

"My Lord; I should be wanting "in gratitude were I to omit return- "ing you my most sincere thanks for "your disinterested endeavours on "my behalf, and I assure your Lord- "ship I do not feel the less grateful "because they were unsuccessful.— "Your Lordship will perhaps ex- "cuse me if I mention a few circum- "stances in my case of which I think "I am justified in complaining, and "particularly as Mr. Attorney Gene- "ral asserted that I had suffered no "material hardships.—In the first "place, I did not seek the barter or "exchange which formed the subject "of the accusation against me, the "plan was laid by the Mint Solicitors "to tempt me to the bargain, and "then to prosecute me.—Pursuant to "this arrangement, a foreigner was "employed, who came to my house "as the interpreter to another man, in "his company; they stated, that they "were recommended to me to make "the purchase, and, after urging me "to deal with them, officers came into "my house, seized me and my money, "and, at a late hour in the evening, "I was hurried from my family to a "loathsome prison, (the Poultry "Counter) and there kept three days "and three nights in custody without "bail being admitted. At length, on "the final examination, I was dis- "charged on giving bail to a large "amount, which I had some difficulty "in procuring; and had I not been "able to obtain them, I must have "remained in custody 18 months, the "period this question has been pend- "ing. Lastly, the expence and anxiety "I have sustained has been enormous, "some through the solicitors for the "prosecution, for, after going through "all the necessary forms of law to "bring the first Indictment against "me to issue, and, indeed, when it "stood for trial, the prosecutors moved "to quash it and prefer another, be- "cause they had misrecited the pro- "clamation.—A second Indictment "was accordingly found, and this also "I proceeded in, until it was coming "on for trial, at the Old Bailey, when, "to my great mortification and as- "tonishment, it was removed by the "prosecutors into the Court of King's "Bench, by which means, I had, as "it were, my defence again to com- "mence.—Being in very moderate "circumstances, and having a family "to support, I have necessarily sus- "tained many deprivations in conse- "quence of the great law expences "incurred in defending myself against "this accusation, and, I fear, it will "be a considerable time before I can "recover myself from the injuries I "have sustained.—I will not further "trouble your Lordship, but con- "clude with observing, that I hum- "bly conceive the Law Officers of the "great public bodies and of Govern- "ment, having, as they must, the best "means of information on legal points, "ought to be somewhat more circum- "spect and accurate in their expound- "ing acts of parliament, before they "distress and bear down an humble "individual and expend the public "money, by harrassing and groundless prosecutions.—I am, my Lord, "with the greatest respect, your most "obedient and very humble Servant,

JAMES DE YOUNG."

107, Houndsditch, 17th July, 1811.

LETTER XXVIII.

"I looked upon the Bullion Report as likely to load to what would be likely to secure the country from the "natural consequences of that overwhelming corruption, which I regarded as the fruit of the paper "system; and, as I have the accomplishment of this great object deeply at heart; as I look upon the happiness and honour of my country as of far greater value to me than any other worldly possession, I "said, and I still say, that the Bullion Report has given me more pleasure than I should derive from "being made the owner of the whole of Hampshire. As to any idea of a *party* nature, I shall, I am sure, "be believed, when I say, that I did not care one straw to what party the Committee belonged. If I had "a wish as to party, it certainly would be, that *no change of ministry should take place*; for, without "prejudice to the OUTS, who, I think, would do the thing full as well with a little more time, I am "quite satisfied, that the present people will do it as *neatly* and as *quickly*, as any reasonable man can "expect."——POLITICAL REGISTER, Vol. XVIII. p. 427, Sept. 22nd, 1810.

Progress of Lord Stanhope's Bill—Effects of its Provisions—Mr. Brougham's Resolutions—The Justice of Lord King's Claim insisted on—Illustrated by the Grants to the King and the Additions to the Pay of the Judges.

GENTLEMEN,

THE Bill is past! And, be you assured, that the *die is cast!* When I wrote the passage, which I have taken for my motto to this letter, I did expect to see what I hinted at in the close of that passage; but, I must confess, that I did not expect the progress to have been *quite so rapid* as it has been. For the future my calculations will be more likely to keep pace with events.

Well, the Bill of Lord Stanhope is now become *a law*. We will, therefore, take a short view of the rise and progress of it; and, when we have so done, we will examine its provisions, and endeavour to point out its consequences.

The Bill was brought into the House of Lords and, read a first time on the 27th of June, when no division took place, and when an intimation was given by the ministers, that they should *oppose* it. On the second of July, it was read a second time, and, being now *supported* by the ministers, the question for the second reading was carried, 36 for it, 12 against it. On the 8th of July, it was read a third time and passed, 43 for it and 16 against it. In the Honourable House, it was read a first time on the 9th of July, and, upon a division on the question, there appeared 64 for it and 19 against it. On the 15th of July it was read a second time, 133 for it, and 35 against it. On the 17th of July it went through a committee of the House, and, on the 19th of July, it was read a third time and passed with the amendments, relating to the *penalties*. On the 22nd of July, the amendments introduced by the Commons were agreed to by the Lords. On the 24th of July it received the Royal Assent by Commission; and thus it is become A LAW; thus a new *penal law* has been added to the almost endless number already in existence. Many hundreds of the people of this country have been banished, or put to death, for *imitating* the promissory notes of the Bank Company; and now the people are liable to be punished *for passing them for what they may deem their worth,* though they be their *own property*.

The provisions of the Bill are not numerous: it is a pithy affair The first part relates to the passing of coin and paper, and the second to the recovery of rents. It will be best to insert the words. Those of the first part are as follows: "Be it enacted, "that from and after the passing of "this Act, no person shall receive or "pay for any gold coin lawfully current within the realm, any more in "value, benefit, or advantage, than "the true lawful value of such coin, "whether such value, benefit, profit "or advantage be paid, made, or taken "in lawful money, or in any note or "notes, bill or bills of the Governor "and Company of the Bank of England, or in any silver token or "tokens issued by the said Governor "and Company, or by any or all of "the said means wholly or partly, or "by any device, shift, or contrivance "whatsoever. And be it further enacted, by the authority aforesaid, "that no person shall by any device, "shift, or contrivance, whatsoever, "receive or pay any note or notes, "bill or bills of the Governor and "Company of the Bank of England, "as of less value in money, except "lawful discount, than the sum expressed therein, to be thereby made "so payable." Thus it stood as it went from the Lords. There were, I believe, some trifling verbal alterations made in the Honourable House, who also added the *penalty*, and made it a *misdemeanour* to disobey this part of the law; of course, offenders against it may be punished by *fine* and *imprisonment*, or, as I am, by *both*, at the discretion, perhaps, of the Judges; but, of this I am not sure, not having, as yet, seen the Act in its finished state.

Thus, then, the Bank Company, after having applied to the Government to issue an Order in Council, after having subsequently applied for acts of Parliament, to screen them against the consequences of refusing to pay their promissory notes in coin, now see a law passed making it *criminal*, for any one to get rid of any of those notes that he may happen to possess for their real worth in coin!

This law does what the laws already in existence could not do in the case of DE YONGE; or, at least, it *attempts* to do it. It forbids and punishes the selling of gold coin for more than its nominal worth in Bank Notes, which was precisely what DE YONGE did. But, do you believe, Gentlemen, that this will put a stop to the traffick? I should think, that nobody could believe this; and, if any one were inclined to believe it, he need only consider the little effect produced by the conviction of DE YONGE to convince him of the contrary. That gentleman was found *guilty* of the crime of selling guineas at *Twenty two shillings and sixpence* each, and, while he lay under that conviction, the price of the guinea rose to *Twenty six or Twenty seven shillings*. This is a pretty good proof that the price of the guinea is not to be kept down by penal laws. But, if the law should put an end to all purchases of gold coin in *Bank of England notes*, it cannot have any such effect with regard to *Country Bank Notes*. Suppose, for instance, that one of you had a fancy for a hundred guineas to lay snugly aside, and I had them to dispose of; the price would be 135*l*., but, say we, the bargain must not take place in notes of the Governor and Company in Threadneedle Street, for so says Lord Stanhope's law. But the law does not say, that such bargains shall not be made in *Country Bank* notes; and therefore, you give me 135*l*. in the notes of Paperkite and Co. which notes will, in all probability, answer my purpose full as well as the London notes, or better if I want to pay them away in the country; and, if they should not answer my purpose quite so well, what have I to do but go to the country banker and get them changed for Bank of England notes? I keep the country bank notes if I please, and if I please I change them. This is one way, then, and a most effectual way too, of rendering the Bill of no use as to its main apparent object.

But, how many are the ways, in which such a law may, must, and will be evaded? It is a law intended to make people part with their property for *less* than it is worth in the one case, and to make them obtain for it *more* than it is worth in the other case. The old adage of "a thing is "*worth* what it will *bring*" is, by this law, to be totally destroyed after having lived in the world ever since purchase, or even barter, was known amongst men. According to this law, a thing, in one case will be *worth more* than it is to be suffered *to bring*, and, in the other case, a thing will not bring *so much* as it is to be asserted *to be worth*. It is a law, in short, to compel men to dispose of certain articles of their property (if they dispose of them at all) at a price fixed on by the Government; and is such a law as never was heard of before, except in France, during the times of Robespierre and Danton and Marat. It is, as Mr. BROUGHAM has called it, in his Resolutions, a law of *maximum* as to gold coin; but, it is a law, which cannot be generally *enforced*, and which can have only a temporary and partial effect, if any at all, in checking the traffic in coin against paper; and to whatever extent it is efficient, it will be efficient in driving all the coin out of the kingdom, excepting such portion as people are enabled to *hoard*; for, if I have a guinea, or any thing else, that is worth 27 shillings, and if there be a law which prevents me from getting at present in England more than 21 shillings for it, I shall certainly hoard it 'till I can get the worth of it, if I have no safe means of sending it abroad. Where is the man who will not do this? I am sure that there is not a man amongst you who would not do it. Yes, I am sure, that there is not one single farmer in all England, who will not hoard a guinea rather than exchange it for a bank note of twenty one shillings. So that, as I have observed to you before, and as has been very well expressed in Mr. BROUGHAM's Resolutions, this law will, as far as it shall be efficient, drive the little remains of gold coin into hoards or out of the country, and, by preventing a free and open and unrestrained *competition* between the coin and the paper, will, as far as it has effect, prevent the operation of the only cure for the evil of a depreciated paper money.*

---

* It was on the 19th of July, that Mr. BROUGHAM proposed his RESOLUTIONS to the House of Commons. They were *negatived*: and, gentlemen, I beseech you to compare them with such resolutions as were *agreed to* by that House. These Resolutions are well worthy of attention, containing as they do what will become a memorable protest against the law, which is now the subject of discussion, and which will be a subject of observation with our children, if any trace of it shall remain beyond our own times.

I. That by the Law and Constitution of these Realms, it is the undoubted right of every man to sell, or otherwise dispose of his property for whatever he deems to be its value, or whatever consideration he chuses to accept. And that every man possessed of a Bank Note, or other security for the payment of money, has an undoubted right to give it away for nothing, or in exchange for whatever sum of money he pleases; or if he cannot obtain what he demands, to retain possession of it.

II. That any statute, having for its object to restrain this right, would be contrary to the principles of the British Constitution, and a flagrant violation of the most sacred Rights of Property, and the ancient and inalienable Liberties of the People.

III. That any statute, having for its object to prevent the Bank, or other Paper Currency of the Country from being exchanged against the lawful money of the Realm below a certain rate, would, if it could be carried into effect, cause the lawful money of the realm to disappear, and would, in proportion to its efficacy, preclude the application of the most appropriate remedies for the present derangement in the circulation of the country.

I have before observed, that, in all *ready-money* transactions, this law must be nugatory, and I have given an instance of a farmer having a pig to sell at market. It will, of course, be the same in all other bargains for ready-money; and, even in cases of credit, amongst friends and neighbours, the same will take place. Some roguery may be, in this respect, created by the law, but the law will never compel men to give the guinea and receive the note at their nominal value, one compared with the other. In that place, where, of all others, one might expect to see the dispositions of men concur with this law; I mean, the *Stock Exchange*, a distinction between coin and paper is already made; for Stock has frequently been bought with guineas at a price much lower than the rate of the day, which rate is regulated upon the supposition that paper-money is to be the medium. And, who is to prevent this, without a general law of *maximum;* that is to say, a law putting a price upon all commodities whatever, and punishing men for selling them for more than the price so fixed? This present law, therefore, is nothing *of itself.* It is nothing unaccompanied with a *maximum* of prices. Those who have begun in this path, must keep on, and go the whole length, or they do nothing at all, *except drive coin out of the country or into the hoards*, and, perhaps, in many cases, cause a breach of contracts between man and man. To a maximum they must come at last, or what is done will be of no effect at all.

The other provision of the Bill relates to *distress for rent,* and is as follows: "And be it enacted, by "the authority aforesaid, that in case "any person shall proceed by dis-"tress to recover from any tenant "or other person liable to such dis-"tress, any rent or sum of money "due from such tenant or other per-"son, it shall be lawful for such te-"nant or other person, in every "such case, *to tender notes of the "Governor and Company of the "Bank of England,* expressed to "be payable on demand, to the "amount and in discharge of such "rent or sum so due to the person "on whose behalf such distress is "made, or to the officer or person "making such distress on his behalf; "and in case such tender shall be ac-"cepted, or in case such tender shall "be made and refused, *the goods "taken in such distress shall be forth-"with returned to the party distressed "upon,* unless the party distraining "and refusing to accept such tender "shall insist that a greater sum is "due than the sum so tendered, and

IV. That the free exchange of the lawful Money of the realm with the paper currency on such terms as the holders of each may think proper to settle among themselves, is not only the undoubted right of the subject, but affords the best means of restoring the circulation of the country to its sound and natural state, by establishing two prices for all commodities, whensoever the one currency is from any causes depreciated below the other.

V. That no law whatsoever can alter the real value of the paper currency in relation to the lawful money of the realm, nor alter the real value of either kind of currency, in relation to all other commodities; and that any attempt to fix the rates at which paper and coin shall pass current, must, in proportion to its success, interfere with the just and legal execution of all contracts already existing, without the possibility of affecting the terms upon which contracts shall be made in time to come.

VI. That it is the bounden duty of the Commons House of Parliament, as the guardians of the rights of the people, to discountenance and resist a scheme which has for its immediate objects the establishment of a maximum in the money-trade of the realm, and the dissolution of the obligations already contracted by numerous classes of the community, but which has for its groundwork principles leading to an universal law of maximum, and the infraction of every existing contract for the payment of money; and that a Bill touching the gold coin which has lately been brought from the Lords, has all the said objects, and proceeds upon the said principles.

"in such case the parties shall proceed as usual in such cases; but if "it shall appear that no more was "due than the sum so tendered then "the party who tendered such sum "shall be entitled to the costs of all "subsequent proceedings: Provided "always, that the person to whom "such rent or sum of money is due "*shall have and be entitled to all such* "*other remedies for the recovery* "*thereof, exclusive of distress, as such* "*person had or was entitled to at the* "*time of making such distress, if* "*such person shall not think proper* "*to accept such tender so made as* "*aforesaid:* Provided also, that nothing herein contained shall affect "the right of any tenant, or other "such person as aforesaid, having "such right to replevy the goods "taken in distress, in case, without "making such tender as aforesaid, he "shall so think fit."——Now, what does this part of the Bill *effect?* It has frequently been said, that the *tenantry* ought to be *protected*, and Lord Stanhope has all along said, that his object was to protect the *tenant*. What, then, has this Bill done for the *tenant?* If the thing leased be a farm, or lands of any sort, *distress* is not the mode that the landlord would pursue. He has other remedies, and those much more efficient than that of distress. So that, in fact, this law affords *no protection* at all to the tenant.

But, though this law will do the tenant *no good*, it may, and, in some cases, will, do him a great deal of *harm*, especially as the minister has avowed his intention of making the bank notes a *legal tender* if this law should prove insufficient for the object in view. Under such circumstances, no man in his senses, will *let a new lease*, or *renew an old one;* for, though a *corn-rent* might possibly serve to guard him against the total loss of his estate, still he will be afraid, and he will think it the safest way to let no lease at all. Tenants for term of years will, therefore, become tenants at will, and will have their rents raised upon them every year agreeably to the depreciation of money and the rise in prices; and, another consequence will be, that landlords will, whenever it is practicable, take the lands into their own possession and use, seeing that even a yearly letting may, in the times that may arise, become dangerous; for, if a law be passed to-day in consequence of a single landlord's demanding his rent according to law, what have not landlords to fear? The safest course, therefore, that they can pursue is to keep, as far as they are able, their farms in their own hands; and this, to a very great extent, they certainly will do. So that this law, as far as it is efficient, will produce a virtual violation of contracts and a discouragement to agriculture.

During the discussions upon this measure, several hints were thrown out as to the *courts of law setting their faces* against those who should demand payment in gold. Sir SAMUEL ROMILLY observed upon what Mr. Manning said about the *law* being *too strong* for the *landlords*, that it alarmed him to hear such language; and that he thought it dangerous in the extreme to expose men to such an uncertainty as to the real meaning of the law. But Mr. FULLER and Lord STANHOPE, as appears from the reports of the newspapers, came to the point at once. The former is reported to have said, in the debate of the 9th of July, that "he wondered to "hear any doubt of the solvency "of Government; and Government "surely had ships and stores, and "plenty of valuables besides. He "(Mr. Fuller) did not understand the "objects of the persons who had "brought forward the question, but "he was convinced they were something sinister. *(A laugh.)* As to "Bank notes, if any landlord was "offered payment in them, and he "wanted gold, he (Mr. Fuller) did "not know what might be done; but "of this he was sure, that THE "WHOLE TENANTRY OF "THE COUNTRY WOULD "MEET AND TOSS HIM IN "A BLANKET. *(laughing.)*" And the latter is reported to have said, in the House of Lords, on the 22nd of July, that, "his Noble Friend "(Earl of Lauderdale) had called the "Bill a legislative HINT; but it "was a pretty broad hint, too. He "did not know whether his Noble "Friend had been educated at any "of the Universities: but he believed "not at Oxford. There was a story "there about a broad hint, which they "called "*John Keale's broad hint.*" "There was a man that John Keale "did not like; John gave him a hint "that he did not like his company: "but he would not go away. "What "did you do, then," says one to "John? "Do," says John Keale, "why, I kicked him down stairs. "That was a pretty broad hint!!!" "*(laughing.)* So he, (Earl Stanhope) had given Lord King *a hint;* "and *if he followed up this business,* "why, when next Session came, he "would give him a BROAD hint! "*(a laugh.)*" Quite a *wit,* I declare: "Quite a sea-wit, Mr. Benjamin!" Well, you know, Gentlemen, that there is a *time* for all things, and, of course, a time for *laughing.* But, it is well worthy of remark, that this war (for it is the same that began in 1793) was waged in the "PRESERVATION OF LIBERTY "AND PROPERTY AGAINST "REPUBLICANS AND LEVELLERS," that was the title of the Association at the Crown and Anchor. This is well worthy of remark; *now* is the time to make such remark. This war has now been going on eighteen years; this war for the support of *order* and *law* and *property,* and now, behold, we hear, in the two Houses of Parliament, the supporters of this system, talk of *tossing a landlord in a blanket* and *kicking him down stairs,* if he should persist in demanding payment of his rents *agreeably to the contract in his leases!*

Gentlemen, if you have read the reports of the debates in Parliament, upon this subject, you must have observed, that the people in the ministry have very loudly disapproved of the conduct of LORD KING for demanding of his tenants payment in gold, or in notes in sufficient amount *to make up for the depreciation of money.* Now, observe; they have brought forward, several times, propositions for *large grants to the King and to others,* on account of the *rise in prices,* which, as I have already explained to you is only another name for the *depreciation of money.* I beg you to mark well what I am now going to state to you; because it will give you a clear insight into this whole matter.

In 1802, eight years ago, a large sum of money, no less a sum than 990,053*l.* (why not have made it a *round million?*) was granted by Parliament "to the King to discharge "the arrears and debts due upon the "CIVIL LIST on the 5th of January, 1802." The *Civil List,* Gentlemen, is the King's establishment of servants and officers of different sorts, and, in short, of all his expences. The King had a permanent allowance, fixed by Act of Parliament, of 800,000*l.* a year for these purposes; but, in 1802 (the time we are now speaking of) the Civil List had got into debt; and the then Minister, Addington, taking advantage of the national satisfaction at the Peace of Amiens, proposed a grant of the above sum, for the purpose of paying off this debt. Mr. FOX and others opposed the grant; but it was supported by PITT, GEORGE ROSE and the majority, and upon a division here were 226 for it and only 51 against it. And, let it be borne in mind, that the grant was justified by PITT on this ground: that it did not make an increase to the Civil List equal in proportion "to the *increase of* "*the price of commodities*, and to "THE DEPRECIATION OF "MONEY." So he said; so they all said; and the assertion was sanctioned by a vote of the House granting 990,053*l.* to the King. Now, then, if the King was to have a grant like this on account of the *past depreciation of money*, why should Lord King be reviled, why should he be *tossed in a blanket*, or *kicked down stairs*, for demanding payment in such a way as to give him some securi- for *future depreciation of money*, especially when we consider, that he only demanded the *fulfilment of a bargain*, while the grant to the King was *over and above the fulfilment of a bargain made with him by the public?*

But, did the demands for the King *stop here?* Very far from it; for, in the year 1804 (only *two years* afterwards), PITT, who was then come back into power, called for another grant for a similar purpose, to no less an amount than 591,842*l.* 3*s.* 10½*d.* How scrupulously exact the Gentleman was! To a halfpenny, you see! Oh, wondrous financier! This grant also was made, and without any division of the House, though it was strenuously opposed by SIR FRANCIS BURDETT, upon the ground of its being a departure from a bargain with the public, and of the practice of making such grants being calculated to render the Royal Family absolutely dependent upon the Minister of the day. This grant also was justified upon the ground that *money had depreciated* and the *prices of all commodities increased*. This grant was accompanied with a *permanent addition* to the Civil List of 60,000*l.* a year; and, indeed, the annual sum, *now* paid by the people on that account is 958,000*l.* exclusive of 295,968*l.* 1*s.* 8½*d.* in allowances and pensions to the Royal Family, besides the amount of sinecure places and military offices that some members of the Family enjoy; the propriety or impropriety of none of which I am discussing, but it is necessary to state them in order to enable you to judge of the fairness of the attacks upon Lord KING, who only wanted a *bare fulfilment of contract* with regard *to his own private estate;* who only wanted to save himself from ruin from the *future* depreciation of money, and who gave up to his tenants all they had gained from him by the *past*.

Now, Gentlemen, I beg you to observe, that this second grant to the King; this grant of £591,842 was to pay off what he had lost in *two years* by the depreciation of money; and, you will also observe, and mark it well, that these *are two out of the nine years that have elapsed since Lord King let the Estate respecting the rent of which you have seen his notice to his tenant.* The King, in 1802, had a fixed allowance of £.800,000 a year out of the public money; and at the end of *only two* years, his advisers find him to require a grant of £.591,842 on account of the depreciation of money; that is to say, £,295,921 in each of the two years. *More than* 30 *per cent. per annum!* And, is Lord King, after having silently suffered under the gradual depreciation for *nine years*, to be attacked in this manner; is he to be lumped along with *Jews* and *Pedlars* and *Smugglers;* is he to have a hint that he will be *kicked down stairs* or *tossed in a blanket*, because he now, when he sees the guinea selling at 25, or 26, or 27*s.* is resolved to have a fulfilment of his bargain, and not to be wholly

Entered at Stationers' Hall.

Printed by W. MOLINEUX, 5, Bream's Buildings, Chancery Lane; Published by W. COBBETT Jun. No. 8, Catherine Street, Strand: and Retailed at No. 192, Strand.

ruined by this depreciation of money?

But, Gentlemen, this principle of augmenting allowances out of the *public treasure*, on account of the depreciation of money, has not been confined to the King and his family. It has been acted upon in almost all the departments under the Government, the army and navy excepted, where, as far as relates to the Commissioned Officers especially, little augmentation has taken place. I will, however, here confine myself to one particular class of persons, namely, **THE JUDGES**, and I do it the rather because it has been hinted pretty *broadly*, that the *Courts of Law* would set their faces against the efforts of those, who might attempt to *enforce* payment in gold.

Be it known to you, then, Gentlemen, that the Judges' pay has had *two lifts* since the Bank stopped its payments in gold and silver. The first was, in the year 1799, two years only after the passing of our famous Bank *Restriction* Act. The two *Chief* Judges, whose incomes were very large, underwent no augmentation by Act of Parliament; but, the pay of all the rest was augmented by the Act, Chapter 110, of the 39th year of the King's reign; and, no trifling augmentation did their pay receive, it being upon an average nearly, if not quite, *half the whole amount of their former pay*. The Chief Baron of the Exchequer had £.1,000 a year added to his former £.3,000 a year; and all the nine Puisne Judges had £.1,000 each added to their former pay, which was, in some cases a little more and in some cases a little less than £.2,000 a year before. And, besides this, the Act enabled *the King*, that is to say, his advisers, to make a permanent provision for any judge that might become *superannuated*, and it fixed on great pensions for them in this case, which pensions can, in consequence of that Act, *be granted without any particular consent of the Parliament, which was not the case before.* Mr. TIERNEY opposed this measure in a very able manner. He said, that the House of Commons would thus lose all check and controul as to such remunerations; and that the influence of the Crown would be thus greatly and most fearfully enlarged. The measure was, however, adopted; and thus the Judges, in Scotland as well as in England, received *an ample compensation for the depreciation of money*, up to the year 1797.

Having gone on with this pay for ten years, it appears to have been thought time to give them *another lift*, and, accordingly an Act for this purpose was passed in the year 1809, of which the people seem to have taken not the least notice. It seems to have escaped every body's attention; but, indeed, the Acts now passed are so numerous, that it is next to impossible for any single man to be able to pay attention to them all, or to a quarter part of them. This Act, which is Chapter 127 of the 49th year of the King's reign, makes an addition of £.1,000 a year, to the pay of the Chief Baron of the Exchequer; also an addition of £.1,000 a year, to each of the nine Puisne Judges; and it gives an additional £.400 a year to each of the Welsh Judges. Thus, at the end of twelve years from the time when the Bank stopped paying in gold, the pay of the English Judges was nearly doubled; and, shall my Lord King be represented as a *pedlar*, a *jew*, and a *smuggler*, because, at the end of *nine years* of depreciation of

W. Molineux, Printer, Bream's Buildings, Chancery Lane.]

money, he wishes to put a stop to the ruinous progress? And shall he be threatened with the hostility of these same Judges, in case he should attempt to enforce his legal claim? Shall he be told about being fought off in the Courts, and about the law being *too strong* for him?

At the time when these Acts were passed for augmenting the pay of the Judges, one of the arguments was, that such augmentation was necessary to support the DIGNITY of the office of Judge. Now, in what way was an increase of pay to produce such an effect? Certainly in no other way than that of enabling the Judge to augment his expences of living; for, as to his authority, as to his powers, as to his station, the money would make no alteration at all in them. This being the case, there appears to have been no good reason for augmenting the Judges' pay any more than the pay of the officers of the Navy, or of any other persons in the public employ. Mr. TIERNEY used, at the time when the first augmentation was proposed, an argument very applicable to our present purpose: "If," said he, "an augmentation of "income be necessary to support the "station of the Judge, has the country "no interest in enabling the officers "of the Army and Navy, of the "Ministers of the Church, or the "Magistrates, to maintain their station "of society? If the circumstances of "a Judge, who has £.2,000 a year, "require that he should have an additional £.1,000 we know very well "what must be the situation of a "private Gentleman with an income "of £.2,000 a year."

This argument applies precisely to Lord King. The answer to Mr. Tierney was, that the private Gentleman, if his estate was in land, would, of course, raise his rents in order to make his income keep pace with the depreciation of money. But the reply to this is, that, if his estate was let upon lease, as Lord King's is, he could not raise his rents, till the expiration of that lease; and if he let a farm upon a fourteen years' lease in the year 1798, he has been receiving money at the rate of that time, during the last thirteen years, whereas the pay of the Judges has been *doubled* in the space of twelve of those years. This is, in fact, the situation of Lord King. Either, thefore, it was not necessary, and it was not just to augment the pay of the Judges in any degree; or, it is extremely unjust that Lord King should be prevented from augmenting his income. Indeed he has had, till now, all the legal means of making his income keep pace with the depreciation of money, by demanding his rents in gold; that is to say, agreeably to the terms of the contract, in good and lawful money of the realm.

This legal, this equitable, this fair, this honest, this indubitable claim, he was preparing to inforce, when my Lord Stanhope steps forward with the proposition of a law avowedly intended to prevent him from so doing; to throw impediments in his way; to interfere in the management of his estates; to take from him part of the legal means which he before possessed of preserving his property; and, for having signified his intention to use those means, he is held forth as a *jew*, a *pedlar*, and a *smuggler*. I have observed, that Mr. SHERIDAN has taken part upon this occasion with those who have censured Lord King. And this is the more remarkable as he has seldom taken part in any discussion whatever. Is Mr. SHERIDAN aware of the consequences to which this may lead? It is hardly necessary to tell him, that the day may not be far distant, when the CIVIL LIST will have to be settled anew; and, I should be glad to know whether, in that settlement, it is likely to be the wish of the parties concerned, that the sum should be fixed as if it were to be paid in gold. Whether, in short, the amount of the Civil List would be fixed for the future, at its present amount. But, if that were not to be the case, how could a *larger amount* be proposed or supported by those who have now railed at the conduct of Lord King?

Endless are the difficulties, into which those have plunged themselves, who have reprobated the conduct of this nobleman as unjust, or who have represented it as unwise. Such persons will hardly muster up the resolution to make a frank acknowledgement of their error; and yet, if they do not do this, with what face can they propose, or support, or sanction, either expressly or tacitly, any measure which shall have for its object, the preservation of the Crown, the Royal Family, the Army, the Navy, the Courts of Justice, or any department of the state, against the effects of the depreciation of money? The measure of Lord King fell far short of the justice due to himself, for, though the money had depreciated considerably at the date of his oldest leases, still, it has gone on depreciating further from that time to this. He, therefore, would have been fairly entitled to payment in Gold, and nothing else, for the remainder of those old leases. But, pursuing a moderate and liberal course, he restrained his demands far within their legal bounds. With a considerateness that does him great honour, he suffered his tenants quietly to retain what they had gained during the past, and only required of them a due fulfilment of contract for the future, which was not less necessary to the welfare o. his tenants, than it was to his own protection; because without such a measure, it was impossible they ever could obtain a renewal of their leases.

Much, during the discussions upon this famous Bill has been said about *patriotism*: and Lord King has been charged with a want of that quality, because he made the demand, of which so much has been said. But, if Lord King, in barely demanding the fulfilment of a contract in order to protect himself against the effects of the depreciation of money; if Lord King, in barely appealing to the law already in existence for his protection against this ruinous effect of paper money; if, for this, Lord King is to be accused of a want of *patriotism*, and is to be lumped with Jews, Pedlars, and Smugglers, what will be the inference with regard to the King and Royal Family, and my Lords the Judges, to protect whom against the effects of depreciation *laws have been passed*, laws proposed by the *minister* of the day and sanctioned by the *majority*. Lord King comes for *no law* to protect him; he asks for no law *against his tenants*; he only wants his due according to the existing law; and yet, he is, and by the very people, too, who approved of the above-mentioned large grants to the King and the Judges, accused of *a want of patriotism!*

The venal prints have not failed to join in the accusations against Lord King, whom the COURIER, on the 5th instant, charges with motives of "*base lucre*," as the ATTORNEY GENERAL did me, and with precisely the same degree of justice. The article here referred to in the COURIER concludes with some observations as to the duty of patriotism, in this case; and says, that, "On an "occasion in which ALL SUFFER, "the man who first *abandons the* "*general cause* for his own personal "interests, must needs make a very "sorry figure before the world, just "like the *coward who is the first to* "*fly in battle*, while victory is doutful. "But if this man were an high officer, "a Legislator, an hereditary Coun-"sellor of his Sovereign, whose "peculiar duty it is to *set an example* "*of bravery, of fortitude, of contempt* "*for personal consequences* in the "general cause, with what feelings "could we view his conduct? Now, it is to be observed here, that all this talk about the public cause is most shocking nonsense, and what no man in the world besides one of these hirelings would be found to put upon paper. But, if to demand merely the fulfilment of contracts in order to preserve his fortune against the effects of depreciation of money, if this be to "*abandon the general cause for his* "*own personal interests*," if this be to resemble "*a coward who is the first to* "*flee in battle*," how will this venal man speak of the *King* and *Royal Family* and *the Judges?* The King has, since the year 1799, had *two* great grants in augmentation of the sum allowed him, the Junior Branches of the Royal Family have had *one* additional grant (in 1806) and the Judges have, as we have above seen, had their pay *doubled* actually *doubled*, since that time. And yet this venal man accuses Lord King of "BASE "LUCRE" because he is endeavouring to get what is *his due;* because he is endeavouring to get *his own;* because he is trying to protect himself against that ruin which he foresees will come upon him, if he does not now begin to obtain the fulfilment of his contracts.

"On an occasion," says this venal man, in "which ALL suffer." No: not all. The *King* has not suffered from the depreciation, nor have the *Judges*, whose pay has been, as we have seen, actually *doubled* since the stoppage of cash payments took place, and who, of course, would be now as well off as they were before that time, if the pound bank note were worthy only *ten shillings*, and Mr. HORNER tells us it is yet worth about *sixteen shillings*. "ALL" do not suffer, then. The Judges, so far from *suffering* have *gained* very greatly; and yet, no one has ever charged *them* with motives of "BASE LUCRE." The Judges of England alone have received, since the year 1799, in virtue of the two Acts above-mentioned, no less a sum than £.120,000, that is, one hundred and twenty thousand pounds of principal money, more than they would have received had not these two grants been made to them; and if we include the interest, as in all such calculations we must, they have received, since 1799, over and above their former pay, about £.145,000. And, yet, my Lord King is, by this venal scribe, accused of motives of "BASE LUCRE," because he wishes to prevent *the whole of his income from being sunk in the depreciation of money.* The Judges have actually put in their pockets this large sum of money; they have actually touched it, since the year 1799, and, of course, the *National Debt is so much the greater on that account;* the interest upon that Debt is so much the greater on that account; the quantity of bank notes to pay the Dividends are so much the greater on that account; and, of course, these two Acts of Parliament have tended, in some degree, to hasten the depreciation, and to produce the very effect which now threatens to ruin Lord King, and to find out a *remedy* for which puzzles so many men who think themselves wise. Lord King's measure does not tend to add to the *national Debt:* it tends to produce no addition to the Dividends or the bank paper; it is a mere measure of management of his private affairs, which does not trench upon the public good in any way whatever; and yet, he is lumped along with Jews, Pedlars, and Smugglers, and is accused of a want of patriotism!

This writer tells us, that it was the duty of such a man as Lord King to set an example of "*contempt of per-* "*sonal consequences*," meaning, of course, *pecuniary* consequences. But, was it *more* his duty than it was the duty of *the King*, the *Royal Family*, and *the Judges?* He says that Lord King ought to have done it, as being an hereditary counsellor of the crown. If Lord King had had much to do in counselling the Crown, the present subject would, perhaps, never have been discussed; but, be that as it may, was it *more* his duty to set an example of *contempt of pecuniary consequences* than it was of the King? Was it *more* his duty than it was *the duty of the Judges?* Was no example of this sort to be expected from *them*, while it was to be expected from *him?* And, I beg you to observe the wide difference between the case of the Judges and that of Lord King. No new law is made to favour the interests of the latter; but a new law is made, and afterwards another new law, to favour the interests of the former. Lord King does not attempt to obtain any *real addition* to his original rents; but there is granted to the Judges a very large *real addition* to their original pay. The COURIER calls upon Lord KING to suffer quietly for the good of his country. His suffering would not do the country any good, but a great deal of harm. But, upon the supposition that it would do the country good, what does the same man say about the augmentation of the pay of the Judges? When the augmentation to the pay of these persons was under discussion, Mr. PERCEVAL (who was then a *barrister*) argued, that the Judges ought to have quite enough to maintain them in all their state *without touching their private fortunes;* and, observe, this he said *at the very time*, in that very year, 1799, when Old George Rose, who was then one of the Secretaries of the Treasury at £.4,000 a year, and who had another good £.4,000 a year in sinecure places, was preaching up to "the *most thinking* people of all Europe," his doctrine of *sacrifices* and *salvage*, a specimen of which I gave you in my last Letter. "The *imperious* and "*awful* necessity of the present "crisis," said GEORGE, unavoidably "subjects US to heavy burdens. It "has been said, that they ought to be "considered as a SALVAGE for "the remaining part of OUR property. The metaphor though just "is inadequate; for what Tariff shall "settle the difference between the "BLESSED COMFORTS OF "RELIGION and the GLOOMY "DESPAIR OF ATHEISM." George talks of "US" and of "OUR" property; but HE was gaining all the while; aye, and he got his great sinecure place, with reversion to his eldest son, while "*imperious* and "*awful* necessity," was calling upon the nation for sacrifices. GEORGE's doctrine of SALVAGE was for the use of others, and not at all for his own use; nor did this doctrine of SALVAGE apply to the Judges, who, we have seen, received an *addition* to their pay out of the public money, during the times of this "*imperious* and *awful* necessity;" during the time that George Rose was calling upon the people, for the love of God, not to spare their money. "Oh!" said George, "it would be a *slander* "to the *sense* and *virtue* of the people "to suppose an abatement in that "*spirit* which has *enabled* the Govern- "ment to *call forth those resources.*" And, at this very time he was receiving upwards of £.8,000 a year out of the taxes raised upon that same people, and Mr. TIERNEY, who opposed the augmentation to the pay of the Judges, was told, that they ought to be enabled to maintain all their dignity and state, that is to say, to live and keep their families, *without touching their private fortunes.* And, yet, Lord King is to be lumped with Jews, Pedlars, and Smugglers; he is to have a hint about tossing in blankets and kicking down stairs; and, what is still more serious, he is to see a law passed avowedly to counteract his measures with regard to the management of his own estate; he is to be accused of motives of *base lucre;* he is to be held forth as an enemy to his country; and all this because he wishes to obtain what is legally and equitably his due; what is his due as fairly as the produce of their fields is the due of his tenants.

I have now, Gentlemen, to apologize to you for having taken up so much of your time in illustrating what was so clear itself. The additional grants to the Civil List, and the augmentation of the pay of the Judges, did not properly belong to our subject; but, when my Lord King was reviled, and when a law was avowedly levelled at him, because he sought, in 1811, to protect himself and family against the ruinous effects of depreciation, justice demanded of me, if I wrote at all upon the subject, to shew what has been done in behalf of the King and the Judges in 1799, 1802, 1804, and 1809, and especially as these measures in behalf of the King and the Judges were approved of and supported by some of those who now reprobate the conduct of Lord King.

In my next Letter, which will be *the last of the series*, I shall have to offer you some observations of a more general nature, and in the mean while, I remain,

Gentlemen,

Your friend,

WM. COBBETT.

State Prison, Newgate, Friday, 26th, July, 1811.

LETTER XXIX.

"The true way of convincing your enemy, that his war upon your finances will be useless, is, to state explicitly to the world, that you are not at all afraid of the consequences of a *national bankruptcy*: for, while you endeavour to make people believe, that such an event *cannot possibly happen*, they will certainly think, that you regard it, if it should happen, as *irretrievable ruin and destruction*; and, therefore, as you never can quite overcome their apprehensions, the best way is to be silent upon the subject, or to set the terrible bugbear at defiance."—*Political Register, 18th June, 1803.*

What is to be the end of all this?—Paper-Money is not the cause of Sunshine and Showers—We may exist without Paper-Money—England did very well before Paper-Money was heard of—What is to become of the Fundholders?—The Sale of the Royal Plate and of the Church Property in Austria—Let what will happen in England the Jacobins and Levellers will not merit any Share of the Blame—Conclusion.

GENTLEMEN,

WHAT, then, is to be the *end* of all this? What are to be the ultimate effects produced upon *the nation* by this depreciation of the paper-money?—The PITTITE party tell us, that there is not gold to be had; that the Bank cannot pay in gold; and that the matter must be left to *better times* and to *better fortune*. The other party tell us, that, if they had the power of adopting what measures they pleased, they would *cause the Bank to pay again in gold*; that thy would restore the paper to its former estimation; and, in short, retrieve the whole system. I have, I think, shewn you very clearly, that to cause the Bank to pay again in gold *is impossible*; and that, let what will happen, let what will take place as to commerce, or as to war, the Bank Paper will never regain any part of what it has lost, *as long as the national debt shall exist*; or, rather, as long as the *dividends shall be paid* upon the interest of that debt.

Now, if I have shewn this to your satisfaction, the question, and the only question, that remains to be discussed, is, what would be the CONSEQUENCES of a cessation in the payment of the dividends; that is to say, the total destruction of the National Debt; the total breaking up of the Funds and the Bank Note system. This is the only question that now remains to be discussed; but a very important question it is, and one which, I hope, will receive your patient attention.

To hear the greater part of people talk upon this subject, one would imagine, that the Bank Notes were the meat, drink, and clothing of the inhabitants of this island; and, indeed, that they gave us sun-shine and showers and every thing necessary to our existence. One would really suppose, that the general creed was, that the Bank Directors were the Gods of the country, that they were our Sustainers if not actually our Makers, that from them we derived the breath in our nostrils, that in and through them we lived, moved, and had our being. No wonder, then, that there should be an *apprehension* and even a *horror* inspired by the idea of a total destruction of the paper-money; no wonder, that, when I began, about eight years and a half ago, to write against the Funding System, I should have been regarded as guilty of blasphemy, and should have been accused thereof by that devout man, Mr. SHERIDAN; no wonder that some men's knees should knock together and their teeth chatter in their head upon being told, that the day is, probably, not far distant, when a guinea, a real *golden* guinea, will buy a hundred pounds' worth of three per cents.

But, Gentlemen, is there any *ground* for these apprehensions? Are such apprehensions to be entertained by *rational* men? No: the corn and the grass and the trees will grow without paper-money; the Banks may all break in a day, and the sun will rise the next day, and the lambs will gambol and the birds will sing and the carters and country girls will grin at each other, and all will go on just as if nothing had happened.

"Yes," says some besotted Pittite, "we do not suppose, that the destruction of the paper-system would "put out the light of the sun, prevent "vegetation, or disable men and women to propagate their species: we "are not fools enough to suppose "that." Pray, then, *what* are you fools enough to suppose? *What* are you fools enough to be *afraid of?* For, if the destruction of the paper produces, and is calculated to produce, none of these effects, how can it be a thing to excite any very *general* apprehension? *Who* would it *hurt?* "Oh! it would create universal *uproar* and *confusion:* it would destroy all property; it would introduce anarchy and bloodshed, and "annihilate *regular government, social order*, and our *holy religion.*" Thse are the words that JOHN BOWLES, the Dutch Commissioner, used to make use of. This is the declamatory cant, by the means of which the people of this country have been deceived and deluded along from one stage of ruin to another, till, at last, they have arrived at what they now taste of. If, when JOHNNY BOWLES, or any of his tribe, had been writing in this way, a plain tradesman, who gets his living by fair dealing and who has no desire to share in the plunder of the publ'c, had gone to the writer, and, taking him fast by the button, had said to him: "Come, come! tell "me, in definite terms, what you "mean, and shew me *how I should* "*be a loser by* this thing that *you* appear so much to dread. None of "your *rant;* none of your *horrifying* "descriptions; but come, JOHN, tell "me HOW I should be made worse "of in this world, and HOW I "should be more exposed to go to "Hell, if that which you appear to "dread were actually to take place:" if any such man had so addressed this Treasury scribe, the scribe would have been puzzled much more than he was by his per cents. about the Dutch Commission.

Why, Gentlemen, should the total destruction of the paper-money produce any of these effects? Why should it destroy all *property;* why produce *bloodshed;* why destroy our *holy religion?* I have before told you, that the paper-money was unknown in England, till within about 107 years. England did very well before that time. The people of England were brave and free, happy at home and dreaded abroad, long before paper-money was heard of. Why, then, should they now believe, that, without paper-money, they would be reduced to a state of barbarism and slavery? The Church, as is now established, existed long before paper-money was thought of, and so did *all those laws,* which we yet *boast* of as the great bulwark of our freedom; and, what is more, I defy any man to shew me one single law, *in favour of the liberties of the people,* which has been passed *since* the establishment of the Paper-Money System, while numerous laws have been passed hostile to those liberties. Before the existence of the National Debt and the Bank, the House of Commons used frequently to refuse to grant the money called for by the Crown; since they have existed, no grant of the kind has ever been refused by that House. Before the Paper System existed, there was no standing army in England; Before the Paper System existed, there were not more than *two hundred thousand paupers* in England and Wales: there are now *twelve hundred thousand.*

Why, then, should we alarm ourselves at what appears to indicate the appoaching destruction of this System? "Oh, but," says the Minister (Perceval), "without the Paper System "we could not have had the *victories* "recently won in Spain and Portu-"gal:" to which he might have added the achievements at *Quiberon,* at *Dunkirk,* at the *Helder,* at *Ferrol,* at *Buenos Ayres,* in *Hanover,* in *Leon* and *Gallicia,* at *Corunna,* at *Walcheren,* &c. &c. The list might be swelled out to three times this length; but this is long enough. If what the Minister calls the "recent *victories*" are the fruit of the Paper System, so are all the achievements to which I have here called your recollection. Indeed they were so; for, the wars themselves proceeded from the same source. The *American War* grew out of the Paper System; and so did the Antijacobin war, which began in 1793, and which has finally produced the state of things which we now have before us. So that, as to the *use* of the Paper System in this way, there can, I think, be very little doubt.

"Well, but, after all," some one will say, "*what is to become of the* "*Fund-holder?* How is he to get "*re-paid?*" My answer to this is, that, it does not appear to be a matter in which *the people,* I mean the *mass of the nation,* have much to do or to say. For, what is the *Fund-holder* or *Stock-holder?* Why, he is a man, who, choosing a large rather than a small interest for his money, has lent it to some persons in power, under an agreement, that he shall be paid interest upon it out of the taxes raised upon the people. A man, who lends money, knows, of course, or, at least, he ought to know, the *sufficiency of the borrower;* or, if he does not know that, he, of course, takes the *risk* into his calculation; and he can have no right to complain if the chances should happen to turn up against him. Upon this principle SIR JOHN MITFORD (now Lord Redesdale) went in defending the first Bank Restriction Bill, when, in answer to those who contended, that it would be a *breach of faith* to compel the Fund-holder to take payment in paper, he said, that the Fund-holder, *when he lent his money, knew that a case like this might happen,* and that, therefore, he had no reason to complain. Till I read this, I thought that I was the only one who had held the doctrine, so that my satisfactian at seeing my opinions corroborated by such high legal authority was somewhat diminished by the reflection, that I had lost what I had deemed my undivided claim to originality.

I do not, however, see any reason why the Fundholders, or, at least, that part of them, who have been *compelled* to suffer their property to be thus vested, should not, in any case, *have a just compensation*. And *how?* Whence is this compensation to come? In Austria, our old and faithful and august ally, the Emperor, is acting the part of a very honest man. The paper-money in Austria has fallen to a fourteenth part of its nominal value, *in spite of several Edicts prohibiting the passing of it for less than its nominal value.* A *hundred florins* in silver were worth *fourteen hundred and fifty three florins* in paper when the last advices came away; and, perhaps, *one* florin in silver, is, by this time, worth *fifty* florins in paper. Of course the Government creditors, or Austrian Fundholders, must be ruined, unless something be done to obtain a compensation for them. The Emperor, therefore, like an honest man, has, as the newspapers tell us, sent all his plate, all his gold and silver, in whatever shape, to the mint to be melted down and turned into coin for the payment of the people who have lent him and his Government their money. And, besides this, the *Clergy*, animated by a zeal for their sovereign truly worthy of example, *have given up their estates to be sold for the same honest purpose*, which, doubtless, they have been the more disposed to do, when they reflected, that the debts of the Government were incurred in carrying on a war for "regular government, social order, and "their holy religion," and in the producing and prolonging of which war they themselves had so great a hand, as well as in persecuting all those who were opposed to the system. Accordingly, we see accounts in the public prints of the SALES OF CHURCH LANDS going on in Austria. They are said to sell remarkably well;* and, it is stated, that, these sales, together with the meltings of the Royal Plate, will yield enough to satisfy all the Government Creditors; or, at least, to afford them the means of living beyond the reach of misery.

But, methinks, I see start forth a Courtier on one side of me and a Parson on the other, and, with claws distended ready to lay hold of my cheek, exclaim: "What, cold blooded "wretch! are *these*, then, your means "of compensation for the *English* "Fund-holder? Softly! Softly! Give me time to speak. Do not tear my eyes out before you hear what I have to say. Stop a little, and I will tell you what I mean.

Now, why should you be in such a rage with me? If I were to propose that the same should be done here as is now doing in Austria, what would there be, in my proposition, injurious to either the station or character of the *king* or the *clergy?* Am I to suppose, that the Crown depends upon the possession of a parcel of *plate* by the King and Royal Family; that a throne, the seat of kingly power, is supported by a waggon load, perhaps, of gold and silver dishes and plates and spoons and knives and forks and salvers and candlesticks and sauce-boats and tea-pots and cream-jugs? Good Heavens! What a vile opinion

* VIENNA, JULY 6—"A second sale of "ecclesiastical estates will soon take place. "On the 2[illegible]d will be sold, the estate of "Keixendorf; and on the 26th, those of St. "George and Baumgarten. As there are "many competitors, the sums produced by "these sales have greatly surpassed what the "lands were estimated at. The body of "merchants in this city published, some "days since, a memoir in their defence, "against the charges objected to them, of "having contributed to the depreciation of "the paper money. The memoir has been "transmitted to the Minister of Finance, "and presented to his Majesty the Em-"peror."

must they have of the throne, who look upon such things as tending to its support! And then, as to the Church, what could her sons wish for more earnestly than an opportunity of giving us a proof of their disregard of things temporal? Besides, there would be, in this case, a striking proof of the truth of the good maxim, that "Justice, "though *slow*, is *sure*;" for, it is well known, that the Paper System, which would thus draw upon the Church, was the *invention of* A BISHOP *of that same Church!*

But, the Courtiers and the Clergy may be tranquil; for I do not think it at all likely that such measures will become necessary in England, though they have been adopted at Vienna, and, as would seem, with such singular success. I am of opinion, that there would be found ample means, *elsewhere*, for a due compensation to those Fundholders, who had been *compelled* to vest their property in that way. In short, I am quite satisfied, that we have nothing at all to *fear* from the destruction of the paper-system if that should take place; and, as the friends of the system assert, that we have nothing to fear from its continuing to exist, we are, I think, *tolerably safe*. The RUIN of *America* and *France* were foretold because their paper-money was falling; but, the prophecy proved false. They were both victorious, both became prosperous; and, what is odd enough, both have since become receptacles of the coin that is gone from England; aye, from that country, who hoped to triumph over them by the means of that same coin! How many times did PITT predict the time when France would be what he called *exhausted*, and how was he hallooed on by his numerous understrappers of all sorts, verbally as well as in print! Has she been *ruined?* Has she lost in population or in power? Is she *exhausted?* Has she become *feeble*? We are still *struggling* with her; and do we find her grow *weaker* and *weaker?*

Well, this doctrine of RUIN from a depreciated paper-money is a false doctrine. It was engendered in a shallow brain, and brought forth by arrogant emptiness. But, suppose it to be sound as applied to us; suppose, for argument's sake, that the destruction of the paper system should take place, and should prove the utter ruin of the country; or, suppose, at any rate, that it should send all the Fundholders into beggary, should cause all the Church and Collegiate property to be sold as in Austria, should send the Royal Plate to the Mint, should annihilate all the remaining feudal rights and tenures; and, in short, should produce a species of revolution. I say, that it *need* do none of this: I say, that not one of these is a *necessary* consequence of the overthrow of the paper system; but, for argument's sake, *suppose* the contrary, and suppose that such overthrow were to take place; WHO, *in that case, would be to blame*?

This is a question that every man ought, as soon as may be, to answer in his own mind; for, if any of these consequences were to come upon us, it would be of the greatest utility to be able to say, at once, who it was that had been the real authors of the calamity. Certainly, then, the *Reformers*, commonly called *Jacobins* and *Levellers*, have had nothing to do with the matter. They have had *no power*. They have been carefully shut out from all authority. They have filled no offices of any sort. They have been held forth as a sort of enemy in the bosom of the country. There is no creature who has had power, of any sort, no matter what, who has not employed that power upon them. They have been either killed, banished, ruined, or, at the least, beaten down and kept down. Well, then, *they* will not come in for any of the blame, if things should turn out wrong at last. They have had no hand in declaring war against the regicides of France; they have had no hand in forming leagues, in voting subsidies, in sending out expeditions; they have had no hand in making loans or grants; and, therefore, they will, surely, not come in for any share of the blame which shall attach to the consequences. They have been represented as an ignorant and factious herd, "*a low, degraded crew;*" while those who have thus described them have had all the powers and the resources of the country at their command; and, therefore, let what will happen, the Reformers will have to bear no portion of the blame. The full-blooded Anti-Jacobins; the members of the Pitt Club; all the numerous herd of the enemies to Reform may be fairly called upon for a share of responsibility; but, to the Reformers who have had no power, and who have been hardly able to exist in peace, no man can reasonably look.

I shall now, Gentlemen, after nearly a twelvemonth's correspondence, take my leave of you, and with the conviction, that I have done much towards giving you a clear view of the subject, of which I have been treating. I had long entertained the design to make the subject familiar; to put my countrymen in general beyond the reach of deception on this score; to enable them to avoid being cheated, if they chose to avoid it; and a sufficiency of *time* for the purpose being furnished me, it would have been greatly blameable in me, if I had neglected to avail myself of it: I have not been guilty of this neglect; I have, with great care and research, brought together what appears to me to be the whole, or very nearly the whole, of the useful information relating to the paper system; I have laboured most zealously and anxiously for the accomplishment of the great object in view; and it more than repays me for every thing to hear, to see, to know, that *I have not laboured in vain.*

In the course of these Letters, I have clearly expressed my opinions as to the fate of the paper-money; those opinions are in direct opposition to many of those persons, in parliament as well as out of parliament, who have delivered their sentiments upon the subject: TIME, the trier of all things, must now decide between us; and, if I am wrong, I have, at least, taken effectual means to make my error as conspicuous and as notorious as possible. One thing, above all others, however, I am desirous of leaving strongly impressed upon your minds, and that is, that it is my decided opinion, that, let what will be the fate of the paper-money, that fate, however destructive, does not necessarily include any, even the smallest, danger to the independence of England, or to the safety of the throne, or to the liberties or the happiness of the people.

I remain,
Gentlemen,
Your friend
and obedient Servant,
WM. COBBETT.

State Prison, Newgate, Friday, 2d August, 1811.

LETTER XXX.

The Bullion Committee's two years twice expired.—The Peace of 1814 saw the Bank Protection Bill renewed—All the pretexts were vanished.—Ominous opinions.—New issue joined between the Author on the one part and the Paper partizans on the other.

GENTLEMEN,

IN renewing my correspondence with you, after a lapse of more than four years, and after the wonderful events of the years 1814 and 1815, it may be necessary for me to remind you of the state, in which we left the question of Paper against Gold, in the summer of 1811, when I remained at issue with the Bullion Committee and also with the partizans of Paper-Money, appealing to TIME, the trier of all things, to decide between us. Four years is a considerable space of *time*; and, we shall see now, on which side TIME, thus far, has decided.

The Bullion Committee proposed to the House of Commons to compel the Bank to pay in gold and silver *at the end of two years from* 1810. The Ministry opposed this proposition; and asserted, that, *when peace returned*, specie would return, and the payment of it at the Bank would take place, *as a matter of course*, because the law, which protected the Bank against demands of payment in cash, would, of itself, *expire* at the end of six months after peace should be made. This Act was passed in December, 1803. See page 254.

Now, in opposition to these two assertions, I was satisfied, that I *proved* it to be impossible for the Bank to pay in real money, in war or in peace, as long as the dividends on the Debt continued to be paid. Well, Gentlemen, what has since been done? Has the Bank yet paid in Gold and Silver, though four years instead of two have passed over our heads? You know well that it has not.

But, observe, peace was made in May, 1814. And what did the Ministry then do? Did they suffer the Act to expire, "*as a matter of course?*" Did they make good their assertion, that Gold and Silver should come back with peace? They assured us, that it was the power of Napoleon which had robbed us of our gold and silver; and that, in order to get them back again, we must go on, fighting and paying, till that power should be diminished. It was not only diminished in 1814; but it was destroyed. Napoleon was dethroned and banished, and the long-sighed-for event, the restoration of the Capets, took place. A Congress met at Vienna; all was so arranged, that peace in Europe promised to last for our lives, and peace with America had taken place too. *Now*, then, was the time to suffer the Bank Act to die that *natural death*, of which the minister had so boldly talked in 1810. But, instead of this, what did the Ministry do? Why, they *renewed the Act for another year!* And, you will please to observe, that, though this renewal did not actually become *a law* till after the return of Napoleon from Elba, it was distinctly stated by the Ministry, *before that time*, that the renewal would be proposed to the Parliament; and, Ministers in England seldom *propose*, as you know very well, any measure, which the Houses refuse to adopt.

Therefore there is no shadow of excuse for the renewal of the Act, except, that the Bank cannot, in *peace* any more than in war, pay in Gold and Silver. This is a very good reason for renewing the Act but this is completely fulfilling my prediction; completely proving, and that by Act of Parliament too, the soundness of my former reasoning.

The Parliament and, indeed, the country, were, as to this question, divided into two parties: one said, that the Bank would be able to pay in specie in two years: the other said, that the Bank was *always able* to pay, but that it would not be *prudent* to suffer the Bank to pay, till *peace* came. I gave it as my opinion, that peace would not enable the Bank to pay; or, at any rate, that her Ladyship would not pay in Gold and Silver when peace should come. Thus far, then, time has proved me to have been right.

We must now wait for TIME again; but, happily, we shall not have to wait *long*. Peace is now again come; and come in a way, too, that seems to defy even chance to interrupt its duration. Not only is Napoleon down, but he is in our hands; he is banished to a rock, of which we have the sole command and possession; he is as completely in the power of our Government as if they had him in the Tower of London. Therefore, this great obstacle to Gold and Silver payments is swept away. The Capets, or the *Bourbons*, as they call themselves, are restored. Spain has regained that beloved Ferdinand, in whose cause we were so zealous, and he has restored the Inquisition and the Jesuits. The Pope, to the great joy of loyal protestants, is again in the Chair of Saint Peter; has again resumed his Keys and his Shepherd's crook. In short, our Government, so far from dreading any enemy, is in *strict alliance* with every sovereign in Europe.

Now, then, are come the halcyon days. Now John Bull is to sit down in peace under his own vine and his own fig-tree with no one to make him afraid. *Now* there will be; there *can* be, no need of armies or navies. *Now*, then, my good neighbours, we shall, surely, see Gold and Silver return. Which of you will *bet* any thing on the affirmative of this proposition? My opinion is, that we shall not see it return; that we not see the Bank pay in Gold and Silver; that we shall not hear the Minister say, that the Old Lady is ready with her csah. In short, my opinion is, that another and another Act of Parliament, will convince even the most stupid and credulous, that, as long as the dividends on the National Debt are paid, so long will they be paid in Bank Notes, so long will the law to protect the Bank against demands in real money remain in full force: for, the man that needs more than two more Acts of Parliament to produce this conviction in his mind must be *an idiot*.

Let us wait, then, with patience for two years more; but, let us keep our eye steadily fixed on the movements of the Ministry and the Bank. Let us listen quietly to all they say, without seeming to take any notice of what they are about. If they *do* pay in cash at the end of two years, and still continue to pay the dividends, or the interest of the Debt, I will frankly acknowledge, that I ought to pass for an ignorant pretender all the remainder of my life. If they *do not* pay in cash at the end of two years more, then, what *they* ought to pass for I shall leave my readers to decide.

As to giving them a longer tether, that is wholly out of the question. Twelve years is the average length, it is said, of the life of man. I have already given them *four*. I will allow them two more; but, as the grey hairs begin to thicken, very fast upon my head, as my sons and daughters begin to walk faster than their father and mother, I certainly shall not lengthen the tether; but, at the end of two years from this first day of the month of September, 1815, I shall, if I still hold a pen, and the Old Lady does not pay the dividends in cash, assume it as a notoriously admitted fact, *that she never will and never can*.

Before I conclude this letter, however, I will just notice the strange doctrines which are beginning to be held. We hear people saying, and in print too, that *Paper Money* is a *better thing* than gold and silver coin. That it is more *commodious*; that it cannot be *sent out of the country* (which last is very true); that it is so much *clear gain to the nation*; that the nation would be *ruined*, if it were to use gold and silver coin instead of paper-money. These are ugly notions. They seem to be thrown out *to feel the pulse* of John Bull. They do not come forth *officially*; but they come from sources that render them rather more than suspicious. The *friends of Government*; that is to say, those who, in some way or other, *gain by the taxes*, promulgate them; and hence we may pretty safely conclude, that they are not very disagreeable to the Government itself. There is one person connected with the Old Lady, who has put forth such doctrines. Very natural, you will say. Yes, but it is not so very natural that we should adopt them into our political creed. These doctrines do not argue much in favour of our expectations of gold and silver payments. They put one in mind of Goldsmith's friend's high eulogium on liver and bacon just when he was about to announce to his guest the absence of a promised venison pasty.

With these hints; with these motives to watchfulness, let us now lay aside the subject of Paper against Gold, and proceed to inquire what *good* this nation has derived from the late wars, in which we are said to have acquired glory that calls for thanksgivings and monuments. This inquiry shall be the subject of future letters.

I am,

Gentlemen,

Your faithful friend,

W^M. COBBETT.

Botley,
September 1st, 1815.

LETTER XXXI.

What is the condition of Great Britain, compared to what it would have been, if the wars against the French had not taken place.

GENTLEMEN,

THE war, which began in 1793, is now over. The troops are not all come home, the ships are not all paid off, the account is not wound up; but, the war is over. Social Order is restored; the French are again under the power of the Bourbons; the Revolution is at an end; no change has been effected in England; our Boroughs, and our Church Nobility and all have been preserved; our Government tell us, that we have covered ourselves with glory. And now let us see what we have *gained* by this long war; what *we*, the people of England, Ireland, and Scotland, who pay taxes for the support of the people in office, the army, the navy, the sinecure placemen, the pensioners, and the royal family, have gained by this war.

But, here I shall be met at the threshold by Old George Rose, who will say; that is not "a fair way of putting the question." George, who is a person of such well-known merit, that he has sinecure places worth about 4,000*l.* a year, the greater part of which descends in reversion to his eldest son. George, who is very long-sighted, and can perceive conclusions which are greatly at a distance from the premises, will meet me at the very out-set, and cry "hold! hold! it is not of what "the poor fellows have *gained* that "you ought to talk to them. You "ought to ask them *how much more* "*they would have lost than they have* "*lost*, had it not been for the war, "now happily terminated amidst such "a blaze of glory."

George sees what I am going at. *He* knows, if you do not, what a picture I am going to draw, and how clearly I shall trace our Debts, Taxes, Paupers, and manifold miseries, now only beginning to be seriously felt, to the war; and, therefore, he would make you believe (as he has endeavoured to do in print long ago), that it would have been still *worse* for you, if the war had not taken place.

Gentlemen, I will leave even George Rose nothing to complain of. I will take the question in his own way; and I shall, for argument's sake, voluntarily make admissions in his favour, for which he (though that is saying a great deal) would not have the conscience to ask.

It is impossible to say, or even to form any thing like a correct estimate of, what would have been the consequences, in England, of remaining at peace in 1793, instead of going to war against the French people. But, it is easy to name some things, which would *not* have taken place, even if peace had been preserved. For instance, the earth of England would still have retained its former qualities; the sun, the moon, the stars, the rains, the frosts, the snows, would not have been obstructed by peace. The animals, of all sorts, would have continued breeding. Young people would have continued to grow up and see their parents buried. We should, in short, have the same air to breathe, and the same kinds of food and drink, and the same kinds of clothes to wear.

There are some of the most resolute Antijacobins, who will assert the contrary of the greater part of all this. They will insist, that all nature would have suffered; and that England would have become a wild waste, inhabited by savage men and savage beasts. This, however, we will not believe. We must confine our admissions, great as they are to be, far within this compass.

I will admit, then, that, if the People of France had been suffered to remain at peace, that, as far as the circumstances of the two nations were, previous to the French revolution, alike, *so far* the People of England would have followed their example. The Jacobins, as the friends of Reform, were called, were very active. The success of the People of France, in overturning a most horrid despotism, had produced great pleasure in England amongst the mass of the people; and, I have no doubt, that, had our Government continued at peace with France; that had it not adopted any of its hostile measures in 1792; that, if it had continued the former relationships of peace, commerce, and intercourse with France, some *very great changes* would have taken place in England.

What, then, according to the above supposition, would those changes have been? We are told of the burning of country houses, of the demolition of gentlemen's property, of the pillaging of Aristocrats, of the massacres and guillotinings of the French. But, first let it be observed, that, all these, which took place after July 1792, are fairly to be ascribed to *the war*, that *war* which the Bourbons and Aristocrats, and the Prussians and Austrians made upon the French, in order to compel them to return to a submission to that despotism, which they had overturned. Previous to this time, though there were many acts of unjustifiable violence on the part of some of the people, there were none of those bloody scenes, which took place *after* the invasion of France by the Aristocrats and the Prussians, with the Duke of Brunswick at their head, in 1792, when the king was alive, and was enjoying as much power, as many very wise men think a king ought to enjoy. It was, therefore, not till *war* was begun against the French People, that those bloody scenes ensued, which are, by the Aristocrats, ascribed to the *revolution*, when they ought to be, and are by all just men, ascribed to *the war* waged against the French People.

In seeking, therefore, to ascertain what changes would have taken place in England, we must always bear in mind how far the French had gone, *previous to their being attacked by the*

Emigrants of the Allies; and, previous to our hostile measures against them, indicating intentions of war. Because, all the changes which the French made *after that,* we have a right to suppose they would *not have* made *had it not been for the war;* that very war, of which we were the main supporters, and which has only now come to a close after twenty-two years duration.

What, then, *were the changes,* which the French (whose *example,* observe, it was said we should follow) made previous to the war? But, before I come to state these, I must notice, that the situation of England, at the commencement of the French revolution, was very different from that of France. The sufferings of the latter had been so much greater, that it is not reasonable to suppose, that the people here would have gone such lengths, in the way of resentment, as the people of France went. This leads us to call to our recollection what the sufferings of the people of France really were.

It is notorious, that, for ages, previous to the French revolution, we, in this country, constantly described the French as slaves; our histories, our moral essays, our political writings, our poems, our plays, all describe them as slaves, and as cowards for submittting to such a government as then existed. *Now,* indeed, our conductors of news-papers, with a degree of impudence absolutely without parallel, abuse the French people for having destroyed the PATERNAL *sway of the Bourbons!*——Let us now see, then, what was the nature of that "*paternal sway;*" and, when we have taken a full view of it, and of its effects, we shall be able to judge, whether it be probable, that the people of France will listen to those who are endeavouring to bring them back to blessings of that "*paternal* sway."—But, how are we to get at a *true* account of the nature and effects of the Bourbon government? We must resort to some *authority:* to somebody's word, whose word is to be relied on.—The authority, to which I am about to refer, is that of Mr. ARTHUR YOUNG, who is, and who has been, for many years past, *Secretary to the Board of Agriculture,* with a salary, paid by the public, of 500*l.* a year.—Mr. Young is, in the first place, a man of great talents; and, perhaps, it is impossible to find out a person so fit to be referred to as Mr. Young. His studies had been of that kind, which peculiarly fitted him for an inquiry of this description; and, he was in France at precisely the time for making it. He made, during the years 1787, 1788, and 1789, an agricultural and politico-œconomical survey of the kingdom of France. He was there when the revolution began; he was there during its progress until the new constitution was formed. He was not only living in great intimacy with many of the most respectable leaders in that work; but, he himself, crossing the kingdom in all directions, made himself minutely acquainted by the means of personal inquiry and the evidence of his senses, of every particular, relating to the nature and effects of those "*ancient Ordinances* "*and Customs,*" of which the partizans of the war now boast.—During his travels, he gives an account of these, by citing numerous instances, of the abominable tyranny, under which the people groaned; and, at the close of his work, he publishes *reflections on the Revolution,* beginning with a summary description of

Entered at Stationers' Hall.

Printed by W. MOLINEUX, 5, Bream's Buildings, Chancery Lane; Published by W. COBBETT, Jun. No. 8, Catherine Street, Strand: and Retailed at No. 192, Strand.

the state of the people under the Bourbon government, and, to the evidences of his own observation, adding, as he proceeds, the complaints contained in the *Cahiers*, that is to say, the lists of complaints, made to the National Assembly by the most respectable people of the different provinces, to which *Cahiers*, he refers in the notes.—This part of Mr. Young's work, I am now about to insert. I beg you to go through it with attention. You will see how every part of it applies to the subject on which we are, and also to the present crisis.

ON THE REVOLUTION OF FRANCE.

"The gross infamy which attended *letters de cachet* and the Bastile, during the whole reign of Louis XV. made them esteemed in England, by people not well informed, as the most prominent features of the despotism of France. They were certainly carried to an excess hardly credible; to the length of being sold, with blanks, to be filled up with names at the pleasure of the purchaser; who was thus able, in the gratification of private revenge, to tear a man from the bosom of his family, and bury him in a dungeon, where he would exist forgotten, and die unknown!*—But such excesses could not be common in any country; and they were reduced almost to nothing, from the accession of the present King. The great mass of the people, by which I mean the lower and middle ranks, could suffer very little from such engines, and, as few of them are objects of jealousy, had there been nothing else to complain of, it is not probable they would ever have been brought to take arms. The abuses attending the levy of taxes were heavy and universal. The kingdom was parcelled into generalities, with an intendant at the head of each the whole power of the crown was delegated for every thing except the military authority; but particularly for all affairs of finance. The generalities were subdivided into elections, at the head of which was a *sub-délegué*, appointed by the intendant. The rolls of the *taille, capitation, vingtiemes*, and other taxes, were distributed among districts, parishes, and individuals, at the pleasure of the intendant, who could exempt, change, add, or diminish, at pleasure. Such an enormous power, constantly acting, and from which no man was free, must, in the nature of things, degenerate in many cases into absolute tyranny. It must be obvious, that the friends, acquaintances, and dependants of the intendant, and of

* An anecdote, which I have from an authority to be depended on, will explain the profligacy of Government, in respect to these arbitrary imprisonments. Lord Albemarle, when ambassador in France, about the year 1753, negociating the fixing of the limits of the American colonies, which, three years after, produced the war, calling one day on the minister for foreign affairs, was introduced, for a few minutes, into his cabinet, while he finished a short conversation in the apartment in which he usually received those who conferred with him. As his lordship walked backwards and forwards, in a very small room (a French cabinet is never a very large one), he could not help seeing a paper lying on the table, written in a large legible hand, and containing a list of the prisoners in the Bastile, in which the first name was Gordon. When the minister entered, Lord Albemarle apologized for his involuntarily remarking the paper; the other replied, that it was not of the least consequence, for they made no secret of the names. Lord A. then said, that he had seen the name of Gordon first in the list, and he begged to know, as in all probability the person of this name

W. MOLINEUX, Printer, Bream's Buildings, Chancery Lane.

all his *sub-delegués,* and the friends of these friends, to a long chain of dependance, might be favoured in taxation at the expense of their miserable neighbours; and that noblemen, in favour at court, to whose protection the intendant himself would naturally look up, could find little difficulty in throwing much o. the weight of their taxes on others, without a similar support. Instances, and even gross ones, have been reported to me in many parts of the kingdom, that made me shudder at the oppression to which numbers must have been condemned, by the undue favours granted to such crooked influence. But, without recurring to such cases, what must have been the state of the poor people paying heavy taxes, from which the nobility and clergy were exempted? A cruel aggravation of their misery, to see those who could best afford to pay, exempted, because able!—The inrolments for the militia, which the *cahiers* call *an injustice without example*†, were another dreadful scourge on the peasantry; and, as married men were exempted from it, occasioned in some degree that mischievous population, which brought beings into the world, in order for little else than to be starved. The *corvées,* or police of the roads, were annually the ruin of many hundreds of farmers; more than 300 were reduced to beggary in filling up one vale in Lorraine: all these oppressions fell on the *tiérs etat* only; the nobility and clergy having been equally exempted from *tailles,* militia, and *corvées.* The penal code of finance makes one shudder at the horrors of punishment inadequate to the crime‡. A few features will sufficiently characterize the old government.

1. Smugglers of salt, armed and assembled to the number of five, in Provence, *a fine* of 500 liv. *and nine years gallies;*—in all the rest of the kingdom, *death.*

2. Smugglers armed, assembled, but in number under five, *a fine of* 300 liv. *and three years gallies.* Second offence, *death.*

3. Smugglers, without arms, but with horses, carts, or boats; *a fine of* 300 liv. *if not paid, three years gallies.* Second offence, 400 liv. *and nine years gallies.*—In Dauphiné, second offence, *gallies for life.* In Provence, *five years gallies.*

4. Smugglers, who carry the salt on their backs, and without arms, *a fine of* 200 liv. *and, if not paid, are flogged and branded.* Second offence, *a fine of* 300 liv. *and six years gallies.*

5. Women, married and single, smugglers, first offence, *a fine of* 100 liv. Second, 300 liv. Third, *flogged, and banished the kingdom for life.*

---

was a British subject, on what account he had been put into the Bastile. The minister told him, that he knew nothing of the matter, but would make the proper enquiries. The next time he saw Lord Albemarle, he informed him, that, on inquiring into the case of Gordon, he could find no person who could give him the least information; on which he had had Gordon himself interrogated, who solemnly affirmed, that he had not the smallest knowledge, or even suspicion, of the cause of his imprisonment, but that he had been confined thirty years; however, added the minister, I ordered him to be immediately released, and he is now at large. Such a case wants no comment.

† *Nob. Briey,* p. 6, &c. &c.

‡ It is calculated by a writer (*Recherches et Consid. par M. le Baron de Cormeré,* tom. ii. p. 187,) very well informed on every subject of finance, that, upon an average, there were annually taken up and sent to prison or the gallies; Men, 2,310. Women, 896. Children, 201. Total, 3,437; 300 of these to the gallies (tom. i. p. 112). The salt confiscated from these miserables amounted to 12,633 quintals, which, at the mean price of 8 liv. are.................... 101,064 liv.

2,77½lb. of salted flesh, at 10*s.*	1,386
1,086 horses, at 50 liv.......	54,300
52 carts, at 150 liv.......	7,800
Fines.....................	53,207
Seized in houses............	105,530
	323,287

Husbands responsible both in fine and body.

6. Children smugglers, the same as women.—*Fathers and mothers responsible; and for defect of payment, flogged.*

7. Nobles, if smugglers, *deprived of their nobility; and their houses rased to the ground.*

8. Any persons in employments, (I suppose employed in the salt-works or the revenue), if smugglers, *death.* And such as assist in the theft of salt in the transport, *hanged.*

9. Soldiers smuggling, with arms, are *hanged;* without arms, *gallies for life.*

10. Buying smuggled salt to resell it, *the same punishment as for smuggling.*

11. Persons in the salt employments, *empowered, if two, or one with two witnesses, to enter and examine houses, even of the privileged order.*

12. All families, and persons liable to the *taille,* in the provinces of the *Grandes Gabelles* inrolled, and their consumption of salt for the *pot and saliere* (that is, the daily consumption, exclusive of salting meat, &c. &c.) estimated at 7lb. a head per annum, which quantity they are forced to buy, whether they want it or not, under the pain of various fines, according to the case.

The *Capitaineries* were a dreadful scourge on all the occupiers of land. By this term, is to be understood the paramountship of certain districts, granted by the king, to princes of the blood, by which they were put in possession of the property of all game, even on lands not belonging to them; and, what is very singular, on manors granted long before to individuals; so that the erecting of a district into a *capitainerie,* was an annihilation o. all manerial rights to game within it. This was a trifling business, in comparison of other circumstances; for, in speaking of the preservation of the game in these *capitaineries,* it must be observed, that by game must be understood whole droves of wild boars, and herds of deer, not confined by any wall or pale, but wandering, at pleasure, over the whole country, to the destruction of the crops; and to the peopling of the gallies by the wretched peasants, who presumed to kill them, in order to save that food which was to support their helpless children. The game in the *capitainerie* of Montceau, in four parishes only, did mischief to the amount of 184,263 liv. per annum.* No wonder then that we should find the people asking '*Nous demandons à grand cris la destruction des capitaineries & celle de toute sorte de gibier*'.† And what are we to think of demanding, as a favour, the permission—'*De Nettoyer ses grains, de faucher les prés artificiels, et d'enlever ses chaumes sans égard pour la perdrix ou tout autre gibier.*'‡ Now, an English reader will scarcely understand it without being told, that there were numerous edicts for preserving the game, which prohibited weeding and hoeing, lest the young partridges should be disturbed; steeping seed, lest it should injure the game; manuring with night-soil, lest the flavour of the partridges should be injured by feeding on the corn so produced; mowing hay, &c. before a certain time, so late as to spoil many crops; and taking away the stubble, which would deprive the birds of shelter. The tyranny exercised in these *capitaineries,* which extended over 400 leagues of country, was so great, that many *cahiers* demanded the utter sup-

* *Cahier du tiers etat de Meaux,* p. 49.

† *De Mantes* and *Meulan,* p. 40.—Also, *Nob. & Tier Etat de Peronne,* p. 42.—*De Trois ordres de Montfort,* p. 28.—That is: "We most earnestly pray for the suppression of the Capitaineries, and that of all the game laws."

‡ *De Mantes* and *Meulan,* p. 33.—That is to say, "the *favour* to weed their corn, to mow their upland grass, and to take off their stubble, without consulting the convenience of the partridges, or any other sort of game."

pression of them.* Such were the exertions of arbitrary power which the lower orders felt directly from the royal authority; but, heavy as they were, it is a question whether the others, suffered circuitously through the nobility and the clergy, were not yet more oppressive? Nothing can exceed the complaints made in the *cahiers* under this head. They speak of the dispensation of justice in the manerial courts, as comprising every species of despotism: the districts indeterminate—appeals endless—irreconcileable to liberty and prosperity—and irrevocably proscribed in the opinion of the public†—augmenting litigations—favouring every species of chicane—ruining the parties—not only by enormous expenses on the most petty objects, but by a dreadful loss of time. The judges commonly ignorant pretenders, who hold their courts in *cabarets*, and are absolutely dependant on the seigneurs.‡ Nothing can exceed the force of expression used in painting the oppressions of the seigneurs, in consequence of their feudal powers. They are "*vexations qui sont le plus grand fléau des peuples.*§—*Esclavage affligeant.*‖—*Ce regime desastreuse.*¶———That the *feodalité* be for ever abolished. The countryman is tyrannically enslaved by it. Fixed and heavy rents; vexatious processes to secure them; appreciated unjustly to augment them: rents, *solidaires*, and *revenchables*; rents, *chéantes*, and *levantes*; *fumages*. Fines at every change of the property, in the direct as well as collateral line; feudal redemption *(retraite)*; fines on sale, to the eighth and even the sixth penny; redemptions *(rachats)* injurious in their origin, and still more so in their extension: *banalité* of the mill,* of the oven, and of the wine and cyder-press; *corveés* by custom; *corveés* by usage of the fief; *corveés* established by unjust decrees; *corveés* arbitrary, and even phantastical; servitudes; *prestations*, extravagant and burthensome; collections by assessment incollectable; *aveux, minus, impunissemens*; litigations ruinous and without end: the rod of of seigneural finance for ever shaken over our heads; vexation, ruin, outrage, violence, and destructive servitude, under which the peasants, almost on a level with Polish slaves, can never but be miserable, vile, and oppressed.† They demand also, that the use of hand-mills be free; and hope that posterity, if possible, may be ignorant that feudal tyranny in Bretagne, armed with the judicial power, has not blushed even in these times at breaking hand-mills, and at selling annually to the miserable, the faculty of bruising between two stones a measure of buck-wheat or barley.‡ The very terms of these complaints are unknown in England, and untranslatable; they have probably arisen long since the feudal system ceased in this kingdom. What are these tortures of the peasantry in Bretagne, which they call *chevanchés, quintaines, soules, saut de poison,*

* *Clergé de Provins* & *Montereau*, p. 35.—*Clergé de Paris*, p. 25.—*Clergé de Mantes* & *Meulan*, p. 45, 46. *Clergé de Laon*, p. 11.—*Nob. de Nemours*, p. 17.—*Nob. de Paris*, p. 22.—*Nob. d'Arras*, p. 29.

† *Rennes*, art. 12. ‡ *Nevernois*, art. 43.

§ *Tiers Etat de Vennes*, p. 24.—That is "Vexations which are the greatest scourge "of the people."

‖ *T. Etat Clermont Ferrand*, p. 52.—That is: "Cruel Slavery."

¶ *Tiers Etat. Auxerre*, art 6.—That is: "This ruinous system of governing."

* By this horrible law, the people are bound to grind their corn at the mill of the seigneur only; to press their grapes at his press only; and to bake their bread in his oven; by which means the bread is often spoiled, and more especially wine, since in Champagne those grapes which, pressed immediately, would make white wine, by waiting for the press, which often happens, make red wine only.

† *Tiers Etat Rennes*, p. 159.

‡ *Rennes*, p. 57.

*baiser de mariées; chansons; transporte d'œuf sur un charette; silence des grenouilles;** *corvée a misericorde; milods; leide; couponage; cartelage; barage; fouage; marechaussée; ban vin; ban d'aout; trousses; gelinage; civerage; taillabilitié; vingtain; sterlage; bordelage; minage; ban de vendanges; droit d'accapte?** In passing through many of the French provinces, I was struck with the various and heavy complaints of the farmers and little proprietors, of the feudal grievances, with the weight of which their industry was burthened; but I could not then conceive the multiplicity of the shackles which kept them poor and depressed. I understood it better afterwards, from the conversation and complaints of some grand seigneurs, as the revolution advanced; and I then learned, that the principal rental of many estates consisted in services and feudal tenures; by the baneful influence of which, the industry of the people was almost exterminated. In regard to the oppressions of the clergy, as to tithes, I must do that body a justice, to which a claim cannot be laid in England. Though the ecclesiastical tenth was levied in France more severely than usual in Italy, yet was it never exacted with such horrid greediness as is at present the disgrace of England. When taken in kind, no such thing was known in any part of France, where I made inquiries, as a tenth: it was always a twelfth, or a thirteenth, or even a twentieth of the produce. And in no part of the kingdom did a new article of culture pay any thing; thus turnips, cabbages, clover, chicorée, potatoes, &c. &c. paid nothing. In many parts, meadows were exempt. Silk-worms nothing. Olives in some places paid—in more they did not. Cows nothing. Lambs from the 12th to the 21st. Wool nothing.—Such mildness, in the levy of this odious tax, is absolutely unknown in England. But mild as it was, the burden to people groaning under so many other oppressions, united to render their situation so bad that no change could be for the worse. But these were not all the evils with which the people struggled. The administration of justice was partial, venal, infamous. I have, in conversation with many very sensible men, in different parts of the kingdom, met with something of content with their government, in all other respects than this; but upon the question of expecting justice to be really and fairly administered, every one confessed there was no such thing to be looked for. The conduct of the parliaments was profligate and atrocious. Upon almost every cause that came before them, interest was openly made with the judges: and woe betided the man who, with a cause to support, had no means of conciliating favour, either by the beauty of a handsome wife, or by other methods. It has been said, by many writers, that property was as secure under the old government of France as it is in England; and the assertion might possibly be true, as far as any violence from the King, his ministers, or the great was concerned; but for all that mass of property, which comes in every country to be litigated in courts of justice, there was not even the shadow of security, unless the parties were totally and equally unknown, and totally and equally honest; in every other case, he who had the best interest with the judges, was sure to be the winner. To reflecting minds, the cruelty and abominable practice attending such courts are sufficiently apparent. There was also a circumstance in the constitution of

* This is a curious article: when the lady of the seigneur lies in, the people are obliged to *beat the waters* in marshy districts, to keep the frogs silent, that she may not be disturbed; this duty, a very oppressive one, is commuted into a pecuniary fine.

† *Resume des cahiers*, tom. iii. p. 316, 317.

these parliaments, but little known in England, and which under such a government as that of France, must be considered as very singular. They had the power, and were in the constant practice of issuing decrees, without the consent of the crown, and which had the force of laws through the whole of their jurisdiction; and of all other laws, these were sure to be the best obeyed; for as all infringements of them were brought before sovereign courts, composed of the same persons who had enacted these laws (a horrible system of tyranny!) they were certain of being punished with the last severity. It must appear strange, in a government so despotic in some respects as that of France, to see the parliaments in every part of the kingdom making laws without the King's consent, and even in defiance of his authority. The English whom I met in France in 1789, were surprised to see some of these bodies issuing arrets against the export of corn out of the provinces subject to their jurisdiction, into the neighbouring provinces, at the same time that the King, through the organ of so popular a minister as Mons. Necker, was decreeing an absolutely free transport of corn throughout the kingdom, and even at the requisition of the National Assembly itself. But this was nothing new; it was their common practice. The parliament of Rouen passed an arret against killing of calves: it was a prosperous one, and opposed by administration; but it had its full force; and had a butcher dared to offend against it, he would have found, by the rigour of his punishment, who was his master. Inoculation was favoured by the court in Louis XV.'s time; but the parliament of Paris passed an arret against it, much more effective in prohibiting, than the favour of the court in encouraging that practice. Instances are innumerable, and I may remark, that the bigotry, ignorance, false principles, and tyranny of these bodies were generally conspicuous; and that the Court (taxation excepted), never had a dispute with a Parliament, but the Parliament was sure to be wrong. Their Constitution, in respect to the administration of justice, was so truly rotten, that the members sat as judges, even in causes of private property, in which they were themselves the parties, and have, in this capacity, been guilty of oppressions and cruelties, which the crown has rarely dared to attempt.

It is impossible to justify the excesses of the people on their taking up arms; they were certainly guilty of cruelties; it is idle to deny the facts, for they have been proved too clearly to admit of a doubt. But is it really the people to whom we are to impute the whole?—Or to their oppressors, who had kept them so long in a state of bondage? He who chooses to be served by slaves, and by ill-treated slaves, must know that he holds both his property and life by a tenure far different from those who prefer the service of well treated freemen; and he who dines to the music of groaning sufferers, must not, in the moment of insurrection, complain that his daughters are ravished, and then destroyed; and that his sons' throats are cut. When such evils happen, they surely are more imputable to the tyranny of the master, than to the cruelty of the servant. The analogy holds with the French peasants—the murder of a seigneur, or a chateau in flames, is recorded in every news-paper; the rank of the person who suffers, attracts notice; but where do we find the register of that seigneur's oppressions of his peasantry, and his exactions of feudal services, from those whose children were dying around them for want of bread? Where do we find the minutes that assigned these starving wretches to some vile petty-fogger to be fleeced by impositions, and a mockery of justice, in the seigneural courts? Who gives us the awards of the intendant and his *sub-delegués*, which took off the taxes of a man of fashion, and laid them with accumulated weight, on the poor, who were so unfortunate as to be his neighbours? Who has dwelt sufficiently upon explaining all the ramifications of despotism, legal, aristocratic, and ecclesiastical, pervading the whole mass of the people; reaching, like a circulating fluid, the most distant capillary tubes of poverty and wretchedness? In these cases, the sufferers are too ignoble to be known; and the mass too indiscriminate to be pitied. But should a philosopher feel and reason thus? Should he mistake the cause for the effect? and giving all his pity to the few, feel no compassion for the many, because they suffer in his eyes not individually, but by millions? The excesses of the people cannot, I repeat, be justified; it would undoubtedly have done them credit, both as men and Christians, if they had possessed their new acquired power with moderation. But let it be remembered, that the populace in no country ever use power with moderation; excess is inherent in their aggregate constitution; and as every Government in the world knows, that violence infallibly attends power in such hands, it is doubly bound in common sense, and for common safety, so to conduct itself, that the people may not find an interest in public confusions. They will always suffer much and long, before they are effectually roused; nothing, therefore, can kindle the flame, but such oppressions of some classes or order in the society, as give able men the opportunity of seconding the general mass; discontent will soon diffuse itself around; and if the Government take not warning in time, it is alone answerable for all the burnings, and plunderings, and devastation, and blood that follow. The true judgment to be formed of the French revolution, must surely be gained, from an attentive consideration of the evils of the old Government: when these are well understood—and when the extent and universality of the oppression under which the people groaned—oppression which bore upon them from every quarter, it will scarcely be attempted to be urged, that a revolution was not absolutely necessary to the welfare of the kingdom. Not one opposing voice* can, with reason, be raised against this assertion: abuses ought certainly to be corrected, and corrected effectually: this could not be done without the establishment of a new form of government; whether the form that has been adopted were the best, is another question absolutely distinct. But that the above-mentioned detail of enormities practised on the people required some great change, is sufficiently apparent."

THUS we have the *causes* of those violences, which the people of France committed at the beginning of the revolution. Mr. Young has fairly stated them. They were produced by those

* Many opposing voices have been raised: but so little to their credit, that I leave the passage as it was written long ago. The abuses that are rooted in all the old Governments of Europe, give such numbers of men a direct interest in supporting, cherishing, and defending abuses, that no wonder advocates for tyranny, of every species, are found in every country, and almost in every company. What a mass of people, in every part of England, are some way or other interested in the present representation of the people, tithes, charters, corporations, monopolies, and taxation! and not merely to the things themselves, but to all the abuses attending them; and how many are there, who derive their profit, or their consideration in life, not merely from such institutions, but from the evils they engender! The great mass of the people, however, is free from such influence, and will be enlightened by degrees; assuredly they will find out, in every country in Europe, that by combinations, on the principles of liberty and property, aimed equally against regal, aristocratical, and mobbish tyranny, they will be able to resist successfully, that variety of combination, which, on principles of plunder and despotism, is every where at work to enslave them.

Nobles, Priests, and that Bourbon family, to seat whom in their power again we have saddled ourselves with an everlasting Debt.

Now, unless we are ready to admit, that we are *worse* than the French naturally; that we are a more foolish, or a more wicked, or more sanguinary race, it can never be supposed, that we should have gone *so far* as the French went previous to the war of 1792; because we certainly had not, at that time, such oppressions to complain of and avenge. Indeed, all that the people of England complained of was, that they were not represented in Parliament; and this had been complained of by PITT in terms more strong than by any other man that ever lived. He had gone so far as to say, that, without a reform in the Parliament, it was *impossible*, that any Minister, in England, should be a Minister and an honest man. This grievance had long been complained of by the whole nation, those who were interested in the abuse excepted, and even these seemed to object more to the time and the manner of the proposed reform than to the thing itself.

At the breaking out of the French Revolution the people of England were, at first, astonished: but, they soon began to perceive, that this event would compel the conceding of that reform in the Parliament, which they had so long petitioned for in vain. Those in power saw it too. All communication was, by war, cut off between the two countries; reform did not take place; our system of government was new-steeled, instead of being softened; and by divers laws, still in existence, the liberties of the people were abridged, instead of being enlarged.

But, do I suppose, that the people would have stopped at the end of a Reform in the Commons House of Parliament? Frankly to speak, I do not believe they would. I think it would have been wise for them to stop there, but I do not think they would. The *Established Church* would have been abolished. There was, and there is, nobody who approves of *tythes*. We even *now* hear the land-occupiers, and even the land-holders, including many of the nobility, respecting tythes as one of the causes of our inability to sell corn so cheap as the French; and, thus, after all, and even while we are paying armies to put down the French revolutionists, inculcating the wisdom of following their example in this very material point. So that, if to this dislike of tythes amongst the Church people themselves, amongst those whose relations, sons, fathers, brothers, own the tythes, what might not have been expected from the dissenters? From all those numerous sects, who look upon the Established Church, not only as a heavy burden to them, but as a great injury to religion itself? What mercy could she, as to her property, reasonably expect from these millions, whom she had so long kept in a state of depression, and whose teachers she had so long filled with envy.

The *Nobility* would have stood but little better chance. The nation was too full of knowledge; there were too many men of wealth and talent, not belonging to the Noblesse; there were too many opulent merchants and manufacturers and others, to have suffered the Nobility to remain. The Orders of Nobility would therefore, have been, in all likelihood, abolished. There is no doubt, that, either by a reformed Parliament, or in consequence of popular menaces, the whole of the Sinecure Placemen, and nearly the whole of the Pensioners and Grantees would have been dismissed without a penny of compensation; and there is as little doubt that the Game-laws would have been wholly swept away.

I will allow, too, that the powers and expenses of the King and his family would have been greatly abridged; that they would have been reduced to be merely the Chief Magistrates of the country; that they would no longer have enjoyed Droits of Admiralty; and that all magnificence and show must have been laid aside. Whether this would have been wise or not is another question. Such was the temper of the time, that, I think, had it not been for the war, it would inevitably have taken place.

But, when I have made these admissions, I am sure, that even George Rose cannot ask me to allow, that the people of England would have gone further; that they would have proceeded, as the French did, to the burning of Noblemen's houses, to the pillaging of their farms, the murder of themselves and their families, to the personal ill-treatment and robbery of the houses of the Clergy. To allow this would be to allow, that the people would have done that without provocation, which the people of France did with provocation; and this would be to allow, that the people of England are, by nature, a great deal less just and humane than the people of France.

I say *without provocation*, because, though the people of England had to complain of the want of being duly represented in Parliament, and though they did complain of the law of tythes and some other grievances, all their complaints, in 1792, put together, did not amount to almost any one of the hundreds of oppressions, under which the French people had groaned for centuries. The Clergy, in England, if they had great possessions, owed their preferment, in most cases, to patronage solely; if many of them were fox-hunters, or men of fashion, they were yet, generally speaking, very little inclined to oppression of any sort, and were as mild in their manners, and as kind and as liberal, in all respects, as any other gentlemen in the country. They were at the head of no intolerant Church. They had never murdered people for the love of Christ. If people went to hear them, it was well; if not, it was also well. Never was there in the whole world so inoffensive a Church.

The Nobility, with few exceptions, had long been in the habit of mixing indiscriminately amongst the opulent of all descriptions. In the chace, on the turf, at the gaming table, at the Bible Societies, at agricultural meetings, in Societies, and Clubs and Parties of all sorts, they had had the good sense to mix with the nation at large. They were, in general, the best and kindest landlords and masters, as they are still. And, which was more than all the rest in their favour, they joined to their affability and liberality their fair share of learning and talent.

In short, there was nothing in these two orders of men to call forth the hatred or vengeance of the people. Yet, such was their alarm at the abolishing of the Church and of tythes in France, that they instantly *acted as if they had been of the same description as the persecuting Priests and petty lay Tyrants of that country*, who were also called *Clergy* and *Nobility*, but who no more resembled ours than the poison-tree resembles the vine.

What have been the consequences of this their decision, as to the freedom and happiness of France, the Continent of Europe, and of England; and what will, in all human probability, be the final consequences of it, to our Church and Nobility themselves, who, by this time, must begin to be frightened at their own success, is a subject into which I will not now enter. We all know, that there is an English army in France; that Hanoverian and other German armies, subsidized by us are there also; that the Bourbons are again upon the throne of that country; and that the Roman Catholics, stimulated by their Priests, are again, as during the reigns of former Bourbons, cutting the throats, mangling and burning the bodies of Protestants. And, it is for us now to inquire, "how "much *more* WE should have *lost*, "than we *have lost*, if the war had "not taken place."

Our losses are these: 1st, all that part of our incomes, or fruit of our labour, which have been taken away during the war for the purpose of carrying it on. 2nd. All that part of our property, which has been taken and actually sold, or is now for sale, by the Government, under what is called the redemption of the Land Tax. 3rd. All that part of our property, or fruit of our labour, which is required to pay the interest of about eight hundred millions of Debt, *occasioned solely by the war*, and which will be required for ever. 4th. All that part of our property and the fruit of our labour which is required to maintain that increased standing army and those innumerable pensioners and and half-pay officers, naval and military, who have been created by the war. 5th. The permanent supply of Manufactures to the United States of America, which are now able to manufacture for themselves, and this *solely* in consequence of the war, because the Orders in Council, Impressments from American ships, Non-importations, Embargoes, and finally war with America, were all produced by our war against the French. 6th. That state of comparatively light taxation, and ease and plenty, and cheapness, which left our rich people no reason to wish to migrate to foreign countries, which enabled our farmers to sell their produce as cheap as the French, and which enabled our manufacturers to undersell all the world. These, as no one can deny, *are our losses* by the war. By peace, I allow, that our Nobility *might* have lost their titles, our Clergy their tythes, our Sinecure placemen and Pensioners their incomes from those sources, our King and Royal Family much of their power and splendour; and that we should have lost the *Borough System* I am quite certain. Whether what we *might* thus have lost by peace would have been greater than what we *have lost* by war, I must now leave for you to decide.

"Aye," some one may say, "but "you have forgotten our *gains* by the "war. You have forgotten the im-"mense mass of *glory*." I really do not see, that of military or naval glory we have gained a single particle by this war. Nay, I think we have *lost*.

The war in Spain and Portugal exhibited a mere *branch* of the army in France fighting nearly the whole of our military means, aided by immense fleets, and aided by the chief part of the people of those two countries. That war continued many years. There were Spanish armies and Portuguese armies to assist us. The two Governments were on our side. We had fleets in every harbour. The French were in an enemy's country. And they were not driven out, at last, 'till all the rest of Europe were pouring their armies into France on the East and on the North.

We were victorious at the battle of Waterloo; but we had with us an immense army of Hanoverians, Belgians, and Prussians, and, what is more, we were fighting, as all the people of France thought, *for* the King of France. We have now an army in France; but, it is there by the aid of allies and troops subsidized by us, amounting to *one million and eleven thousand men*. In short, our army is in France with the armies of all the rest of Europe at their back, and with France divided in itself besides. Is this the *harvest of glory*, of which we have heard so much talk? And is it this glory which is to compensate us for all our sufferings and all our losses? When English Kings sailed from Southampton with bands of English followers, landed in France, fought battles there, defeated the Kings of France, and finally caused the King of England to be crowned at Paris, and to reign as King of France by his Vice-Roys for several years, that was, indeed, *military glory*; but, in this war, the very *title of King of France*, which served to perpetuate the recollection of that glory, has been given up, and that too, observe, as a preparative for peace, with Napoleon, who, it was clearly foreseen, would not have acknowledged the title, though the Bourbons had always acknowledged it. And, is it, then, for us, Englishmen, whose ancestors really conquered France, as the French had before really and more effectually conquered England, to brag about the *glory* of getting to Paris along with a million of German troops? And that, too, after we have so recently seen the French, unaided by any other nation, sally forth, and really conquer every state on the continent of Europe, Russia only excepted, and that excepted only because France was then co-operating with the German allies.

But, have the English army given no proofs of their determined bravery, during these long wars? Oh! yes, a great many. They have acted like very gallant men. Their officers, of all ranks, have discovered great talents, and wonderful zeal. But is this any thing *new?* When were the people of these Islands not brave? When were they not true to their colours? Did it need the battles in Egypt, in Naples, or in Spain, to acquire a character for valour, for those whose ancestors had conquered Canada; and who, before that, had fought under Marlborough? Whence comes the notion, and what can be its *motive*, that *valour* is something *new* in the English, Scots, and Irish character? Besides, to say nothing about our many reverses in Europe, and especially that of the *Helder*, are we to be made forget what has passed in America? And if there has been a balance of accounts on the side of Canada, can we quite overlook the famous battle of *New Orleans?* In that battle there were engaged from ten to twelve thousand British troops, sent from France, under General Pakenham, who had been so much extolled for his exploits in the Peninsula of Europe. This army was furnished with all the means of destruction. A great fleet, with its seamen and marines aided it in all its operations. The American General Jackson, a lawyer by profession (who had never before, I believe, seen a single regiment in the character of an enemy), with the inhabitants of New Orleans aided by the militia of Tennese and Kentucky, had assigned to him the task of defending the city against the army of regulars, and, as they were called, of invincibles. With his untutored bands, even whose officers were not in uniform, he, with inferior numbers, attacked the British army twice, in the night-time, before they were ready for the main attack on him. On the 8th of January, 1815, they advanced to that attack, with rockets, bombs, an immense train of artillery, and with all the apparatus for storming, the soldiers and sailors having been previously stimulated, and steeled against relaxation, by assurances the most gratifying to their tastes and wishes. They finally arrived at the point of onset: the faggots, which they carried to make them a road over the works, were just tossing into a ditch: in idea the city with all its spoils were in their possession. At that moment the brave and prudent enemy, with as much coolness as if he had been aiming at harmless birds, opened his fire upon them, and swept them down like grass before the scythe of the mower. He sallied in pursuit, marching over blood and brains and mangled carcasses, and finally, to use the words of his countrymen, "drove the survivors to "their ships, and bad them carry to "England the proof of the fact, that "the soil of freedom was not to be "invaded with impunity." There were more than half as many British soldiers and sailors killed and wounded in this battle as in the battle of Waterloo. And, is this battle to pass for nothing? Is this to form no item in the account of *glory?* Is there no deduction to be made here from the *gain of glory* by the war.

As to our *Navy*, when was it not victorious over all its enemies? When did it not, since the days of the Stuarts, drive the navies of the French, Dutch, and Spaniards from the ocean? When was it not thought disgraceful for an English ship to yield to a force considerably superior to her own? When was it thought glorious for an English squadron to take a single frigate? When was it known that English ships yielded, one after another, in every part of the ocean, to ships of the same class and force? When was it dreamt of, that whole squadrons of English ships of war would be beaten and captured by squadrons of inferior force? *Never, till the late war against America*; which war, we must always bear in mind, grew out of, and formed a part of, the war against the French.

Thus, then, stands the account of *glory*. How that of *National Prosperity* stands, we shall see in another Letter.

I am,

Your faithful Friend,

WM. COBBETT.

Botley,

3d September, 1815.

LETTER XXXII.

The Costs of the War in the Articles of Funds, Debt, Expenses, Taxes, and Paupers.—Conclusion.

GENTLEMEN,

HAVING now seen, in the aggregate, what we have gained in the way of *Glory* as well as in the way of civil and religious liberty, and what we have lost in the way of *Prosperity*, it will be necessary, as to the latter, to enter into some details; because, with regard to the debt, the taxes, the funds, the trade, population, and pauperism of our country, we are able to refer to documents which the Government itself own to be correct.

An inquiry of this sort is peculiarly necessary in a case like the present, because it is notorious, that the war was begun under the pretext of its being *necessary* to the preservation of our *property*, which, we were told, would all be taken away from us (though it was not said very particularly *by whom*) unless we made war upon the French nation. In talking of *glory*, too, we must bear in mind, that our *glory* is, in great part, a *purchased* article. We are not like the French and the Americans, who *fight their battles themselves*, and who resemble those tradesmen who carry on their business themselves, having no journeymen under them. England is like a *master* tradesman, who, though he now and then puts his hand to the mallet, does, in fact, carry on his trade by means of journeymen. During the first war against the Americans, we had Brunswickers, Hanspachers, Hessians, Dramstadters, and other troops in our pay, as to much *per man* per month, and so much *per life*, if killed or lost while in our service. During the war against the French, we have had in our employ and pay, Russians, Prussians, Dutchmen, Autrians, Neapolitans, Papal troops, Sicilians, Spaniards, Portuguese, Switzers, Savoyards, Hessians, Hanspachers, Brunswickers, Danes, Swedes, French Royalists, Hanoverians, Blacks, and I do not know how many other nations. Our *glory*, therefore is much more an affair of *money* than of *arms*. Indeed this idea was very well illustrated at the Winchester meeting against the renewal of the Income Tax, by a country gentleman (who, by the by, is paper-maker to the Bank of England) who plainly stated in his speech, that those who had paid the taxes to carry on the war ought to *share in the honours*, then recently conferred on the new Knights of the Bath. He was very right, for it was owing to those taxes, and those taxes only, that the victories by the hands of Spaniards, Portuguese, Swedes, Hessians, Prussians, Hanoverians, &c. were gained. When a prize is awarded to a farmer for rearing the best ox, for instance, it is very well known that the ox has been reared, not *by him*, but by his labourers, who are supported by his money, and who are put in movement at his instigation; but, as, according to the rule of the law, that *he who does a thing by another does the thing itself*, so the farmer receives the reward, and the labourers receive their wages.

Upon this principle it is, doubtless, that our newspapers claim for us the whole of the *glory* of the recent successes, and of all that is now doing against the French people. But, upon the same principle, the greater part of the glory falls fairly to the share of the *taxes*, and that admirable money machine, the Bank, in Threadneedle-street. It was that venerable Old Lady, who brought the Russians and Prussians, and Austrians and Hanoverians into the field, who inspired them with patriotic and loyal feelings, and who filled their hearts with valour. And, if her Ladyship's merit does not find a distinguished place upon the great *Waterloo Column*, there is no justice left amongst men.

It is agreed on all hands, that the war has cost a great deal of money, and the country is now beginning to feel the effect of that cost; but, the amount of the whole cost has never been, as far as I know of, clearly stated at one time. The divers items have been stated at different times, and in different shapes; but the whole has never been brought into one concise view. This is what I shall now attempt, beginning with the state, or value of the FUNDS.

We will take 3 *per cents.* as the standard of the whole. During the *peace*, which ended in 1793, the average price of the 3 per cents. for years, had been 96. The average *peace-price* is now 58, and that, too, in paper-money. So that, in fact, every person, who held funded property in 1792, and who, or whose heirs or successors, still hold that same property, have actually lost *one half* of it by depreciation in value, and 10 *per cent.* in addition out of that half, which is now stopped out of the dividends in the shape of *Property Tax*.—This is the cost of the war with regard to the Funds.

The DEBT, which is commonly called the *National Debt*, or the *Public Debt*, demanded, in 1792, nine millions to pay the interest of it. It now demands £43,723,149 to pay the interest of this debt; and, therefore, the property and labour of the nation are mortgaged for 34 millions a year more than they stood mortgaged for before the war.—This is the cost of the war in the article of debt.

As to EXPENSES, which are to be expenses of *peace*, exclusive of the debt, they are not precisely known; but the Minister has told us, that they will amount, Civil List and all, to about 22 millions a year. Before the war, they amounted to six millions a year. This, therefore, is the cost of the war in the article of permanent Peace Expenses.

The TAXES of 1792 amounted to 15 millions a year. They must now, in *peace*, amount to 62 millions a year. That they *must* be severely felt is certain. From every class of persons complaints against them have come. They now are so heavy, that the *direct* taxes alone upon a farm exceed in amount *all that it takes to pay and feed all those who labour on that farm.*—The consequence is, that ruin is spreading around in every direction.—You are now driving your sheep to sell them to us in the richer soils. Only two years ago, you would not condescend to look at us, if we had not 300 pounds in our pocket to give you for 100 ewes. You now pull off your hats to us if we have got 125 pounds, to give you for the same number. But we have not more to give; our taxes remain *the same*, or are augmented, and yours remain *the same*, though your ewes are fallen (taking all the sorts together) from 60*s*. to 25*s*. Bear in mind, however, that this is the fair and honest price of the *war*, for which ninety-nine hundredths of you were advocates. This is the fair and honest price of that *glory*, on the acquirement of which you made bonfires, and *roasted sheep* and *oxen*. You may now roast *all* your sheep and oxen; for we have no money to give you for them. The tax-gatherer takes away all that our corn amounts to, except what goes to keep our labourers and our poor.

The POPULATION of the kingdom, to have kept pace with the Taxes, ought now to have been 51 millions, and excluding those persons, brought thither by the war, and who are now gone away, it is not 10 millions. Nay, so great has been, and is, the emigration, that if a census of the actual residents were now taken, there is every reason to believe, that it is of lower amount than in 1792.

The PAUPER part of the population have increased in the proportion of from one to 18 to one to 7. This is a fact, which I have *proved* in detail twenty times; and, I have never been answered by any one, who did not make the increase higher.

The NAVIGATION, COMMERCE, and MANUFACTURES, as they are represented in the *Official* accounts, have *increased* in the proportion of nearly one half. But, these accounts relate to *a state of war*, and a war of so singular a character as to have been, for the time, advantageous to all these. In *peace* it seems impossible that they can maintain their present ground. But, admit that they do, here is an increase of these to the amount of *a half*, while the increase of evils has been to the amount of rather more than *four-fifths*.

Such, my friends and neighbours, has been, to us, the consequences of our harvest of *Glory!* Such has been, to us, the consequences of having succeeded in restoring the Bourbons to the throne of France, and of throwing the French people back in their pursuit of freedom. It is now hoped, by some persons, that the restoration of the Pope, the Inquisition, the Jesuits, and the Bourbons, will so far brutalize the people of the Continent of Europe, that we shall have no rivals in the arts of peace; and that, thus, we shall be left to enjoy a monopoly of Navigation, Commerce, and Manufacturers; and be, thereby, enabled to pay the interest on our Debt and to meet the enormous annual expenses of our Government. Without stopping to comment on the morality and humanity of this hope, entertained in a country, abounding in Bible Societies, I venture to give it as my decided opinion, that the hope is fallacious. Russia, Denmark, Sweden, Holland, Austria, Spain, the Italian States, and even the Bourbons, will all push forward for their *share* of the benefits of the arts of peace. While our purse is open to them all, they will be subservient to us; but that cannot be for ever. It cannot be for many months longer. And, mark my words, that, as soon as we cease *to pay*, so soon shall we cease to have *friends* so very complaisant as our friends now are.

Thus, Gentlemen, I close this long series of Letters; too long, I am afraid, for your patience; but, I am of opinion, that occasions will frequently arise, when a recurrence to their contents will be of service to most persons, who pay attention to the politics and political economy of our country.

I am your faithful friend,
And most obedient Servant,
WM. COBBETT.

Botley,
12th September, 1815.

THE END.

Entered at Stationers' Hall.

Printed by W. MOLINEUX, 5, Bream's Buildings, Chancery Lane; Published by W. COBBETT, Jun. No. 8, Catherine Street, Strand: and Retailed at No. 192, Strand.

www.ingramcontent.com/pod-product-compliance
Ingram Content Group UK Ltd.
Pitfield, Milton Keynes, MK11 3LW, UK
UKHW020656091025
8309UKWH00043B/996

9 781016 61795